797,885 Books

are available to read at

www.ForgottenBooks.com

Forgotten Books' App
Available for mobile, tablet & eReader

ISBN 978-1-333-86916-8
PIBN 10573409

This book is a reproduction of an important historical work. Forgotten Books uses state-of-the-art technology to digitally reconstruct the work, preserving the original format whilst repairing imperfections present in the aged copy. In rare cases, an imperfection in the original, such as a blemish or missing page, may be replicated in our edition. We do, however, repair the vast majority of imperfections successfully; any imperfections that remain are intentionally left to preserve the state of such historical works.

Forgotten Books is a registered trademark of FB &c Ltd.
Copyright © 2015 FB &c Ltd.
FB &c Ltd, Dalton House, 60 Windsor Avenue, London, SW19 2RR.
Company number 08720141. Registered in England and Wales.

For support please visit www.forgottenbooks.com

1 MONTH OF FREE READING

at

www.ForgottenBooks.com

By purchasing this book you are eligible for one month membership to ForgottenBooks.com, giving you unlimited access to our entire collection of over 700,000 titles via our web site and mobile apps.

To claim your free month visit:
www.forgottenbooks.com/free573409

* Offer is valid for 45 days from date of purchase. Terms and conditions apply.

English
Français
Deutsche
Italiano
Español
Português

www.forgottenbooks.com

Mythology Photography **Fiction** Fishing Christianity **Art** Cooking Essays Buddhism Freemasonry Medicine **Biology** Music **Ancient Egypt** Evolution Carpentry Physics Dance Geology **Mathematics** Fitness Shakespeare **Folklore** Yoga Marketing **Confidence** Immortality Biographies Poetry **Psychology** Witchcraft Electronics Chemistry History **Law** Accounting **Philosophy** Anthropology Alchemy Drama Quantum Mechanics Atheism Sexual Health **Ancient History Entrepreneurship** Languages Sport Paleontology Needlework Islam **Metaphysics** Investment Archaeology Parenting Statistics Criminology **Motivational**

FIG. 1.—Frontispiece to the Epistle of St. Jerome in the Book of Durrow Specimen of ancient Irish penwork. (From Miss Stokes's Early Christian Art in Ireland.)

A SMALLER
SOCIAL HISTORY

OF

ANCIENT IRELAND

TREATING OF

The Government, Military System, and Law;
Religion, Learning, and Art; Trades, Industries, and Commerce;
Manners, Customs, and Domestic Life,
of the Ancient Irish People

BY

P. W. JOYCE, M.A., LL.D., T.C.D.; M.R.I.A.

One of the Commissioners for the Publication of the Ancient Laws of Ireland
Honorary President of the Royal Society of Antiquaries of Ireland

WITH 213 ILLUSTRATIONS

LONGMANS, GREEN, & CO.
LONDON, NEW YORK, AND BOMBAY
DUBLIN: M. H. GILL & SON, LTD.
1906

Printed at the

By Ponsonby & Gibbs

Sculpture over a doorway, Cormac's Chapel, Cashel: Centaur shooting at a lion. (From Petrie's Round Towers.)

PREFACE

This book is an abridgment of my larger work, "A Social History of Ancient Ireland." It consists mainly of simple exposition: most of the illustrative quotations and proofs, which are given in detail in the larger work, and nearly all the numerous references to authorities, are here omitted.* Yet the book is something more than a mere dry array of fact-statements; and I hope it will be found, not only instructive, but readable and interesting.

The social condition of most of those ancient nations that have made any figure in the world has been investigated and set forth in books; and perhaps it will be acknowledged that Ireland deserves to be

---

* From this it will be understood that for all the important statements in this book, authorities, references, and illustrative quotations will be found in the larger Social History.

similarly commemorated. For, besides the general importance of all such studies in elucidating the history of the human race, the ancient Irish were a highly intellectual and interesting people; and the world owes them something, as I hope to be able to show. In this book an attempt is made to picture society, in all its phases, as it existed in Ireland before the Anglo-Norman Invasion; and to accomplish this work, every authentic source of information within my reach has been turned to account.

The society depicted here—as the reader will soon discover for himself—was of slow and methodical growth and development; duly subordinated from the highest grades of people to the lowest; with clearly-defined ranks, professions, trades, and industries; and in general with those various pursuits and institutions found in every well-ordered community: a society compacted and held together by an all-embracing system of laws and customs, long established and universally recognised.

From the account here given, and from the evidences adduced in this and in the larger work, we may see that the ancient Irish were as well advanced in civilisation, as orderly, and as regular, as the people of those other European countries of the same period that—like Ireland—had a proper settled government; and it will be shown farther on that they were famed throughout all Europe for Religion and Learning.

The subject of the social condition of Ancient Ireland has been to some extent treated of by other writers, notably by Ware, O'Curry, and Sullivan; and I have taken full advantage of their learned labours. But they deal with portions only: my Essay aims at opening up the entire field.

This book does not deal with pre-historic times, except by occasional reference, or to illustrate the historic period. My survey generally goes back only so far as there is light from living record—history or tradition.

I have taken occasion all along to compare Irish Social Life with that of other ancient nations, especially pointing out correspondences that are the natural consequence of common Aryan origin: but want of space precluded much indulgence in this very desirable direction.

The writer who endeavours to set forth his subject —whatever it may be—in "words of truth and soberness," is sure to encounter the disapproval or hostility of those who hold extreme opinions on either side. In regard to my subject, we have, on the one hand, those English and Anglo-Irish people —and they are not few—who think, merely from ignorance, that Ireland was a barbarous and half-savage country before the English came among the people and civilised them; and, on the other hand, there are those of my countrymen who have an exaggerated idea of the greatness and splendour of the ancient Irish nation. I have not been in the least influenced by writers belonging to either class. Following trustworthy authorities, I have tried to present here a true picture of ancient Irish life, neither over-praising nor depreciating. I have not magnified what was worthy of commendation, nor suppressed, nor unwarrantably toned down, features that told unfavourably for the people: for though I love the honour of Ireland well, I love truth better.

The Irish race, after a long-protracted struggle, went down before a stronger people; and in addition to this, from causes which it would be out of place to discuss here, they suffered almost a total eclipse at home during a period nearly coincident with the eighteenth century. Chiefly for these reasons the old Irish people have never, in modern times, received the full measure of credit due to them for their early and striking advance in the arts of civilised life, for their very comprehensive system of laws, and for their noble and successful efforts, both at home and abroad, in the cause of religion and learning. Of late indeed we can perceive, among Continental and British writers, something like a spontaneous movement showing a tendency to do them justice; but the essays in this direction, though just, and often even generous, as far as they go, are fragmentary, scattered, and fitful. Those who are interested in this aspect of the subject will perhaps be pleased to have the whole case presented to them in one Essay.

I am glad to be able to say that the large Social History has been successful even beyond what I had expected. But as it is too expensive for the general run of readers, I am induced to bring out this abridgment, which can be sold at a price that places it within reach of all. For, irrespective of mere personal considerations, it seems to me very desirable that a good knowledge of the social condition of Ancient Ireland, such as is presented here, should be widely diffused among the people: more especially now, when there is an awakening of interest in the Irish language, and in Irish lore of every kind, unparalleled in our history. This smaller book, however, is not designed to supersede the larger work, but rather to lead up to it.

The numerous Illustrations relate directly to the several current parts of the text: and I hope they will be found an instructive and pleasing feature of the book.

I am indebted to Dr. Kuno Meyer—the well-known distinguished Celtic scholar — for many valuable corrections and suggestions. These were given in connexion with the larger Social History, but many of them are reflected in this book.

Mr. J. T. Gibbs, of the University Press, read the proof-sheets all through, and suggested many useful verbal corrections and alterations.

The old Irish writers commonly prefixed to their books or treatises a brief statement of "Place, Time, Person, and Cause." My larger Social History, following the old custom, opens with a statement of this kind, which may be appropriately repeated here, only with the "Time" changed:—

> *The Place, Time, Author, and Cause of Writing, of this book, are:—Its place is Lyre-na-Grena, Leinster-road, Rathmines, Dublin; its time is the year of our Lord one thousand nine hundred and six; the author is Patrick Weston Joyce, Doctor of Laws; and the cause of writing the same book is to give glory to God, honour to Ireland, and knowledge to those who desire to learn all about the Old Irish People.*

PREFACE.

I have now to discharge the pleasant duty of recording my thanks for help towards illustrating both this book and the larger Social History.

The Councils of the Royal Irish Academy, and of the Royal Society of Antiquaries, Ireland, gave me the use of the blocks of great numbers of the illustrations in their respective publications, and where the blocks were not available, permitted me to copy any of their illustrations I wanted. That the book is so well illustrated is mainly owing to the liberality of these two distinguished Societies. There is no need to enter into detail here, as under every illustration in the book is mentioned the source from which it is derived: but I wish to direct attention to the number of valuable and accurate figures I have borrowed from Wilde's "Catalogue of Irish Antiquities," belonging to the Royal Irish Academy.

Messrs. Hodges, Figgis, & Co., of Dublin, placed at my disposal the blocks of as many of Petrie's and Wakeman's beautiful drawings as I chose to ask for.

Colonel Wood-Martin lent me the blocks of many of the illustrations in his "Pagan Ireland" and "Traces of the Elder Faiths of Ireland."

From the Board of Education, South Kensington, I have received permission to use electrotypes from the original blocks of nearly a dozen of the admirable illustrations in Miss Stokes's "Early Christian Art in Ireland."

The Controller of His Majesty's Stationery Office, London, allowed me to reproduce some of the illustrations in Sir John T. Gilbert's "Facsimiles of Irish National Manuscripts."

I am indebted to the late Mr. Bernard Quaritch, of London, for leave to reproduce the beautiful illuminated page of the Book of MacDurnan, from Westwood's "Facsimiles of Anglo-Saxon and Irish Manuscripts."

PREFACE.

Messrs. George Bell & Sons lent me the blocks of some of the illustrations in Miss Stokes's "Three Months in the Forests of France," and "Six Months in the Apennines."

I had the permission of the Rev. Dr. Abbott, s.f.t.c.d., to copy some of the figures in his "Reproductions of Portions of the Book of Kells."

Lord Walter FitzGerald gave me leave to copy some of the illustrations in the "Journal of the County Kildare Archæological Society."

The Editor of the "Revue Celtique" has given me permission to reproduce two of the figures in that periodical.

Besides the above, a number of illustrations have been taken from books having no copyright, and others have been purchased from the proprietors of copyright works · all of which are acknowledged in the proper places. And there are a good many original sketches appearing here now for the first time.

Dr. Petrie and Miss Margaret Stokes have been the chief illustrators of the Scenery and Antiquities of Ireland ; and even a casual glance will show to what an extent I have been enabled to enrich this book with their beautiful and accurate drawings.

P. W. J.

Dublin,
    October, 1906.

Sculpture on a Column, Church of the Monastery, Glendalough.
(From Petrie's Round Towers.)

CONTENTS.

PART I.

GOVERNMENT, MILITARY SYSTEM, AND LAW.

CHAPTER I.

	PAGE
A Preliminary Bird's-eye View,	3

CHAPTER II.

Government by Kings,	13
Section	
1. Territorial Subdivision,	13
2. Classes of Kings,	17
Election and Inauguration,	18
Revenue and Authority,	22
Privileges,	23
Limitations and Restrictions,	25
3. Household, Retinue, and Court Officers,	25
4. The Over-Kings,	31

CHAPTER III.

Warfare,	32
Section	
1. Foreign Conquests and Colonisations,	32
2. Military Ranks, Orders, and Services,	38
3. Arms, Offensive and Defensive,	49
4. Strategy, Tactics, and Modes of Fighting,	62

CHAPTER IV

	PAGE
THE BREHON LAWS, ...	70
Section	
1. THE BREHONS, ...	70
2. THE SENCHUS MÓR AND OTHER BOOKS OF LAW,	73
3. SUITABILITY OF THE BREHON LAWS, . . .	76
4. STRUCTURE OF SOCIETY, ...	77
5. THE LAWS RELATING TO LAND, ...	81
6. THE ADMINISTRATION OF JUSTICE, ...	86

PART II.

RELIGION, LEARNING, AND ART.

CHAPTER V.

PAGANISM, ...	95
Section	
1. DRUIDS: THEIR FUNCTIONS AND POWERS, . .	95
2. POINTS OF AGREEMENT AND DIFFERENCE BETWEEN IRISH AND GAULISH DRUIDS, ...	101
3. SORCERERS AND SORCERY, ...	102
4. MYTHOLOGY: GODS, GOBLINS, AND PHANTOMS,	104
5. WORSHIP OF IDOLS, ...	118
6. WORSHIP OF THE ELEMENTS, ...	121
7. THE PAGAN HEAVEN AND A FUTURE STATE, .	124
8. TURNING DEISIOL OR SUNWISE, ...	127
9. THE ORDEAL, ...	128
10. THE EVIL EYE, ...	130
11. GEASA, OR PROHIBITIONS, ...	131

CHAPTER VI.

CHRISTIANITY, ...	133
Section	
1. CHRISTIANITY BEFORE ST. PATRICK'S ARRIVAL,	133
2. THE THREE ORDERS OF IRISH SAINTS, . . .	135
3. THE FIRST ORDER: PATRICIAN SECULAR CLERGY,	136

Chapter VI.—*continued*.

Section   PAGE
   4. THE SECOND ORDER: MONASTIC CLERGY,   138
   5. THE THIRD ORDER: ANCHORITES OR HERMITS, AND HERMIT COMMUNITIES, ... 152
   6. BUILDINGS, AND OTHER MATERIAL REQUISITES, 155

CHAPTER VII.

LEARNING AND EDUCATION, ... 168
  Section
   1. LEARNING IN PAGAN TIMES: OGHAM, . . . 168
   2. MONASTIC SCHOOLS, ... 174
   3. LAY SCHOOLS, ... 178
   4. SOME GENERAL FEATURES OF BOTH CLASSES OF SCHOOLS, ... 180
   5. THE MEN OF LEARNING, ... 184
   6. HONOURS AND REWARDS FOR LEARNING, 190
   7. THE KNOWLEDGE OF SCIENCE, ... 191

CHAPTER VIII.

IRISH LANGUAGE AND LITERATURE, ... 197
  Section
   1. DIVISIONS AND DIALECTS OF CELTIC, . . . 197
   2. WRITING, AND WRITING MATERIALS, . . . 202
   3. ANCIENT LIBRARIES, ... 205
   4. EXISTING BOOKS, ... 208
   5. IRISH POETRY AND PROSODY, ... 214

CHAPTER IX.

ECCLESIASTICAL AND RELIGIOUS WRITINGS, . . . 217

CHAPTER X.

ANNALS, HISTORIES, AND GENEALOGIES, ... 224
  Section
   1. HOW THE ANNALS WERE COMPILED, . . . 224
   2. TESTS OF ACCURACY, ... 225
   3. PRINCIPAL BOOKS OF ANNALS, ... 228
   4. HISTORIES: GENEALOGIES: DINNSENCHUS, 231

CHAPTER XI.

	PAGE
HISTORICAL AND ROMANTIC TALES,	233
Section	
1. CLASSES, LISTS, AND NUMBERS,	233
2. CHRONOLOGICAL CYCLES OF THE TALES,	234
3. GENERAL CHARACTER OF THE TALES,	236
4. STORY-TELLING AND RECITATION,	238

CHAPTER XII.

ART,	239
Section	
1. PENWORK AND ILLUMINATION,	239
2. GOLD, SILVER, AND ENAMEL, AS WORKING MATERIALS,	244
3. ARTISTIC METAL WORK,	246
4. STONE CARVING,	249

CHAPTER XIII.

MUSIC,	251
Section	
1. HISTORY,	251
2. MUSICAL INSTRUMENTS,	254
3. CHARACTERISTICS, CLASSES, STYLES,	259
4. MODERN COLLECTIONS OF ANCIENT IRISH MUSIC,	262

CHAPTER XIV

MEDICINE AND MEDICAL DOCTORS,	264
Section	
1. MEDICAL DOCTORS,	264
2. MEDICAL MANUSCRIPTS,	268
3. DISEASES,	270
4. TREATMENT,	273

PART III.
SOCIAL AND DOMESTIC LIFE.

CHAPTER XV.

	PAGE
THE FAMILY,	283
Section	
1. MARRIAGE,	283
2. POSITION OF WOMEN AND CHILDREN,	284
3. FOSTERAGE,	286
4. FAMILY NAMES,	288

CHAPTER XVI.

THE HOUSE,	289
Section	
1. CONSTRUCTION, SHAPE, AND SIZE,	289
2. INTERIOR ARRANGEMENTS AND SLEEPING ACCOMMODATION,	300
3. OUTER PREMISES AND DEFENCE,	306
4. DOMESTIC VESSELS,	314
5. ROYAL RESIDENCES,	320

CHAPTER XVII.

FOOD, FUEL, AND LIGHT: PUBLIC HOSTELS,	343
Section	
1. MEALS IN GENERAL,	343
2. DRINK,	348
3. COOKING,	351
4. FLESH MEAT AND ITS ACCOMPANIMENTS,	354
5. MILK AND ITS PRODUCTS,	359
6. CORN AND ITS PREPARATION,	361
7. HONEY,	363
8. VEGETABLES AND FRUIT,	365
9. FUEL AND LIGHT,	369
10. FREE PUBLIC HOSTELS,	372

CHAPTER XVIII.

		PAGE
Dress and Personal Adornment,	. . . .	376
Section		
1. THE PERSON AND THE TOILET,	. . . .	376
2. DRESS,	. . . .	382
3. PERSONAL ORNAMENTS,	. . . .	399
4. ROUGH CLASSIFIED LIST OF THE GOLD OBJECTS IN THE NATIONAL MUSEUM, DUBLIN,	. . .	420

CHAPTER XIX.

Agriculture and Pasturage,	. . . . .	421
Section		
1. FENCES,	. . . .	421
2. LAND, CROPS, AND TILLAGE,	. . . .	425
3. SOME FARM ANIMALS,	. . . . .	428
4. HERDING, GRAZING, MILKING,	. . . .	430

CHAPTER XX.

Workers in Wood, Metal, and Stone,	. . .	433
Section		
1. CHIEF MATERIALS,	. . . . . .	433
2. BUILDERS,	. . . .	435
3. BRASIERS AND FOUNDERS,	. . . .	437
4. THE BLACKSMITH AND HIS FORGE,	. . .	440
5. CARPENTERS, MASONS, AND OTHER CRAFTSMEN,	.	444
6. PROTECTION OF CRAFTS AND SOCIAL POSITION OF CRAFTSMEN,	. . . . . .	452

CHAPTER XXI.

Corn Mills and Querns,	. . . . . .	456
Section		
1. MILLS,	. . . .	456
2. QUERNS AND GRAIN RUBBERS,	. . . .	459

CHAPTER XXII.

Trades and Industries connected with Clothing	PAGE 462
Section	
1. WOOL AND WOOLLEN FABRICS,	462
2. FLAX AND ITS PREPARATION,	465
3. DYEING,	466
4. SEWING AND EMBROIDERY.	469
5. TANNING AND TANNED LEATHER,	471

CHAPTER XXIII.

Measures, Weights, and Mediums of Exchange,	472
Section	
1. LENGTH AND AREA,	472
2. CAPACITY,	474
3. WEIGHT,	474
4. STANDARDS OF VALUE AND MEDIUMS OF EXCHANGE,	475
5. TIME,	478

CHAPTER XXIV.

Locomotion and Commerce,	480
Section	
1. ROADS, BRIDGES, AND CAUSEWAYS,	480
2. CHARIOTS AND CARS,	483
3. HORSE-RIDING,	487
4. COMMUNICATION BY WATER,	491
5. FOREIGN COMMERCE,	494

CHAPTER XXV.

Public Assemblies, Sports, and Pastimes,	496
Section	
1. THE GREAT CONVENTIONS AND FAIRS,	496
2. THE FAIR OF CARMAN,	500
3. GENERAL REGULATIONS FOR MEETINGS,	502
4. SOME ANIMALS CONNECTED WITH HUNTING AND SPORT,	504
5. RACES,	509

CHAPTER XXV.—*continued.*

Section   PAGE
6. CHASE AND CAPTURE OF WILD ANIMALS, . . . 510
7. CAMÁN OR HURLING, AND OTHER ATHLETIC GAMES, 513
8. CHESS, ... 514
9. JESTERS, JUGGLERS, AND GLEEMEN, . . . 516

CHAPTER XXVI.

VARIOUS SOCIAL CUSTOMS AND OBSERVANCES, . . . 518
  Section
1. SALUTATION, ... 518
2. PLEDGING, LENDING, AND BORROWING, . . . 519
3. PROVISION FOR OLD AGE AND DESTITUTION, . . 520
4. LOVE OF NATURE AND OF NATURAL BEAUTY, . 521
5. SOMETHING FURTHER ABOUT ANIMALS, . . . 524
6. ANIMALS AS PETS, ... 525
7. THE CARDINAL POINTS, ... 526
8. THE WIND, ... 527
9. THE SEA, ... 528
10. BISHOP ULTAN AND THE ORPHANS, . . . 530

CHAPTER XXVII.

DEATH AND BURIAL, ... 531
  Section
1. WILLS, ... 531
2. FUNERAL OBSEQUIES, ... 532
3. MODES OF BURIAL, ... 534
4. CEMETERIES, ... 537
5. SEPULCHRAL MONUMENTS, ... 540

INDEX, ... 551

Portion of a Bell-shrine found in the River Bann. (From Miss Stokes's Christian Inscriptions.)

LIST OF ILLUSTRATIONS.

FIG.	PAGE
1. Frontispiece to the Epistle of St. Jerome in the Book of Durrow, . *Frontispiece*	
2. Cormac's Chapel on the Rock of Cashel, . .	xxiv
3. Ruins on Inishcaltra in Lough Derg, . . .	8
4. Specimen of ancient Irish Bookbinding, . . .	10
5. Aill-na-Meeran, . . .	14
6. Irish Kings and Archers, thirteenth century,	24
7. Dun-Dalgan, Cuculainn's residence, near Dundalk,	40
8. Rath-Keltair at Downpatrick, ...	41
9. Flint Arrow-head, .	50
10. Do. do.,	50
11. Do. do.,	50
12. Bronze head of Battle-mace,	51
13. Bronze Spear-head, .	52
14. Do. do., .	52
15. Do. do., .	53
16. Do. do., .	53
17. Do. curved Sword,	53
18. Ancient bronze Sword,	55
19. Bronze Scabbard,	55
20. Metallic Celt or Battle-axe,	56
21. Do. do.,	56
22. Celt on handle, . .	57
23. Do. do., . . .	57
24. Dermot Mac Murrogh,	58
25. Two Galloglasses,	58
26. Front of bronze Shield,	61

FIG.	PAGE
27. Back of bronze Shield,	61
28. Soldier receiving charge, .	67
29. Two Galloglasses on tomb,	68
30. Capital L from Book of Kells, ...	70
31. Facsimile of Senchus Mór,	74
32. A Fairy Hill, . . .	105
33. A Fairy Moat, . . .	107
34. Amulet, .	123
35. Killeen Cormac in Wicklow,	134
36. Doorway of St. Erc's Hermitage, ...	137
37. Ancient Baptismal Font of Clonard, ...	138
38. St. Columb's House at Kells, ...	140
39. Irish Shrine, . . .	147
40. St. Dicuil's Holy Well at Lure, France,	151
41. Gougane Barra in Cork, .	154
42. St. Mac Dara's Church, .	155
43. St. Doulogh's Church near Dublin, .	156
44. Ancient Church Doorway, .	157
45. Kilmallock Abbey, . .	159
46. Round Tower, Clonmacnoise, ...	161
47. Round Tower, Devenish, .	162
48. Round Tower, Drumcliff, .	163
49. St. Patrick's Bell, . .	166
50. Shrine of St. Patrick's Bell,	167
51. Mac Aiello's Bell, . .	168
52. Ogham Alphabet, . .	170
53. Ogham Stone, . . .	170

LIST OF ILLUSTRATIONS.

FIG.		PAGE
54.	Two Irish-Roman Alphabets,	173
55.	John Scotus Erigena,	176
56.	Tombstone of the "Seven Romans,"	177
57.	Alphabet cut on Stone,	183
58.	Astronomical Diagram,	192
59.	Scribe writing,	204
60.	Facsimile of part of Book of Dun Cow,	210
61.	Dysert Aengus in Limerick,	221
62.	Noah's Ark,	223
63.	Tubbrid Church in Tipperary,	231
63A.	Illuminated page of Book of Mac Durnan, *facing*	241
64.	Outlines of illuminated page,	241
65.	Ornamented page, Gospel of St. John,	243
66.	The Ardagh Chalice,	247
67.	The Tara Brooch,	248
68.	The Cross of Cong,	250
69.	Harp-player,	255
70.	Irish Piper,	256
71.	Harp- and Pipe-players,	257
72.	Group of Irish Trumpets,	258
73.	Ornamental bronze Trumpet-plate,	259
74.	Sweating-house,	279
75.	Trim Castle,	291
76.	Coloured Glass Ornament,	294
77.	Coloured Porcelain Pin-head,	294
78.	Coloured Glass Circular Disk,	294
79.	Carrickfergus Castle,	296
80.	King John's Castle, Limerick,	297
81.	Plan of Irish Homestead,	299
82.	Plan of Irish Dwelling-house,	301
83.	Castle of Athlone,	304
84.	The Moat of Kilfinnane,	307
85.	Staigue Fort in Kerry,	308
86.	Dun-Aengus in Aranmore,	309
87.	Carlow Castle,	311
88.	Dundrum Castle, Co. Down,	312
89.	Stone Drinking-cup,	314

FIG.		PAGE
90.	Bronze Drinking-vessel,	315
91.	The Kavanagh Horn,	315
92.	Ancient wooden vessel,	316
93.	Figure of a Man drinking,	317
94.	Wooden Mether,	318
95.	Do. do.,	318
96.	Wooden Bucket,	318
97.	Earthenware glazed Pitcher,	319
98.	Plan of Tara,	322
99.	The Forrad Mound, Tara,	324
100.	Dinnree Fort,	333
101.	North Moat, Naas,	335
102.	Carbury Castle, Kildare,	336
103.	The Rock of Cashel,	338
104.	Caher Castle,	339
105.	Small ancient Table,	346
106.	Bronze Strainer,	349
107.	Bronze Caldron,	352
108.	Do. do.,	353
109.	Ancient Butter-print,	359
110.	Firkin of Bog-butter,	360
111.	Bronze Figures of Ecclesiastics,	378
112.	Ancient Ornamented Comb,	379
113.	Do., do.,	379
114.	Do. do.,	379
115.	Bronze Razor,	380
116.	Small gold Box,	382
117.	Angel: from Book of Kells,	386
118.	Evangelist: from Book of Kells,	387
119.	Group showing Costume,	389
120.	Figures showing the Kilt,	390
121.	Figures showing *Trews* or Trousers,	391
122.	Enamelled bronze Button,	392
123.	Decorated bronze Pin,	392
124.	Do. do.,	392
125.	Do. do.,	392
126.	Do. do.,	392
127.	Do. do ,	392
128.	Do. do.,	392
129.	Gentleman of high class in costume of 1600,	393
130.	Lady of high class in costume of 1600,	393
131.	Lady of middle class in costume of 1600,	393

FIG.		PAGE
174.	Mould for Forge Furnace,	444
175.	Bronze Adze,	446
176.	Bronze Chisel,	448
177.	Do.,	448
178.	Do.,	448
179.	Do.,	448
180.	Bronze Gouge,	449
181.	Round Tower of Devenish,	451
182.	Window of Castledermot Abbey,	452
183.	Doorway of Rahan Church,	454
184.	Upper Stone of Quern,	459
185.	Quern,	460
186.	Grain-Rubber,	461
187.	Specimen of Wool-weaving,	464
188.	Do. do.,	464
189.	Two bronze Needles,	469
190.	Ancient Steelyard	475
191.	Bracteate Coin,	476
192.	Do.,	476
193.	Small *Bunne*, used as Money,	
194.	Ancient Irish Chariots,	486
195.	Horseman,	488
196.	Horseman using Horse-rod,	489
197.	Skeleton of Irish Elk	507
198.	Pronged Fishing-spear,	512
199.	Bone Chessman,	515
200.	The Twelve Winds, ,	528
201.	Cinerary Urn of Stone,	535
202.	Cinerary Urn of baked Clay,	535
203.	New Grange Mound,	538
204.	Burial Mound near Clonard,	541
205.	Sepulchral Chamber with Sarcophagus,	542
206.	Sepulchral Stone Enclosure,	543
207.	Great Cromlech at Kilternan,	544
208.	Phœnix Park Cromlech,	545
209.	King Dathi's Grave and Pillar-stone,	547
210.	Lugnaed's Headstone,	548
211.	Stronghow's Monument in Christchurch,	549
212.	Tomb of Felim O'Conor, King of Connaught,	550

Fig. 2.

Cormac's Chapel on the Rock of Cashel. Example of Irish Romanesque Architecture. (From Miss Stokes's Early Christian Architecture in Ireland.)

PART I.

GOVERNMENT, MILITARY SYSTEM, AND LAW.

IRELAND.

Specially drawn to illustrate Dr Joyce's Histories of Ireland.

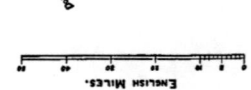

English Miles.

PRESENT DIVISION INTO PROVINCES AND COUNTIES.

LEINSTER. Louth, Meath, Dublin, Wicklow, Wexford, Westmeath, Longford, King's County, Queen's County, Kildare, Carlow, Kilkenny.

ULSTER. Donegal, Londonderry, Antrim, Down, Armagh, Monaghan, Tyrone, Fermanagh, Cavan.

CONNAUGHT. Galway, Mayo, Sligo, Leitrim, Roscommon.

MUNSTER. Waterford, Cork, Kerry, Clare, Limerick, Tipperary.

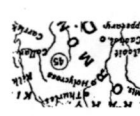

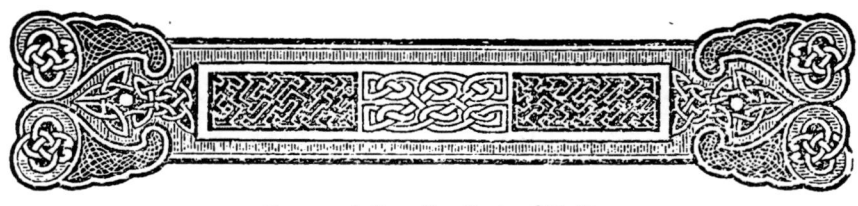

Composed from the Book of Kells

CHAPTER I.

A PRELIMINARY BIRD'S-EYE VIEW.

IRELAND, from the sixth to the twelfth century of the Christian era, presented an interesting spectacle, which, viewed through the medium of history, may be sketched in broad outline as follows.

In those early times the physical aspect of Ireland was very different from what it is at present. All over the country there were vast forests, and great and dangerous marshes, quagmires, and bogs, covered with reeds, moss, and grass. But though bogs existed from the beginning, many districts, where we now find them lying broad and deep, were once forest land: and the bog grew up after the surface had, in some manner, become denuded of trees. Buried down at a depth of many feet in some of our present bogs great tree trunks are often found, the relics of the primeval forest.

But outside forest and bog, there were open plains, valleys, and hillsides, under cultivation and pasturage, and all well populated. The woods and waste places were alive with birds and wild animals of all kinds, and the people were very fond of hunting and fishing; for there was plenty of game, both large and small, and the rivers and lakes teemed with fish. Sometimes they hunted hares and foxes for mere sport. But they had much grander game: wild boars with long and dangerous tusks, deer in great herds, and wolves that lurked in caves and thick woods. There were the same broad lakes, like inland seas, that still remain; but they were generally larger then than they are now; and they were surrounded with miles of reedy morasses: lakes and marshes tenanted everywhere by vast flocks of cranes, wild geese, wild swans, and other fowl. Kites and golden eagles skimmed over the plains, peering down for prey; and the goshawks, or falcons, used in the old game of hawking, were found in great abundance.

A person traversing those parts of the country that were inhabited found no difficulty in getting from place to place; for there were roads and bridle-paths everywhere, rough indeed, and not to be compared with the roads of our day, but good enough for the travel and traffic of the time. If the wayfarer did not choose to walk, there were plenty of ox-waggons; and among the higher classes rough springless chariots, drawn by one or two horses. Horse-riding, though sometimes adopted, was not in those times a very general mode of travelling. What with rough conveyances, and with roads and paths often full of ruts, pools, and mire, a journey, whether by walking, driving, or horse-riding, was a slow, laborious, and disagreeable business, and not always free from danger. Rivers were crossed by means of wooden bridges, or by wading at broad shallow fords, or by little ferry-boats, or, as a last resource, by swimming: for in those days of openair life everyone could swim. Fords were, however, generally very easy to find, as the roads and paths usually impinged on them, and in many places lights were kept burning beside them at night.

In the inhabited districts the traveller experienced little difficulty on the score of lodging; for there were open houses of hospitality for the reception of strangers, where bed and food were always ready. If one of these happened not to be within reach, he had only to make his way to the nearest monastery. where he was sure of a warm welcome: and, whether in monastery or hostel, he was entertained free of charge. Failing both, there was small chance of his having to sleep out: for hospitality was everywhere enjoined and practised as a virtue, and there was always a welcome from the family of the first private house he turned into.

The people were divided into tribes and clans, each group, whether small or large, governed by a king or chief; and at the head of all was the high king of Ireland. But these kings could not do as they pleased: for they had to govern the country or the district in accordance with old customs, and had to seek the advice of the chief men on all important occasions—much the same as the limited monarchs of our own day. There were courts of justice presided over by magistrates and judges, with lawyers to explain the law and plead for their clients.

The houses were nearly all of wood, and oftener round than quadrangular, the dwelling of every comfortable family being surrounded by a high rampart of earth with a thorn hedge or strong palisade on top, to keep out wild animals and robbers. Beside almost every homestead was a kitchen-garden for table vegetables, and one or more enclosed spaces for various purposes, such as out-door games, shutting in cattle at night, or as haggards for corn-stacks. In some places the dwellings were clustered in groups or hamlets, not huddled close as the houses in most of our present villages, but with open spaces between. The large towns—which, however, were very few—lay open all round, without any attempt at fortification.

The people were bright and intelligent and much given to intellectual entertainments and amusements. They loved music and singing, and took delight in listening to poetry, history, and romantic stories, recited by professional poets and shanachies; or, in the absence of these, by good non-professional story-tellers, who were everywhere to be found among the peasantry. They were close observers of external nature, too, and had an intense admiration for natural beauty—a peculiarity everywhere reflected in their literature, as well as in their place-names.

In most parts of the country open-air meetings or fairs were held periodically, where the people congregated in thousands, and, forgetting all the cares of the world for the time, gave themselves over to unrestrained enjoyment—athletic games and exercises, racing, music, recitations by skilled poets and storytellers, jugglers' and showmen's representations, eating and drinking, marrying and giving in marriage. So determined were they to ward off all unpleasantness on these occasions, that no one, at the risk of his life, durst pick a quarrel or strike a blow: for this was one of the rules laid down to govern all public assemblies. An Irish fair in those times was a lively and picturesque sight. The people were dressed in their best, and in great variety; for all, both men and women, loved bright colours; and from head to foot every individual wore articles of varied hues. Here you see a tall gentleman walking along with a scarlet cloak flowing loosely over a short jacket of purple, with perhaps blue trousers and yellow headgear, while the next showed a colour arrangement wholly different; and the women vied with the men in variety of hues. Nay, single garments were often particoloured; and it was quite common to see the long outside mantle, whether worn by men or women, striped and spotted with purple, yellow, green, or other dyes.

But outside such social gatherings, and in ordinary life, both chiefs and people were quarrelsome and easily provoked to fight. Indeed they loved fighting for its own sake; and a stranger to the native character would be astonished to see the very people who only a few days before vied with each other in good-natured enjoyment, now fighting to the death on some flimsy cause of variance, which in all likelihood he would fail to understand if he made inquiry. These everlasting jars and conflicts—though not more common in Ireland than in England and Scotland—brought untold miseries on the people, and were the greatest obstacle to progress. Sometimes great battles were fought, on which hung the fate of the nation, like those we have seen contested in Ireland within the last two or three hundred years. But the martial instincts of the people were not always confined within the shores of Ireland; for Irish leaders often carried war into the neighbouring countries both of Great Britain and the Continent.

In all parts of the country were monasteries, most of them with schools attached, where an excellent education was to be had by all who desired it, for small payment, or for nothing at all if the student

FIG. 3.

Ruins on Inishcaltra or Holy Island in Lough Derg on the Shannon. Island Monastery founded by St. Camin (died 653) Here was one of the Munster Colleges where many distinguished men were educated. From Kilk. Archæol. Journ.

was poor; and besides these there were numerous lay schools where young persons might be educated in general learning and for the professions. The teaching and lecturing were carried on with life and spirit, and very much in the open air when the weather permitted. In the monasteries and schools, as well as in some private houses, there were libraries of manuscript books containing all the learning then known : but when you walked into the library room, you saw no books on shelves ; but numbers of neat satchels hanging on hooks round the walls, each containing one or more precious volumes and labelled on the outside.

Learning of every kind was held in the highest estimation; and learned men were well rewarded, not only in the universal respect paid to them, but also in the solid worldly advantages of wealth and influence. Professional men—physicians, lawyers, builders, &c.—went on their visits, each attended by a group of scholars who lived in his house and accompanied him to learn their profession by actual practice.

Some gave themselves up to the study and practice of art in its various forms, and became highly accomplished: and specimens of their artistic work remain to this day, which are admitted to be the most perfect and beautiful of the kind existing in any part of the world.

In numerous districts there were minerals, which, though not nearly so abundant as in the neighbouring island of Great Britain, were yet in sufficient quantity to give rise to many industries. The mines were worked too, as we know from ancient documents; and the remains of old mines of copper, coal, and other minerals, with many antique mining tools, have been discovered in recent times in some parts of Ireland. Gold was found in many places, especially in the district which is now called the county Wicklow ; and the rich people wore a variety of gold ornaments, which they took great pride in. Many rivers produced the pearl mussel, so that Ireland was well known for its pearls, which were unusually

Fig. 4.
Specimens of the Ancient Irish Art of Bookbinding. From Miss Stokes's Early Christian Art in Ireland.

large and of a very fine quality: and in some of the same rivers pearls are found to this day.

Though there were no big factories, there were plenty of industries and trades in the homes of the people, like what we now call cottage industries.

Coined money was hardly known, so that all transactions of buying and selling were carried on by a sort of barter, values being estimated by certain well-known standards, such as cows, sacks of corn of a fixed size, ounces of gold and silver, and such like. To facilitate these interchanges, the people had balances and weights not very different from those now used.

The men of the several professions, such as medical doctors, lawyers, judges, builders, poets, historians; and the tradesmen of various crafts—carpenters, smiths, workers in gold, silver, and brass, ship- and boat-builders, masons, shoemakers, dyers, tailors, brewers, and so forth—all worked and earned their bread under the old Irish laws, which were everywhere acknowledged. Then there was a good deal of commerce with Britain and with Continental countries, especially France; and the home commodities, such as hides, salt, wool, etc., were exchanged for wine, silk, satin, and other goods not produced in Ireland.

As the population of the country increased, the cultivated land increased in proportion. But until a late time there were few inhabited districts that were not within view, or within easy reach, of unreclaimed lands—forest, or bog, or moorland: so that the people had much ado to protect their crops and flocks from the inroads of wild animals.

All round near the coast ran, then as now, the principal mountain ranges, with a great plain in the middle. The air was soft and moist, perhaps even more moist than at present, on account of the great extent of forest. The cleared land was exceedingly fertile, and was well watered with springs, streamlets, and rivers, not only among the mountainous districts, but all over the central plain. Pasture lands were luxuriant and evergreen, inviting flocks and herds without limit. There was more pasture than tillage, and the grass land was, for the most part, not fenced in, but was grazed in common.

Some of the pleasing features of the country have been well pictured by Denis Florence M'Carthy in his poem of " The Bell Founder " :—

" O Erin! thou broad-spreading valley, thou well-watered land of fresh streams,
When I gaze on thy hills greenly sloping, where the light of such loveliness beams,
When I rest on the rim of thy fountains, or stray where thy streams disembogue,
Then I think that the fairies have brought me to dwell in the bright Tirnanogue."

Ireland, so far as it was brought under cultivation and pasture in those early days, was—as the Venerable Bede calls it—" a land flowing with milk and honey"; a pleasant, healthful, and fruitful land, well fitted to maintain a prosperous and contented people.

Though the period from the sixth to the twelfth century has been specified at the opening of this chapter, the state of things depicted here continued, with no very decided changes, for several hundred years afterwards; and many of the customs and institutions, so far from being limited backwards by the sixth century, existed from prehistoric times.

All these features, and many others not noticed here, will now be examined in the following chapters of this book.

Composed rom tıe Book of Kells.

CHAPTER II.

GOVERNMENT BY KINGS.

SECTION I. *Territorial Subdivision.*

BEFORE entering on the subject of Government, it will be useful to sketch the main features of the ancient territorial divisions of the country. It was parcelled out into five provinces from the earliest times of which we have any record:—Leinster; East Munster; West Munster; Connaught; and Ulster: a partition which, according to the legend, was made by the five Firbolg brothers, the sons of Dela.* Laigin or Leinster originally extended—in coast line—from Inver Colpa (the mouth of the Boyne at Drogheda) to the river Suir : East Muman or Munster from the Suir to the Lee at Cork: West Munster from the Lee round to the Shannon: Olnegmacht or Connaught from Limerick and the Shannon to the little river Drowes, which issues from Lough Melvin and flows between the counties

---

* See Joyce's Short Hist. of Ireland, p. 125.

of Leitrim and Donegal: and Ulaid or Ulster from this round northwards to the Boyne.

This division became modified in course of time. The two Munsters, East and West, gradually ceased to be distinguished, and Munster was regarded as a single province. A new province, that of Mide [Mee] or Meath, was formed in the second century

FIG. 5.

Aill-na-Meeran, the 'Stone of the Divisions; now often called the "Cat Stone." (From a photograph. Man put in for comparison.)

of the Christian era by Tuathal [Thoohal] the Acceptable, king of Ireland. Down to his time the provinces met at a point on the hill of Ushnagh (in the present county Westmeath) marked by a great stone called *Aill-na-Mirenn* [Aill-na-Meeran], the 'Stone of the Divisions,' which stands there a conspicuous object still. Round this point Tuathal formed the new province by cutting off a portion of each of the others. It was designed to be the mensal land or personal estate of the *Ard-ri* or supreme king of Ireland, that he might be the better able to maintain his court with due state and dignity. Previous to his time the king of Ireland had only a small tract—a single *tuath* (see next page)—for his own use. This new province was about half the size of Ulster, extending from the Shannon eastwards to the sea, and from the confines of the present county Kildare and King's County on the south to the confines of Armagh and Monaghan on the north. The present counties of Meath and Westmeath retain the name, but comprise only about half the original province.

At the time of Tuathal's accession—A.D. 130—there were four places belonging severally to the four provinces, situated not far from each other, which for centuries previously had been celebrated as residences and as centres for great periodical meetings for various purposes:—Tara in Leinster; Tailltenn in Ulster (now Teltown on the Blackwater, midway between Navan and Kells); Tlachtga in Munster (now the Hill of Ward near Athboy in Meath); and Ushnagh in Connaught, nine miles west of Mullingar in the present county Westmeath. All these were included in the new province; and Tuathal built a palace in each, of which some of the mounds and fortifications remain to this day. After his time the five provinces generally recognised and best known in Irish history were Leinster, Munster, Connaught, Ulster, Meath.

Besides the formation of a new province, there

were several minor changes. The district forming the present county Louth was transferred from Ulster to Leinster; the present county Cavan, which originally belonged to Connaught, was given to Ulster; and the territory now known as the county Clare was wrested from Connaught and annexed to Munster. Down to the time of Tuathal, Connaught included a large tract east of the Shannon, a part of the present counties of Longford and Westmeath (nearly as far as Mullingar); but in accordance with his arrangements, the Shannon, in this part of its course, became the eastern boundary of that province. The most ancient division of Munster, as has been said, was into East and West: but a later and better known partition was into Thomond or North Munster, which broadly speaking included Tipperary, Clare, and the northern part of Limerick; and Desmond or South Munster, comprising Kerry, Cork, Waterford, and the southern part of Limerick. In later times, however, the name Thomond has been chiefly confined to the county Clare, the patrimony of the O'Briens, who are usually known by the tribe-name of Dalcassians. Recently Meath has disappeared as a province: and the original provinces now remain—Leinster, Munster, Connaught, and Ulster.

The provinces were subdivided into territories of various sizes. The political unit, *i.e.* the smallest division with a single government, under a chief or king, was the *Tuath* [Thooa]. A tuath contained about 177 English square miles, and might be represented in area by an oblong district, sixteen miles by eleven. There were 184 tuaths in all Ireland.

Sometimes three, four, or more tuaths were united to form one large territory under a king: this was called a *Mór-tuath,* or great tuath.

2. *Classes of Kings.*

The government of the whole country, as well as that of each division and subdivision, was in the hands of a king or chief, who had to carry on his government in accordance with the immemorial customs of the country or sub-kingdom: and his authority was further limited by the counsels of his chief men. The usual name for a king in the ancient as well as in the modern language is *ri* [ree], genitive *righ* [ree]. A queen was, and is, called *rioghan* [reean]. Over all Ireland there was one king, who, to distinguish him from others, was designated the Ard-ri, or over-king (*árd,* 'high'). The over-kings lived at Tara till the sixth century A.D.; after that, elsewhere: hence the *Ard-ri* was often called "King of Tara," even after its abandonment. The last over-king was Roderick O'Conor. After his death, in 1198, there were no more supreme monarchs: but the provinces and the smaller kingdoms continued to be ruled by their native kings in succession down to a much later period.

There was a king over each of the five provinces—an arrangement commonly known as the Pentarchy. The provinces, again, included many sub-kingdoms, some consisting of a single *tuath* and some of more, as has been said. The tuath was the smallest territory whose ruler could claim the title of *ri,* or king; but all the 184 tuaths had not kings.

From this it will be seen that, speaking in a general sense, there were four classes of kings:—the king of the *tuath*; the king of the *mór-tuath*; the king of a province; and the king of all Ireland: forming a regular gradation, kingdom within kingdom.

The kings of the provinces were subject to the over-king, and owed him tribute and war-service. A similar law extended to all the sub-kingdoms: in other words, the king of each territory, from the tuath upwards to the province, was—at all events nominally—subject to the king of the larger territory in which it was included. Some of the sub-kingdoms were very large, such as Tyrone, Tirconnell, Thomond, Desmond, Ossory, Hy Many, &c., each of which comprised several tuaths and several tribes.

3. *Election and Inauguration.*

Election.—The king or ruling chief was always elected from members of one *finĕ* or family, bearing the same surname (when surnames came into use); but the succession was not hereditary in the present sense of the word: it was elective, with the above limitation of being confined to one family. Any freeborn member of the family was eligible, provided that both his father and paternal grandfather had been *flaiths* or nobles, and that he was free from all personal deformities or blemishes likely to impair his efficiency or to lessen the respect of the people for him. The successor might be son, brother, nephew, cousin, &c., of the chief. That member was chosen who was considered the best able to lead in war and govern in peace; which of course implied that he should be of full age.

The proceedings at the election, which were carried on with much ceremony and deliberation, are described in the law. Every freeman of the rank of *aire* [arra] or chief had a vote. If there were several candidates, a court was held for the election in the house of the chief *brewy* or hosteller of the district—or in the palace, if it was for a high-class king—to which all the chiefs about to take part in the election proceeded, each with his full retinue: and there they remained in council for three days and three nights, at the end of which time the successful candidate was declared elected.

With the object of avoiding the evils of a disputed succession, the person to succeed a king or ruling chief was often elected by the chiefs convened in formal meeting during the lifetime of the king himself: when elected he was called the **tanist**, a word meaning *second*, i.e. second in authority. Proper provision was made for the support of the tanist by a separate establishment and an allowance of land, a custom which continued, in case of the tanists of provincial and minor kings, till the time of Elizabeth, and even later. He was subordinate to the king or chief, but was above all the other dignitaries of the state. The other persons who were eligible to succeed in case of the tanist's failure were termed *Roy-damna*, that is to say 'king-material.'

The **Inauguration** or *making* of a king, after he had been elected, was a very impressive ceremony. Of the mode of inaugurating the pagan kings we know hardly anything, further than this, that the kings of Ireland had to stand on an inauguration stone at Tara called *Lia Fail*, which *uttered a roar*, as was believed, when a king of the old Milesian race stood on it.

But we possess full information of the ceremonies used in Christian times. The mode of inaugurating was much the same in its general features all over the country, and was strongly marked by a religious character. But there were differences in detail; for some tribes had traditional customs not practised by others. There was a definite formula, every portion of which should be scrupulously carried out in order to render the ceremony legal. Some of the observances that have come within the ken of history, as described below, descended from pagan times. Each tribe, or aggregation of tribes, had a special place of inauguration, which was held in much respect—invested indeed with a half sacred character. It was on the top of a hill, or on an ancestral carn (the sepulchre of the founder of the race), or on a large *lis* or fort, and sometimes under a venerable tree, called in Irish a *bile* [billa]. Each tribe used an inauguration stone—a custom common also among the Celts of Scotland. Some of the inauguration stones had the impression of two feet, popularly believed to be the exact size of the feet of the first chief of the tribe who took possession of the territory. Sometimes there was a stone chair, on which the king sat during part of the ceremony. The inauguration chair of the O'Neills of Clannaboy (a branch of the great O'Neills) is still preserved in the Belfast Museum. On the day of the inauguration the sub chiefs of the territory, and all the great officers of state, with the brehons, poets, and historians, were present, as also the bishops, abbots, and other leading ecclesiastics.

The hereditary historian of the tribe read for the elected chief the laws that were to regulate his conduct; after which the chief swore to observe them, to maintain the ancient customs of the tribe, and to rule his people with strict justice. Then, while he stood on the stone, an officer—whose special duty it was—handed him a straight white wand, a symbol of authority, and also an emblem of what his conduct and judicial decisions should be—straight and without stain. Having put aside his sword and other weapons, and holding the rod in his hand, he turned thrice round from left to right, and thrice from right to left, in honour of the Holy Trinity, and to view his territory in every direction. Then one of the sub-chiefs appointed for this purpose pronounced in a loud voice his surname—the surname only, without the Christian name—which was afterwards pronounced aloud by each of the clergy, one after another, according to dignity, and then by the sub-chiefs. He was then the lawful chief; and ever after, when spoken to, he was addressed "O'Neill"— "Mac Carthy More"—"O'Conor," &c.; and when spoken of in English, he was designated "The O'Neill," &c., a custom existing to this day, as we see in "The O'Conor Don," "The Mac Dermot," and in Scotland "The Mac Callum More."

The main parts of the inauguration ceremony were performed by one or more sub-chiefs: this office was highly honourable, and was hereditary. The inaugurator had a tract of land and a residenc free, which remained in the family. The O'Neills of Tyrone were inaugurated by O'Hagan and O'Cahan at Tullaghoge, near Dungannon, where the fine old inauguration moat still remains; the O'Donnells of Tirconnell by O'Freel, at the Rock of Doon, near Kilmacrenan. Near Quin in Clare is the fort of *Magh Adhair* [Mah-ire], on which the Dalcassian kings were made; and Carnfree, the mound on which the O'Conors, kings of Connaught, were inaugurated, is to be seen in the townland of Carns, near Tulsk, in Roscommon.

4. *Revenue and Authority.*

The revenue of the king or ruling chief, of whatever grade, which enabled him to support his court and household, was derived from three main sources. *First*: he was allowed, for life or for as long as he continued chief, a tract of land, which varied in size according to the rank of the king. *Second*: payments from the individual chiefs, farmers, and artisans, over whom he ruled: all according to their means. These were almost always paid in kind:—cattle and provisions, plough-oxen, hogs, sheep, with mantles and other articles of dress, dyestuffs; and sometimes gold and silver reckoned in ounces. *Third*: payment for lending stock, as described in chap. iv., sect. 5. But in addition to all this he might have land as his own personal property: and there were other minor sources of income.

A king usually secured the allegiance of his sub-kings and chiefs by taking hostages; so that every king had hostages residing in his palace, who all lived in one particular house, specially allotted to them.

5. *Privileges.*

Kings enjoyed many privileges, and were bound by many restrictions. A king's evidence in a brehon's court against all of a rank below him was accepted without question, as they had not the right to be heard in evidence against him : but this privilege did not hold against a bishop, a doctor of learning, or a pilgrim, all of whom were regarded as of equal rank with himself—so far as giving evidence was concerned.

When a king of any grade ascended the throne, he usually made a visitation or royal progress through his kingdom, to receive allegiance and hostages from his sub-kings. He moved very leisurely in a roundabout, sunwise, *i.e.* from left to right; and during the whole journey, he was to be entertained, with all his retinue, free of charge, by those sub-chiefs through whose territories he passed: so that these visitations were called "Free Circuits."

In old times it was the belief of the Irish that when a good and just king ruled—one who faithfully observed in his government the royal customs and wise precepts followed by his ancestors—the whole country was prosperous: the seasons were mild, crops were plentiful, cattle were fruitful, the waters abounded with fish, and the fruit trees had to be propped owing to the weight of their produce. The same belief prevailed among the Greeks and Romans.

The ancient Irish had a very high ideal of what a king should be : and we meet with many statements throughout our literature of the noble qualities expected from him. He should be "free from falsehood, from the betrayal of his nobles, from unworthy conduct towards his people." "For what is a prince selected over a country?" asks Carbery of King Cormac, who replies: "For the goodness of his form and race, and sense, and learning, and dignity, and utterance: he is selected for his goodness and for his wisdom, and strength, and forces, and valour in

Fig. 6.

Irish Kings and Archers, thirteenth century. From frescoes in Abbey Knockmoy, Galway. (Drawn by Petrie.)

fighting." A just sovereign "exercises not falsehood, nor [unnecessary] force, nor oppressive might. He has full knowledge of his people, and is perfectly righteous to them all, both weak and strong."

A king should, according to law, have at least three chief residences; and he lived in them by turns as suited his fancy or convenience. On state occasions he sat upon a throne, called in Irish *righshuidhe* [ree-hee], "royal seat," slightly elevated so as to enable him to view the whole assembly. He wore a crown or diadem, called a *minn*, which will be described farther on.

6. *Limitations and Restrictions.*

Irish kings were not despotic: they were all, from the supreme monarch down to the king of the *tuath*, in every sense, limited monarchs; they were subject to law like their own free subjects. We have seen that at their inauguration they had to swear that they would govern their people with strict justice, and in accordance with the ancient customs of the kingdom; and their duties, restrictions, and privileges were strictly laid down in the Brehon code. This idea pervades all our literature, from the earliest time.

There were certain things which a king was forbidden to do, as being either dangerous or unbecoming. He was neither to do any work nor concern himself about servile work of any kind. It was not permitted to a king, or even to a noble, to keep pigs: that is to have them managed for him round or near his house by any of his immediate dependents. But swineherds living in their own homes at a distance from the palace, fed great herds of swine in the woods for the king.

7. *Household, Retinue, and Court Officers.*

Under the king, of whatever grade, and forming part of his household, persons held various offices of trust, with special duties, all tending to support the dignity or ensure the safety of the king; just as we find in royal households of modern times. The persons appointed to each office always belonged to some particular family, in whom the office was hereditary; and all were paid liberal allowances for their services.

The higher the king's status the more numerous were the offices and the more important the positions of the persons holding them. Some of these were in constant attendance, and lived in or about the palace: others attended only on special great occasions: and these commonly lived at a distance in their own territories—for they were themselves generally sub-chiefs or sub-kings with their own retinues and office-holders. Most of the higher class of officers, such as professional men (who will be treated of farther on), who were supposed to give their whole —or nearly their whole—time to the service, had land and houses for their support, not far from the royal residence. On state occasions, all these officers attended in person on the monarch, and were assigned their proper places in the great hall. In accordance with an ordinance made by King Cormac Mac Art, the Ard-ri, or king of Ireland, was at all times—and not merely on state occasions—to be accompanied by a retinue of at least ten persons:—a *flaith* or noble; a brehon or judge; a druid; a *sai* or doctor; a poet; a historian; a musician; and three servants—all to exercise their several professional functions when required. This arrangement continued in force till the death of Brian Boru in 1014, except that in Christian times a bishop took the place of a druid.

A few picked men commonly accompanied the king as personal and immediate guards, and stood beside him when he sat down, with swords or battle-axes in their hands: for Irish kings were not less liable to assassination than others, from ancient times to the present day. This custom continued down to the sixteenth century: for the Four Masters have left us a description of Shane O'Neill's body-guard, which has the antique flavour of the period of the Red Branch Knights. In front of Shane's tent burned a great fire, " and a huge torch, thicker than a man's body, was constantly flaring at a short distance from the fire; and sixty grim and redoubtable galloglasses, with sharp keen axes, terrible and ready for action, and sixty stern and terrific Scots [hired soldiers from Scotland], with massive broad and heavy-striking swords in their hands [ready] to strike and parry, were watching and guarding O'Neill."

The king commonly kept in his retinue a *trén-fher* [trainar], a 'strong man,' or *cath milid*, 'battle-soldier,' his champion or chief fighting man, to answer challenges to single combat. Concobar Mac Nessa's champion Triscatal, who lived in the palace of Emain, is described in an ancient tale in the Book of Leinster in terms that remind us of the English writer's description of a much later *trén-fher*, John de Courcy, whose very look—on the day of single combat before King John of England and King Philip of France—so frightened the French champion that he " turned round and ranne awaie off the fielde."* Triscatal was a mighty broad-fronted,

---

* This whole story about John de Courcy and the French champion is told in my Reading Book in Irish History.

shaggy-haired man, with thighs as thick as an ordinary man's body, wearing a thick leathern apron from his armpits down : his limbs were bare, and his aspect was so fierce that he killed men by his very look.

We know that St. Patrick kept a household in imitation of the ancient Irish custom : and one of his attendants was his *trén-fher* or 'strong man,' St. Mac Carthen, afterwards first bishop of Clogher, whose peaceful function was to carry the aged saint on his back across fords and other difficult places, on their missionary journeys.

At the entrance to the royal palace or council chamber stood the doorkeepers to scan and interrogate all visitors. There was a *Rechtaire* [3-syll.] or house-steward, whose office was a very dignified one. The house-steward of King Conari's household is described as wearing a fleecy mantle, and holding in his hand his "wand of office," which was no small ornamental rod—no "silver wand of state"—but a huge black beam "like a mill-shaft." He arranged the guests in their proper places at table, assigned them their sleeping-apartments, and determined each morning the supplies of food for the day. If a dispute arose on any matter connected with the arrangements for receiving, placing, or entertaining the guests, he decided it; and his decision was final. When he stood up to speak, all were silent, so that a needle might be heard if it dropped on the floor. From this description it will be seen that the *rechtaire* corresponded closely with the Anglo-Norman seneschal, major-domo, or house-steward, of later times.

A particular officer had charge of the king's (or queen's) *séds*, 'jewels,' or personal treasures, which were generally kept in a *corrbolg*, or large round ornamental satchel, or in a number of such receptacles. One man, and sometimes two, had charge of the chessboard and chessmen. The board was enclosed in some sort of case, and the men were often kept in a bag of wire netting. There was a master of the horse who had charge of the king's stables and horses, under whom were one or more grooms. We find mentioned, among the other officials, chief swineherds and chief cooks, whose positions were considered of importance. Runners, *i.e.*, messengers or couriers, were always kept in the king's or chief's employment; and not unfrequently we find women employed in this office.

A king kept in his court an ollave of each profession:—poet, historian, storyteller (or most commonly one ollave combining these three professions), physician, brehon, builder, &c. Each of these gave his services to the king, for which an ample stipend was allowed, including a separate dwelling-house and free land. The whole institution flourished in the time of Camden (sixteenth century), who correctly describes it:—" These lords [*i.e.*, the Irish kings and chiefs] have their historians about them, who write their acts and deeds:—they have their physicians, their rymers whom they call bards, and their harpers: all of whom have their several livelihoods, and have lands set out for them." Fools, jugglers, and jesters were always kept in the king's court for the amusement of the household and guests. They and their functions will be described in chapter xxv. Each chief, of whatever grade, kept a household after the manner of a king, but on a smaller scale, with the several offices in charge of the members of certain families.

From the description given at pp. 17, 18, it will be seen that there was a regular gradation of authority. The king of the *tuath* owed allegiance to the king of the *mór-tuath* : the king of the *mór-tuath* to the provincial king ; the provincial king to the *ard-rí* of all Ireland. But this was very imperfectly carried out. The authority of the supreme monarch over the provincial kings was in most cases only nominal, like that of the early Bretwaldas over the minor kings of the Heptarchy. He was seldom able to enforce obedience, so that they were often almost or altogether independent of him. There never was a king of Ireland who really ruled the whole country: the king that came nearest to it was Brian Boru. In like manner the under-kings often defied the authority of their superiors. The people grouped into families, clans, tribes, and *kinels*, with only slight bonds of union, and with their leaders ever ready to quarrel, were like shifting sand. If the country had been left to work out its own destinies, this loose system would probably in the end have developed into one strong central monarchy, as in England and France. As matters stood it was the weak point in the government. It left the country a prey to internal strife, which the supreme king was not strong enough to quell ; and the absence of union rendered it impossible to meet foreign invasion by effectual resistance.

8. *The Over-Kings.*

According to the ancient bardic legends, five successive colonies arrived in Ireland many centuries before the Christian era:—the Parthalonians, the Nemedians, the Firbolgs, the Dedannans, and the Milesians.* The bards say that government by monarchy began with the Firbolgs; whose first king —and the first king of Ireland—was Slainge [two-syll.: Slang-a]. From the time of his accession down to the birth of Christ, they allow 107 monarchs, of whom 9 were Firbolgs; 9 Dedannans; and 89 Milesians. The last king of the period before the Christian era was Nuada Necht or Nuada the White: and his successor, Conari the First, or Conari the Great, was the first king belonging to the Christian era. The Milesian kings continued to reign till the time of Roderick O'Conor, the last over-king of Ireland, who died in 1198; and who, according to the bardic accounts, was the 193rd monarch of Ireland. A list of the over-kings, with dates, is given in the larger Social History, vol. i., p. 68.

As to the records of the very early kings, they cannot, of course, be received as history: but neither should they be rejected altogether: it is as much of a fault to be too sceptical as to be too credulous.

---

* For these see my Short History of Ireland, p. 123.

Sculpture on Chance Arch, Monastery Church, Glendalough; drawn, 1845.
(From Petrie's Round Towers)

CHAPTER III.

WARFARE.

SECTION 1. *Foreign Conquests and Colonisations.*

LIKE their ancestors the Continental Celts, the Irish, from the earliest ages, had a genius for war and a love of fighting. In the writings of classical Latin and Greek authors are found many passages that indicate the warlike character the ancient Irish had earned for themselves among foreign nations. They were not contented with fighting at home, but made themselves formidable in other lands. Their chief foreign conquests were in Wales and Scotland: but they not unfrequently found their way to the Continent. In those times the Scots, as the Irish were then called, seem to have been almost as much dreaded as the Norsemen were in later ages. Irish literature of every kind abounds in records of foreign invasions and alliances; and the native accounts are corroborated by Roman writers, so far as they touch on these matters.

All who have read the histories of England and Rome know how prominently the "Picts and Scots" figure during the first four centuries of our era, and how much trouble they gave to both Romans and Britons. The Picts were the people of Scotland: the Scots were the Irish Gaels. As a protection against these two tribes, the Romans, at different intervals in the second and third centuries, built those great walls or ramparts from sea to sea between Britain and Alban, so well known in the history of those times, the ruins of which still remain. For three or four centuries the Irish continued their incursions to Britain and Scotland, sometimes fighting as invaders against the Picts, sometimes combining with them against Romans and Britons; and as a consequence there were several settlements of colonies from Ireland in Wales and Scotland.

Criffan the Great, who reigned in Ireland from A.D. 366 to 379, is celebrated for his conquests in Britain, in all the Irish histories and traditions dealing with that time, so that he is often called Criffan the Great, " king of Ireland and of Alban to the Ictian Sea ": " Alban " here meaning, not Scotland, but Great Britain; and the " Ictian Sea," the English Channel. His reign is almost exactly coincident with the command of the Roman general Theodosius (father of the emperor Theodosius the Great), who, according to the Roman historians, checked the career of the Gaels and their allies. The Irish accounts of Criffan's invasion of Britain are in the main corroborated by the Roman poet Claudian, in those passages of his poem that celebrate the victories of Theodosius. The continual attacks of the three tribes—Scots, Picts, and Saxons—became at last so intolerable that the Roman government was forced to take defensive measures. In 367, the year after Criffan's accession, Theodosius was appointed to the military command of Britain; and, after two active campaigns, he succeeded in delivering that country for the time from the invaders.

Criffan was succeeded as king of Ireland by Niall of the Nine Hostages (A.D. 379 to 405), who was still more distinguished for foreign conquests than his predecessor. Moore (Hist. I. 150) thus speaks of his incursions into Wales:—" An invasion of Britain, on a far more extensive and formidable scale than had yet been attempted from Ireland, took place towards the close of the fourth century under Niall of the Nine Hostages, one of the most gallant of all the princes of the Milesian race." He collected a great fleet, and landing in Wales, carried off immense plunder: but was at last forced to retreat by the valiant Roman general Stilicho. On this occasion Claudian, when praising Stilicho, says of him— speaking in the person of Britannia:—" By him was I protected when the Scot [*i.e.* Niall] moved all Ireland against me, and the ocean foamed with their hostile oars." The Irish narratives of Niall's life and actions add that he invaded Gaul, which was his last exploit; for he was assassinated (A.D. 405) on the shore of the river Loire by one of his own chiefs, the king of Leinster, who shot him dead with an arrow.

The extensive scale of these terrible raids is strikingly indicated by no less an authority than St. Patrick, who, in his "Confession," speaking of the expedition—probably led by Niall—in which he himself was captured, says:—"I was then about sixteen years of age, being ignorant of the true God; I was brought captive into Ireland, *with so many thousand men*, according as we had deserved."

Welsh scholars, from Lhuyd of two centuries ago, to Principal Rhys of the present day, as well as historical inquirers of other nationalities, have investigated this question of the Irish conquests in Wales, quite independently of Irish records: and they have come to the conclusion that, at some early time, extensive districts of Wales were occupied by the Irish; and, as a consequence, numerous places in Wales have to this day names commemorating the invaders: as, for instance, the Welsh name of Holyhead, *Cerrig y Gwyddell*, the 'Rocks of the Goidels or Gaels'; and the Welsh language still contains many Irish words, or words evidently derived from Irish. After careful examination of all the evidence, Dr. Jones, a Welshman, bishop of St. David's, in a book written by him on this subject, comes to the conclusion that the Gaels from Ireland once occupied the whole of Anglesey, Carnarvon, Merioneth, and Cardiganshire, and parts of Denbighshire, Montgomery, and Radnor. But besides all this, ancient Welsh literature—history, annals, tales, legends—like that of Ireland, abounds with references to invasions of Wales and other parts of Britain by Irishmen. In those early days too, as might be expected, a continual intimate relationship by intermarriage was kept up between the Irish kings and chiefs on the one side, and the ruling families of western and northern Britain on the other, which is fully set forth in our ancient books of genealogy.

About the period of the series of expeditions to

Wales, the Irish also mastered the Isle of Man: and Irish literature abounds with references to the constant intercourse kept up by the parent people with those of their little insular colony. Though the Norsemen wrested the sovereignty of the island from them in the ninth century, they did not succeed in displacing either the Gaelic people or their language. The best possible proof of the Irish colonisation and complete and continued occupation of the island is the fact that the Manx language is merely a dialect of Irish, spelled phonetically, but otherwise very little altered. There are also still to be seen, all over the island, Irish buildings and monuments, mixed up, however, with many of Norse origin: and the great majority of both the place-names and the native family-names are Gaelic.

Niall's successor Dathi [Dauhy], king of Ireland, A.D. 405 to 428, followed in the footsteps of his predecessors, and, according to Irish authorities, invaded Gaul: but was killed by a flash of lightning at the foot of the Alps, after his followers had destroyed the hermitage of a recluse named Formenius or Parmenius. Although this legend looks wild and improbable, it is in some respects corroborated by continental authorities, and by present existing names of places at the head of Lake Zurich: so that there is very likely some foundation for the story.

We will now go back in point of time to sketch the Irish colonisation of north Britain, the accounts of which, however, are a good deal mixed with those of the Welsh settlements. From very early ages, the Irish of Ulster were in the habit of crossing the narrow sea to Alban or Scotland, where colonies were settled from time to time: and constant intercourse was kept up between the two countries down to a late period. The authentic history of these expeditions and settlements begins in the early part of the third century, during the reign of Conari II. (A.D. 212–220). This king had three sons, Carbery Musc, Carbery Baskin, and Carbery Riada. At this time a great famine devastated Munster; and Carbery Riada led a number of his Munster people to Ulster and to the south-west of Scotland, in both which places they settled down permanently.

These Irish narratives are confirmed by the Venerable Bede in his Ecclesiastical History, where he says:—"In course of time, besides the Britons and Picts, Britain received a third nation, the Scots, who, migrating from Ireland under their leader Reuda, obtained for themselves, either by friendly agreement or by force of arms, those settlements among the Picts which they still hold. From the name of their commander they are to this day called Dalreudini: for in their tongue *dal* signifies a part." The "Dalreudini" of Bede is the Dalriada of Irish history.

These primitive settlers increased and multiplied; and, supported from time to time by contingents from the mother country, they held their ground against the Picts. But the settlement was weak and struggling till the reign of Lewy, king of Ireland (A.D. 483 to 512), about three centuries after the time of Carbery Riada. In the year 503 three brothers named Fergus, Angus, and Lorne, sons of a chief named Erc, a direct descendant of Carbery Riada, led a colony to Scotland from their own district in the Irish Dalriada (in the present Co. Antrim: see map): descendants of the Munster settlers of three centuries before. They appear to have met with little or no opposition, and being joined by the previous settlers, they took possession of a large territory, of which Fergus, commonly called Fergus mac Erc, and also known as Fergus More (the Great), was the first king. The descendants of these colonists ultimately mastered the whole country; and from them its name was changed from Alban to Scotia or Scotland. Fergus was the ancestor of the subsequent kings of Scotland; and from him, in one of their lines of genealogy, descend, through the Stuarts, our present royal family.

2. *Military Ranks, Orders, and Services.*

At different periods of our early history the kings had in their service bodies of militia, who underwent a yearly course of training, and who were at call like a standing army whenever the monarch required them. The most celebrated of these were the " Red Branch Knights" of about the time of the Incarnation, and the "*Fianna* or Fena of Erin," who flourished in the third century. Though the accounts that have come down to us of these two military organisations are much mixed up with romance and fable, there is sufficient evidence to show that they really existed and exercised great influence in their day.

The **Red Branch Knights** belonged wholly to Ulster, and in the ancient Tales they are represented as in the service of Concobar mac Nessa, king of that province, but not king of Ireland. The king's palace was Emain or Emania near Armagh, of which a description will be found in chap. xvi., sect. 5, below.

Every year during the summer months, various companies of the Knights came to Emain under their several commanders, to be drilled and trained in military science and feats of arms. The greatest Red Branch commander was Cuculainn, a demigod, the mightiest of the heroes of Irish romance. The other, chief heroes were Conall Kernach; Laegaire (or Laery) the Victorious; Keltar of the Battles; Fergus mac Roy: the poet Bricriu "of the venom tongue," who lived at Loughbrickland, where his fort still remains near the little lake; and the three sons of Usna—Naisi, Ainnle, and Ardan. All these figure in the ancient literature.

The Red Branch Knights had a passion for building great duns or forts, many of which remain to this day, and excite the wonder and awe of visitors. Besides Emain itself, there is the majestic fort of Dun-Dalgan, Cuculainn's residence, a mile west of the present town of Dundalk. This dun consists of a high mound surrounded by an earthen rampart and trench, all of an immense size, even in their ruined state; but it has lost its old name, and is now called the Moat of Castletown, while the original name Dundalgan, slightly altered, has been transferred to Dundalk. Another of these Red Branch Knights' residences stands beside Downpatrick: viz. the great fort anciently called (among other names) Dun-Keltair, or Rath-Keltair, where lived the hero, Keltar of the Battles. It consists of a huge embankment of earth, nearly circular, with the usual deep trench outside it, enclosing a great mound, all covering a space of about ten acres. Still another,

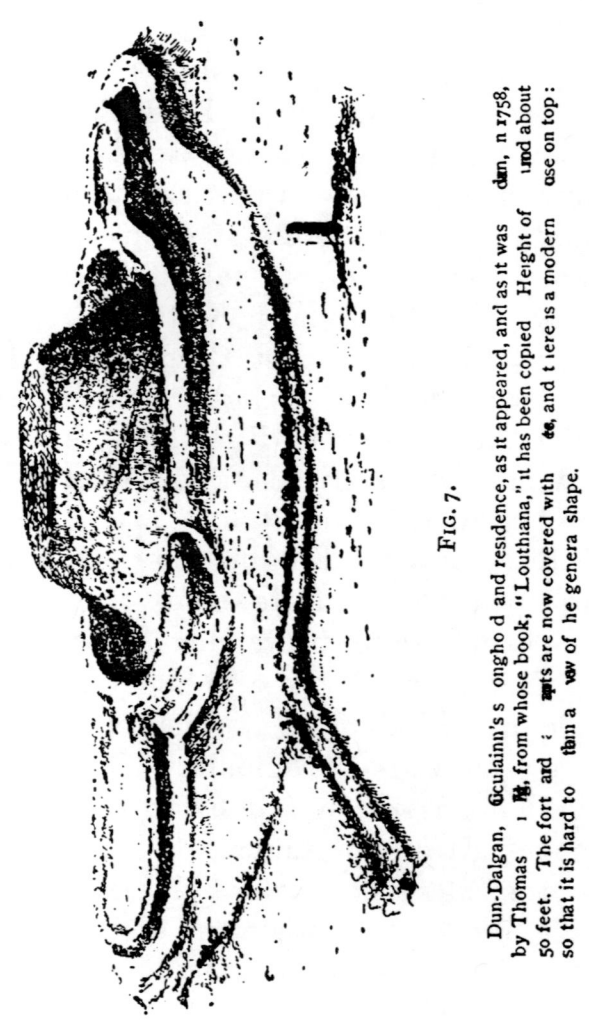

Fig. 7.

Dun-Dalgan, Cuculainn's stronghold and residence, as it appeared, and as it was drawn, in 1758, by Thomas Wright, from whose book, "Louthiana," it has been copied and about 50 feet. The fort and its appendants are now covered with trees, and there is a modern house on top: so that it is hard to obtain a view of the general shape.

which figures much in the old romances under its ancient name *Dun-da-benn*—but now called Mountsandall—crowns the high bank over the Cutts

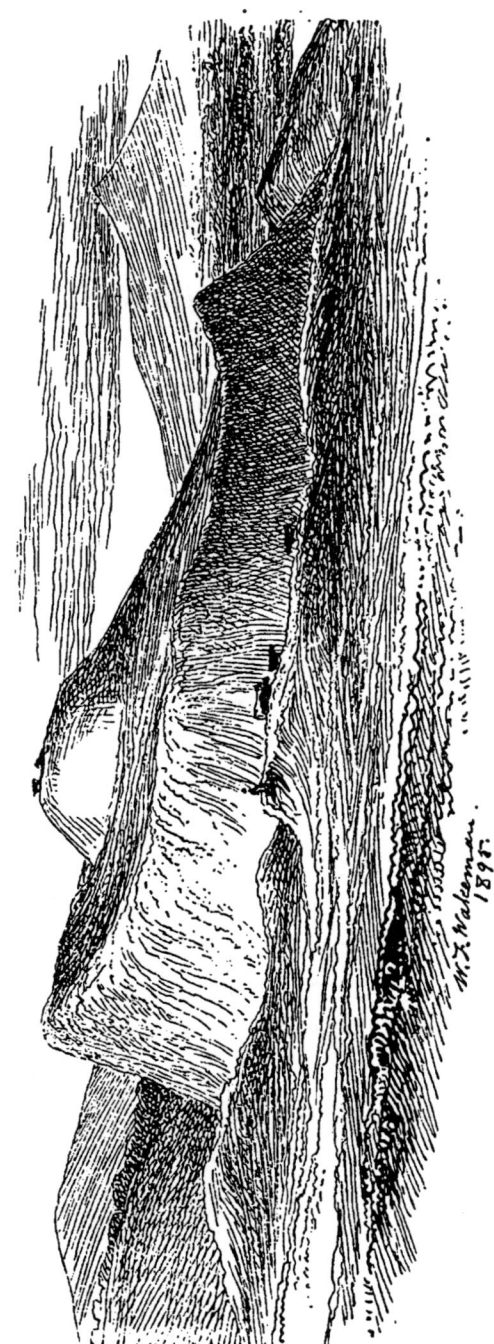

FIG. 8.

Rath-Ketara, Downpatrick. From Co Wood-Martin's Traces of the Elder Faiths of Ireland.

waterfall on the Bann, near Coleraine. Four miles west of this is a similar fortress, now known by the name of the "Giant's Sconce," which is the ancient *Dun Cethern* [Doon-Kehern], so called from "Cethern of the Brilliant Deeds," a famous Red Branch Knight. John de Courcy's original Castle of Dundrum, in Down, was built on the site of one of the most formidable of all—Dun-Rury—the immense earthworks of which still remain round the present castle, at the base of the rock, though the original dun-mound on the top was levelled by the castle-builders.

Contemporary with the Red Branch Knights were the **Degads** of Munster—but of Ulster extraction—whose chief was Curoi mac Dáirĕ, king of South Munster; and the **Gamanraide** [Gowanree] of Connaught, commanded by Keth mac Magach and by the renowned hero Ferdiad. Curoi lived in a *caher* or stone fort on a rocky shelf 2050 feet over the sea, on the mountain of Caherconree, near Tralee, whose ruins remain there to this day. As a still further evidence that the old legends and romances about Curoi rest on a foundation of fact, not only is the old stone fortress there to witness, but, like *Emain* and *Creeveroe* (the "Red Branch": for which see chap. xvi., sect. 5), in the north, it retains its ancient name, which has been extended to the whole mountain, and which commemorates the mighty hero himself: for "Caherconree" correctly represents the sound of the Irish name *Cathair-Chonroi*, the caher or stone fortress of Curoi.

The Red Branch Knights, as well as those of Munster and Connaught, used chariots both in battle and in private life. Chariot-racing too was one of their favourite amusements: and the great heroes are constantly described in the tales as fighting from their chariots.

The **Fianna** or **Fena of Erin**, so far as we can trace their history with any certainty, lasted for about a century. They attained their greatest power in the reign of Cormac mac Art (254 to 277) under their most renowned commander Finn, the son of Cumal, or Finn mac Coole as he is commonly called, King Cormac's son-in-law, who is recorded in the Annals to have been killed beside the Boyne, when an old man.

The chief heroes under Finn, who figure in the tales, were:—Oisin or Ossian, his son, the renowned hero-poet to whom the bards attribute—but we know erroneously—many poems still extant; Oscar the brave and gentle, the son of Ossian; Dermot O'Dyna, unconquerably brave, of untarnished honour, generous and self-denying, the finest character in all Irish literature, perhaps the finest in any literature; Goll mac Morna, the mighty leader of the Connaught Fena; Cailte [Keelta] mac Ronan the swift-footed: Conan Mail or Conan the Bald, large-bodied, foul-tongued, boastful, cowardly, and gluttonous.

Before admission to the ranks, candidates were subjected to certain severe tests, both physical and mental, one of which deserves special mention here:—No candidate was allowed to join unless he had mastered a certain specified and large amount of poetry and tales: that is to say, he had to prove that he was a well-educated man, according to the standard of the times: a provision that anticipated by seventeen centuries the condition of admission to the higher posts of our present military service, designed to ensure that every commissioned officer of the army shall be a man of good general education. This—whether history or legend—shows what was regarded as the general standard of education in Ireland in those times. The physical tests consisted of running, leaping, defence against an attack of armed spearmen, and such like.

Of all the heroes of ancient Ireland Finn is most vividly remembered in popular tradition. He had his chief residence on the summit of the Hill of Allen, a remarkable flat-topped hill, lying about four miles to the right of the railway as you pass Newbridge and approach Kildare, rendered more conspicuous of late years by a tall pillar erected on the top, on the very site of Finn's house. So far as we can judge from the old accounts, the house was built altogether of wood—like the "Red Branch"—without any earthen rampart round it: and accordingly no trace of a rampart or earthen dun remains. At this day the whole neighbourhood round the hill teems with living traditions of Finn and the Fena.

When not employed in training or fighting, the Fena spent the six months of summer—from the 1st of May to the 31st of October—hunting, and lived on the produce of the chase, camping out all the time: during the remaining six months they were billeted on the well-to-do people all over the country—fed and lodged free. After King Cormac's death they became openly rebellious, claiming in some respects to rule even the monarch of Ireland. At last the king—Carbery of the Liffey, Cormac

mac Art's son, who came to the throne A.D. 279 — marched against them, and annihilated them in the bloody battle of Gavra, near Skreen in Meath (A.D. 297): but was himself slain in the battle.

We have seen that the Red Branch Knights, and their contemporary heroes of Munster and Connaught, fought, rode, and raced in chariots; and that they erected immense duns or forts. In both these respects the Fena of Erin stand in complete contrast. In none of the tales or other literature of the Fena is it mentioned that they used chariots in battle, and they scarcely ever used them in any way, though during the whole period of their existence chariots were used all through Ireland. Then as to duns: while we have still remaining the majestic ruins of many of the forts erected by the Red Branch Knights, as shown at page 39, there are, so far as I can find out, no corresponding forts in any part of Ireland attributed to the Fena in the ancient tales. Even on the Hill of Allen, where if anywhere we might expect to find a mighty fortification like that at Downpatrick, there is no vestige of a rath. No forts, large or small, that I know of, commemorate any others of the great leaders—Ossian, Oscar, Dermot O'Dyna, Goll mac Morna, Cailte mac Ronain, or Conan Mail, such as we have for Cuculainn, Keltar of the Battles, Cethern of the Brilliant Deeds, Curoi mac Dáire, and others; though during their time forts were built by chiefs and people all over the country.

To come to strictly historic times:—**Ordinary War Service** was of several kinds. Every man who held land in any sort of tenancy was obliged to bear a part in the wars of the tribe and in the defence of their common territory. The number of days in the year that each should serve was strictly defined by law: and when the time was ended, he might return to his home—unless some very special need arose. A chief or king, if required, was bound to send a certain number of men, fully armed, for a fixed time periodically, to serve his superior in war. The men of the superior king's own immediate territory, with the contingents supplied to him from the several subordinate tribes by their chiefs, went to form his army. The tributary chief again made up the contingent to be sent to his superior, partly from his own household troops, and partly by small contingents from his sub-chiefs.

The king had in his service a champion or chief fighting man, called *Airĕ-echta*—always a *flaith* or noble (see page 77, *below*)—whose duty it was to avenge all insults or offences offered to the families of the king and tribe, particularly murder: like the "avenger of blood" of the Jews and other ancient nations. In any expected danger from without he had to keep watch—with a sufficient force—at the most dangerous ford or pass—called *bearna baoghaill* [barna beel] or "gap of danger"—on that part of the border where invasion was expected, and prevent the entrance of any enemy.

Kings and great chiefs almost always kept bodies of mercenary soldiers—commonly small in number and often as a mere bodyguard—under regular pay, something like the soldiers of our present standing army. These men hired themselves wherever they could get the best pay. Hired soldiers are constantly mentioned in our ancient records. Bodies of Scotchmen, and of Welshmen, were very often in the service of Irish kings: and we also find companies of Irish under similar conditions serving in Wales and Scotland.

The maintenance and pay of such soldiers was called in Irish *buanacht*, whence men serving for pay and support were often called "bonnaghts" by English writers of the time of Elizabeth. The practice of hiring foreign mercenaries, which was commenced at a very early period, was continued down to the sixteenth century: and we have already seen (p. 27, *supra*) that Shane O'Neill had a number of fierce soldiers from Scotland as bodyguard.

These several bodies constituted a small standing army. But where large armies had to be brought into the field, the men of the tribe or tribes owing allegiance and service were called upon to serve. It was understood, however, that this was only for the single campaign, or for some specified time, as already stated, at the end of which they were free to return to their homes. An army of men on campaign usually consisted of men of all the different kinds of service.

Military Asylums—According to the "Battle of Rossnaree," in the Book of Leinster, there was an asylum for the old warriors of the Red Branch—in some manner corresponding with the present Chelsea Hospital, and with the Royal Hospital in Dublin—where those who were too old to fight were kept in ease and comfort: and it was under the direction of one governor or commander. It was probably supported partly at the public expense, and partly by payments from the inmates: but on this point there is no information.

Knighthood.—As far back as our oldest traditions reach there existed in Ireland an institution of knighthood. The Red Branch Knights have already been mentioned: and it appears that admission to their ranks was attended with much formality. It was usual to knight boys at an early age, commonly at seven years. This was the age, according to the statement of Tigernach—and also of the Tales—at which the young hero Cuculainn was admitted: and his example as to age was often followed in subsequent times. The young candidate was given a number of little spears suitable to his age and strength, which he hurled against a shield; and the more spears he broke the more credit he received. These are the native Irish accounts; and they are strikingly corroborated by Froissart, who tells us that the same custom still existed in Ireland when King Richard II. visited this country in 1494. This historian moreover states that the custom of knighting boys at seven, with ceremonies like those of the Irish, existed among the Anglo-Saxon kings. But in Ireland the rule of the seven years was not universally, or even generally, followed—except perhaps in case of the sons of kings or great nobles. The ceremony was commonly put off till the candidate was able to fight. The usual Irish words for a knight are *curad* [curra] and *ridire* [riddera], of which the last is the same as the German *ritter*, and is probably borrowed. "Assuming knighthood" is commonly expressed in Irish by "taking valour."

3. *Arms, Offensive and Defensive.*

Handstone.—Among the missive weapons of the ancient Irish was the handstone, which was kept ready for use in the hollow of the shield, and flung from the hand when the occasion came for using it. Handstones were specially made, and were believed to possess some sort of malign mystical quality, which rendered them very dangerous to the enemy. The handstone was called by various names, such as *cloch, lia, lec,* &c.

Sling and Sling-stones.—A much more effective instrument for stone-throwing was the sling, which is constantly mentioned in the Tales of the Táin, as well as in Cormac's Glossary and other authorities, in such a way as to show that it formed an important item in the offensive arms of a warrior. The accounts, in the old writings, of the dexterity and fatal precision with which Cuculainn and other heroes flung their sling-stones, remind us of the Scriptural record of the 700 chosen warriors of Gibeah who could fight with left and right hand alike, and who flung their sling-stones with such aim that they could hit even a hair, and not miss by the stone's going on either side (Judges xx. 16).

The Irish used two kinds of sling. One, which was called by two names *teilm* and *taball* [tellim taval] consisted of two thongs attached to a piece of leather at bottom to hold the stone or other missile: a form of sling which was common all over the world, and which continues to be used by boys to this day. The other was called *crann-tabaill,* i.e. 'wood-sling'

50 GOVERNMENT, MILITARY SYSTEM, AND LAW. [PART I.

or 'staff-sling,' from *crann*, 'a tree, a staff, a piece of wood of any kind'; which indicates that the sling so designated was formed of a long staff of wood with one or two thongs—like the slings we read of as used by many other ancient nations. David killed Goliath with a staff-sling. Those who carried a sling kept a supply of round stones, sometimes artificially formed. Numerous sling-stones have been found from time to time—many perfectly round—in raths and crannoges, some the size of a small plum, some as large as an orange, of which many specimens are preserved in museums.

Though the Irish had the **Bow and Arrow**, it was never a favourite weapon with them. They used only the long bow, which was from four to five feet in length, and called *fidbac* [feevak], signifying 'wood-bend,'

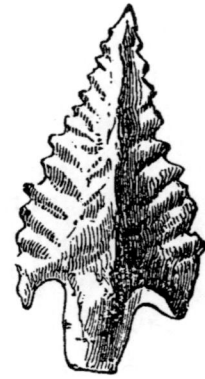

FIG. 9.   FIG. 10.   FIG. 11.

Flint arrow-heads. Fig. 9 shows arrow with a piece of the shaft and the tying gut as it was found. (From Wilde's Catalogue.)

from *fid*, 'wood,' and *bac*, 'a bend.' The arrow, which was called *saiged* [sy'-ed], was tipped with flint or metal. A supply of arrows was kept in a quiver, called *saiged-bolg*, meaning 'arrow-bag.' Arrow-heads, both of flint and of bronze, are constantly found in every part of Ireland, and may be seen in vast numbers in the National Museum. Those of bronze are usually made with a hollow *cro* or socket into which the wood was inserted.

The Mace—The club or mace—known by two names—*matan* and *lorg*—though pretty often mentioned, does not appear to have been very generally used. In the Tales, a giant or an unusually strong and mighty champion, is sometimes represented as armed with a mace. There can be no doubt that the mace was used: for in the National Museum in Dublin there are several specimens of bronze mace-heads with projecting spikes. One of them is here represented, which, fixed firmly on the top of a strong *lorg* or handle, and wielded by a powerful arm, must have been a formidable weapon.

FIG. 12.

Bronze head of Irish battle-mace, now in the National Museum, Dublin. The handle was fastened in the socket. Picture half size.

Spear.—The Irish battle-spears were used both for thrusting and for casting. They were of various shapes and sizes: but all consisted of a bronze or iron head, fixed on a wooden handle by means of a hollow *cro* or socket, into which the end of the handle was thrust and kept in place by rivets. The manufacture of spear-heads was carried to great perfection in Ireland at a very early age—long before the Christian era—and many of those preserved in our museums are extremely graceful and beautiful in design and perfect in finish: evidently the work of trained and highly skilled artists. The iron spears were hammered into shape: those of bronze were cast in moulds, and several specimens of these moulds may be seen in the National Museum (see chapter xx., section 3, *infra*). Both bronze and iron spear-heads are mentioned in our oldest literature.

In the National Museum in Dublin there is a collection of several hundred spear-heads of all shapes and sizes, the greater number of bronze, but some of iron, and some of copper; and every other museum in the country has its own collection. They vary in length from 36 inches down. Some of the Irish names for spear-heads designated special shapes, while others were applied to spears of whatever shape or size.

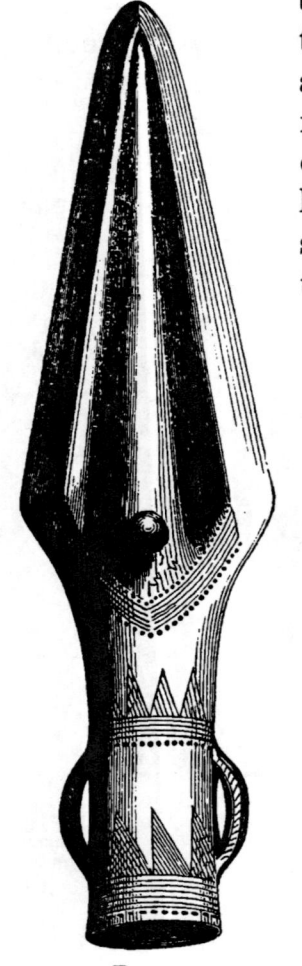

FIG. 13.   FIG. 14.

Specimens of bronze spear-heads in the National Museum, Dublin. (From Wilde's Catalogue.)

CHAP. III.] WARFARE. 53

The words *qae, ga,* or *gai*; *faga* or *foga*; and *sleg* (now written *sleagh*: pron. sla) were sometimes used as terms for a spear or javelin in general. Among the spears of the Firbolgs was one called *fiarlann* [feerlann], 'curved blade' (*fiar*, 'curved'; *lann*, 'a blade'), of which many specimens are to be seen in the National Museum. The *fiarlann* was rather a short sword than a spear.

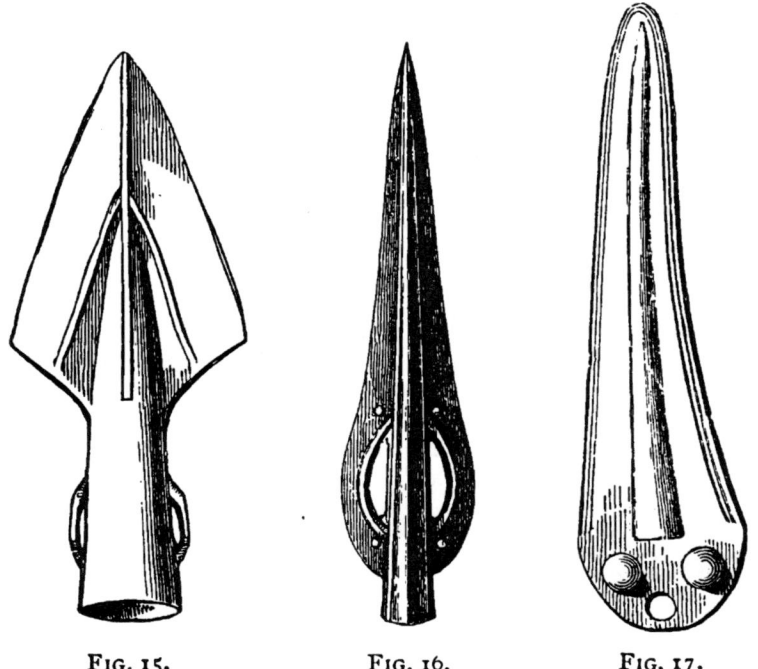

FIG. 15. FIG. 16. FIG. 17.

Fig. 15, a Firbolg spear-head; fig. 16, a Dedannan one; fig. 17, a Fiarlann. Now in the National Museum, Dublin.

In the ancient Irish battle-tales a sharp distinction is made between the spears of the Firbolgs and of the Dedannans respectively: to which O'Curry first drew attention. The Firbolg spears are described as broad and thick, with the top rounded and sharp-edged, and having a thick handle. The spear used by the Dedannans was very different, being long, narrow, and graceful, with a very sharp point. Whether these two colonies are fictitious or not, a large number of spear-heads in the National Museum answer to those descriptions.

The Irish casting-spear was usually furnished with a loop of string called *suanem* or *suaineamh* [soonev] attached to the handle near the middle, and made of silk or flax. The Greeks and Romans had a loop of a similar kind on their spears—called *amentum* by the Latins: but how exactly the loop was used by Greeks, Romans, or Irish, or what its effect was, is a matter of conjecture. We only know that, like the Roman soldier, the Irish warrior put his forefinger in the loop in the act of casting.

Some of the spears of the heroes of the Red Branch and other great champions are described in the old legends as terrible and mysterious weapons. The spear of Keltar of the Battles, which was called *Lón* or *Luin*, twisted and writhed in the hand of the warrior who bore it, striving to make for the victim whose blood was ready for spilling. Some spears were regularly seized with a rage for massacre; and then the bronze head grew red-hot, so that it had to be kept near a caldron of cold water, or, more commonly, of black poisonous liquid, into which it was plunged whenever it blazed up with the murder fit. The Greeks of old had the same notion; and those fearful Irish spears remind us of the spear of Achilles, as mentioned by Homer, which when the infuriated hero flung it at Lycaon, missed the intended victim, and, plunging into the earth, " stood in the ground,

CHAP. III.] WARFARE. 55

hungering for the flesh of men." So also another Greek hero is made to say·— "My spear rageth in my hands," with the eagerness to plunge at the Trojans.

Sword.—The Irish were fond of adorning their swords elaborately. Those who could afford it had the hilt ornamented with gold and gems. But the most common practice was to set the hilts round with the teeth of large sea-animals, especially those of the sea-horse—a custom also common among the Welsh. This practice was noticed by the Roman geographer Solinus in the third century A.D.:—"Those [of the Irish] who cultivate elegance adorn the hilts of their swords with the teeth of great sea-animals."

The usual term for an ordinary sword was *cloidem* [cleeve]: and one of the largest size was called *cloidem-mór*, a name which the Scotch retain to this day in the Anglicised form "claymore," which nearly

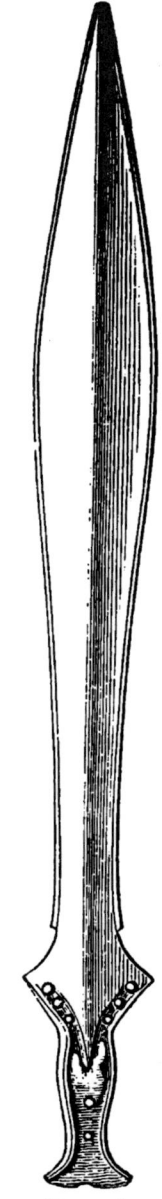

FIG. 18.
Ancient Irish bronze sword: 22½ in long: in Nat Mus, Dub. The hilt was riveted on. (From Wilde's Catalogue.)

FIG. 19.
Bronze scabbard; now 19½ in. long. (From Kilk. Arch. Journ.)

represents the proper sound. Many warriors practised to use the sword with the left hand as well as with the right, so as to be able to alternate, or to fight with one in each hand as occasion required. Some made it a practice to sleep with their favourite sword lying beside them under the bed-clothes. A short sword or dagger was much in use among the Irish, called a *scian* [skean], literally a 'knife.'

The blade (*lann*) was kept in a sheath or scabbard. Sometimes the sheath was made of bronze: and several of these are preserved in museums. The beautiful specimen figured on last page was found in a crannoge.

The **battle-axe** (*tuag* or *tuagh*, pron. tooa) has been in use from prehistoric times in Ireland; as is evident from the fact that numerous axe-heads of stone, as well as of bronze, copper,

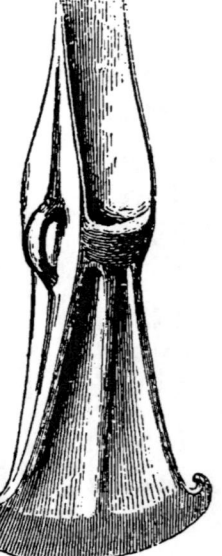
Fig. 20.

Fig. 21.

Two types of metallic celts or early battle-axes   (From Wilde's Catalogue)

and iron, have been found from time to time, and are to be seen in hundreds in the National Museum and elsewhere. These are now commonly called *celts*, of which the illustrations on last page will give a good idea.

In later times the Irish were noted for their fatal dexterity with the battle-axe. Giraldus mentions that among other weapons they had a heavy axe excellently well wrought and tempered; and he goes on to say:—" They make use of but

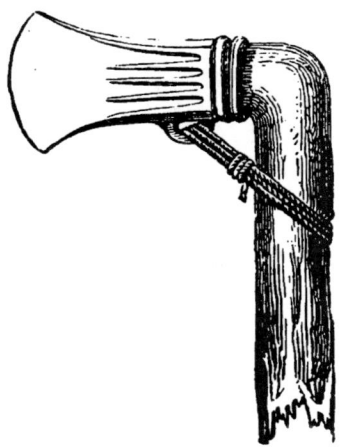

FIG. 22.   FIG. 23.

To show how the metallic celts or axe-heads were fastened on handles. Fig. 23 shows one found in its original handle, as seen in the illustration. It has a loop underneath, which is partly eaten away by rust. Fig. 22 is a conjectural restoration of the fastening of this kind of celt. (From Wilde's Catalogue.)

one hand to the axe when they strike, and extend the thumb along the handle to guide the blow from which neither the crested helmet can defend the head, nor the iron folds of the armour the rest of the body. From whence it has happened, even in our times, that the whole thigh of a soldier, though cased in well-tempered armour, hath been lopped off by a single blow of the axe." There were two kinds of battle-axes: a broad one, generally used by galloglasses, and a long, narrow one, called a *sparra* or *sparth*: examples of both are illustrated in figures 24 and 25. The narrow axe seems to have been the earlier form.

FIG. 24.

FIG. 25.

Fig. 24, Dermot Mac Murrogh, with the narrow battle-axe called "sparra" or "sparth." In a MS. of Giraldus Cambrensis (From Wilde's Catalogue.) Fig. 25, two galloglasses depicted on a map of Ireland of 1567: showing the broad battle-axe. One of the two galloglasses in fig. 29 below holds a broad axe.

Armour.—We know from the best authorities that at the time of the invasion—*i.e.*, in the twelfth century—the Irish used no metallic armour. Giraldus says:—"They go to battle without armour, considering it a burden, and deeming it brave and honourable to fight without it."

The Danes wore armour: and it is not unlikely that the Irish may have begun to imitate them before the twelfth century: but, if so, it was only in rare cases. They never took to it till after the twelfth century, and then only in imitation of the English.

But the tales describe another kind of protective covering as worn by Cuculainn, and by others; namely, a primitive corslet made of bull-hide leather stitched with thongs, " for repelling lances and sword-points, and spears, so that they used to fly off from him as if they struck against a stone." Greaves to protect the legs from the knee down were used, and called by the name *asán*.

Helmet.—That the Irish wore a helmet of some kind in battle is certain: but it is not an easy matter to determine the exact shape and material. It was called *cathbharr* [caffār], *i.e.*, ' battle-top,' or battle-cap, from *cath* [cah], ' a battle,' and *barr*, ' the top.' It was probably made of hard tanned leather, possibly chequered with bars of iron or bronze. The warriors often dyed their helmets in colours: and there was commonly a crest on top.

Shield.—From the earliest period of history and tradition, and doubtless from times beyond the reach of both, the Irish used shields in battle. The most ancient shields were made of wicker-work, covered with hides: they were oval-shaped, often large enough to cover the whole body, and convex on the outside. It was to this primitive shield that the Irish first applied the word *sciath* [skeé-ă], which afterwards came to be the most general name for a shield of whatever size or material. These wicker shields—of various sizes—continued in use in Ulster even so late as the sixteenth century, and in the Highlands of Scotland till 200 years ago.

Shields were ornamented with devices or figures, the design on each being a sort of cognisance of the owner to distinguish him from all others. These designs would appear to have generally consisted of concentric circles, often ornamented with circular rows of projecting studs or bosses, and variously spaced and coloured for different shields. As generally confirming the truth of these accounts, the shields in the Museum have a number of beautifully wrought concentric circles formed either of continuous lines or of rows of studs; as seen in the illustration. Sometimes figures of animals were painted on shields.

Shields were often coloured according to the fancy of the wearer. We read of some as brown, some blood-red; while many were made pure white. This fashion of painting shields in various colours continued in use to the time of Elizabeth.

Hide-covered shields were often whitened with lime or chalk, which was allowed to dry and harden, as soldiers now pipeclay their belts. Hence we often find in the Tales such expressions as the following:—" There was an atmosphere of fire from [the clashing of] sword and spear-edge, and a cloud of white dust from the *cailc* or lime of the shields."

The shields in most general use were circular, small, and light, of wickerwork, yew, or more rarely of bronze, from 13 to 20 inches in diameter, as we see by numerous figures of armed men on the high crosses and in manuscripts, all of whom are repre-

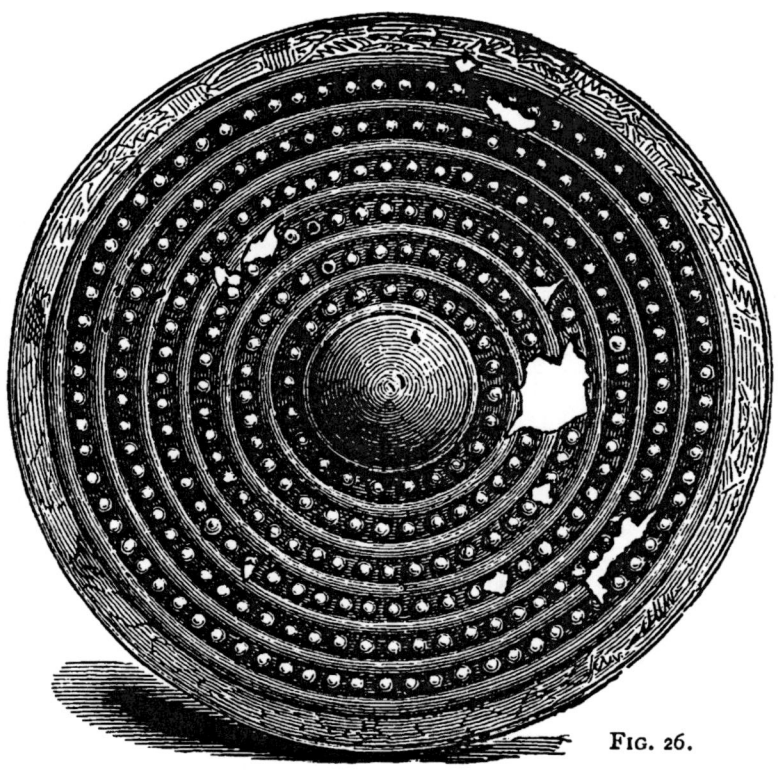

FIG. 26.

Bronze Shield. Fig. 26, front or outside; fig. 27, back or inside.

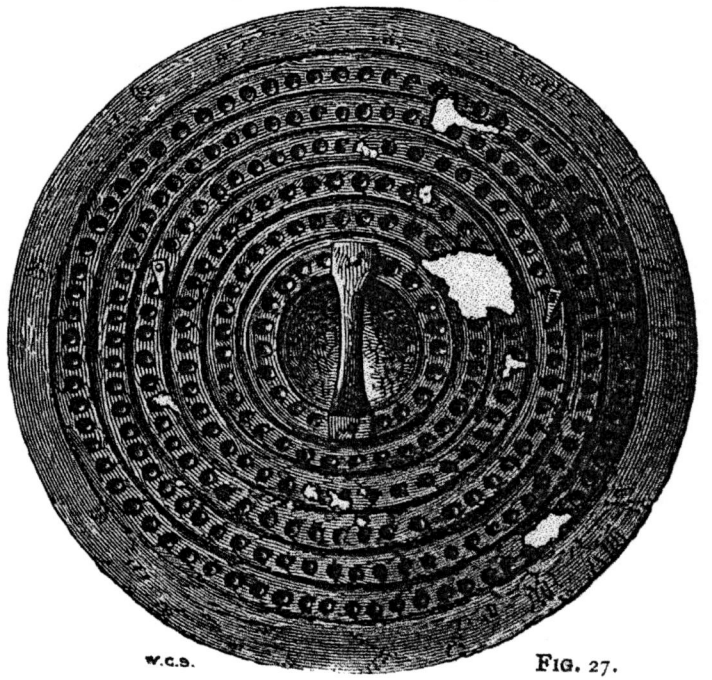

FIG. 27.

sented with shields of this size and shape. I do not remember seeing one with the large oval shield. Specimens of both yew and bronze shields have been found, and are now preserved in museums. Shields were cleaned up and brightened before battle. Those that required it were newly coloured, or whitened with a fresh coating of chalk or lime: and the metallic ones were burnished—all done by gillies or pages.

The shield, when in use, was held in the left hand by a looped handle or crossbar, or by a strong leather strap, in the centre of the inside, as seen in fig. 27, above. But as an additional precaution it was secured by a long strap, called *iris* or *sciathrach* [skiheragh], that went loosely round the neck. When not in use, it was slung over the shoulder by the strap from the neck.

In pagan times it was believed that the shield of a king or of any great commander, when its bearer was dangerously pressed in battle, uttered a loud melancholy moan which was heard all over Ireland, and which the shields of other heroes took up and continued. The shield-moan was further prolonged; for as soon as it was heard, the "Three Waves of Erin" uttered their loud melancholy roar in response. (For the Three Waves, see chap. xxvi., sect. 9.)

4. *Strategy, Tactics, and Modes of Fighting.*

Subordination of Ranks.—Though the discipline of the Irish in time of war and on the field of battle was very inferior to that of the Anglo-Normans, we are not to conclude that they were ignorant or careless of the Science and Art of War. On the contrary, military science was studied with much care. The whole army was divided into *catha* [caha] or battalions, each *cath* consisting of 3000 men with a commander; and these again were parcelled into smaller companies, down to nine, with officers regularly descending in rank.

Encampment.—During marches the leaders were very particular about their encampments. Even when the halt was only for a night or two, careful arrangements were made as to tents, sitting-places, sleeping accommodation, bathing, cooking, etc.: and everything was done to make the encampment comfortable and enjoyable. In all cases the camp was fortified, so far as the time permitted: and of course sentinels were set while the army slept. Where the sojourn was likely to be pretty long, more elaborate arrangements were made.

Sentinels and Watchmen.—In the early stages of society, when wars were frequent, look-out points were very important: sometimes they were on the seashore, so that the sentinel might catch sight of invaders from the sea.

Immediately beside the palace, or the temporary residence, of every king or great chief, a sentinel or watchman kept watch and ward day and night. In time of battle or campaign, warriors slept at night with a single weapon by their side for use in any sudden alarm, their principal arms hanging on the racks in the proper place.

Heralds.—In the course of warfare, heralds or envoys were often employed, as among all other nations. When on their mission, they were regarded as sacred and inviolable, and were treated with the utmost respect, even by the bitterest enemies : exactly as Homer describes the heralds of the Greeks. Heralds had a special dress by which they were at once recognised ; and they commonly carried in one hand a white wand or hand-staff, and in the other a sword, symbolical of the alternative to be accepted—peace or war.

Banners, Flags, and Standards.—From the earliest period of their history the Irish used banners or standards, which were borne before the army when going into battle, or on ordinary marches : a custom common to the Celts and Romans, but unknown to the Homeric Greeks. In Ireland the office of standard-bearer to each king or chief was hereditary, like all other important functions.

A banner is denoted by the word *méirge* [mair-ya]. In the accounts of many of the ancient Irish battles, there are descriptions of the standards borne by each chief or clan. The commander-in-chief had his own banner, and so had each captain under his command : and each usually bore some device or figure, so that the several captains and companies could be distinguished from a distance ; and their deeds recorded by the shanachies who attended the army. The attendant shanachies of those old times answered in some sort to the war correspondents of our own day. The standard of Ulster was a yellow lion on green satin ; that of Dalaradia, yellow satin ; of O'Sullivan, a spear with an adder entwined with it ; and so on.

Cathach or 'Battler.'—In Christian times it was usual for the ruler of a clan, tribe, or sub-kingdom, to have a relic, commonly consecrated by the patron saint of the district, which the chief brought to battle with him, in the hope that it would ensure victory: somewhat as the Jews used the Ark of the Covenant. Such a relic was called a *cathach* [caha], i.e. *præliator* or 'battler.' The usual formula for the use of the *cathach* was to cause it to be carried *desiol* or sunwise —commonly by an ecclesiastic—three times round the army before the battle began.

The most celebrated of these battle-relics was the *cathach* or battle-book of the O'Donnells of Tirconnell, which may now be seen in the National Museum in Dublin. It is a small square box or shrine made of silver gilt, with enamel and precious stones, containing a copy of a portion of the Psalms, once believed to have been written by St. Columkille, the patron of the Kinel Connell, or O'Donnell family. The permanent *cathach* or battle-relic of each tribe was placed in the keeping of some particular family. This was considered a great honour; and the family had usually a tract of land free of rent, as well as other perquisites, as payment for the faithful discharge of their duty as custodians.

Chivalry.—In Ireland, in ancient times, people as a general rule declined to take advantage of surprises or stratagems in war. They had a sort of chivalrous feeling in the matter, and did not seek to conceal—and sometimes even gave open notice of— intended attacks, or came to an agreement with their adversaries as to the time and place to fight the matter out. In later ages, and at the present day, such plain, unsophisticated dealing would be looked upon as bad generalship. But not unfrequently a general rose up with unusual military genius and with less scrupulous notions of chivalry, who did not hesitate to employ ambush and other stratagems. and many victories are recorded as obtained by these means.

Medical Attendance in Battle.—A number of physicians or surgeons always accompanied an army going to battle to attend to the wounded, who were brought to them at the rear during the fight. This was quite an established institution from the most remote times—a fact of which there can be no doubt, notwithstanding the number of fables and exaggerations that are mixed up with the accounts of their cures. We are now familiar with the humane practice in war of giving medical aid after the battle to the wounded, without distinction of friend or enemy: and it is interesting to observe that the same idea was equally familiar to the writers of the Táin Bó Quelna. When Cethern [Kehern], a famous Ulster warrior, returned from a fight against the Connaught forces, all covered with wounds, a request was sent to the Connaught camp—the enemy's—for physicians for him, as it happened that none of the Ulster physicians were at the moment available: and physicians were at once despatched with the messenger.

Military Formation and Marching.—In going to battle the Irish often rushed pell-mell in a crowd without any order. But they sometimes adopted a more scientific plan, advancing in regular formation, shoulder to shoulder, forming a solid front with shields and spears. On the morning of the day of battle each man usually put as much food in a wallet that hung by his side as was sufficient for the day. When a commander had reason to suspect the loyalty or courage of any of his men in a coming battle, he sometimes adopted a curious plan to prevent desertion or flight off the field. He fettered them securely in pairs, leg to leg, leaving them free in all other respects.

Horse and Foot.—Cavalry did not form an important feature of the ancient Irish military system: we do not find cavalry mentioned at all in the Battle of Clontarf, either as used by the Irish or Danes. But kings kept in their service small bodies of horse-soldiers, commonly called in Irish "horse-host." The chief men, too, often rode in battle, and the leaders fought on horseback. After the Anglo-Norman Invasion cavalry came into general use. Each horseman had at least one footman to attend him—called a *gilla* or *dalteen*—armed only with a dart or javelin. In later times each horseman had two and sometimes three attendants.

FIG. 28.

Foot-soldier preparing to receive charge. One of several grotesque figures in the illustrations of the Book of Kells (seventh or eighth century) This shows that when receiving a charge, the Irish soldiers—sometimes at least—went on one knee. (From Wilde's Catalogue)

Two kinds of foot-soldiers are often mentioned in Irish records, the kern and galloglasses. The kern were light-armed soldiers: they wore headpieces, and fought with a *skian* (a dagger or short sword) and with a javelin.

The galloglasses appear only in later times—after the Anglo-Norman Invasion. They are not met with in ancient Irish writings. They were heavy-armed infantry, wearing a coat of mail and an iron helmet, with a long sword by the side, and carrying in the hand a broad, heavy, keen-edged axe. They are usually described as large-limbed, tall, and

FIG. 29.

Two of the eight galloglasses on King Felim O'Conor's tomb in Roscommon Abbey (thirteenth century). (From Kilk. Archæol Journ)

fierce-looking. It is almost certain that the galloglasses, and the mode of equipping them, were imitated from the English.

Trumpets.—The Irish constantly used bronze war-trumpets in battle, as will be found mentioned in the chapter on Music ; and from a gloss written by an Irishman in the eighth century we know that even at that early time the trumpeters had different notes or musical phrases to direct different movements—for battle, for unyoking, for marching, for retiring to sleep, for going into council, etc.

War-Cries.—The armies charged with a great shout called *barrán-glaed* [barran-glay], 'warrior-shout'—a custom which continued until late times. The different tribes and clans had also special war-cries; and the Anglo-Normans fell in with this custom, as they did with many others. The war-cry of the O'Neills was *Lamh-derg aboo*, i.e. 'the Red-hand to victory' (*lamh*, pron. lauv, 'a hand'), from the figure of a bloody hand on their crest or cognisance: that of the O'Briens and Mac Carthys, *Lamh-laidir aboo*, 'the Strong-hand to victory' (*laidir*, pron. lauder, 'strong'). The Kildare Fitz Geralds took as their cry *Crom aboo*, from the great Geraldine castle of Crom or Croom in Limerick; the Earl of Desmond, *Shanit aboo*, from the castle of Shanid in Limerick. The Butlers' cry was *Butler aboo*. Most of the other chiefs, both native and Anglo-Irish, had their several cries. Martin found this custom among the people of the Hebrides in 1703; and in Ireland war-cries continued in use to our own day.

CHAPTER IV.

THE BREHON LAWS.

Section 1. *The Brehons.*

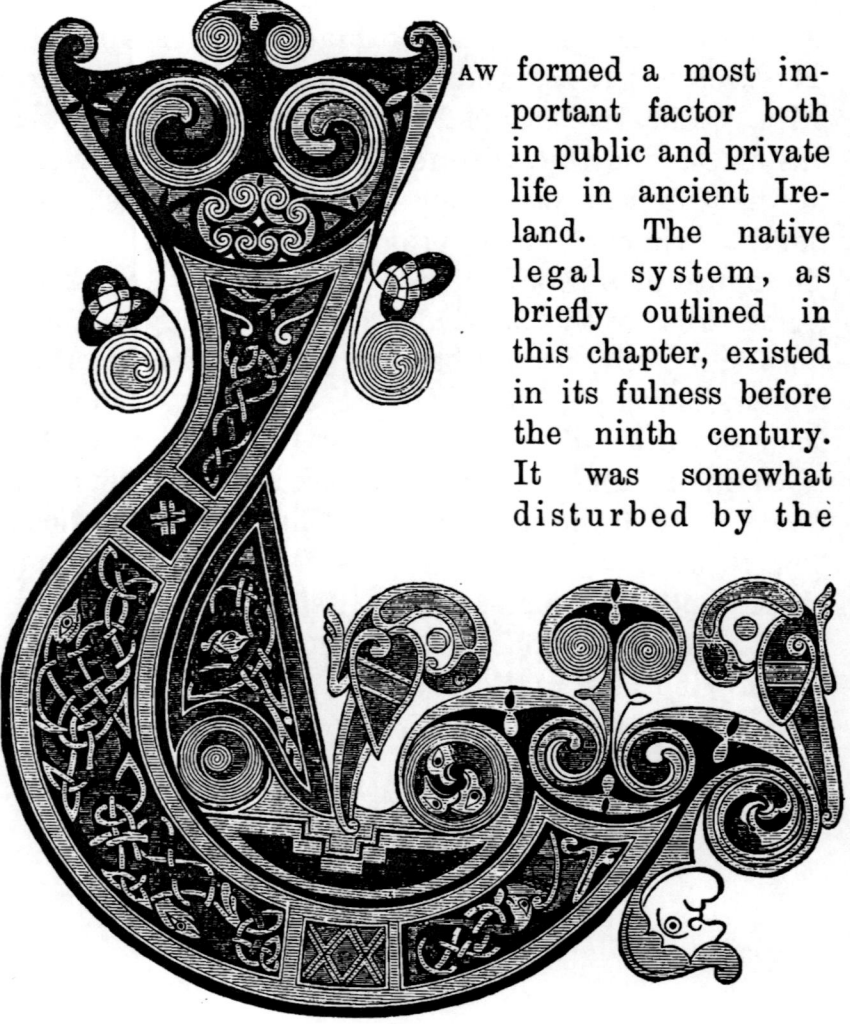

Law formed a most important factor both in public and private life in ancient Ireland. The native legal system, as briefly outlined in this chapter, existed in its fulness before the ninth century. It was somewhat disturbed by the

Fig. 30.

Capital L in Book of Kells: full size. (From Miss Stokes's Early Christian Art in Ireland.)

Danish and Anglo-Norman invasions, and still more by the English settlement; but it continued in use till finally abolished in the beginning of the seventeenth century. In this short chapter I merely attempt a popular sketch of the main features of the Brehon laws, devoid of technical legal terms.

In Ireland a judge was called a **brehon**, whence the native Irish law is commonly known as the "Brehon Law"; but its proper designation is **Fénechas**, *i.e.* the law of the *Féine* or *Féne*, or free land-tillers. The brehons had absolutely in their hands the interpretation of the laws and the application of them to individual cases. They were therefore a very influential class of men; and those attached to chiefs had free lands for their maintenance, which, like the profession itself, remained in the same family for generations. Those not so attached lived simply on the fees of their profession, and many eminent brehons became wealthy. The legal rules, as set forth in the Law Books, were commonly very complicated and mixed up with a variety of technical terms; and many forms had to be gone through and many circumstances taken into account, all legally essential: so that no outsider could hope to master their intricacies. The brehon had to be very careful; for he was himself liable for damages, besides forfeiting his fee, if he delivered a false or an unjust judgment.

To become a brehon a person had to go through a regular, well-defined course of study and training. It would appear that the same course qualified for any branch of the legal profession, and that once a man had mastered the course, he might set up as

a brehon or judge proper, a consulting lawyer, an advocate, or a law-agent. In very early times the brehon was regarded as a mysterious, half-inspired person, and a divine power kept watch over his pronouncements to punish him for unjust judgments:—"When the brehons deviated from the truth, there appeared blotches upon their cheeks." The great brehon, Morann, son of Carbery Kinncat (king of Ireland in the first century), wore a *sin* [sheen] or collar round his neck, which tightened when he delivered a false judgment, and expanded again when he delivered the true one. All this agrees with the whole tenor of Irish literature, whether legendary, legal, or historical, which shows the great respect the Irish entertained for justice pure and simple according to law, and their horror of unjust decisions. It was the same at the most ancient period as it was in the beginning of the seventeenth century, when Sir John Davies—an Englishman—the Irish attorney-general of James I., testified:—
"For there is no nation of people under the sunne that doth love equall and indifferent [*i.e.* impartial] justice better then the Irish; or will rest better satisfied with the execution thereof, although it bee against themselves: so as they may have the protection and benefit of the law, when uppon just cause they do desire it." But later on the Penal Laws changed all that, and turned the Irish natural love of justice into hatred and distrust of law, which in many ways continues to manifest itself to this day.

2. *The Senchus Mór and other Books of Law.*

The brehons had collections of laws in volumes or tracts, all in the Irish language, by which they regulated their judgments, and which those of them who kept law-schools expounded to their scholars; each tract treating of one subject or one group of subjects. Many of these have been preserved, and of late years the most important have been published, with translations, forming five printed volumes (with a sixth consisting of a valuable Glossary to the preceding five). Of the tracts contained in these volumes, the two largest and most important are the **Senchus Mór** [Shanahus More] and the **Book of Acaill** [Ack'ill].

In the ancient Introduction to the Senchus Mór the following account is given of its original compilation. In the year 438 A.D. a collection of the pagan laws was made at the request of St. Patrick; and Laegaire [Laery], king of Ireland, appointed a committee of nine learned and eminent persons, including himself and St. Patrick, to revise them. At the end of three years these nine produced a new code, from which everything that clashed with the Christian doctrine had been carefully excluded. This was the Senchus Mór.

The very book left by St. Patrick and the others has been long lost. Successive copies were made from time to time, with commentaries and explanations appended, till the manuscripts we now possess were produced. The existing manuscript copies of the Senchus Mór consist of:—1. The original text, written in a large hand with wide spaces between the lines: 2. An introduction to the text:

74 GOVERNMENT, MILITARY SYSTEM, AND LAW. [PART I.

3. Commentaries on the text, in a smaller hand:
4. Glosses or explanations on words and phrases of the text, in a hand still smaller: commentaries and glosses commonly written in the spaces between the

FIG. 31.

Facsimile specimen of the Senchus Mór. The four lines of large text are a part of the Senchus Mór proper; and they are to be read in the order, second, first, third, fourth. The commentary (i.e the small text) consists of seventeen lines and, supposing them to be numbered from top to bottom, they are to be read in this way.—Begin at line 8 (which comments on the line of larger text right under it); then 7, 6, 5, part of 4 and part of 3 (both as far as the curve; the rest of 4, the rest of 3; then 2, 1 Resume at 9 and go on in like manner—sometimes upwards, sometimes downwards—to the end. the reader being guided all through by the context No glosses occur on this facsimile

lines of the text, but often on the margins. Of these the text, as might be expected, is the most ancient.

The laws were written in the oldest dialect of the Irish language, called *Bérla Féini* [Bairla-faina], which even at the time was so difficult that persons about to become brehons had to be specially instructed in it. Even the authors of the Commentaries and Glosses who wrote hundreds of years ago, and were themselves learned brehons, were often quite at fault in their attempts to explain the archaic text: and their words show that they were fully conscious of the difficulty. It will then be readily understood that the task of translating these laws was a very difficult one, rendered all the more so by the number of technical terms and phrases, many of which are to this day obscure, as well as by the peculiar style, which is very elliptical and abrupt—often incomplete sentences, or mere catch-words of rules not written down in full, but held in memory by the experts of the time. Another circumstance that greatly adds to the difficulty of deciphering these MSS. is the confused way in which the Commentaries and glosses are written in, mainly with the object of economising the expensive vellum. The explanatory note under fig. 31 will give some idea of this.

The two great Irish scholars—O'Donovan and O'Curry—who translated the Laws included in the five printed volumes, were able to do so only after a life-long study; and in numerous instances were, to the last, not quite sure of the meaning. As they had to retain the legal terms and the elliptical style, even the translation is hard enough to understand, and is often unintelligible. It is, moreover, imperfect for another reason: it was only a preliminary and provisional translation, containing many imperfections and errors, to be afterwards corrected; but the translators did not live to revise it, and it was printed as they left it.

3. *Suitability of the Brehon Laws.*

The Brehon Code forms a great body of civil, military, and criminal law. It regulates the various ranks of society, from the king down to the slave, and enumerates their several rights and privileges. There are minute rules for the management of property, for the several industries—building, brewing, mills, water-courses, fishing-weirs, bees and honey—for distress or seizure of goods, for tithes, trespass, and evidence. The relations of landlord and tenant, the fees of professional men—doctors, judges, teachers, builders, artificers,—the mutual duties of father and son, of foster-parents and foster-children, of master and servant, are all carefully regulated. In that portion corresponding to what is now known as criminal law, the various offences are minutely distinguished :—murder, manslaughter, assaults, wounding, thefts, and all sorts of wilful damage ; and accidental injuries from flails, sledge-hammers, machines, and weapons of all kinds ; and the amount of compensation is laid down in detail for almost every possible variety of injury.

The Brehon Law was vehemently condemned by English writers ; and in several acts of parliament it was made treason for the English settlers to use it. But these testimonies are to be received with much reserve as coming from prejudiced and interested parties. We have good reason to believe that the Brehon Law was very well suited to the society in which, and from which, it grew up. This view is confirmed by the well-known fact that when the

English settlers living outside the Pale adopted the Irish manners and customs, they all, both high and low, abandoned their own law and adopted the Brehon Code, to which they became quite as much attached as the Irish themselves.

4. *Structure of Society.*

Five main Classes of People.—The lay people were divided into classes, from the king down to the slave, and the Brehon Law took cognizance of all—setting forth their rights, duties, and privileges. The leading, though not the sole, qualification to confer rank was property; the rank being, roughly speaking, in proportion to the amount. Under certain conditions, persons could pass from one class to the next above, always provided their character was unimpeachable.

There were five main classes of people :—1. Kings of several grades, from the king of the *tuath* or cantred up to the king of Ireland: 2. Nobles, which class indeed included kings: 3. Non-noble Freemen with property: 4. Non-noble Freemen without property, or with some, but not sufficient to place them among the class next above: 5. The non-free classes. The first three—Kings, Nobles, non-noble Freemen with property—were the privileged classes; a person belonging to these was an **aire** [arra] or chief. Kings have been treated of in chapter ii.

Flaiths or Nobles.—The Nobles were those who had land as their own property, for which they did not pay rent: they were the owners of the soil—the aristocracy. An *aire* of this class was called a

Flaith [flah], *i.e.* a noble, a chief, a prince. There were several ranks of nobles, the rank depending chiefly on the amount of landed property.

Non-noble Freemen with Property.—A person belonging to the other class of *aire*—a non-noble rent-paying freeman with property (No. 3, above)—had no land of his own, his property consisting of cattle and other movable goods; hence he was called a **Bo-aire**, *i.e.* a 'cow-chief' (*bo*, 'a cow'). He should rent a certain amount of land, and possess a certain amount of property in cattle and other goods, to entitle him to rank as an *aire*. As in the case of the nobles, there were several classes of bo-aires, ranking according to their property. If a person belonging to the highest class of bo-aires could prove that he had twice as much property as was required for the lowest rank of noble, and complied with certain other conditions and formalities, and also provided his father and grandfather had been *aires* who owned land, he was himself entitled to take rank as a noble of the lowest rank.

The three preceding main classes—kings, nobles, and *bo-aires*—were all aires, chiefs, or privileged people: the first two being *flaiths* or noble aires, the third, non-noble aires, *i.e.* free tenants, with property sufficient to entitle them to the position of aire. All three had some part in the government of the country and in the administration of the law, as kings, tanists, nobles, military chiefs, magistrates, and persons otherwise in authority; and they commonly wore a *flesc* or bracelet on the arm as a mark of their dignity.

Non-noble Freemen without Property.—The next class—the fourth—the freemen with little or with no property, were *céiles* [kailas] or free tenants. They differed from the *bo-aires* only in not being rich enough to rank as *aires* or chiefs; for the bo-aires were themselves céiles or rent-payers; and accordingly a man of the fourth class could become a bo-aire if he accumulated property enough: the amount being laid down in the Brehon Law. These *céiles* or tenants, or free rent-payers—corresponding with the old English *ceorls* or churls—formed the great body of the farming class. They were called *aithech* [ah'-egh], *i.e.* 'plebeian,' 'farmer,' 'peasant,' to distinguish them from the *aires* or chieftain grades: and the term *féini* or *féne* [fainĕ], which means much the same as *aithech*, was also applied to them.

The land held by the féine or free tenants was either a part of the tribe-land (for which see p. 82, below), or was the private property of some *flaith* or noble, from whom they rented it. Everywhere in the literature, especially in the laws, the féine or free farming classes are spoken of as a most important part of the community—as the foundation of society, and as the ultimate source of law and authority.

Tradesmen formed another very important class of freemen. The greater number belonged to the fourth class—freemen without property. Some crafts were 'noble' or privileged, of which the members enjoyed advantages and privileges beyond those of other trades: and some high-class craftsmen belonged to the class *aire* or chief.

The Non-free Classes.—So far we have treated of freemen, that is those who enjoyed all the rights of the tribe, of which the most important was the right to the use of a portion of the tribe-land and commons (for which see p. 83, below). We now come to treat of the non-free classes. The term 'non-free' does not necessarily mean that they were slaves. The non-free people were those who had not the full rights of the free people of the tribe. They had no claim to any part of the tribe-land, though they were permitted, under strict conditions, to till little plots for mere subsistence. This was by far the most serious of their disabilities. Their standing varied, some being absolute slaves, some little removed from slavery, and others far above it. That slavery pure and simple existed in Ireland in early times we know from the law-books as well as from history; and that it continued to a comparatively late period is proved by the testimony of Giraldus Cambrensis—twelfth century—who relates that it was a common custom among the English to sell their children and other relatives to the Irish for slaves—Bristol being the great mart for the trade. From this, as well as from our own records, we see that some slaves were imported. But the greater number were native Irish, who, from various causes had lost their liberty and had been reduced to a state of slavery.

Groups of Society.—The people were formed into groups of various sizes, from the family upwards. The **Family** was the group consisting of the living parents and all their descendants. The **Sept** was a larger group, descended from common parents long since dead: but this is an imported word, brought into use in comparatively late times. All the members of a sept were nearly related, and in later times bore the same surname. The **Clan** or **house** was still larger. *Clann* means 'children,' and the word therefore implied descent from one ancestor. The word *finè* [finna] usually meant a group of persons related by blood within certain degrees of consanguinity, all residing in the same neighbourhood; but it was often applied in a much wider sense. The **Tribe** (*tuath*) was made up of several septs, clans, or houses, and usually claimed, like the subordinate groups, to be descended from a common ancestor. The adoption of strangers—sometimes individuals, sometimes whole groups—into the family or clan was common; but it required the consent of the *finè* or circle of near relations—formally given at a court meeting. From all this it will be seen that in every tribe there was much admixture; and the theory of common descent from one ancestor became a fiction, except for the leading families, who kept a careful record of their genealogy.

5. *The Laws relating to Land.*

Land originally common Property.—It would appear that originally—in prehistoric times—the land was all common property, belonging to the tribe, not to individuals, and chief and people were liable to be called on to give up their portions for a new distribution. But as time went on, this custom was gradually broken in upon; and the lands held by some, after long possession, came to be looked upon as private property. As far back as our records go, there was some private ownership in land.

Five ways of holding Land.—Within historic times the following were the rules of land tenure, as set forth chiefly in the Brehon Laws, and also in some important points by early English writers. The tribe (or aggregate of tribes), under the rule of one king or chief, held permanently a definite district of the country. The tribe was divided, as already described, into smaller groups—clans or septs—each of which, being governed by a sub-chief under the chief of the tribe, was a sort of miniature of the whole tribe; and each clan was permanently settled down on a separate portion of the land, which was considered as their separate property, and which was not interfered with by any other clans or septs of the tribe. The land was held by individuals in some one of **five** different ways.

First.—The chief, whether of the tribe or of the sept, had a portion as mensal land, for life or for as long as he remained chief (for which, see p. 22, *supra*).

Second.—Another portion was held as private property by persons who had come, in various ways, to own the land.

Third.—Persons held, as tenants, portions of the lands belonging to those who owned it as private property, or portions of the mensal land of the chief—much like tenants of the present day: these paid what was equivalent to rent—always in kind. The term was commonly seven years, and they might sublet to under-tenants.

Fourth.—The rest of the arable land, which was called the **Tribe-land**—equivalent to the *folc* or folk land of England—forming by far the largest part of the territory, belonged to the people in general, the several subdivisions of it to the several septs, no part being private property. This was occupied by the free members of the sept, who were owners for the time being, each of his own farm. Every free man had a right to his share—a right never questioned. Those who occupied the tribe-land did not hold for any fixed term, for the land of the sept was liable to gavelkind (page 86, below) or redistribution from time to time—once every three or four years. Yet they were not tenants at will, for they could not be disturbed till the time of gavelling; even then each man kept his crops and got compensation for unexhausted improvements; and though he gave up one farm, he always got another.

Fifth.—The non-arable or waste land—mountain, forest, bog, &c.—was **Commons-land**. This was not appropriated by individuals; but every free man had a right to use it for grazing, for procuring fuel, or for the chase. There was no need of subdividing the commons by fences, for the cattle of all grazed over it without distinction. This custom still exists in many places all through Ireland.

The portion of territory occupied by each clan or sept commonly included land held in all the five ways here described. It should be observed that the individuals and families who owned land as private property were comparatively few, and their possessions were not extensive: the great bulk of both people and land fell under the conditions of tenure described under the Fourth and Fifth headings.

Tenants: their Payments and Subsidies.—Every tribesman had to pay to his chief certain subsidies according to his means. Those who held portion of the tribe-land, and who used the commons-land for grazing or other purposes, paid these subsidies of course; but beyond this they had no rent to pay to any individual for land held or used under headings *four* and *five* described above.

The tribesman who placed himself under the protection of a chief, and who held land, whether it was the private property of the lessor or a part of the general tribe-land, was, as already explained, a **Céile** [cail'eh] or tenant; also called *féinĕ* and *aithech*, i.e. a plebeian, farmer, or rent-payer. But a man who takes land must have stock—cows and sheep for the pasture-land, horses or oxen to carry on the work of tillage. A small proportion of the céiles had stock of their own, but the great majority had not. Where the tenant needed stock it was the custom for the chief to give him as much as he wanted at certain rates of payment. This custom of giving and taking stock on hire was universal in Ireland, and was regulated in great detail by the Brehon Law.

Every tenant and every tradesman had to give his chief a yearly or half-yearly tribute, chiefly food-supplies—cows, pigs, corn, bacon, butter, honey, malt for making ale, &c.—the amount chiefly depending on the quantity of land he held and on the amount of stock he hired. Some tenants were obliged to give **coinmed** [coiney]. that is to say, the chief was privileged to go with a retinue, for one or more days to the house of the tenant, who was to lodge and feed them for the time. This was an evil custom, liable to great abuse; and it was afterwards imitated by the Anglo-Norman chiefs, who called it

coyne and livery; which they chiefly levied from their own people, the English settlers. They committed great excesses, and their coyne and livery was far worse than the Irish *coinmed*, so that it came at last to be forbidden by the English law.

There was a numerous class of very poor unfree tenants called **fudirs**, who were generally in a very wretched condition. They were tenants at will, having no right in their holdings. A fudir was completely at the mercy of his chief, who might turn him off at any time, and who generally rackrented him so as to leave barely enough for subsistence.

The ancient rights of the tenants, *i.e.* of the *céiles* or freemen, were chiefly three·—A right to some portion of the arable or tribe-land, and to the use of the commons: a right to pay no more than a fair rent, which, in the absence of express agreement, was adjusted by the Brehon Law: a right to own a house and homestead, and (with certain equitable exceptions) all unexhausted improvements. Among the freemen who held farm land there was no such thing as eviction from house or farm, for there was a universal conviction that the landlord was not the absolute owner, so that all free tenants had what was equivalent to fixity of tenure. If a man failed to pay the subsidy to his chief, or the rent of land held in any way, or the debt due for stock, it was recovered, like any other debt, by the processes described in next section, never by process of eviction.

Descent of Land.—In Ireland the land descended in three different ways.

First, as **private property.**—When a man had land understood to be his own, it would naturally pass to his heirs; or he might if he wished divide it among them during his life—a thing that was sometimes done.

Second.—The land held by the chief as mensal estate descended, not to his heir, but to the person who succeeded him in the chiefship. This is what is known as descent by **Tanistry**.

Third, by **Gavelkind**.—When a tenant who held a part of the tribe-land died, his farm did not go to his children: but the whole of the land belonging to the *finè* or sept was redivided or *gavelled* among all the male adult members of the sept—including the dead man's adult sons. The domain of the chief, and all land that was private property, were exempt. The redistribution by gavelkind on each occasion extended to the clan or sept—not beyond. Davies complains, with justice, that this custom prevented the tenants from making permanent improvements.

The two customs of Tanistry and Gavelkind formerly prevailed all over Europe, and continued in Russia till a very recent period: and Gavelkind, in a modified form, still exists in Kent. They were abolished and made illegal in Ireland in the reign of James **I.**; after which land descended to the next heir according to English law.

6. *The Administration of Justice.*

The Law of Compensation.—In very early times, beyond the reach of history, the **law of retaliation** prevailed, as in most other countries—"an eye for an eye, a tooth for a tooth"—in other words, every man or every family that was injured might take direct revenge on the offender. But this being found inconsistent with the peace and well-being of the community—especially in cases of homicide, which were frequent enough in those days—gradually gave place to the **law of compensation,** which applied to every form of injury. In Ireland the process was this :—The injured party sued the offender in proper form, and, if the latter responded, the case was referred to the local brehon, who decided according to law. The penalty always took the form of a fine to be paid by the offender to the person or family injured, and the brehon's fee was usually paid out of this fine.

Procedure by Distress.—If the offender refused to submit the case to the usual tribunal, or if he withheld payment after the case had been decided against him, or if a man refused to pay a just debt of any kind—in any one of these cases the plaintiff or the creditor proceeded by **Distress**; that is to say, he *distrained* or seized the cattle or other effects of the defendant. We will suppose the effects to be cattle. There was generally an **anad** or stay of one or more days on the distress; that is, the plaintiff went through the form of seizing the cattle, but did not remove them. During the stay the cattle remained in the possession of the defendant or debtor, no doubt to give him time to make up his mind as to what course to take, viz. either to pay the debt or to have the case tried before the brehon: but the plaintiff had all the time a claim on them. If the debt was not paid at the end of the lawful stay, the plaintiff, in the presence of certain witnesses, removed the animals and put them in a pound, the expense of feeding and tending being paid out of the value of the cattle. If the debtor persisted in refusing to settle the case, the creditor sold or kept as many of the cattle as paid the debt.

Procedure by Fasting.—In some cases before distress was resorted to, a curious custom came into play:—the plaintiff "**fasted** on" the defendant. It was done in this way. The plaintiff, having served due notice, went to the house of the defendant, and, sitting before the door, remained there without food; and as long as he remained, the defendant was also obliged to fast. It may be inferred that the debtor generally yielded before the fast was ended, *i.e.* either paid the debt or gave a pledge that he would settle the case. This fasting process—which exists still in India—was regarded with a sort of superstitious awe; and it was considered outrageously disgraceful for a defendant not to submit to it. It is pretty evident that the man who refused to abide by the custom, not only incurred personal danger, but lost all character, and was subject to something like what we now call a universal boycott, which in those days no man could bear. He had in fact to fly and become a sort of outlaw.

Eric or Compensation Fine.—Homicide or bodily injury of any kind was atoned for by a fine called **Eric** [errick]. The injured person brought the offender before a brehon, by whom the case was tried and the exact amount of the eric was adjudged. Many modifying circumstances had to be taken into account—the actual injury, the rank of the parties, the intention of the wrong-doer, the provocation, the amount of set-off claims, &c.—so that the settlement called for much legal knowledge, tact, and technical skill on the part of the brehon—quite as much as we expect in a lawyer of the present day.

In case of homicide the family of the victim were entitled to the eric. If the culprit did not pay, or absconded, leaving no property, his *finè* or family were liable. If he refused to come before a brehon, or if, after trial, the eric fine was not paid by him or his family, then he might be lawfully killed. The eric for bodily injury depended, to some extent, on the "dignity" of the part injured: if it was the forehead, or chin, or any other part of the face, the eric was greater than if the injured part was covered by raiment. Half the eric for homicide was due for the loss of a leg, a hand, an eye, or an ear; but in no case was the collective eric for such injuries to exceed the "body-fine"—*i.e.* the eric for homicide.

The principle of compensation for murder and for unintentional homicide existed among the Anglo-Saxons, as well as among the ancient Greeks, Franks, and Germans. In the laws of the English king Athelstan, there is laid down a detailed scale of prices to be paid in compensation for killing persons of various ranks of society, from an archbishop or duke down to a churl or farmer; and traces of the custom remained in English law till the early part of the last century..

Modes of Punishment.—There was no such thing as a sentence of death passed by a brehon in a court of law, no matter what the crime was: it was always compensation; and the brehon's business was to determine the amount. Capital punishment was known well enough, however, and practised, outside the courts of law. Kings claimed the right to put persons to death for certain crimes. Thus we are told, in the Tripartite Life of St. Patrick, that neither gold nor silver would be accepted from him who lighted a fire before the lighting of the festival fire of Tara, but he should be put to death; and the death-penalty was inflicted on anyone who, at a fair-meeting, killed another or raised a serious quarrel. We have seen that if for any cause homicide was not atoned for by eric, then the criminal's life was forfeit.

Various modes of putting criminals to death were in use in ancient Ireland. Sometimes they were hanged. Sometimes the culprit was drowned by being flung into water, either tied up in a sack or with a heavy stone round his neck.

Where the death penalty was not inflicted for a crime, various other modes of punishment were resorted to, though never as the result of a judicial process before a brehon. Blinding as a punishment was very common, not only in Ireland but among many other nations. A very singular punishment was to send the culprit adrift on the open sea in a boat, without sail, oar, or rudder; as, for instance, in case of homicide, if it was unintentional. A person of this kind cast on shore belonged to the owner of the shore until a *cumal* was paid for his release.

Courts of Justice.—Courts for the trial of legal cases, as well as meetings of representative people to settle local affairs, were often held in the open air —sometimes on green little hills, and sometimes in buildings. There was a gradation of courts, from the lowest—something like our petty sessions—to the highest, the great national assembly—whether at Tara or elsewhere—representing all Ireland. Over each court a member of the chieftain or privileged classes presided : the rank of the president corresponded to the rank of the court; and his legal status, duties, powers, and privileges were very strictly defined. The over-king presided over the National *Féis* or assembly.

In each court—besides the brehon who sat in judgment—there were one or more professional lawyers, advocates, or pleaders, called, in Cormac's Glossary, *dálaighe* [dawlee] and *dai*, who conducted the cases for their clients; and the presiding brehon-judge had to hear the pleadings for both sides before coming to a decision. Whether the court was held in a building or in the open air, there was a platform of some kind on which the pleader stood while addressing the court.

With regard to evidence, various rules were in force, which may be gathered from detached passages in the laws and general literature. In order to prove home a matter of fact in a court of justice, at least two witnesses were required. If a man gave evidence against his wife, the wife was entitled to give evidence in reply; but a man's daughter would not be heard against him in like circumstances. Any freeman might give evidence against a fudir; but the fudir was not permitted to give evidence in reply. A king's evidence was good against all other people, with the three exceptions mentioned at page 23. The period at which a young man could give legal evidence was when he was seventeen years of age, or when he began to grow a beard.

The Irish delighted in judgments delivered in the form of a sententious maxim, or an apt illustration

—some illustration bearing a striking resemblance to the case in question. The jurist who decided a case by the aid of such a parallel was recognised as gifted with great judicial wisdom, and his judgment often passed into a proverb. Several judgments of this kind are recorded, of which one is given here. When Cormac mac Art, the rightful heir to the throne of Ireland, was a boy, he lived at Tara in disguise; for the throne was held by the usurper Mac Con, so that Cormac dared not reveal his identity. There was at this time living near Tara a female *brewy*, named Bennaid, whose sheep trespassed on the royal domain, and ate up the queen's valuable crop of *glaisin* [glasheen] or woad-plants for dyeing. The queen instituted proceedings for damages; and the question came up for decision before the king, who, after hearing the evidence, decided that the sheep should be forfeit in payment for the *glaisin*. "Not so," exclaimed the boy Cormac, who was present, and who could not restrain his judicial instincts: "the cropping of the sheep should be sufficient for the cropping of the *glaisin*—the wool for the woad—for both will grow again." "That is a true judgment," exclaimed all · "and he who has pronounced it is surely the son of a king"—for kings were supposed to possess a kind of inspiration in giving their decisions. And so they discovered who Cormac was, and in a short time placed him on the throne, after deposing the usurper.

PART II

RELIGION, LEARNING, AND ART.

Ornament on top of Devenish Round Tower   (From Petrie's Round Towers.)

CHAPTER V

PAGANISM.

SECTION 1. *Druids: their Functions and Powers.*

Druidism. — No trustworthy information regarding the religion of the pagan Irish comes to us from outside: whatever knowledge of it we possess is derived exclusively from the native literature. There were many gods, but no supreme god, like Zeus or Jupiter among the Greeks and Romans. There was little of prayer, and no settled general form of worship. There were no temples: but there were altars of some kind erected to idols or to the gods of the elements (the sun, fire, water, &c.), which must have been in the open air. The religion of the pagan Irish is commonly designated as Druidism: and in the oldest Irish traditions the druids figure conspicuously. All the early colonists had their druids, who are mentioned as holding high rank among kings and chiefs. There were druids also in Gaul and Britain; but the Gaels of Ireland and Scotland were separated and isolated for many centuries from the Celtic races of Gaul; and thus their religious system, like their language, naturally diverged, so that the druidism of Ireland, as pictured forth in the native records, differed in many respects from that of Gaul.

In pagan times the druids were the exclusive possessors of whatever learning was then known. They combined in themselves all the learned professions: they were not only druids, but judges, prophets, historians, poets, and even physicians. There were druids in every part of Ireland, but, as we might expect, Tara, the residence of the over-kings of Ireland, was, as we are told in the Life of St. Patrick, "the chief seat of the idolatry and druidism of Erin." The druids had the reputation of being great magicians; and in this character they figure more frequently and conspicuously than in any other. In some of the old historical romances we find the issues of battles sometimes determined not so much by the valour of the combatants as by the magical powers of the druids attached to the armies.

Perhaps the most dreaded of all the necromantic powers attributed to them was that of producing madness. In the pagan ages, and down far into Christian times, madness was believed to be often brought on by malignant magical agency, usually the work of some druid. For this purpose the druid prepared a "madman's wisp," that is, a little wisp of straw or grass, into which he pronounced some horrible incantations, and, watching his opportunity, flung it into the face of his victim, who at once became insane or idiotic.

Madness was often produced by the rage of battle. For, during a bloody battle, it sometimes happened that an excitable combatant ran mad with fury and horror: and occurrences of this kind are recorded in the romantic accounts of nearly all the great battles fought in Ireland. There was a most curious belief —a belief that still lingers in some parts of the country—that during the paroxysm a madman's body became as light as air, so that as he ran distractedly, he scarcely touched the ground, or he rose into the air, still speeding on with a sort of fluttering motion. There is a valley in Kerry called Glannagalt, ' the glen of the *galts* or lunatics': and it is believed that all lunatics, if left to themselves, would find their way to it, no matter from what part of Ireland. When they have lived in its solitude for a time, drinking of the water of Tobernagalt ('the lunatics' well'), and eating of the cresses that grow along the little stream, the poor wanderers get restored to sanity. At the entrance to Lough Foyle, on the strand near Inishowen Head in Donegal, there is a well called Stroove Bran, which was thought to possess the same virtue as Tobernagalt, and to which all the deranged people in the surrounding district were wont to resort.

It was believed that the druids could pronounce a malign incantation, not only on an individual, but on a whole army, so as to produce a withering or enervating effect on the men; and they were sometimes employed to maledict a hostile army, as Balaam was employed by Balak. They could give a drink of forgetfulness, so as to efface the memory of any particular transaction. They were the intermediaries with the fairies, and with the invisible world in general, which—as they asserted—they could influence for good or evil; and they could protect people from the malice of evil-disposed spirits of every kind; which explains much of their influence with the people. They could—as the legends tell—bring on snow-storms, or showers of fire and blood, and cover the land with blinding clouds and mists.

Divination.—An important function of the druid was divination—forecasting future events—which was practised by the pagan Irish—like the Greeks and Romans—in connexion with almost all important affairs, such as military expeditions. Laegaire's druids foretold the coming of St. Patrick. The druids forecasted, partly by observation of natural objects or occurrences, and partly by certain artificial rites: and in the exercise of this function the druid was a *fáith* [faw] or prophet.

They drew auguries from observation of the clouds, and of the heavenly bodies; and for purposes of divination they often used a rod of yew with Ogham words cut on it. They professed to be able to find out the lucky or unlucky days, and the period of suitable weather for beginning any business or enterprise, and to discern the future in general, from the voices of birds, from sneezing, and from the interpretation of dreams.

Divination by the voices of birds was very generally practised, especially from the croaking of the raven and the chirping of the wren: and the very syllables they utter, and their interpretation, are given in the old books. The wren in particular was considered so great a prophet that, in an old Life of St. Moling, one of its Irish names, *drean*, is fancifully derived from *drui-én*, meaning the 'druid of birds.' When St. Kellach, Bishop of Killala, was about to be murdered, the raven croaked, and the grey-coated scallcrow called, the wise little wren twittered ominously, and the kite of Cloon-O sat on his yew-tree waiting patiently to carry off his talons-full of the victim's flesh. But when, after the deed had been perpetrated, the birds of prey came scrambling for their shares, everyone that ate the least morsel of the saint's flesh dropped down dead. The Welsh birds of prey knew better when they saw the bodies of the slaughtered druids :—

> " Far, far aloof th' affrighted ravens sail;
> The famished eagle screams, and passes by."
> *The Bard*: by GRAY.

Just before the attack by Ingcel and his band of pirates on Da Derga's Hostel, the howl of Ossar, King Conari's *messan* or lapdog, portended the coming of battle and slaughter. The clapping of hands was used in some way as an omen; and also an examination of the shape of a crooked, knotted tree-root. Sometimes animals were sacrificed as part of the ceremony. In the performance of these and of all other important functions, the druids wore long white robes; like the Gaulish druid, who, as Pliny states, wore a white robe when cutting the mistletoe from the oak with a knife of gold.

Trees reverenced.—We know that the Gaulish druids regarded the oak, especially when mistletoe grew on it, with much religious veneration; but I cannot find that the Irish druids had any special veneration for the oak: although, like other trees, it occasionally figures in curious pagan rites. The mistletoe is not a native Irish plant: it was introduced some time in the last century. The statement we so often see put forward that the Irish druids held their religious meetings, and performed their solemn rites, under the sacred shade of the oak, is pure invention. But they attributed certain druidical or fairy virtues to the yew, the hazel, and the quicken or rowan-tree—especially the last—and employed them in many of their superstitious ceremonials. We have already seen that yew-rods were used in divination. On some occasions, witches or druids, or malignant phantoms, cooked flesh—sometimes the flesh of dogs or horses—on quicken-tree spits, as part of a diabolical rite for the destruction of some person obnoxious to them.

Druids as Teachers and Counsellors.—A most important function of the druids was that of teaching: they were employed to educate the children of kings and chiefs—they were indeed the only educators; which greatly added to their influence. The chief druid of a king held a very influential position: he was the king's confidential adviser on important affairs. When King Concobar mac Nessa contemplated avenging the foray of Queen Maive, he sought and followed the advice of his "right illustrious" druid Cathbad as to the time and manner of the projected expedition. And on St. Patrick's visit to Tara, King Laegaire's proceedings were regulated by the advice of his two chief druids Lucetmail and Lochru.

Druidesses.—The ancient Irish had druidesses also, like their relatives the Gauls. A druidess was called a *ban-drui* [ban-dree], *i.e.* a 'woman druid': and many individual druidesses figure in the ancient writings. Amongst the dangers that St. Patrick (in his Hymn) asks God to protect him from are " the spells of women, and smiths, and druids," where the "women" are evidently druidesses. In one of St. Patrick's canons, kings are warned to give no countenance to magi (*i.e.* 'druids'), or *pythonesses*, or augurers, in which it is obvious from the context that the *pythonesses* were druidesses. The Greek word 'pythoness,' which corresponds to the Irish *ban-drui*, was the name of the priestesses of the oracle of Apollo at Delphi.

2. *Points of Agreement and Difference between Irish and Gaulish Druids.*

Chief Points of Agreement. — 1. They had the same Celtic name in both countries: 'Druid.' 2. They were all wizards—magicians and diviners. 3. They were the only learned men of the time: they were judges, poets, professors of learning in general. 4. They were teachers, especially of the children of kings and chiefs. 5. Their disciples underwent a long course of training, during which they got by heart great numbers of verses. 6. They were the king's chief advisers: they were very influential, and held in great respect, often taking precedence even of the kings. 7. Among both the Irish and Gauls there were druidesses. 8. They had a number of gods; and many of the Irish gods were identical, both in names and chief functions, with those of Gaul.

Chief Points of Difference.—1. The Gaulish druids were under one head druid, with supreme authority: and they held periodical councils or synods. There was no such institution in Ireland:

though there were eminent druids in various districts, with the influence usually accorded to eminence. 2. The Gaulish druids held the doctrine of the immortality of the soul, as applying to all mankind: the soul of every human being passing, after death, into other bodies, *i.e.* of men, not of the lower animals. There is no evidence that the Irish druids held the souls of all men to be immortal. But in case of a few individuals—palpably exceptional—it is related that they lived on after death, some reappearing as other men, some as animals of various kinds, and a few lived on in Fairyland, without the intervention of death. 3. Human sacrifice was part of the rite of the Gaulish druids, sometimes an individual being sacrificed and slain: sometimes great numbers together. There is no record of any human sacrifice in connexion with the Irish druids: and there are good grounds for believing that direct human sacrifice was not practised at all in Ireland. 4. The Gaulish druids prohibited their disciples from committing to writing any part of their lore, regarding this as an unhallowed practice. There is no mention of any such prohibition among Irish druids. 5. The Gaulish druids revered the oak, and the mistletoe when growing on it: the Irish druids revered the yew, the hazel, and the quicken-tree or rowan-tree.

3. *Sorcerers and Sorcery.*

"**One foot, one hand, one eye.**"—Spells of several kinds are often mentioned in our ancient writings, as practised by various people, not specially or solely by druids. But all such rites and incantations, by whomsoever performed—magical practices of every kind—had their origin in druidism. Usually while practising his spell, the sorcerer was "on one foot, one hand, and one eye," which, I suppose, means, standing on one foot, with one arm outstretched, and with one eye shut. While in this posture, he uttered, in a loud voice, a kind of incantation or curse, called *glám dichenn*, commonly extempore, which was intended to inflict injury on the maledicted person or persons. There are many notices of the exercise, by druids or others, of this necromantic function; and a similar posture was often adopted in other ceremonies besides the *glám dichenn*.

Celtar: Fe-fiada.—The druids and other 'men of might' could make a magic mantle that rendered its wearer invisible: called a *celtar* [keltar].

In an Irish version of the Aeneid, the writer, following his own native Irish legend, tells us that when Venus was guiding Aeneas and his companions to Dido's city, she put a "celtar" round them, so that they went unseen by the hosts till they arrived within the city: just as Athene threw a mist of invisibility round Ulysses as he entered the city of the Phæacians.

Druids and others could raise or produce a *Fe-fiada*, which rendered people invisible. The accounts that have reached us of this *Fe-fiada* are very confused and obscure. Sometimes it appears to be a poetical incantation, which rendered the person that repeated it invisible. Often it is a mantle: occasionally a 'magic fog,' or a spell that hid natural objects—such an object as a well—and that might be removed by Christian influences. Every *shee* or fairy palace had a *Fe-fiada* round it, which shut it out from mortal vision. At the Battle of Clontarf (1014), the banshee Eevin gave the Dalcassian hero Dunlang O'Hartigan a *fe-fiada* or mantle, which, so long as he wore it, made him invisible, and protected him from harm during the battle; but when he threw it off, he was slain.*

4. *Mythology : Gods, Goblins, and Phantoms.*

Gods in general.—In the Irish language there are several names for God in general, without reference to any particular god. The most general is *dia*, which, with some variations in spelling, is common to many of the Aryan languages. It was used in pagan as well as in Christian times, and is the Irish word in universal use at the present day for God. In Irish literature, both lay and ecclesiastical, we sometimes find vague references to the pagan gods, without any hint as to their identity or functions. The 'gods' are often referred to in oaths and asseverations: and such expressions as "I swear by the gods that my people swear by" are constantly put into the mouths of the heroes of the Red Branch.

Individual Gods.—But we have a number of individual gods of very distinct personality who figure in the romantic literature, some beneficent and some evil. The names of many of them have been identified with those of ancient Gaulish gods—a thing that might be anticipated, inasmuch as the

---

* See the episode of Eevin and Dunlang O'Hartigan at the Battle of Clontarf in my Short History of Ireland.

Gaelic people of Ireland and Scotland are a branch of the Celts or Gauls of the Continent, and brought with them, at their separation from the main stock, the language, the traditions, and the mythology of their original home.

Shee or Fairies and their Dwellings.—The pagan Irish worshipped the *side* [shee], *i.e.* the earth-gods, or fairies, or elves. These *side* are closely

FIG. 32.

A fairy hill: an earthen mound at Highwood, near Lough Arrow, in Co. Sligo.

mixed up with the mythical race called Dedannans, to whom the great majority of the fairy gods belonged. According to our bardic chroniclers the Dedannans were the fourth of the prehistoric colonies that arrived in Ireland many centuries before the Christian era. They were great magicians, and were highly skilled in science and metal-working. After inhabiting Ireland for about two hundred years, they were conquered by the people of the fifth and last colony—the Milesians. They then arranged that the several chiefs, with their followers, were to take up their residence in the pleasant hills all over the country—the *side* [shee] or elf-mounds—where they could live free from observation or molestation; and Bodb Derg [Bove Derg] was chosen as their king. Deep under ground in these abodes they built themselves glorious palaces, all ablaze with light, and glittering with gems and gold. Sometimes their fairy palaces were situated under wells or lakes, or under the sea.

From what has been said it will be observed that the word *side* is applied to the fairies themselves as well as to their abodes. And *shee*, as meaning a fairy, is perfectly understood still. When you see a little whirl of dust moving along the road on a fine calm day, that is called *shee-geeha*, 'wind-fairies,' travelling from one *lis* or elf-mound to another.

The ideas prevalent in the ninth, tenth, and eleventh centuries, as to what the people's beliefs were, regarding the fairies before the time of St. Patrick, are well set forth in the concluding paragraph of the tale of "The Sick Bed of Cuculainn" in the Book of the Dun Cow: "For the demoniac power was great before the faith: and such was its greatness that the demons used to tempt the people, and they used to show them delights and secrets, and how they might become immortal. And it was to these phantoms the ignorant used to apply the name *side*."

Numbers of fairy hills and sepulchral carns are scattered over the country, each with a bright palace deep underneath, ruled by its own chief, the tutelary deity. They are still regarded as fairy haunts, and are held in much superstitious awe by the peasantry.

The fairies possessed great preternatural powers. They could make themselves invisible to some persons standing by, while visible to others: as Pallas showed herself to Achilles, while remaining invisible to the other Greeks (Iliad, I.). But their powers were exercised much oftener for evil than for good. They were consequently dreaded rather than loved; and whatever worship or respect was paid to them was mainly intended to avert mischief. It is in this sense that they are now often called 'Good people.'

FIG. 33.

Fairy moat at Patrickstown, near Oldcastle, County Meath.
(From Journ. Roy. Soc. Antiqq Irel., 1898)

They could wither up the crops over a whole district, or strike cattle with disease. To this day the peasantry have a lurking belief that cattle and human beings who interfere with the haunted old *lisses* or forts, are often fairy-struck, which brings on paralysis or other dangerous illness, or death.

Manannan mac Lir, whose epithet *Mac Lir* signifies 'Son of the Sea,' was the Irish sea-god. He is usually represented in the old tales as riding on the sea, in a chariot, at the head of his followers. When Bran the son of Febal had been at sea two days and two nights, "he saw a man in a chariot coming towards him over the sea," who turns out to be Manannan mac Lir, and who, as he passed, spoke in verse, and said that the sea to him was a beautiful flowery plain:—

> "What is a clear sea
> For the prowed skiff in which Bran is,
> That is to me a happy plain with profusion of flowers,
> [Looking] from the chariot of two wheels."

Manannan is still vividly remembered in some parts of Ireland. He is in his glory on a stormy night: and on such a night, when you look over the sea, there before your eyes, in the dim gloom, are thousands of Manannan's white-maned steeds, careering along after the great chief's chariot. According to an oral tradition, prevalent in the Isle of Man and in the eastern counties of Leinster (brought from Leinster to Man by the early emigrants: p. 36, *supra*), Manannan had three legs, on which he rolled along on land, wheel-like, always surrounded by a 'magic mist': and this is the origin of the three-legged figure on the Manx halfpenny.

The Dadga was a powerful and beneficent god, who ruled as king over Ireland for eighty years.

Bodb Derg [Bove-Derg], the Dedannan fairy king, son of the Dagda, had his residence—called *Side Buidb* [Shee Boov]—on the shore of Lough Derg, somewhere near Portumna.

Aengus Mac-in-Og [Oge], another son of the Dagda, was a mighty magician, whose splendid palace at 'Brugh of the Boyne' was within the great sepulchral mound of Newgrange, near Drogheda.

Brigit, daughter of the Dagda, was the goddess of Poets, of Poetry, and of Wisdom. She had two sisters, also called Brigit: one was the goddess of medicine and medical doctors; the other the goddess of smiths and smithwork.

Ana, also called **Dana** or **Danann,** was the mother of three of the Dedannan gods, whom she nursed and suckled so well that her name 'Ana' came to signify plenty; and from her the Dedannans derived their name — *Tuatha De Danann,* ' the *tuatha* [Thooha] or tribes of the goddess Dana.' She was worshipped in Munster as the goddess of plenty: and the name and nutritive function of this goddess are prominently commemorated in the ' Two Paps of Danann,' a name given to two beautiful adjacent conical mountains near Killarney, which to this day are well known by the name of ' the Paps.'

But there were other fairy chiefs besides those of the Dedannans: and some renowned *shees* belonged to Milesian 'princes, who became deified in imitation of their fairy predecessors. For instance, the Shee of **Aed-Ruad** [Ai-Roo] at Ballyshannon in Donegal. Our ancient books relate that this *Aed Ruad,* or Red Hugh, a Milesian chief, the father of Macha, founder of Emain, was drowned in the cataract at Ballyshannon, which was thence called after him *Eas-Aeda-Ruaid* [Ass-ai-roo], ' Aed-Ruad's Waterfall ' : now shortened to 'Assaroe.' He was buried over the cataract, in the mound which was called from him *Sid-Aeda*—a name still partly preserved in Mullaghshee, ' the hill of the *shee* or fairy-palace.'

This hill has recently been found to contain subterranean chambers, which confirms our ancient legendary accounts, and shows that it is a great sepulchral mound like those on the Boyne. How few of the people of Ballyshannon know that the familiar name Mullaghshee is a living memorial of those dim ages when Aed Ruad held sway, and that the great king himself has slept here in his dome-roofed dwelling for two thousand years.

Another Milesian chief, **Donn**, son of Milesius, was drowned in the magic storm raised by the spells of the Dedannans when the eight brothers came to invade Ireland. But for him it was only changing an earthly mode of existence for a much pleasanter one in his airy palace on the top of Knockfierna, as the renowned king of the fairies: and here he ruled over all the great Limerick plain around the mountain, where many legends of him still linger among the peasantry.

A male fairy was a *fer-side* (*fer*, 'a man'): a female fairy, a *ben-side* or *banshee*, i.e. 'a woman from the fairy-hills.' Several fairy-hills were ruled by banshees as fairy queens. The banshee who presided as queen of the palace on the summit of Knockainy hill, in county Limerick, was **Aine** [2-syll.], daughter of a Dedannan chief, who gave her name to the hill, and to the existing village of Knockainy.

Two other banshees, still more renowned, were **Clidna** [Cleena] of Carrigcleena, and **Aebinn** or **Aibell** [Eevin, Eevil] of Craglea. Cleena is the potent banshee that rules as queen over the fairies of South Munster. In the Dinnsenchus there is an ancient and pathetic story about her, wherein it is related that she was a foreigner from Fairy-land, who, coming to Ireland, was drowned while sleeping on the strand at the harbour of Glandore in South Cork. In this harbour the sea, at certain times, utters a very peculiar, deep, hollow, and melancholy roar, among the caverns of the cliffs, which was formerly believed to foretell the death of a king of the south of Ireland. This surge has been from time immemorial called *Tonn-Cleena*, 'Cleena's wave.' Cleena lived on, however, as a fairy. She had her palace in the heart of a pile of rocks, five miles from Mallow, which is still well known by the name of Carrig-Cleena: and numerous legends about her are told among the Munster peasantry. Aebinn or Aibell, whose name signifies 'beautiful,' presided over North Munster, and was in an especial manner the guardian spirit of the Dalcassians or O'Briens. She had her palace two miles north of Killaloe, in a rock called Crageevil, but better known by the name of Craglea, 'grey rock.' The rock is situated in a silent glen, under the face of a mountain: and the people affirm that she forsook her retreat when the woods which once covered the place were cut down.

The old fort under which the banshee **Grian** of the Bright Cheeks had her dwelling still remains on the top of Pallas Grean hill in the county Limerick. One of the most noted of the fairy-palaces is on the top of Slievenamon in Tipperary. But to enumerate all the fairy-hills of Ireland, and relate fully the history of their presiding gods and goddesses, and the superstitious beliefs among the people regarding them, would occupy a good-sized volume.

In modern times the word 'banshee' has become narrowed in its meaning, and signifies a female spirit that attends certain families, and is heard *keening* or crying at night round the house when some member is about to die. At the present day almost all raths, cashels, and mounds—the dwellings, forts, and sepulchres of the Firbolgs and Milesians, as well as those of the Dedannans—are considered as fairy haunts.

Shees open at Samain.—On Samain Eve, the night before the 1st of November, or, as it is now called, All Hallows Night, or Hallowe'en, all the fairy hills were thrown wide open; for the *Fe-fiada* was taken off. While they remained open that night, any mortals who were bold enough to venture near might get a peep into them. No sooner was the *Fe-fiada* lifted off than the inmates issued forth, and roamed where they pleased all over the country: so that people usually kept within doors, naturally enough afraid to go forth. From the cave of Cruachan or Croghan in Connaught issued probably the most terrific of all those spectre hosts; for immediately that darkness had closed in on Samain Eve, a crowd of horrible goblins rushed out, and among them a flock of copper-red birds, led by one monstrous three-headed vulture: and their poisonous breath withered up everything it touched: so that this cave came to be called the 'Hell-gate of Ireland.' That same hell-gate cave is there still, but the demons are all gone—scared away, no doubt, by the voices of the Christian bells. The superstition that the fairies are abroad on Samain Night exists at the present day, both in Ireland and in Scotland.

There were **war-goddesses** or **battle-furies**, who were usually called by the names *Mórrigan* [more-reean] and *Badb* [Baub or Bauv] : all malignant beings, delighting in battle and slaughter. The *Badb* often showed herself in battle in the form of a *fennog*, *i.e.* a scallcrow, or royston crow, or carrion crow, fluttering over the heads of the combatants.

The *Badb* or *Mórrigan*, sometimes as a bird, and sometimes as a loathsome-looking hag, figures in all the ancient battles, down even to the Battle of Clontarf (A.D. 1014). In the midst of the din and horror she was often seen busily flitting about through the battle-cloud overhead: and sometimes she appeared before battle in anticipation of slaughter. Just before the Battle of Moyrath (A.D. 637), the grey-haired *Mórrigan*, in the form of a lean, nimble hag, was seen hovering and hopping about on the points of the spears and shields of the royal army who were victorious in the great battle that followed. Before the Destruction of Bruden Da Choca, the *Badb* showed herself as " a big-mouthed, swarthy, swift, sooty woman, lame, and squinting with her left eye."

"**Neit**," says Cormac's Glossary, "was the god of battle with the pagans of the Gael: **Nemon** was his wife." They were malignant beings:—"Both are bad: a venomous couple, truly, were they," says Cormac.

The *Badbs* were not the only **war-goblins**. There was a class of phantoms that sometimes appeared before battles, bent on mischief. Before the Battle of Moylena (second century), three repulsive-looking witch-hags with blue beards appeared before the armies, hoarsely shrieking victory for Conn the Hundred Fighter, and defeat and death for the rival king Eoghan. Before the Banquet of *Dun-nan-ged*, two horrible black spectral beings, a man and a woman, came to the assembly, and having devoured an enormous quantity of food, cursed the banquet, after which they rushed out and vanished. But they left their baleful trail: for at that feast there arose a deadly quarrel which led to the Battle of Moyrath (A.D. 637).

In many remote, lonely glens there dwelt certain fierce apparitions — females — called *Geniti-glinni*, 'genii or sprites of the valley,' and others called *Bocanachs* (male goblins), and *Bananachs* (females): often in company with *Demna aeir* or 'demons of the air.' At any terrible battle-crisis, many or all of these, with the other war-furies described above, were heard shrieking and howling with delight, some in the midst of the carnage, some far off in their lonely haunts.

In the story of the Feast of Bricriu, we are told how the three great Red Branch champions, Laegaire the Victorious, Conall Cernach, and Cuculainn, contended one time for the *Curathmir*, or 'champion's bit' (chap. xvii., sect. 1, *infra*), which was always awarded to the bravest and mightiest hero; and in order to determine this matter, they were subjected to various severe tests. On one of these occasions the stern-minded old chief, Samera, who acted as judge for the occasion, decided that the three heroes separately should attack a colony of *Geniti-glinni* that had their abode in a neighbouring valley. Laegaire went first; but they instantly fell on him with such demoniac ferocity that he was glad to escape, half-naked, leaving them his arms and battle-dress. Conall Cernach went next, and he, too, had soon to run for it; but he fared somewhat better, for, though leaving his spear, he bore away his sword. Lastly, Cuculainn: and they filled his ears with their hoarse shrieks, and falling on him tooth and nail, they broke his shield and spear, and tore his clothes to tatters. At last he could bear it no longer, and showed plain signs of running away. His faithful charioteer, Loeg, was looking on. Now, one of Loeg's duties was, whenever he saw his master about yielding in a fight, to shower reproaches on him, so as to enrage him the more. On this occasion he reviled him so vehemently and bitterly for his weakness, and poured out such contemptuous nicknames on him, that the hero became infuriated; and, turning on the goblins once more, sword in hand, he crushed and hacked them to pieces, so that the valley ran all red with their blood.

The class of fairies called *siabra* [sheevra], who were also Dedannans—a sort of disreputable poor relations of Manannan and the Dagda—were powerful, demoniac, and dangerous elves. They are mentioned in our earliest literature. To this day the name is quite familiar among the people, even those who speak only English: and they often call a crabbed little boy—small for his age—a "little sheevra" exactly as Concobar mac Nessa, nineteen centuries ago, when he was displeased with the boy Cuculainn, calls him a "little imp of a *sheevra*." The sheevras were often incited by druids and others to do mischief to mortals. In revenge for King Cormac mac Art's leaning towards Christianity, the druids let loose sheevras against him, who choked him with the bone of a salmon, while he was eating his dinner.

The *Leprechán*, as we now have him, is a little fellow whose occupation is making shoes for the fairies; and on moonlight nights you may sometimes hear the tap-tap of his little hammer from where he sits, working in some lonely nook among bushes. If you can catch him, and keep your gaze fixed on him, he will tell you, after some threatening, where to find a *crock* of gold: but if you take your eyes off him for an instant, he is gone. The leprechauns are an ancient race in Ireland, for we find them mentioned in some of our oldest tales. They could injure mortals, but were not prone to do so except under provocation. From the beginning they were of diminutive size; for example, as they are presented to us in the ancient tale of the Death of Fergus mac Leide, their stature might be about six inches. In the same tale the king of the leprechauns was taken captive by Fergus, and ransomed himself by giving him a pair of magic shoes, which enabled him to go under the water whenever, and for as long as, he pleased: just as at the present day a leprechaun, when you catch him—which is the difficulty—will give you heaps of money for letting him go. No doubt, the episode of the ransom by the magic shoes in the old story is the original version of the present superstition that the leprechaun is the fairies' shoemaker.

In modern times the *Pooka* has come to the front as a leading Irish goblin: but I fear he is not native Irish, as I do not find him mentioned in any ancient Irish documents. He appears to have been an immigrant fairy, brought hither by the Danish settlers: and is the same as the English Puck. But, like the Anglo-Norman settlers, he had not long lived in this country till he became " more Irish than the Irish themselves." For an account of his shape, character, and exploits, I must refer the reader to Crofton Croker's "Fairy Legends," and to the first volume of my "Origin and History of Irish Names of Places."

When the Milesians landed in Ireland, they were encountered by mysterious sights and sounds wherever they went, through the subtle spells of the Dedannans. As they climbed over the mountains of Kerry, half-formed spectres flitted dimly before their eyes: for Banba, the queen of one of the three Dedannan princes who ruled the land, sent a swarm of *meisi* [misha], or 'phantoms,' which froze the blood of the invaders with terror: and the mountain range of Slieve Mish, near Tralee, still retains the name of those apparitions.

According to another account, Ireland, before the arrival of St. Patrick, was plagued with multitudes of reptiles and demons. "These venomous and monstrous creatures—the reptiles—used to rise out of the earth and sea, and they wounded both men and animals with their deadly stings, and not seldom rent and devoured their members." "The demons used to show themselves unto their worshippers in visible forms: they often attacked the people, and they were seen flying in the air and walking on the earth, loathsome and horrible to behold."

What with Dedannan gods, with war-gods and goddesses, apparitions, demons, sprites of the valley, ordinary ghosts, spectres, goblins, and demoniac reptiles, fairies of various kinds—sheevras, leprehauns, banshees, and so forth—there appears to have been, in those old pagan days, quite as numerous a population belonging to the spiritual world as of human beings; so that Ireland was then an eerie place to live in: and it was high time for St. Patrick to come.

5. *Worship of Idols.*

Idols were very generally worshipped. The earliest authentic document that mentions idols is St. Patrick's "Confession," in which the great apostle himself speaks of some of the Scots (*i.e.* Irish) who, up to that time, "had worshipped only idols and abominations." Elsewhere in the same document, as well as in many other ancient authorities, the practice of idol-worship is mentioned as a thing well known among the Irish; and the destruction of many idols in various parts of the country was an important part of St. Patrick's life-work.

There was a great idol called **Cromm Cruach**, covered all over with gold and silver, in *Magh Slecht* (the 'Plain of Prostrations'), near the present village of Ballymagauran, in the County Cavan, surrounded by twelve lesser idols, covered with brass or bronze. In our most ancient books Cromm Cruach is mentioned as the chief idol of the whole country, and as being "until the coming of Patrick, the god of every folk that colonised Ireland." In a very old legend, found in the Dinnsenchus in the Book of Leinster, it is related that many centuries before the Christian era, King Tigernmas [Teernmas] and crowds of his people were destroyed in some mysterious way, as they were worshipping it on Samain Eve—the eve of the 1st November. In the main facts regarding *Cromm Cruach*, the secular literature is corroborated by the Lives of St. Patrick. In the Tripartite Life it is stated that this idol was adored by King Laegaire, and by many others; and that Patrick, setting out from Granard, went straight to Magh Slecht, and overthrew the whole thirteen. They were all pillar-stones: and the remains of them were in Magh Slecht at the time of the compilation of the Tripartite Life (eighth to tenth century): for it states that they were then to be seen, buried up to their heads in the earth, as Patrick had left them.

In the Dinnsenchus it is stated that, down to the time of St. Patrick, the Irish killed their children in sacrifice to Cromm Cruach in order to obtain from him plenty of milk, corn, and honey. But this statement is not supported by any other authority, though Cromm Cruach is mentioned often enough: it stands quite alone. In such an important matter the Dinnsenchus is not a sufficient authority, for it is a comparatively late document, and the stories in it, of which this is one, are nearly all fabulous — invented to account for the names. Besides, St. Patrick knew all about this idol; and if children were sacrificed to it down to his time, it would be mentioned in some of the numerous Lives of him. It may then be taken as certain that the Dinnsenchus statement is a pure invention, and that this horrid custom of direct human sacrifice to idols or gods, though practised by the Gauls, never reached Ireland.

As *Cromm Cruach* was the "king-idol" of all Ireland, there was a special idol-god, named *Kermand Kelstach*, that presided over Ulster. This stone-idol was still preserved as a curiosity in the porch of the cathedral of Clogher down to the time of the annalist Cathal Maguire (died 1498), as he himself tells us.

Pillar-stones were worshipped in other parts of Ireland as well as at Moy-Slecht and Clogher. The Dinnsenchus, after speaking of Cromm Cruach and the other twelve, remarks that from the time of Heremon to the coming of the good Patrick of Armagh, there was adoration of pillar-stones in Ireland: a statement which we find also in other old authorities. In the Brehon Laws, one of the objects used for marking the boundaries of land is stated to be "a stone of worship." This interesting record at once connects the Irish custom with the Roman worship of the god Terminus, which god was merely a pillar-stone placed standing in the ground to mark the boundary of two adjacent properties—exactly as in Ireland. Even to this day some of these old idols or oracle-stones are known; and the memory of the rites performed at them is preserved in popular legend.

The Irish—like the Scottish Highlanders—had an idol called *Bél* [Bail], whose worship was celebrated with fire-ceremonies. There was a great meeting held at Ushnagh (in present Co. Westmeath) every year on the 1st May, when two fires were kindled in Bel's name, with solemn incantations, by the druids; and cattle were driven between the fires to protect them against the diseases of the coming year. On this occasion, moreover, the young of cattle were offered to the idol. These pagan ceremonies were practised on May Day, all through Ireland, in imitation of those at Ushnagh, and were continued down to late times.

We know, from Scriptural as well as from other authorities, that the Phœnicians had an idol-god named Baal or Bél, which they worshipped with great fire-ceremonies, and which they introduced to all the surrounding nations. Seeing that Ireland was well known to the Phœnicians, that the Irish god Bél is identical in name with the Phœnician god, and was worshipped with the same fire-ceremonies, it is obvious—though we have no direct authoritative statement on the point—that the Irish derived the name and worship of their god Bél—either directly or indirectly—from the Phœnicians.

The Irish, like the Continental nations of the Middle Ages, paid great reverence to their arms, especially swords, amounting sometimes to downright worship, which accounts for the custom of swearing by them. This oath, which was very usual in Ireland, was quite as binding as that by the elements. The reason is given in "The Sick Bed of Cuculainn":—" Because demons were accustomed to speak to them from their arms; and hence it was that an oath by their arms was inviolable."

6. *Worship of the Elements.*

Elemental Worship in General.—In the Lives of the saints and other ecclesiastical writings, as well as in the lay literature, we have ample evidence that various natural objects were worshipped by the ancient Irish. But this worship was only partial, confined to individuals or to the people of certain districts, each individual or family or group having some special favourite object. We have no record of the universal worship of any element. There is reason to believe that it was not the mere material object they worshipped, but a spirit or genius supposed to dwell in it: for the Celts of Ireland peopled almost all remarkable natural objects with preternatural beings.

Wells.—The worship of water, as represented in wells, is often mentioned. The Tripartite Life, and Tirechan, in the Book of Armagh, relate that St. Patrick, in his journey through Connaught, came to a well called *Slán*, which the heathens worshipped as a god, believing that a certain 'prophet' had caused himself to be buried under it in a stone coffin to keep his bones cool from fire that he dreaded; for 'he adored water as a god, but hated fire as an evil being." This prophet was of course a druid. More than a century later, in the time of St. Columba, as will be found mentioned in next chapter, there was a well in Scotland which the pagan people "worshipped as a divinity." These healing wells were generally called by the appropriate name of *Slán* [slaun], which means 'healing.' It is to be observed that well-worship was not peculiar to Ireland: at one time it prevailed all over Europe.

The Sun.—That the sun was worshipped in Ireland—at least partially, like some other natural objects—is made certain by several passages in our ancient literature. St. Patrick plainly intimates this when he says in his Confession—speaking of the Irish —that all who adore the sun shall perish eternally. This is a contemporary statement: for the saint is evidently denouncing a practice existing in his own time. We have a more specific account in Cormac's

Glossary; but this entry is four centuries later, and records, not contemporary custom, but one existing long before the time of the compilation of the Glossary. It states that *Indelba* ('Images') was the name applied to the altars of certain idols: and that these altars were so called because "they [the pagans] were wont to carve on them the forms (Irish, *delba*) of the elements they adored: for example, the figure of the sun." One of the three last Dedannan kings of Ireland, as we are told, was named *Mac Grena* ('son or devotee of the sun') because his god was the sun.

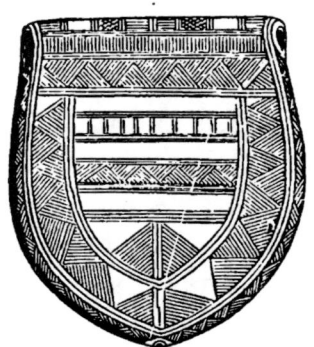

Fig. 34.

Amulet, half the size of the original, which is covered over with a thin plate of gold, beautifully ornamented: the interior is of lead. In the National Museum. (From Wilde's Catalogue.)

Fire.—That fire was worshipped by some of the Irish appears from the statement in the Tripartite Life that Laegaire's druid accused St. Patrick of having fire for a god, which shows that the idea of fire-worship was familiar. We have already seen that fires were kindled by the druids at Ushnagh in honour of the god Bél, and that fire played a prominent part in certain pagan festivals. Many of these fire-ceremonies—now quite harmless—have descended to our own time, some signalising the 1st of May, and some the eve of the 24th June, when the people light open-air fires as soon as dusk comes on, so that the whole country is illuminated.

Elemental Oath.—No doubt this ancient elemental worship was the origin of the very general pagan Irish custom of swearing by the elements, **or**, in other words, giving the elements as guarantee: an oath which it was believed very dangerous to violate, as is shown by the fate of Laegaire, king of Ireland in the time of St. Patrick. In an attempt to exact the Boruma tribute from Leinster, he was defeated and taken prisoner by the Leinstermen: but was released on taking the usual oath, giving as guarantee—*i.e.*, swearing by—the "sun and moon, water and air, day and night, sea and land," that he would never again demand it. But in open violation of his oath he invaded Leinster (A.D. 463) for this same Tribute in less than two years: whereupon—as the Four Masters express it—"the sun and wind killed him because he had violated them ": " for "— says an older authority, the Book of the Dun Cow— " no one durst violate them at that time."

7. *The Pagan Heaven and a Future State.*

Names and Situations. — There was a belief in a land of everlasting youth and peace, beautiful beyond conception, and called by various names: *Tir-nan-óg* [Teernanogue], *i.e.*, the 'Land of the [ever-]youthful people': *I-Bresail*, or *I-Brazil*, the 'Land of Bresal': *Mag Mell* [Moy Mell], the 'Plain of Pleasures': and several others. Sometimes it is described as situated far out in the Western Ocean: sometimes it was deep down under the sea or under a lake or well: sometimes it was in a hollow *shee* or fairy-hill. The inhabitants were the *side* [shee] or fairies, who were immortal, and who lived in perfect peace and in a perpetual round of harmless pleasures.

But it was not for human beings, except a few individuals who were brought thither by the fairies, as will be told below.

This pagan heaven legend did not escape the notice of Giraldus Cambrensis. He tells the story of the Phantom Island, as he calls it, off the western coast, and how, on one occasion when it appeared, some men rowed out towards it, and shot a fiery arrow against it, which fixed it. To this day the legend remains as vivid as ever : and the people believe that if they could succeed in throwing fire on it from their boat, it would fix it, as happened before the time of Giraldus.

Immortality of the Soul.—We know from classical writers that the ancient Gauls or Celts taught, as one of their tenets, that the soul was immortal; and that after death it passed from one human body to another : and this, it appears, applied to all human beings. But in Irish literature I cannot find anything to warrant the conclusion that the pagan Irish believed that the souls of all men were immortal. A few individuals became immortal in Fairyland, and some other few lived on after death, appearing as other men, or in the shapes of animals, as will be presently related. But these are all palpable exceptions, and are put forward as such in the legends.

A few persons were brought by fairies to the happy other world, and became immortal : and the time passed there so obscurely and pleasantly that a whole century appeared only the length of a year or so. Once a person got to Fairyland he could never return, except, indeed, on a short visit, always in a boat or on horseback, merely to take a look at his native land: but if once he touched his mother earth, the spell of youth and immortality was broken, and he immediately felt the consequences. Bran, the son of Febal, had been sailing with his crew among the happy islands for hundreds of years, though they thought it was only the length of an ordinary voyage. When they returned to the coast of Kerry, one man jumped ashore, against solemn warning, but fell down instantly, and became a heap of ashes. Ossian, the son of Finn, did not fare quite so badly when he returned to Ireland riding an enchanted steed, after his 300 years' sojourn in Tirnanoge, which he thought only three years. Traversing his old haunts, the wonder of all the strange people he met, for his size and beauty, he on one occasion, in trying to lift a great stone, overbalanced himself, and had to leap to the ground, when he instantly became a withered, bony, feeble old man, while his fairy steed galloped off and never returned.*

Metempsychosis.—The foregoing observations regarding the pagan Irish notions of immortality after death apply in a great measure to their ideas of metempsychosis. In our romantic literature there are legends of the re-birth of human beings: *i.e*, certain persons, commonly heroes or demigods, were re-born, and figured in the world, with new personality, name, and character. Thus Cuculainn was a re-incarnation of the Dedannan hero-god, Lug of the Long Arms. In other cases human beings, after death, took the shapes of various animals in succession, and re-appeared as human beings. Mongan of Rath-

---

* The whole story will be found in my Old Celtic Romances.

more Moylinny, king of Dalriada, in Ulster, in the seventh century—a historical personage—was fabled to be a re-incarnation of the great Finn mac Cumail of the third century. This same Mongan went, after death, into various shapes, a wolf, a stag, a salmon, a seal, a swan; like the Welsh Taliessin. Fintan, the nephew of Parthalon, survived the deluge, and lived in the shapes of various animals successively for many ages, after which he was re-incarnated in the sixth century as a man named Tuan Mac Cairill. This Tuan was a celebrated sage, and no wonder, for he witnessed all the remarkable things that happened in Ireland from the time of Parthalon, a lapse of some thousands of years, and related everything to St. Finnen of Magh Bile.

These stories are scattered, and have no thread of connexion : they do not coalesce into a system : they are told of individuals, in palpable exception to the general run of people, and many of them are stated to be the result of magical skill. There is no statement anywhere that all persons were re-born as human beings, or underwent transformations after death. Stories of a similar kind are current among most early nations. There are accordingly no grounds whatever for asserting that the ancient Irish believed in the doctrine of general metempsychosis ; and this is also O'Curry's conclusion.

8. *Turning 'Deisiol,' or Sunwise.*

The Celtic people were, and still are, accustomed to turn sunwise—*i.e.* from left to right—in performing certain rites; and the word *deisiol* [deshil] was used to designate this way of turning: from *dess*, now *deas*, 'the right hand': *dessel* or *deisiol*, 'right-hand-wise.' This custom is very ancient, and, like many others, has descended from pagan to Christian times. It was, indeed, quite as common among the Christian people of Ireland as among the pagans : and no wonder ; for the great apostle Patrick, as well as several other eminent Irish saints, showed them the example. For instance, St. Patrick consecrated Armagh, as St. Senan did Scattery Island, each by walking sunwise with his followers in solemn procession round the site.

9. *The Ordeal.*

The use of the ordeal for determining truth or falsehood, guilt or innocence, was developed from prehistoric times in Ireland : but the germs were, no doubt, brought hither by the earliest colonists. The Irish had their own ordeals, in which were some peculiarities not found among other nations of Europe. Most originated in pagan times, but, as in England and elsewhere, the ordeal continued in use for many centuries after the general adoption of Christianity.

In the Book of Ballymote there is a list and description of twelve different kinds of ordeal used by the ancient Irish. Among these were the following :—"Morann's Collar," of which the common version of the legend is this :—The great brehon or judge, Morann, had a collar, which, if placed round his neck, or round the neck of any judge, contracted on his throat if he delivered a false or unjust judgment, and continued to press more tightly, ever till he delivered a righteous one. Placed on the neck of a witness, if he bore false testimony it acted similarly, until it forced him to acknowledge the truth.

"The Adze of Mochta": the metal head of an adze was made red-hot in a fire of blackthorn or of the quicken-tree, "and the [tongue of the accused] was passed over it: it would burn the person who had falsehood: but would not burn the person who was innocent."

The "Three Dark Stones": a bucket was filled with bog-dust, charcoal, and other kinds of black stuff, and three little stones, white, black, and speckled, were put into it, buried deep in the black mass, into which the accused thrust down his hand: if he drew the white stone, he was innocent: if the black one, he was guilty: and if he drew the speckled one, he was half guilty."

The "Caldron of truth" was a vessel of silver and gold. "Water was heated in it till it was boiling; into which the accused plunged his hand: if he was guilty, the hand was burned: if not, it was uninjured. "Lot-casting"—in several forms—was very common as an ordeal "Luchta's iron": the druids having first uttered an incantation over a piece of iron, put it in a fire till it was red-hot. It was then placed in the hand of the accused: and "it would burn him if he had guilt: but would not injure him if innocent." "Waiting at an altar." The person was to go nine times round the [pagan] altar, and afterwards to drink water over which a druid's incantations had been uttered. "If the man was guilty, the sign of his transgression was made manifest in him [by some bodily disfigurement]: if innocent, he remained unharmed." Observe the striking resemblance of this last to the Jewish ordeal for a woman suspected of misconduct, as we read in the Book of Numbers, chapter v.

10. *The Evil Eye.*

From various passages in some very old documents, it may be inferred that the belief in the evil eye was very prevalent in Ireland in old times. The great Fomorian champion, Balor of the Mighty Blows, had a tremendous evil eye called *Birach-derc* ('speary-eye': *bir*, 'a spear'). It was never opened except on the field of battle; and one baleful glance was enough to enfeeble a whole army of his enemies, so as that a few brave men could put them to flight. The Tale of the Second Battle of Moytura relates how he came by his evil eye. When he was a boy, his father's druids used to concoct their spells in a room carefully closed, 'cooking sorcery' over a fire in a caldron, from some horrible ingredients, like Shakespeare's witches in "Macbeth." The boy, curious to know what the druids were at, climbed up and peeped through an opening, when a whiff of foul steam from the caldron blew into his eye, and communicated to it all the baleful influence of the hellish mixture. But this eye, powerful as it was, was not proof against the *tathlum* or sling-ball of his grandson Lug of the Long Arms. At the Second Battle of Moytura, Balor was present, prepared to use his eye on the Dedannan army. But Lug, who was on the side of the Dedannans, kept on the watch; and the moment the lid of the Cyclopean eye was raised, and before the glare had time to work bale, he let fly the hard ball from his sling, which struck the open eye with such force as to go clean through eye, brain, and skull.

These observations may be brought to a close by the remark that the superstition of the evil eye has remained among our people—as among others—down to this day.

11. *Geasa or Prohibitions.*

There were certain acts which people were prohibited from doing under penalty of misfortune or ill luck of some kind. Such a prohibition was called *geis* or *geas* [gesh, gass: *g* hard as in *get, gap*]: plural *geasa* [gassa]. A *geis* was something forbidden. It was believed to be very dangerous to disregard these prohibitions. Because Conari the Great, king of Ireland in the first century of the Christian era, violated some of his *geasa*—most of them unwittingly—the peace of his reign was broken by plunder and rapine; and he himself was finally slain in the sack of Da Derga's Hostel. Some *geasa* were binding on people in general. Thus, on the day of King Laegaire's festival, it was *geis* for the people to light a fire anywhere round Tara till the king's festival fire had first been lighted. It was *geis* for anyone to bring arms into the palace of Tara after sunset.

The most interesting of the *geasa* were those imposed on kings: of which the object of some was obviously to avoid unnecessary personal danger or loss of dignity. For example, it was a *geis* to the king of Emain (*i.e.* of Ulster) to attack alone a wild boar in his den: a sensible restriction. According to the Book of Acaill and many other authorities, it was *geis* for a king with a personal blemish to reign at Tara: so that when king Cormac mac Art lost one eye by an accident, he at once abdicated. The reason of these two *geasa* is plain enough. But there were others which it is not so easy to explain. They appear to be mere superstitions—obviously from pagan times—meant to avoid unlucky days, evil omens, &c. Some kings were subject to *geasa* from which others were free. The king of Emain was forbidden to listen to the singing of the birds of Lough Swilly, or to bathe in Lough Foyle on a May Day. The king of Ireland and the provincial kings had each a series of *geasa*. To the king of Ireland it was forbidden that the sun should rise on him while lying in bed in Tara, *i.e.* he should be up before sunrise; he was not to alight from his chariot on Moy Breagh on a Wednesday; and he was not to go round North Leinster left-hand-wise under any circumstances. Many others of these kingly *geasa* may be seen in my larger "Social History of Ancient Ireland," vol. i., pages 311–312.

It is well known that *geasa* or prohibitions were, and are still, common among all people, whether savage or civilized. They flourish at this day among ourselves. Some people will not dine in a company of thirteen, or remove to a new house on a Saturday, or get married in May: what are these but *geasa*, and quite as irrational as any of those enumerated above?

Composed from the Book of Kells.

CHAPTER VI.

CHRISTIANITY.

SECTION 1. *Christianity before St. Patrick's Arrival.*

THAT there were Christians in Ireland long before the time of St. Patrick we know from the words of St. Prosper of Aquitaine, who lived at the time of the event he records. He tells us that, in the year 431, Pope Celestine sent Palladius "to the Scots believing in Christ, to be their first bishop"· and Bede repeats the same statement. Palladius landed on the coast of the present County Wicklow, and after a short and troubled sojourn he converted a few people, and founded three little churches in that part of the country. One of them is called in the old records *Cill Fine* or *Cill-Fine-Cormaic* [pronounced Killeena-Cormac], where a venerable lonely little cemetery exists to this day, three miles southwest from Dunlavin in Wicklow, and is still called by the old name, slightly changed to Killeen Cormac. There must have been Christians in considerable numbers when the Pope thought a bishop necessary;

FIG. 35.—Killeen Cormac; present appearance: a relic of pre-Patrician Christianity in Ireland. (From Kilk. Archæol. Journ.)

and such numbers could not have grown up in a short time. It is highly probable that the knowledge of Christianity that existed in Ireland before the arrival of Palladius and Patrick (in 431 and 432, respectively) came from Britain, with which the Irish then kept up constant intercourse, and where there were large numbers of Christians from a very early time. However, the great body of the Irish were pagans when St. Patrick arrived in 432; and to him belongs the glory of converting them.

2. *The three Orders of Irish Saints.*

In an old Catalogue, written in Latin by some unknown author, not later than A.D. 750 (possibly in 700), the ancient Irish saints are distinguished into three " Orders "; and much information is given regarding them. The following are the main points of this valuable old document.

Those of " The First Order of Catholic Saints " were all bishops, beginning with St. Patrick: they were "most holy: shining like the sun." They were 350 in number, all founders of churches. "All these bishops "—the Catalogue goes on to say—" were sprung from the Romans, and Franks, and Britons, and Scots"; that is, they consisted of St. Patrick, with the numerous foreign missionaries who accompanied or followed him, and of the Britons and native Scots, or Irish, ordained by him and his successors. This order continued for something more than a century.

Those of " The Second Order were Catholic Priests," numbering 300, of whom a few were bishops. These were "very holy," and "they shone like the moon." They lasted for a little more than half a century.

The Third Order consisted of priests and a few bishops: these were "holy," and "shone like the stars." They continued for a little less than three quarters of a century.

Put into matter-of-fact language, the historical statement is briefly this :—

1. For a little more than a century after St. Patrick's arrival, the work of conversion was carried on by the Patrician clergy and their successors, who were nearly all active missionary priests. Many belonging to this order were foreigners.

2. During the latter half of the sixth century, monasteries spread rapidly over the country, and monastic clergy then and for long afterwards greatly predominated. Nearly all belonging to this Order and the Third were natives.

3. From the end of the sixth century, for seventy or eighty years, eremitical communities, settled in remote and lonely places, became very general. It will be necessary to describe these three religious developments in some detail.

3. *The First Order: Patrician Secular Clergy.*

During the century and a quarter following St. Patrick's arrival, *i.e.*, from A.D. 432 to about 559, the clergy who laboured to spread the faith among the people appear to have been for the most part unconnected with monasteries: in other words, they corresponded to the present secular or parochial clergy. These Patrician clergy, as they may be called, were the First Order of saints. Among them were many distinguished bishops, some of whom are named in the Catalogue. There were monasteries and schools also during the whole of this period, and many of the abbots were bishops: but monasteries did not constitute the main feature of the ecclesiastical system: for the life of St. Patrick, and, it may be added, the life of the First Order of saints in general, was, as the Most Rev. Dr. Healy remarks, "too full of missionary labours to be given to the government or foundation of monasteries." During this period, therefore, the clergy devoted themselves entirely to the home mission — the conversion of the Irish people — which gave them quite enough to do. For more than thirty years they were led by their great master, with all his fiery and tireless energy. After his death, his disciples and their successors continued the work. But the struggle was a hard one: for the druids exerted themselves to the utmost to retard and limit the spread of the faith; and besides this, many unconverted

FIG. 36.

Doorway of hermitage of St. Erc, one of St. Patrick's converts, and first bishop of Slane: beside the Boyne, near Slane: a relic of the Patrician clergy. Present building erected long after St Erc's tune. (From Wilde's Boyne and Blackwater)

pagans still remained in most parts of the country, who naturally supported the druids.

4. *The Second Order: Monastic Clergy.*

Rise of Monasticism.—About the middle of the sixth century a great monastic religious movement

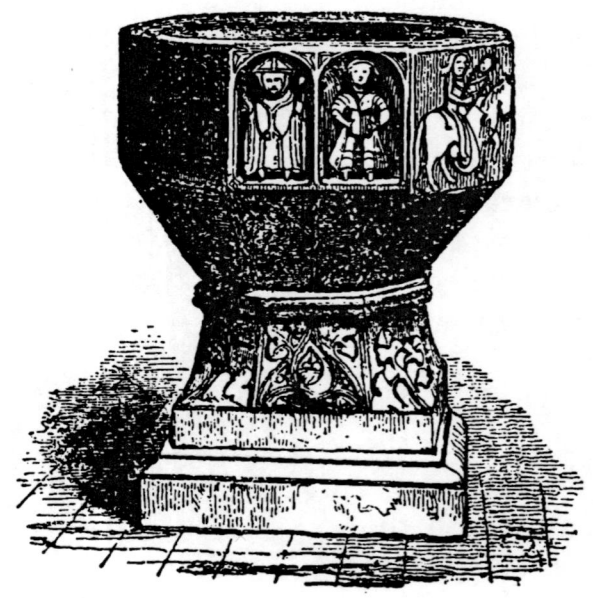

Fig. 37.

Ancient baptismal font of Clonard: three feet high; still preserved in the church there. (From Wilde's Boyne and Blackwater.) Not a vestige of any old building remains on the site of this great monastery.

took its rise, mainly from the monastery and college of Clonard, founded by St. Finnen about the year 527. Soon after his settlement here, great numbers of disciples, attracted by his learning and holiness, gathered round him. Under him were educated and trained for monastic and missionary work many of the most illustrious fathers of the Irish Church, including the "Twelve Apostles of Erin":* so that St. Finnen, who was a bishop, is called "a doctor of wisdom, and the tutor of the saints of Ireland in his time." These men, going forth from Clonard in all directions, founded, in imitation of their master Finnen, numerous monasteries, schools, and colleges, which subsequently became famous throughout all Europe. And now new life and vigour were infused into the Irish missionary Church; and the work of Patrick and his companions was carried on with renewed zeal and wonderful success. The influence of the druids was finally broken down, though they still lingered on, but obscurely and feebly, for many generations. Then also arose the zeal for preaching the Gospel in foreign lands, that gave rise to that vast emigration of Irish missionaries and scholars spoken of farther on.

Monastic Life.—The religious houses of this second class of Irish saints constituted the vast majority of the monasteries that flourished in Ireland down to the time of their suppression by Henry VIII. These are the monasteries that figure so prominently in the ecclesiastical history of Ireland: and it will be interesting to look into them somewhat closely and see how they were managed, and how the monks spent their time

For spiritual direction, and for the higher spiritual functions, such as those of ordination, confirmation, consecration of churches, &c., a bishop was commonly attached to every large monastery and nunnery. The

---

*For the Twelve Apostles of Erin, see the larger work, A Social History of Ancient Ireland, vol. I., p. 322.

monastic discipline was very strict, turning on the one cardinal principle of instant and unquestioning obedience. There was to be no idleness: everyone was to be engaged, at all available times, in some useful work; a regulation which appears everywhere in our ecclesiastical history.

Fig. 38.

"St. Columb's or Columkille's House," at Kells, Co. Meath· interior measurement about 16 feet by 13 walls 4 feet thick. An arched roof immediately overhead inside: between which and the steeply-sloped external stone roof is a small apartment for habitation and sleeping, 6 feet high. A relic of the second order of saints, and probably coeval with St. Columkille, sixth century. (From Petrie's Round Towers)

The monasteries of the Second Order were what are commonly known as "cenobitical" or community establishments: *i.e.*, the inmates lived, studied, and worked in society and companionship, and had all things in common. In sleeping accommodation there was much variety; in some monasteries each monk having a sleeping-cell for himself; in others three or four in one cell. In some they slept on the bare earth: in others they used a skin, laid perhaps on a little straw or rushes. Their food was prepared in one large kitchen by some of their own members specially skilled in cookery; and they took their meals in one common refectory. The fare, both eating and drinking, was always simple and generally scanty, poor, and uninviting: but on Sundays and festival days, and on occasions when distinguished persons visited, whom the abbot wished to honour, more generous food and drink were allowed.

When the founder of a monastery had determined on the neighbourhood in which to settle, and had fixed on the site for his establishment, he brought together those who had agreed to become his disciples and companions, and they set about preparing the place for residence. They did all the work with their own hands, seeking no help from outside. While some levelled and fenced in the ground, others cut down, in the surrounding woods, timber for the houses or for the church, dragging the great logs along, or bringing home on their backs bundles of wattles and twigs for the wickerwork walls. Even the leaders claimed no exemption, but often worked manfully with axe and spade like the rest.

Every important function of the monastery was in charge of some particular monk, who superintended if several persons were required for the duty, or did the work himself if only one was needed. These persons were nominated by the abbot, and held their positions permanently for the time. There was a tract of land attached to almost every monastery, granted to the original founder by the king or local lord, and usually increased by subsequent grants: so that agriculture formed one of the chief employments. When returning from work in the evening, the monks brought home on their backs whatever things were needed in the household for that night and next day. Milk was often brought in this manner in a vessel specially made for the purpose: and it was the custom to bring the vessel straight to the abbot, that he might bless the milk before use. In this fieldwork the abbot bore a part in several monasteries: and we sometimes read of men, now famous in Irish history—abbots and bishops in their time—putting in a hard day's work at the plough.

Those who had been tradesmen before entering were put to their own special work for the use of community and guests. Some ground the corn with a quern or in the mill; some made and mended clothes; some worked in the smith's forge or in the carpenter's workshop; while others baked the bread or cooked the meals.

Attached to every cenobitical monastery was a 'guest house' or hospice, for the reception of travellers. Some of the inmates were told off for this duty, whose business it was to receive the stranger, take off his shoes, wash his feet in warm water, and prepare supper and bed for him. In the educational establishments, teaching afforded abundant employment to the scholarly members of the community. Others again worked at copying and multiplying books for the library, or for presentation outside; and to the industry of these scribes we owe the chief part of the ancient Irish lore, and other learning, that has been preserved to us. St. Columkille devoted every moment of his spare time to this work, writing in a little wooden hut that he had erected for his use at Iona. It is recorded that he wrote with his own hand three hundred copies of the New Testament, which he presented to the various churches he had founded. Some spent their time in ornamenting and illuminating books—generally of a religious character, such as copies of portions of Scripture: and these men produced the wonderful penwork of the Book of Kells and other such manuscripts.

Others were skilled metal-workers, and made crosiers, crosses, bells, brooches, and other articles, of which many are preserved to this day, that show the surpassing taste and skill of the artists. But this was not peculiar to Irish monks, for those of other countries worked similarly. The great English St. Dunstan, we know, was an excellent artist in metal-work. Some of the Irish monks too were skilled in simple herb remedies; and the poor people around often came to them for advice and medicine in sickness. When a monastery was situated on the bank of a large river where there was no bridge, the monks kept a curragh ready to ferry travellers across, free of charge.

In some monasteries it was the custom to keep a fire perpetually burning in a little chapel specially set apart for this purpose, to which the inmates attended in turn to supply fuel, so that the fire might never go out. The perpetual fire of Kildare, which was kept alight from the time of St. Brigit for many centuries, is commemorated in Moore's lines:—

> "Like the bright lamp that shone in Kildare's holy fane,
> And burned through long ages of darkness and storm:"

and there were similar fires in Kilmainham, Seirkieran, and Inishmurray.

Besides the various employments noticed in the preceding pages, the inmates had their devotions to attend to, which were frequent, and often long: and in most monasteries they had to rise at the sound of the bell in the middle of the night, and go to the adjacent church to prayers.

Conversion of England and Northern Scotland.—Towards the end of the sixth century the great body of the Irish were Christians, so that the holy men of Ireland turned their attention to the conversion of other people. Then arose—almost suddenly—an extraordinary zeal for spreading the Gospel in foreign lands: and hundreds of devoted and determined missionaries left our shores. By a curious custom, not found elsewhere, each chief missionary going abroad brought with him twelve companions, but sometimes they went in much larger bodies.

On every side we meet with evidences of the activity of the Irish in Great Britain. Iona was founded in 563 by St. Columkille, a native of Donegal, and from this illustrious centre, he and his monks evangelised northern and western Scotland. The whole western coasts of England and Wales abound in memorials of Irish missionaries. Numbers of the most illustrious of the Irish saints studied and taught in the monastery of St. David in

Wales; St. Dunstan was educated by Irish monks in Glastonbury, as his biographer, William of Malmesbury, testifies; and there is good reason to believe that Cuthbert of Lindisfarne, one of the most illustrious of the saints of Britain, was a native of Ireland. Lanigan, in his "Ecclesiastical History" (II. 174), writes:—

"The Irish clergy and monks undertook the duty [of preaching to the Anglo-Saxons] as soon as a fit opportunity occurred, and have been on that account praised by Bede. It can scarcely be doubted that they were the instruments used by the Almighty for the conversion of those early Anglo-Saxon Christians in Columba's time; and that, with regard to a part of that nation, they got the start of the Roman missionaries in the blessed work of bringing them over to the Christian faith."

The Roman missionaries, under St. Augustine, arrived in England in 597, and succeeded in converting the Anglo-Saxon people of the kingdom of Kent. But in the north of Britain, including the large kingdom of Northumbria, Christianity made little headway till St. Aidan began his labours in Lindisfarne in 634. Aidan was an Irishman descended from the same kingly race as St. Brigit; he was educated at home, and, like so many of his countrymen, entered the monastery of Iona. After some time he was commissioned by the abbot and monks to preach to the Northumbrian Saxons, at the request of their good King Oswald that a missionary might be sent, this king being himself a zealous Christian who had spent some years in exile in Ireland, where he had been converted and received his education. Aidan, who had been consecrated a bishop, chose as his place of residence the little island of Lindisfarne, where he founded the monastery that became so illustrious in after ages. For thirty years—from 634 to 664—this monastery was governed by him and by two other Irish bishops, Finan and Colman, in succession.

Aidan, assisted by a number of his fellow-countrymen, laboured zealously, and with wonderful success, among the rugged Northumbrian pagans. "Many of the Scots"—writes the Venerable Bede—"came daily into Britain, and with great devotion preached the Word to those provinces of the English over which King Oswald reigned." These earnest men had the hearty co-operation and support of the king, of which Bede has given an interesting illustration in a passage where he tells us that as Aidan, on his arrival in Northumbria, was only imperfectly acquainted with the language, King Oswald, who had learned the Irish tongue while in Ireland, often acted as his interpreter to the people.

Montalembert, in his account of this mission, writes:—

"Forty-eight years after Augustine and his Roman monks landed on the shores of pagan England, an Anglo-Saxon prince [Oswald] invoked the aid of the monks of Iona in the conversion of the Saxons of the north. . . . The spiritual conquest of the island [Britain], abandoned for a time by the Roman missionaries, was now about to be taken up by the Celtic monks. The Italians [under Augustine] had made the first step,* and the Irish now appeared to resume the uncompleted work. What the sons of St. Benedict could only begin, was to be completed by the sons of St. Columba."

---

* But we know that the monks from Ireland were beforehand with St. Augustine: see Lanigan's observations above.

Missions to Foreign Lands.—Whole crowds of ardent and learned Irishmen travelled to the Continent in the sixth, seventh, and succeeding centuries, spreading Christianity and secular knowledge everywhere among the people. "What," says Eric of Auxerre (ninth century), in a letter to Charles the Bald, "what shall I say of Ireland, who, despising

Fig. 39.

Shrine, now preserved in Copenhagen, showing the *Opus Hibernicum*: one of the Continental traces of Irish missionaries Made either by an Irish artist, or by one who had learned from Irish artists. (From Journ. Roy Soc. Antiqq Irel)

the dangers of the deep, is migrating with almost her whole train of philosophers to our coasts?" "A characteristic still more distinctive of the Irish monk" —writes Montalembert—"as of all their nation, was the imperious necessity of spreading themselves without, of seeking or carrying knowledge and faith afar, and of penetrating into the more distant regions to watch or combat paganism": and a little further on he speaks of their "Passion for pilgrimage and preaching."

These men, on their first appearance on the Continent, caused much surprise, they were so startlingly different from those preachers the people had been accustomed to. They generally—as we have said—went in companies. They wore a coarse outer woollen garment, in colour as it came from the fleece, and under this a white tunic of finer stuff. They were tonsured bare on the front of the head, while the long hair behind flowed down on the back: and the eyelids were painted or stained black. Each had a long stout *cambutta*, or walking-stick: and slung from the shoulder a leathern bottle for water, and a wallet containing his greatest treasure—a book or two and some relics. They spoke a strange language among themselves, used Latin to those who understood it, and made use of an interpreter when preaching, until they had learned the language of the place.

Few people have any idea of the trials and dangers they encountered. Most of them were persons in good position, who might have lived in plenty and comfort at home. They knew well, when setting out, that they were leaving country and friends probably for ever; for of those that went, very few returned. Once on the Continent, they had to make their way, poor and friendless, through people whose language they did not understand, and who were in many places ten times more rude and dangerous in those ages than the inhabitants of these islands and we know, as a matter of history, that many were killed on the way. Yet these stout-hearted pilgrims, looking only to the service of their Master, never flinched. They were confident, cheerful, and self-helpful, faced privation with indifference, caring nothing for luxuries; and when other provisions failed them, they gathered wild fruit, trapped animals, and fished, with great dexterity and with any sort of next-to-hand rude appliances. They were rough and somewhat uncouth in outward appearance: but beneath all that they had solid sense and much learning. Their simple ways, their unmistakable piety, and their intense earnestness in the cause of religion caught the people everywhere, so that they made converts in crowds.

Irish professors and teachers were in those times held in such estimation that they were employed in most of the schools and colleges of Great Britain, France, Germany, and Italy. The revival of learning on the Continent was indeed due in no small degree to those Irish missionaries; and the investigations of scholars among the continental libraries are every year bringing to light new proofs of their industry and zeal for the advancement of religion and learning. To this day, in many towns of France, Germany, Switzerland, and Italy, Irishmen are venerated as patron saints. Nay, they found their way even to Iceland. We have the best authority for the statement that when the Norwegians first arrived at that island, they found there Irish books, bells, crosiers, and other traces of Irish missionaries; and the Irish geographer Dicuil, who wrote his Geography of the World in 825, records that in 795 some Irish ecclesiastics had sojourned in Iceland from February to August, where—as they told him—during a part of the time, they had sufficient light to transact their ordinary business all night through. Europe was too small for their missionary enterprise. We find a distinguished Irish monk named Augustin in Carthage in Africa, in the seventh century: and a learned treatise by him, written in very elegant Latin, on the "Wonderful Things of the Sacred Scripture," is still extant, and has been published. During his time also two other Irish monks named Baetan and Mainchine laboured in Carthage. There were settlements of Irish monks also in the Faroe and Shetland Islands.

All over the Continent we find evidences of the zeal and activity of Irish missionaries. Twelve centuries after this host of good men had received the reward they earned so well, an Irish pilgrim of our own day—Miss Margaret Stokes—traversed a large part of the scene of their labours in Southern Europe, in a loving and reverential search for relics and memorials of them: and how well she succeeded, how numerous were the vestiges she found—abbeys, churches, oratories, hermitages, caves, crosses, altars, tombs, holy wells, baptismal fonts, bells, shrines, and crosiers, beautiful illuminated manuscripts in their very handwriting, place-names, passages in the literatures of many languages—all with their living memories, legends, and traditions still clustering round them—she has recorded in her two charming books, "Six Months in the Apennines," and "Three Months in the Forests of France." May she be welcomed by those she revered and honoured!

The Irish "Passion for pilgrimage and preaching" never died out: it is characteristic of the race. This great missionary emigration to foreign lands has

CHAP. VI.] CHRISTIANITY. 151

continued in a measure down to our own day: for it may be safely asserted that no other missionaries are playing so general and successful a part in the

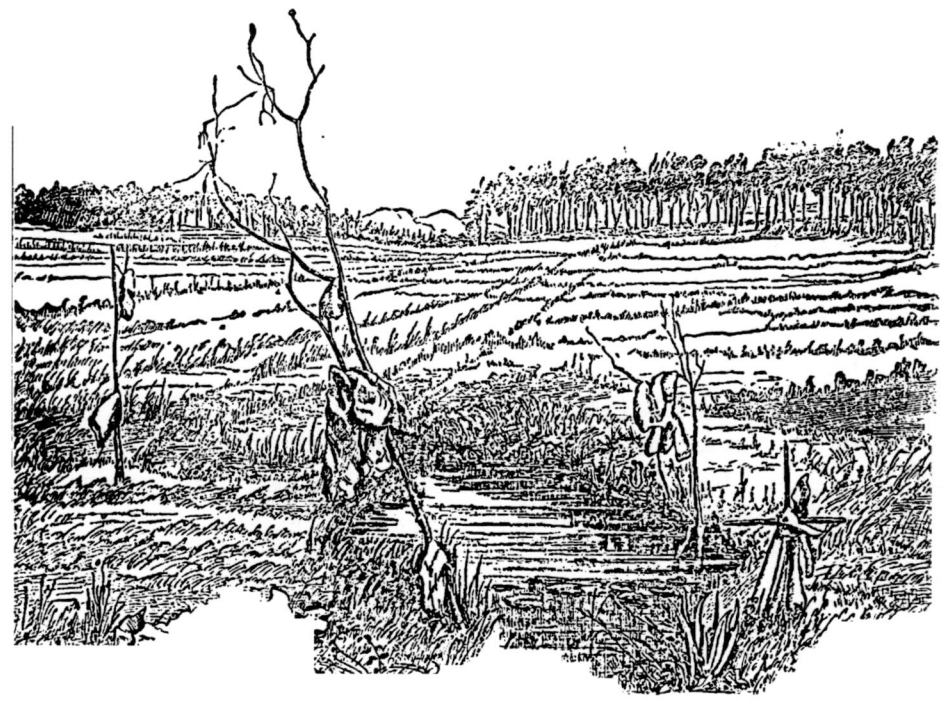

Fig. 40.

Holy Well of St. Dicuil, at Lure, in France: from Miss Stokes's Three Months in the Forests of France. This Dicuil (different from Dicuil the geographer) was a native of Leinster: educated at Bangor in Down: accompanied St. Columbanus to the Continent: founded a Monastery at Lure, where he is now venerated as patron saint: died A.D. 625. Well still called by his name: much resorted to by pilgrims.

conversion of the pagan people all over the world, and in keeping alight the lamp of religion among Christians, as those of Ireland. Take up any foreign ecclesiastical directory or glance through any newspaper account of religious meetings or ceremonies, or bold missionary enterprises in foreign lands; or look through the names of the governing bodies of Universities, Colleges, and Monasteries, in America, Asia, Australia, New Zealand—all over the world—and your eye is sure to light on cardinals, archbishops, bishops, priests, principals, professors, teachers, with such names as Moran, O'Reilly, O'Donnell, Mac Carthy, Higgins, Murphy, Walsh, Fleming, Fitzgerald, Corrigan, O'Gorman, Byrne, and scores of such-like, telling unmistakably of their Irish origin, and proving that the Irish race of the present day may compare not unfavourably in missionary zeal with those of the times of old. As the sons of Patrick, Finnen, and Columkille took a leading part in converting the people of Britain and the Continent, so it would seem to be destined that the ultimate universal adoption of Christianity should be mainly due to the agency of Irish missionaries.

5. *The Third Order: Anchorites or Hermits, and Hermit Communities.*

We have records of numerous individual hermits from the time of St. Patrick down, retiring from the world to spend their days in prayer and meditation in lonely places remote from human society. But the desire for eremitical life became very general about the end of the sixth century. Then not only individuals, but whole communities of monks sought a solitary life. The leader of a colony of intended recluses went with his followers to some remote place, in a deep valley surrounded by mountains, forests, and bogs, or on some almost inaccessible little island, where they took up their abode. Each man built a cell for himself: and these cells, with a little church in the midst, all surrounded by a low *cashel*, *rath*, or wall, formed an eremitical monastery: a monastic group like those known in the East by the name of "Laura." Each monk passed the greater part of his life in his own cell, holding little or no communication with his fellows, except only at stated times in the day or night, when all assembled in the church for common worship, or in the refectory for meals. Their food consisted of fruits, nuts, roots, and other vegetables, which they cultivated in a kitchen-garden: and it must often have gone hard with them to support life. The remains of these little monasteries are still to be seen in several parts of Ireland, both on the mainland and on islands: as, for instance, at Gongane Barra lake, the source of the Lee in Cork, where St. Finbarr, patron of Cork, settled with his hermit community in the end of the sixth century; on Inishmurray off the Sligo coast; on Ardoilen, a little ocean rock off the coast of Galway, where a *laura* was founded by St. Fechin in the seventh century; and on the Great Skellig off the Kerry coast, where there still remains an interesting group of cloghans, *i.e.* beehive-shaped stone houses.

These hermit communities were the Third Order of Saints, who are very correctly described in the old Catalogue. It is stated that they lasted till the time of the Yellow Plague in 664, which broke up the system of eremitical monasteries; but long after this we find numerous records of individual hermits.

There were nuns and convents in Ireland from the

time of St. Patrick, as we know from his "Confession," and from his "Epistle to Coroticus": nevertheless

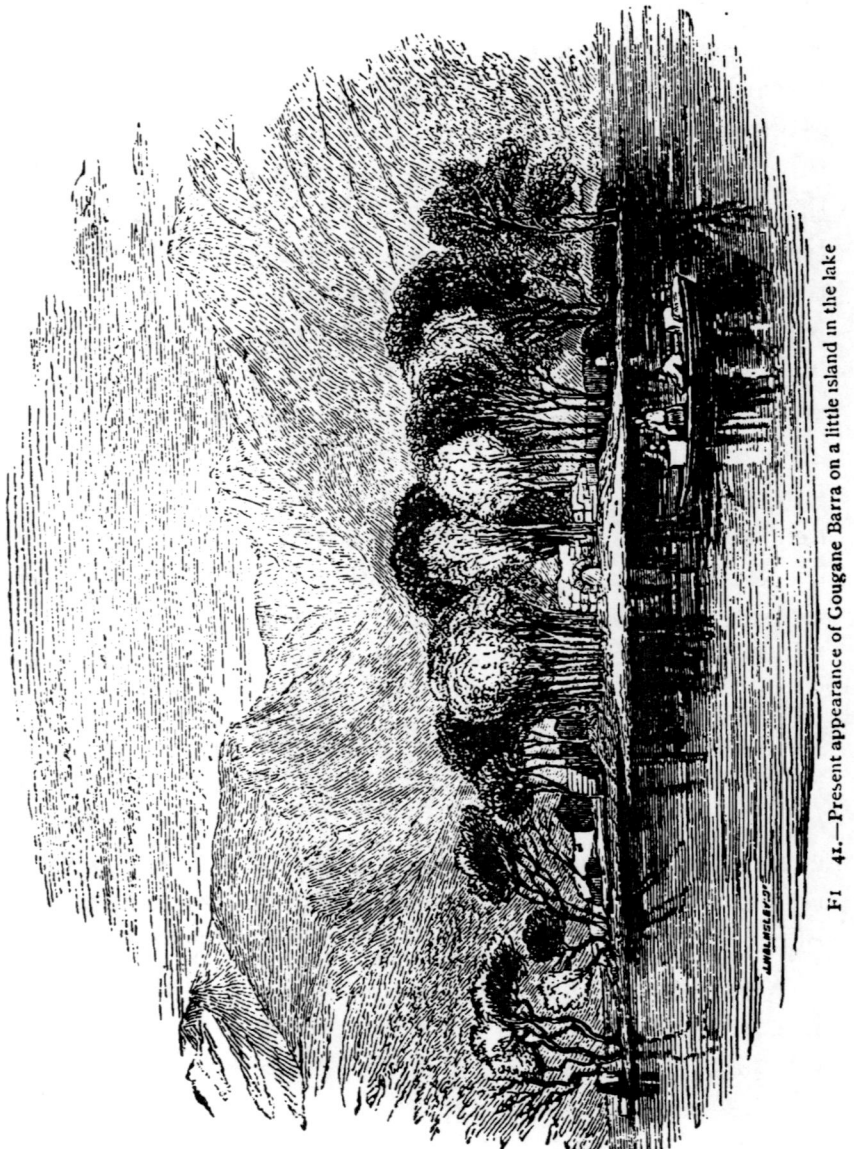

Fig. 41.—Present appearance of Gougane Barra on a little island in the lake

it may almost be said that St. Brigit of Kildare was the founder of the Irish conventual system.

6. *Buildings and other Material Requisites.*

Churches and Monastic Buildings.—Nearly all the churches in the time of St. Patrick, and for several centuries afterwards, were of wood. But this was by no means universally the case; for little

Fig. 42.

St. Mac Dara's primitive church on St. Mac Dara's Island, off the coast of Galway. Interior measurement 15 feet by 11. (From Petrie's Round Towers.)

stone churches were erected from the earliest Christian times. The early churches, built on the model of those introduced by St. Patrick, were small and plain, seldom more than sixty feet long, sometimes not more than fifteen, always a simple oblong, never cruciform; almost universally placed east and west, with the door in the west end.

As Christianity spread, the churches became gradually larger and more ornamental, and a chancel was often added at the east end, which was another

FIG. 43.

St Doulogh's stone-roofed Church, four miles north of Dublin St Dúlech, one of the early Irish saints, settled here and built a church; but the present church (here figured) is not older than the thirteenth century. (From Wakeman's Handbook of Irish Antiquities.)

oblong, merely a continuation of the larger building, with an arch between. The jambs of both doors and windows inclined, so that the bottom of the opening was wider than the top: this shape of door or window is a sure mark of antiquity. The doorways were commonly constructed of very large stones, with almost always a horizontal lintel: the

Fig. 44.

Doorway of Tempull Caimham n Aran, with sloped sides
(From Miss Stokes's Inscriptions)

windows were often semi-circularly arched at top, but sometimes triangular-headed. The remains of little stone churches, of these antique patterns, of ages from the fifth or sixth century to the tenth or eleventh, are still to be found all over Ireland.

The small early churches, without chancels, were often or generally roofed with flat stones, of which Cormac's chapel at Cashel, St. Doulogh's near Dublin (p. 156), St. Columb's house at Kells (p. 140, *supra*), and St. Mac Dara's Church (p. 155, *supra*), are examples. In early ages churches were often in groups of seven—or intended to be so—a custom still commemorated in popular phraseology, as in "The Seven Churches of Glendalough."

In the beginning of the eleventh century, what is called the Romanesque style of architecture, distinguished by a profusion of ornamentation—a style that had previously been spreading over Europe—was introduced into Ireland. Then the churches, though still small and simple in plan, began to be richly decorated. We have remaining numerous churches in this style: a beautiful example is Cormac's chapel on the Rock of Cashel, erected in 1134 by Cormac Mac Carthy, king of Munster (figured on title-page).

Nemed or Sanctuary.—The land belonging to and around a church—the glebe-land—was a sanctuary, and as such was known by the names of *Nemed* [neveh] meaning literally 'heavenly' or 'sacred,' and *Termann* or *Termon*, meaning 'boundary'; for the sanctuary was generally marked off at the corners by crosses or pillar-stones. Once a culprit, fleeing from enraged pursuers, succeeded in getting inside the boundary, he was safe for the time; for no one durst violate the sanctuary by molesting him. But when the immediate occasion passed, he was given up to be dealt with by the ordinary tribunals.

It was usual for the founders of churches to plant trees—oftenest yew, but sometimes oak or ash—for ornament and shelter, round the church and cemetery, and generally within the sanctuary. These little plantations were subsequently held in great veneration, and it was regarded as an outrageous desecration to cut down one of the trees, or even to lop off a branch. They were called *Fidnemed* [finneveh], 'sacred grove,' or grove of the *nemed* or sanctuary: from *fid* (fih), 'a wood or grove.'

The most general term for a church was, and is still, *cill* [kill], derived from **Lat.** *cella*; but there were several other names.

FIG. 45.

Dominican Abbey, Kilnallock: founded in 1291 by Gilbert Fitzgerald.
(From Kilk. Archæol Journ.)

Later Churches.—Until about the period of the Anglo-Norman Invasion all the churches, including those in the Romanesque style, were small, because the congregations were small. But about the middle of the twelfth century the old Irish style of church architecture began to be abandoned, chiefly through the influence of the Anglo-Normans, who were, as we know, great builders. Towards the close of the century, when many of the great English lords had settled in Ireland, they began to indulge their taste for architectural magnificence, and the native Irish chiefs imitated and emulated them; large cruciform churches in the pointed style began to prevail; and all over the country splendid buildings of every kind sprang up. Then were erected—some by the English, some by the Irish—those stately abbeys and churches of which the ruins are still to be seen; such as those of Kilmallock and Monasteranenagh in Limerick; Jerpoint in Kilkenny; Grey Abbey in Down; Bective and Newtown in Meath; Sligo; Quin, Corcomroe, and Ennis in Clare; Ballintober in Mayo; Knockmoy in Galway; Dunbrody in Wexford; Buttevant; Cashel; and many others.

Round Towers.—In connexion with many of the ancient churches there were round towers of stone from 60 to 150 feet high, and from 13 to 20 feet in external diameter at the base: the top was conical. The interior was divided into six or seven stories reached by ladders from one to another, and each story was lighted by one window: the top story had usually four windows. The door was placed 10 or more feet from the ground outside, and was reached by a ladder: both doors and windows had sloping jambs like those of the churches. About eighty round towers still remain, of which about twenty are perfect: the rest are more or less imperfect.

CHAP. VI.] CHRISTIANITY. 161

Formerly there was much speculation as to the uses of these round towers; but Dr. George Petrie, after examining the towers themselves, and—with the help of O'Donovan and O'Curry—searching through all the Irish literature within his reach for allusions to them, set the question at rest in his Essay on "The Origin and Uses of the Round Towers." It is now known that they are of Christian origin, and

FIG. 46.

Great Tower, Clonnacnoise. (From Petrie's Round Towers)

that they were always built in connexion with ecclesiastical establishments. They were erected at various times from about the beginning of the ninth to the thirteenth century. They had at least a two-fold use: as belfries, and as keeps to which the inmates of the monastery retired with their valuables —such as books, shrines, crosiers, relics, and vestments—in case of sudden attack. They were probably used also—when occasion required—as beacons and watch-towers. These are Dr. Petrie's conclusions, but he fixed the date of some few in the fifth century, which recent investigations have shown to be too early. It would appear that it was the Danish incursions that gave rise to the erection of the round towers, which began to be built early in the ninth century simultaneously all over the country. They

FIG. 47.

Round Tower (perfect), Devenish Island, in Lough Erne, near Enniskillen (From Kilk. Archæol Journ) For another view, with church, see chap. xx., sect. 5, *infra*.

were admirably suited to the purpose of affording refuge from the sudden murderous raids of the Norsemen: for the inmates could retire with their valuables on a few minutes' warning, with a good supply of large stones to drop on the robbers from the windows; and once they had drawn up the outside ladder and barred the door, the tower was, for a short attack, practically impregnable. Round towers are not quite peculiar to Ireland; about twenty-two are found elsewhere—in Bavaria, Italy, Switzerland, Belgium, Scotland, and other countries.

Fig. 48.

Remains of Round Tower at Drumcliff, 4 miles north of Sligo town built near the church founded by St. Columkille, but long after his time

Monastic Lis or Rampart.—An Irish monastery, including the whole group of monastic buildings, was generally enclosed by a strong rampart, commonly circular or oval, according to the fashion of the country in the lay homesteads. The rampart was designated by one of the usual Irish names, *rath*, or *lios* [liss], or if of stone, *caiseal* [cashel].

Wells.—Wells have at all times been held in veneration in Ireland by both pagans and Christians; and we have seen that many of the pagan Irish worshipped wells as gods. Some of these were blessed and consecrated to Christian uses by the early saints, of which a very interesting instance is related in Adamnan's Life of St. Columkille. The saint, traversing Scotland, came to a fountain, to which the pagans paid divine honours. But he rescued it from heathenism, and blessed it, so that it was ever after revered as a holy well. In this manner hundreds of the heathen wells were taken over to Christianity and sanctified by the early saints, so that they came to be even more venerated by the Christians than they had been by the pagans. Most of the early preachers of the Gospel established their humble foundations—many of them destined to grow in after-years into great religious and educational institutions—beside fountains, whose waters at the same time supplied the daily wants of the little communities, and served for the baptism of converts.

There are now innumerable holy wells scattered all over the country, most of them called by the names of the noble old missionaries who spent their lives in converting the pagans or in ministering to the spiritual needs of the Christian people of the several localities. In this manner most of our early saints became associated with wells. The practice began with St. Patrick, who, we are told, founded a church at Magh Slecht, in the present County Cavan: " and there [to this day is reverenced] Patrick's well, in which he baptised many."

A well is sometimes met with containing one lone inhabitant—a single trout or salmon—which is always to be seen swimming about in its tiny dominion: and sometimes there are two. They are usually tame; and the people hold them in great respect, and tell many wonderful legends about them. This pretty custom is of old standing, for it originated with the early Irish saints—even with St. Patrick himself. The Tripartite Life states, regarding the well of Aghagower in Mayo, that " Patrick left two salmon alive in the well." The same custom prevailed in the Scottish western islands.

The usual name for a well, both in the old and in the modern Irish language, is *tobar* [tubber].

Bells.—The Irish for a bell is *clog*, akin to the English *clock*. St. Patrick and his disciples constantly used consecrated bells in their ministrations. How numerous they were in Patrick's time we may understand from the fact, that whenever he left one of his disciples in charge of a church, he gave him a bell: and it is recorded that on the churches of one province alone—Connaught—he bestowed fifty. To supply these he had in his household three smiths, whose chief occupation was to make bells. The most ancient Irish bells were quadrangular in shape, with rounded corners, and made of iron: facts which we know both from the ecclesiastical literature, and from the specimens that are still preserved.

The bell of St. Patrick, which is more than fourteen hundred years old, is now in the National Museum in Dublin: it is the oldest of all; and it may be taken as a type of the hammered-iron bells. Its height is $6\frac{1}{2}$ inches: at the mouth the two dimensions are $4\frac{7}{8}$ by $3\frac{7}{8}$ inches. It is made of two iron plates, bent into shape by hammering, and slightly overlapped at the edges for riveting. After the joints had been riveted, the bell was consolidated by the fusion of bronze into the joints and over the surface—probably by dipping into melted bronze—which also increased its resonance. This is the bell known as the "Bell of the Will"; and it is much celebrated in the Lives of St. Patrick. A beautiful and costly shrine was made to cover and protect this venerable relic, by order of Donall O'Loghlin, king of Ireland (died 1121): and this gorgeous piece of ancient Irish art, with O'Loghlin's name and three others inscribed on it, is also preserved in the National Museum. A beautiful drawing of it made by Miss Stokes is shown on the opposite page. Many

FIG. 19.
St. Patrick's Bell called the "Bell of the Will."
(From Miss Stokes's Inscriptions.)

others of these venerable iron bronzed bells, belonging to the primitive Irish saints, are preserved in the National and other Museums, several covered with ornamental shrines.

About the ninth century the Irish artificers began to make bells wholly of cast bronze. A beautiful quadrangular bell of this class, made some short time

FIG. 50.

Shrine of St. Patrick's Bell: now in the National Museum, Dublin.
(From Miss Stokes's Early Christian Art in Ireland.)

before A.D. 900, now known as Mac Ailello's Bell, is to be seen in the National Museum. It tells its own history in an Irish inscription, of which this is a translation :—" A prayer for Cummascach Mac Ailello." This Cummascach, son of Ailill, for

FIG. 51.

Mac Ailello's Bell   (From Miss Stokes's Early Christian Architecture.)

whom the bell was made, was house-steward of the monastery of Armagh, and died A.D. 908.

The very ancient Irish bells, whether of iron or of bronze, were small, and were sounded by a clapper or tongue. All those in the National Museum are furnished inside at top with a ring, from which the clapper was hung, and in some the clapper still remains.

MS. ornamentation. (From Miss Stokes's Early Christian Architecture.)

CHAPTER VII.

LEARNING AND EDUCATION.

SECTION 1. *Learning in Pagan Times·
Ogham.*

ANY passages in our old native literature, both ecclesiastical and secular, state that the pagan Irish had books before the introduction of Christianity. In the memoir of St. Patrick, written by Muirchu in the seventh century, now contained in the Book of Armagh, he relates how, during the contest of the saint with the druids at Tara, King Laegaire [Laery] proposed that one of Patrick's books and one belonging to the druids should be thrown into water, to see which would come out uninjured: a sort of ordeal. Here it will be observed that Muirchu's statement that the druids had books embodies a tradition that was ancient in the seventh century, when he wrote.

The lay traditions, many of them as old as Muirchu's Life, state that the pagan Irish used Ogham writing: and we find Ogham inscriptions constantly referred to as engraved on the tombs of pagan kings and chiefs.

FIG 52 —Oghan Alphabet (Piom Journ. Roy. Soc Antiqq. Irel. for 1902, p 3)
A few other characters were occasionally used.

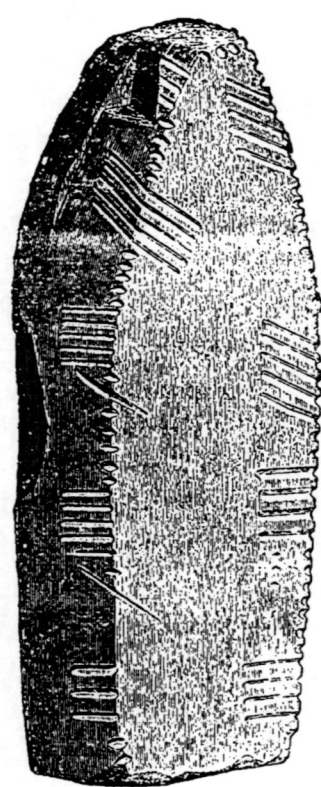

FIG 53 —Ogham stone.
(From Kilk. Archæol. Journal)

Ogham was a species of writing, the letters of which were formed by combinations of short lines and points, on and at both sides of a middle or stem line called a *flesc*. So far as we can judge from the specimens remaining to us, its use was mostly confined to stone inscriptions, the groups of lines and points generally running along two adjacent sides of the stone, with the angle for a *flesc*. Nearly all the Oghams hitherto found are sepulchral inscriptions; which answer exactly to the descriptions given in the old records. Where inscriptions have not been injured or defaced, they can in general be deciphered, so that many have been made out beyond all question. But as the greatest number of Ogham stones are more or less worn or chipped or broken, there is in the interpretation of the majority of the inscriptions some conjecture and uncertainty.

As to the antiquity of Ogham writing, the best authorities now agree that it is a survival from the far distant ages of paganism, and that it was developed before Christianity was heard of in Ireland. But while we know that it originated in pagan times, the custom of engraving Ogham on stones, and of—occasionally—writing in Ogham characters in vellum books, continued far into Christian times. In the ancient tales we find it often stated that Oghams were cut on rods of yew or oak, and that such rods were used as a mode of communication between individuals, serving the same purpose among them as our letters serve now.

There are many other considerations all tending to show that there was some form of written literature before the advent of Christianity; and several circumstances indicate a state of literary activity at the time of the arrival of St. Patrick. Both the native bardic literature and the ancient Lives of Patrick himself and of his contemporary saints concur in stating that he found in the country literary and professional men—all pagans—druids, poets, and antiquarians, and an elaborate code of laws.

We have seen that in the most ancient native literature it is expressly stated that the pagan Irish had books, and the statement is corroborated by an extern writer, a Christian philosopher of the fourth century, named Ethicus of Istria; whose testimony seems indeed decisive. He made a tour of the three continents, writing a description—or "Topography"—

of his journey as he went along, and among other places, he visited the British Islands. From Spain he came direct to Ireland, where, as he says, he spent some time "examining their volumes." This opening statement proves that when he visited—which was at least a century before the time of St. Patrick—he found books among the Irish; and it implies that he found them in abundance, for he remained some time examining them. The fact that there were numerous books in Ireland in the fourth century implies a knowledge of writing for a long time previously.

From all that precedes, we may take it as certain:—

1. That native learning was actively cultivated and systematically developed in Ireland before the introduction of Christianity: and

2. That the pagan Irish had a knowledge of letters, and that they wrote their lore, or part of it, in books, and cut Ogham inscriptions on stone and wood. But when or how they obtained their knowledge of writing, we have as yet no means of determining with certainty.

It is true indeed that no books or writings of any kind, either pagan or Christian, of the time before St. Patrick, remain—with the exception of Ogham inscriptions. But this proves nothing: for in this respect Ireland is circumstanced like most other countries. A similar state of things exists, for instance, in Britain, where, notwithstanding that writing was generally known and practised from the first century down, no manuscript has been preserved of an earlier date than the eighth century.

CHAP. VII.] LEARNING AND EDUCATION. 173

There is nothing, either in the memoirs of St. Patrick, or in Irish secular literature, or in the "Topography" of Ethicus, giving the least hint as to the characters or as to the sort of writing used in the books of the pagan Irish. It could hardly have been Ogham, which is too cumbrous for writing long passages or treatises in books. But whatever characters they may have used in times of paganism

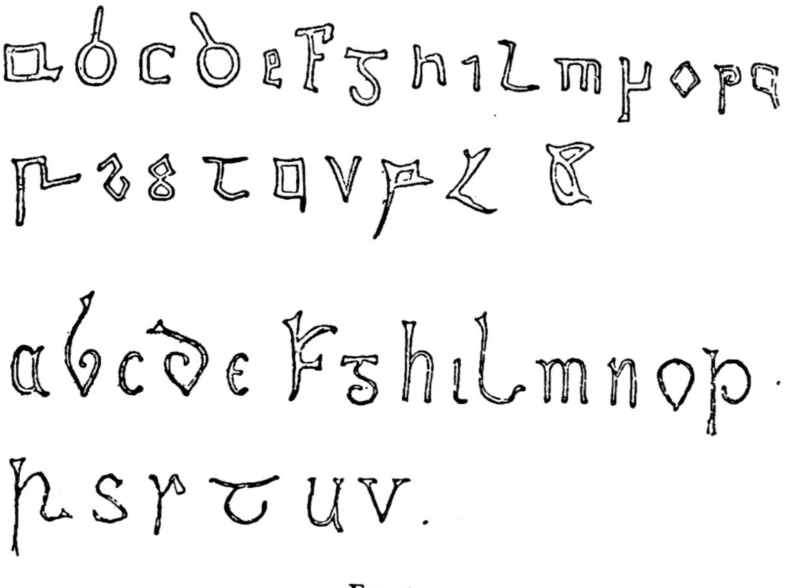

FIG 54.

Two Irish alphabets of Roman letters: the upper one of the seventh century: the lower of the eleventh. The three last characters of the first alphabet are Y, Z, and &c. (Two forms of *s* in each) (From Miss Stokes's Christian Inscriptions, II. 135.)

they adopted the Roman letters in writing their own language after the time of St. Patrick: which are still retained in modern Irish. These same letters, moreover, were brought to Britain by the early Irish Christian missionaries already spoken of, from whom the Anglo-Saxons learned them: so that England received her first knowledge of letters—as she received most of her Christianity—from Ireland. Formerly it was the fashion among the learned to call those letters Anglo-Saxon: but now people know better. Our present printed characters were ultimately developed from those old Irish-Roman letters.

2. *Monastic Schools.*

Two Classes of Schools. — The schools and colleges of ancient Ireland were of two classes, Ecclesiastical and Lay. The ecclesiastical or monastic schools were introduced with Christianity, and were conducted by monks. The lay or secular schools existed from a period of unknown antiquity, and in pagan times they were taught by druids. The Irish monastic schools were celebrated all over Europe in the Middle Ages: the lay schools, though playing an important part in spreading learning at home, were not so well known. These two classes of schools are well distinguished all through the literary history of Ireland, and, without interfering with each other, worked contemporaneously from the fifth to the nineteenth century.

General Features of Monastic Schools.—Even from the time of St. Patrick there were schools in connexion with several of the monasteries he founded, chiefly for the education of young men intended for the church. But when the great monastic movement already spoken of (p. 138) began, in the sixth century, then there was a rapid growth of schools and colleges all over the country : for almost every large monastery had a school attached. Many of these contained great numbers of students. Under each of the three fathers of the Irish Church, St. Finnen in Clonard, St. Comgall in Bangor, and St. Brendan in Clonfert, there were 3000, including no doubt monks as well as students; St. Molaise had 1500; St. Gobban, 1000; and so on down to the school of Glasnevin, where St. Mobi had 50. This last—fifty—was a very usual number in the smaller monastic schools. How such large numbers as those in Clonard, Bangor, and Clonfert obtained living and sleeping accommodation will be found described farther on.

In these schools secular as well as ecclesiastical learning was carefully attended to; for besides divinity, the study of the Scriptures, and classics, for those intended for the church, the students were instructed—as we shall see—in general literature and science. Accordingly, a large proportion of the students in these monastic schools were young men—amongst them sons of kings and chiefs—intended, not for the church, but for ordinary civil or military life, who attended to get a good general education. Those great seminaries were in fact the prototypes of our modern universities.

Extent of Learning in Monastic Schools.—We have ample evidence that both the Latin and Greek languages and literatures were studied with success in Ireland from the sixth to the tenth century; and that the learned men from the Irish schools were quite on a par with the most eminent of the Continental scholars of the time, and not a few of them at the head of all. Columbanus, Aileran the Wise, Cummian, Sedulius, Fergil the Geometer, Duns Scotus, and many others, all Irishmen, and educated in Irish schools, were celebrated throughout Europe for their learning. The most distinguished scholar of his day in Europe was John Scotus Erigena ('John the Irish Scot'), celebrated for his knowledge of Greek, and for his theological speculations. He taught Philosophy in Paris, and died about the year 870.

FIG. 55.
John Scotus Erigena Sculptured in stone at Brasenose College, Oxford: drawn from this by Petrie

Foreign Students.—In all the more important schools there were students from foreign lands, from the Continent as well as from Great Britain, attracted by the eminence of the masters and by the facilities for quiet, uninterrupted study. In the Lives of distinguished Englishmen we constantly find such statements as " he was sent to Ireland to finish his education." The illustrious scholar Alcuin, who was a native of York, was educated at Clonmacnoise. Among the foreign visitors were many princes: Oswald and Aldfrid, kings of Northumbria, and Dagobert II., king of France, were all educated in Ireland. We get some idea of the numbers of foreigners from the ancient Litany of Aengus the Culdee, in which we find invoked many Romans, Gauls, Germans, and Britons, all of whom died in Ireland. To this day there is to be seen, on Great Aran island, a tomb-stone, with the inscription "VII Romani," Seven Romans. It is known that in times of persecution Egyptian monks fled to Ireland; and they have left in the country many traces of their influence. In the same Litany of Aengus mention is made of seven Egyptian monks buried in one place.

Fig 56.

Tomb-stone of the Seven Romans in Aran. (From Petrie's Round Towers.)

The greatest number of foreign students came from Great Britain—they came in *fleet-loads*, as Aldhelm, Bishop of Sherborne (A.D. 705 to 709), expresses it in his letter to his friend Eadfrid, Bishop of Lindisfarne, who had himself been educated in

Ireland. Many also were from the Continent. There is a remarkable passage in the Venerable Bede's "Ecclesiastical History" which corroborates Aldhelm's statement, as well as what is said in the native records, and indeed in some particulars goes rather beyond them. Describing the ravages of the yellow plague in 664, he says:—"This pestilence did no less harm in the island of Ireland. Many of the nobility and of the lower ranks of the English nation were there at that time, who, in the days of Bishops Finan and Colman [Irish abbots of Lindisfarne, p. 146, *supra*], forsaking their native island, retired thither, either for the sake of divine studies, or of a more continent life. . . . The Scots willingly received them all, and took care to supply them with food, as also to furnish them with books to read, and their teaching, all gratis."

Towards the end of the eighth century, it became the custom to appoint a special head professor— commonly called a **Fer-leginn**, *i.e.* 'Man of learning'—to preside over, and be responsible for, the educational functions of the college, while the abbot had the care of the whole institution.

3. *Lay Schools.*

It has been sometimes asserted that, in early times in Ireland, learning was confined within the walls of the monasteries; but this view is quite erroneous. Though the majority of the men of learning, in Christian times, were ecclesiastics, secular learning was by no means confined to the clergy. We have seen that the monastic schools had many lay pupils, and that there were numerous lay schools; so that a considerable body of the lay community must have been more or less educated--able to read and write. Nearly all the professional physicians, lawyers (or *brehons*), poets, builders, and historians, were laymen; a large proportion of the men chronicled in our annals, during the whole period of Ireland's literary pre-eminence, as distinguished in art and general literature, were also laymen; lay tutors were often employed to teach princes; and, in fact, laymen played a very important part in the diffusion of knowledge and in building up that character for learning that rendered Ireland so famous in former times.

It is true that the great body of the people could neither read nor write. But they had an education of another kind—reciting poetry, historic tales, and legends—or listening to recitation—in which all people, high and low, took delight, as mentioned elsewhere. This was true education, a real exercise for the intellect, and a real and refined enjoyment. In every hamlet there were one or more amateur reciters: and this amusement was then more general than newspaper- and story-reading is now. So that, taking education, as we ought, in this broad sense, and not restricting it to the narrow domain of reading and writing, we see that the great body of the Irish people of those times were really educated.

There seems no reason to doubt that there were schools of some kind in Ireland before the introduction of Christianity, which were carried on by druids. After the general spread of Christianity, while monastic schools were growing up everywhere through the country, the old schools still held their ground, taught now by Christian ollaves or doctors—laymen—who were the representatives of the druid teachers of old times.

There were several classes of these schools. Some were known as "Bardic schools," in which were taught poetry, history, and general Irish literature. Some were for law, and some for other special professions. The Bardic schools were the least technical of any: and young laymen not intended for professions attended them—as many others in greater numbers attended the monastic schools—to get a good general education.

4. *Some General Features of both classes of Schools.*

The "Seven Degrees of Wisdom."—In both the ecclesiastical and the secular schools there were **seven degrees** for the students or graduates, like the modern University stages of sizars, freshmen, sophisters, bachelors, moderators, masters, and doctors. The degrees in the lay schools corresponded with those in the ecclesiastical schools; but except in the two last grades the names differed. A man who had attained the seventh or highest grade in either class of school was an **Ollave** or 'Doctor.'

For each degree of both classes of schools there was a specified course of study. In the Bardic schools the minimum length of the whole course was **twelve years**—but it commonly was much longer—each with its subjects set forth: but we do not know the length in the monastic schools. Classics—Latin and Greek—formed a prominent feature of the instruction in the monastic schools, and among the higher class students Latin was spoken quite familiarly in the schools. Much of what they wrote too is a mixture of Gaelic and Latin; both languages being used with equal facility. At first the Bardic schools taught no language but Gaelic: but later on —under the influence of the monastic schools—they admitted Latin and Greek among the subjects of instruction. The graduates of each grade in the Bardic schools had, among their other subjects, to know a number of Romantic and Historical Tales, so as to be able to recite any one of them when called on, for the instruction and amusement of the company. The number was increased year after year of the course. The Ollave had to be master of 350; but these formed only a comparatively small proportion of his acquirements.*

School Life and School Methods.—Some students lived in the houses of the people of the neighbourhood· "poor scholars"—as they came to be called in later times—who, besides being taught free in the schools, were lodged and fed without charge in the farmers' houses all round: a hospitable custom which continued down to a period within my own memory, and which I saw in full work. A few resided in the college itself; but the body of the scholars lived in little houses built mostly by themselves around and near the school. St. Mobi had fifty students in his school at Glasnevin, near Dublin, who had their huts ranged along one bank of the

---

* In my larger work, A Social History of Ancient Ireland, there is a detailed account of the seven degrees or stages in both classes of schools, with their names and programmes of study.

river—the Tolka. Sometimes several lived together in one large house. In the leading colleges, whole streets of these houses surrounded the monastery, forming a collegiate town.

The poorer scholars sometimes lived in the same houses with the rich ones, whom they waited on and served, receiving in return food, clothing, and other necessaries; like the American custom of the present day. But some chose to live in this humble capacity, not through poverty, but as a self-imposed discipline and mortification, like Adamnan, mentioned here. As illustrating this phase of school life, an interesting story is told in the Life of King Finaghta the Festive. A little before his accession, he was riding one day towards Clonard with his retinue, when they overtook a boy with a jar of milk on his back. The youth attempting to get out of the way, stumbled and fell, and the jar was broken and the milk spilled. The cavalcade passed on without noticing him; but he ran after them in great trouble with a piece of the jar on his back, till at last he attracted the notice of the prince, who halted and questioned him in a good-humoured way. The boy, not knowing whom he was addressing, told his story with amusing plainness:—" Indeed, good man, I have much cause to be troubled. There are living in one house near the college three noble students, and three others that wait upon them, of whom I am one; and we three attendants have to collect provisions in the neighbourhood in turn, for the whole six. It was my turn to-day; and lo, what I have obtained has been lost; and this vessel which I borrowed has been broken, and I have not the means to pay for it."

The prince soothed him, told him his loss should be made good, and promised to look after him in the future. That boy was Adamnan, a descendant and relative of princes, subsequently a most distinguished man, ninth abbot of Iona, and the writer of the Life of St. Columba. The prince was as good as his word, and, after he became king, invited Adamnan to his court, where the rising young ecclesiastic became his trusted friend and spiritual adviser.

In teaching a child book-learning, the first thing was, of course, the alphabet. St. Columkille's first alphabet was written or impressed on a cake, which he afterwards ate. This points to a practice, which we sometimes see at the present day, of writing the alphabet, or shaping it in some way, on sweetmeats, as an encouragement and help to what has been, and always will be, a difficult task for a child. Sometimes they engraved the alphabet for

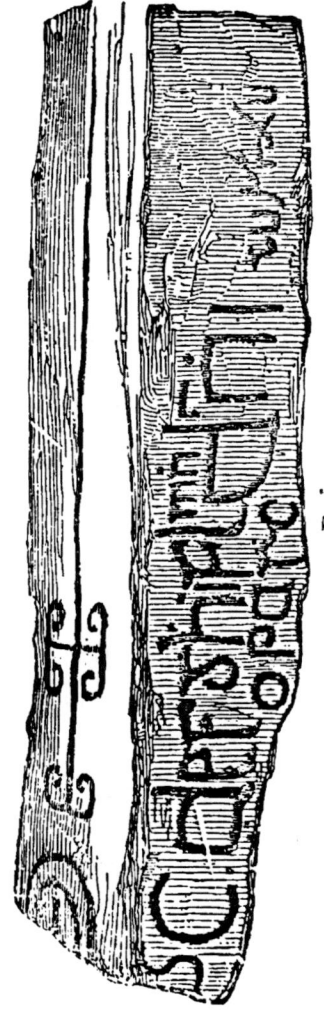

FIG. 57.

Roman Aphabet for learners, on a pillar-stone in the graveyard of Kilnalkeda in Kerry The first letter, A, has been broken off The three large letters near the centre are not part of the alphabet they are DNI, an abbreviation of "Domini," which was on the stone before the alphabet was engraved. (From Petrie's Round Towers

beginners on a large stone, of which an example is shown in fig. 57.

It was the practice of many eminent teachers to compose educational poems embodying the leading facts of history, geography, or other branches of instruction; and a considerable proportion of the metrical compositions preserved in our ancient books belong to this class. These poems having been committed tó memory by the scholars, were commented on and explained by their authors.

Children received a different sort of education in the homes of their parents or foster-parents, which was of a very sensible kind, aiming directly at preparing for the future life of the child. The sons of the humbler ranks were to be taught how to herd kids, calves, lambs, and young pigs; how to kiln-dry corn, to prepare malt, to comb·wool, and to cut and split wood: the girls how to use the needle according to their station in life, to grind corn with a quern, to knead dough, and to use a sieve. The sons of the chiefs were to be instructed in archery, swimming, and chess-playing, in the use of the sword and spear, and horsemanship: the daughters in sewing, cutting-out, and embroidery. All this was compulsory in case of children in fosterage.

5. *The Men of Learning.*

Professions Hereditary.—In ancient Ireland, the professions almost invariably ran in families, so that members of the same household devoted themselves to one particular science or art—Poetry,

History, Medicine, Building, Law, as the case might be—for generations.

Ollamhs or Doctors and their requirements.— *Ollamh* [ollav] was the title of the highest degree in any art or profession: thus we read of an ollave poet, an ollave builder, an ollave goldsmith, an ollave physician, an ollave lawyer, and so forth, just as we have in modern times doctors of law, of music, of literature, of philosophy, of medicine, &c. In order to attain the degree of ollave, a candidate had to graduate through all the lower steps: and for this final degree he had to submit his work—whether literary compositions or any other performance—to some eminent ollave who was selected as judge. This ollave made a report to the king, not only on the candidate's work, but also on his general character, whether he was upright, free from unjust dealings, and pure in conduct and word, *i.e*, free from immorality, bloodshed, and abuse of others. If the report was favourable, the king formally conferred the degree.

Almost every ollave, of whatever profession, kept apprentices, who lived in his house, and who learned their business by the teaching and lectures of the master, by reading, and by actual practice, or seeing the master practise; for they accompanied him on his professional visits. The number under some ollaves was so large as to constitute a little school. There was, of course, a fee; in return for which, as the Brehon Law expresses it:—" Instruction without reservation, and correction without harshness, are due from the master to the pupil, and to feed and clothe him during the time he is at his learning." Moreover the pupil was bound to help the master in old age if poverty came on him. The same passage in the Brehon Law continues:—" To help him against poverty, and to support him in old age [if necessary], these are due from the pupil to the tutor."

Although there were ollaves of the various professions and crafts, this word " ollave " was commonly understood to mean a doctor of Poetry, or of History, or of both combined : for these two professions overlapped a good deal, and the same individual generally professed both. A literary ollave, as a *fili* or poet, was expected to be able to compose a quatrain, or some very short poem, extemporaneously, on any subject proposed on the moment. As a Shanachie or Historian, the ollave was understood to be specially learned in the History, Chronology, Antiquities, and Génealogies of Ireland. We have already seen that he should know by heart 350 Historical and Romantic Stories. He was also supposed to know the prerogatives, rights, duties, restrictions, tributes, &c., of the king of Ireland, and of the provincial kings. As a learned man he was expected to answer reasonable questions, and explain difficulties.

These were large requirements: but then he spent many years of preparation: and once admitted to the coveted rank, the guerdon was splendid; for he was highly honoured, had many privileges, and received princely rewards and presents. Elsewhere it is shown that a king kept in his household an ollave of each profession, who was well paid for his services. The literary ollave never condescended to exercise his profession—indeed he was forbidden to do so—for any but the most distinguished company—kings and chiefs and such like, with their guests. He left the poets of the lower grades to attend a lower class of people.

Poets' Visitations and Sale of Poems.—In Ireland the position of the poets constituted perhaps the most singular feature of society. It had its origin in the intense and universal veneration for learning, which, however, as we shall see, sometimes gave rise to unhealthful developments that affected the daily life of all classes, but particularly of the higher. Every ollave *filè* was entitled to expect and receive presents from those people of the upper classes to whom he presented his poetical compositions: a transaction which the records openly call "selling his poetry." The ollave poet was entitled to go on *cuairt* [coort]—'circuit' or visitation: *i.e.* he went through the country at certain intervals with a retinue of twenty-four of his disciples or pupils, and visited the kings and chiefs one after another, who were expected to lodge and entertain them all for some time with lavish hospitality, and on their departure to present the ollave with some valuable present for his poetry; especially one particular prepared poem eulogising the chief himself, which was to be recited and presented immediately on the poet's arrival.

The poet had also a right to entertainment in the houses of public hospitality. Sometimes an ollave poet, instead of going in person, sent round one of his principal pupils as deputy, with his poetry, who brought home to him the rewards. When a poet of one of the six inferior grades went on visitation, he was allowed a retinue, according to his rank, who were to be entertained with him. This remarkable custom of visitation, which is constantly mentioned in Irish writings of all kinds, existed from the most remote pagan times, and continued down to the beginning of the nineteenth century.

The Satire.—The grand weapon of the poets, by which they enforced their demands, was the *aer*, a sort of satire or lampoon, which—as the people believed—had some baleful preternatural influence for inflicting mischief, physical or mental: so that it was very much dreaded. A poet could compose an *aer* that would blight crops, dry up milch-cows, raise a *ferb* or *bolg*, i.e. an ulcerous blister, on the face, and, what was perhaps worst of all, ruin character and bring disgrace. The dread of these poetical lampoons was as intense in the time of Spenser as it was eight centuries before, as is shown by his words:—"None dare displease them [the poets] for feare to runne into reproach thorough their offence, and to be made infamous in the mouthes of all men."

A poet—it was believed—could kill the lower animals by an *aer*. A story is told of Senchan Torpest, chief poet of Ireland, who lived in the seventh century, that once when his dinner was eaten in his absence by rats he uttered an *aer* on them in his ill-humour, beginning, "Rats, though sharp their snouts, are not powerful in battle," which killed ten of them on the spot. Hence it was believed, even down to late times, that the Irish bards could rhyme rats to death; which is often alluded to by Shakespeare and other English writers of the time of Elizabeth. Some poets devoted themselves exclusively to the composition of satires: these were very much dreaded and generally hated.

All people, high and low, had a sincere admiration and respect for these poets, and, so far as their means permitted, willingly entertained them and gave them presents, of which we find instances everywhere in the literature: and the law made careful provision for duly rewarding them and protecting them from injuries. But, as might be expected, they often abused their position and privileges by unreasonable demands, so that many of them, while admired for their learning, came to be feared and hated for their arrogance.

Their oppression became so intolerable that on three several occasions in ancient times—at long intervals—the people of all classes rose up against them and insisted on their suppression. But they were saved each time by the intervention of the men of Ulster. The last occasion of these was at the convention of Drum-Ketta in the year 574, during the reign of Aed mac Ainmirech, when the king himself and the greater part of the kings and chiefs of Ireland determined to have the whole order suppressed, and the worst among them banished the country. But St. Columkille interposed with a more moderate and a better proposal, which was agreed to through his great influence. The poets and their followers were greatly reduced in number: strict rules were laid down for the regulation of their conduct in the future; and those who were fit for it, especially the ollaves, were set to work to teach schools, with land for their maintenance, so as to relieve the people from their exactions.

Much has been said here about the poets that abused their privileges. These were chiefly the satirists, who were mostly men of sinister tendencies. But we should glance at the other side. At all periods of our history poets are found, of noble and dignified character, highly learned, and ever ready to exert their great influence in favour of manliness, truthfulness, and justice. To these we owe a great number of poems containing invaluable information on the history and antiquities of the country: and such men were at all times respected, loved, and honoured, as will be shown in the next section.

6. *Honours and Rewards for Learning.*

In many other ways besides those indicated in the preceding section, the people, both high and low, manifested their admiration for learning, and their readiness to reward its professors. From the period of myth and romance down to recent times, we trace a succession of learned men in all the professions, to whom the Irish annals accord as honoured places as they do to kings and warriors. An ollave sat next the king at table: he was privileged to wear the same number of colours in his clothes as the king and queen, namely, six, while all other ranks had fewer. The same compensation for injury was allowed for a king, a bishop, and an ollave poet: and they had the same joint at dinner, namely, the *larac* or haunch. We have seen that a king kept at his court an ollave of each profession, who held a very high position, and had ample stipends: and once a family was selected to supply ollaves to the king they were freed from the customary tribute. This veneration for poets and other learned men remained down to a late period, unaffected by wars and troubles. We read of great banquets got up on several occasions to honour the whole body of men of learning, to which all the professional men within reach, both in Ireland and Scotland, were invited. Several such banquets are commemorated in our records, and some were on a vast scale, and lasted for many days.

But all this respect for the poet was conditional on his observance of the rules of his order, one of which was to maintain a high personal character for dignity and integrity. The Senchus Mór lays down that a fraudulent poet may be degraded, *i.e.* a poet who mixes up falsehood with his compositions, or who composes an unlawful satire, or who demands more than his due reward.

The Anglo-Norman lords, after they had settled down in Ireland, became as zealous encouragers of Gaelic learning as the native nobility. They kept moreover in their service ollaves of every profession, brehons, physicians, etc., and remunerated them in princely style like the native chiefs; and they often founded or endowed colleges.

7. *The Knowledge of Science.*

The pure and physical sciences, so far as they were known in the Middle Ages, were taught in the schools and colleges of Ireland. The success of the home teaching appears plain from the distinction gained by several Irishmen on the Continent for their knowledge of astronomy, as will be pointed out farther on : knowledge not acquired abroad, but brought from their native schools.

192 RELIGION, LEARNING, AND ART. [PART II.

The Irish scholars understood astronomy; and we have still several ancient treatises in the Irish language, well illustrated with astronomical diagrams. In the first poem of the Saltair-na-Rann, written

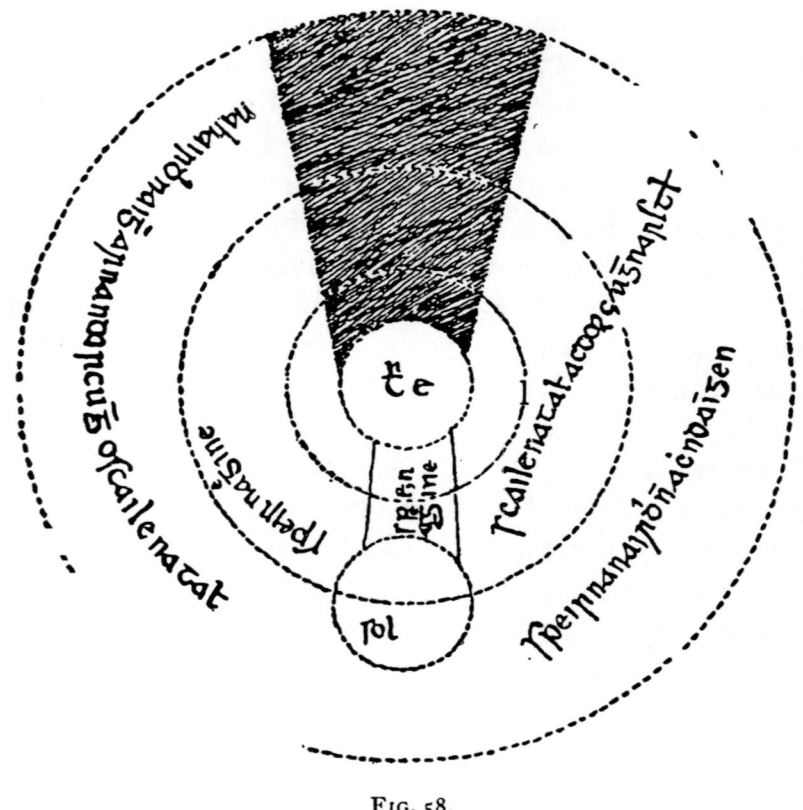

FIG. 58.

Facsimile (by hand) of a diagram in an astronomical tract (about A.D. 1400) in the Royal Irish Academy, Dublin. The lower small circle is the sun (*sol*), the middle small circle is the earth (*terra*), throwing its shadow among the stars.

probably about A.D. 1000, is an account of the creation of the world, with a short description of the universe, showing a knowledge of the theories—some right, some wrong—then prevalent.

The various astronomical cycles were perfectly understood and were familiarly applied to calculations in connexion with chronology and the calendar. Among the many Irish writers who have dealt with those matters may be mentioned Augustin, already referred to (p. 150), who wrote his Essay on the wonders of the Bible, while residing at Carthage. The Irish writers were well acquainted with the solstices, which they called by the descriptive native Irish name *grien-tairisem*—so given in an eighth- or ninth-century gloss in Zeuss—meaning 'sun-standing': and they correctly state that the summer solstice occurs on the 21st June. They had a native name for the autumnal equinox (21st September) which was descriptive and scientifically correct: *Deiseabhair na grene* [Deshoor-na-grena], literally the 'southing' or going south by the sun' (*i.e.* going south of the equinoctial), from *deas*, 'south.'

All this shows that they understood the apparent annual motion of the sun along the ecliptic, half the year north, and the other half south of the equinoctial, and that at the autumnal equinox it enters on the south part of its course. So, also, the real movement of the moon, and the apparent motion of the sun, round the earth—both from west to east— were well understood, as appears from a remark of one of the commentators on Dallan's "Amra on Columkille," that "the moon is before the sun from the first to the fifteenth [of the moon's age], and after the sun from the fifteenth to the first"—a perfectly correct statement.

Irish scholars understood the use and construction of the sundial, for which two words were used, *solam*, which is a native term, and *soiler*, which is borrowed and shortened from the Latin, *solarium*, 'a sundial.' Besides this there is a small Irish MS. book in the monastery of St. Gall in Switzerland, written by some scholarly Irish monk residing there in the eighth century, containing remarks on various scientific subjects, such as the Cycles, the age of the world, and, among others, on the sundial.

Virgil or Virgilius, abbot of Aghaboe in the present Queen's County, who went to the Continent A.D. 745, and became bishop of Salzburg, was one of the most advanced scholars of his day. Pepin, Mayor of the Palace, subsequently king of France, became greatly attached to him, and kept him in the palace for two years. Virgil taught publicly—and was probably the first to teach—that the earth was round, and that people lived at the opposite side—at the antipodes. His Irish name was *Fergil*, which, in a modified form, is common in Ireland to this day (O'Farrell): and he is commonly known in history as Fergil the Geometer.

We have a remarkable testimony to the reputation of Irishmen on the Continent for secular and other learning in those early ages, in the well-known letter written to Charlemagne by the Irish monk Dungal, which came about in this way. It having been stated that two solar eclipses had occurred in one year, A.D. 810, the emperor selected Dungal, who happened to be then in France, as the scholar considered best able to explain such an unusual occurrence, and requested him to do so. Dungal's reply, which explains the matter, so far as the state of knowledge in his time enabled him, shows that he knew of the inclination of the plane of the moon's orbit to that of the ecliptic; and he sets forth the astronomical principle that for an eclipse—whether of sun or moon—to occur, it is necessary that the moon should be in the plane of the ecliptic. This Dungal subsequently resided in Italy, where he became a celebrated teacher, drawing pupils from all the surrounding cities; and he also wrote learnedly on ecclesiastical subjects.

In the year 825, an Irish scholar and traveller named Dicuil wrote a complete Geography of the world, so far as it was then known, which is still extant on the Continent, and which was published in several editions in the eighteenth century by German and French editors.

When learning had declined in England in the ninth and tenth centuries, owing to the devastations of the Danes, it was chiefly by Irish teachers it was kept alive and restored. In Glastonbury especially, they taught with great success; and we are told by many English writers that "they were skilled in every department of learning, sacred and profane"; and that under them were educated many young English nobles, sent to Glastonbury with that object. Among these students the most distinguished was St. Dunstan, who, according to all his biographers, received his education, both Scriptural and secular, from Irish masters there. One writer of his Life,- William of Malmesbury, states that Dunstan studied diligently arithmetic, geometry, astronomy, and music under the Irish teachers, and adds that these sciences were held in great esteem and were much cultivated by them. Even the general mass of intelligent people made use of simple astronomical observations in daily life. Cuculainn, sitting at a feast, says to his attendant:—"Go out, my friend, Loeg, observe the stars of the air, and ascertain when midnight comes" [when Cuculainn would have to leave]. And Loeg did so, and came back at the proper moment to announce that it was midnight. This record shows that all intelligent people of those times could roughly estimate the hour of night throughout the year by the position of the stars: a sort of observation not at all simple, inasmuch as the positions of the stars at given hours change from month to month.

The age of the moon (*aes esca*) is mentioned in Cormac's Glossary, as well as in many other ancient authorities, as a matter quite familiar: and in the Saltair na Rann it is laid down that every intelligent person ought to know the following five things:— The day of the solar or ordinary month; the age of the moon; the time of the flow of the tide [for those living near the sea]; the day of the week; and the chief saints' festival days.

These are a few illustrations—scattered and fragmentary indeed—of the eminence of ancient Irish scholars in science. But the materials for final judgment are not yet available; they are still hidden away in manuscripts among libraries all over Europe. When they are fully brought to light, then, and not till then, we shall be able to accord something approaching the full meed of justice to the learned men of ancient Ireland.

Sculpture on a Capital Priest's House, Glendalough. Beranger, 1779.
(From Petrie's Round Towers)

CHAPTER VIII.

IRISH LANGUAGE AND LITERATURE.

SECTION 1. *Divisions and Dialects of Celtic.*

Six Dialects. — There are **two** main branches of the ancient Celtic language:—The **Goidelic**, or Gaelic, or Irish; and the **British**; corresponding with the two main divisions of the Celtic people of the British Islands. Each of these has branched into three dialects. Those of Gaelic are:—The Irish proper, spoken in Ireland; the Gaelic of Scotland, differing only slightly from Irish; and the Manx, which may be said to be Irish written phonetically with some dialectical variations. The dialects of British are:—Welsh, spoken in Wales; Cornish, spoken till lately in Cornwall; and Breton or Armoric, spoken in Brittany.

Of the whole six dialects, five are still spoken: the Cornish became extinct in the eighteenth century; and Manx is nearly extinct. Four have an ancient written literature:—**Irish, Welsh, Cornish,** and

Armoric. Neither the Gaelic of Scotland nor the Manx has an ancient literature distinct from that of Ireland: but Scotland has a living modern literature.* All these are derived from the Gaulish or Continental Celtic, which in the course of ages, since the separation of the original Gaulish emigrant tribes, has diverged into the two branches and the six dialects named here.

Three Divisions of Irish.—Irish, like all other living languages, has undergone great changes in lapse of time: so that in fact the written language of eleven or twelve hundred years ago, of which many specimens have been preserved, is now all but unintelligible to those who can read only modern Irish. It is usual to divide Irish, as we find it written, into three stages. I. **Old Irish**, from the seventh or eighth to the eleventh or twelfth century. This is the language of the Glosses, of the Irish found in the Book of Armagh, and of some passages in the Book of the Dun Cow; but we have very little Old Irish preserved in Ireland. The oldest, purest, and most cultivated form, as found in the St. Gall and other seventh- or eighth-century glosses, was called the *Bérla féne* [bairla faina], *i.e.* the language of the *Feini* or main body of the free original inhabitants. II. **Middle Irish**, from the twelfth to the fifteenth century, marked by many departures from the Old Irish forms. This is the language of most of our

---

* In Ireland a vigorous attempt is just now being made to re-create a living written Gaelic literature, and to extend the use of spoken Irish, and a knowledge of Irish lore in general. There is a movement also—following the example of Ireland—to revive Manx and Cornish.

present important manuscripts—described farther on (p. 208)—such as the Book of the Dun Cow, the Book of Leinster, the Lebar Brecc, and the Book of Ballymote. III. **Modern Irish**, from the fifteenth century to the present day. This is the language of most of the Ossianic tales. The purest specimens are the writings of Keating, both historical and religious. There is a vast amount of manuscript literature in Modern Irish.

Glosses.—When transcribing or using the classics, or the Latin version of the Scriptures, Irish professors and teachers of the seventh, eighth, and ninth centuries, in order to aid the Irish learners, or for their own convenience, often wrote between the lines or on the margin literal Irish translations of the unusual or most difficult words of the text, or general renderings of the sense into Gaelic phrases. These are what are called Glosses. Numbers of these interesting manuscripts, their pages all crowded with glosses, are preserved to this day in many Continental libraries, mostly written in Ireland, and brought away to save them from destruction (see p. 207, *infra*)—but some written on the Continent: and in them are found older forms of Irish than any we have in Ireland. Many have been recently published, with the Latin words and passages, and the corresponding Gaelic. It is chiefly by means of these glosses that the ancient grammatical forms of the language have been recovered; and the meanings of numbers of Irish words, long obsolete, have been ascertained from their Latin equivalents.

It is interesting to observe that here the original intention is reversed. The scribe wrote the Gaelic, which was the language of his everyday life, to explain the Latin text. But while the Latin, being then, as now, a dead language, has remained unchanged, the Gaelic has suffered those changes spoken of in page 198, so that the Gaelic of the glosses is now in many cases difficult and obscure. Accordingly, instead of the Gaelic explaining the Latin, we now use the Latin to explain the Gaelic.

Zeuss.—The first to make extensive use of the glosses for these purposes was Johann Kaspar Zeuss, a Bavarian; born in 1806; died 1856. He visited the libraries of St. Gall, Wurzburg, Milan, Carlsruhe, Cambrai, and several other cities, in all of which there are manuscript books with glosses in the four Celtic dialects; and he copied everything that suited his purpose. He found the Irish glosses by far the most ancient, extensive, and important of all. Most of them belonged to the seventh or eighth century; some few to the beginning of the ninth. At the end of thirteen years he produced the great work of his life, "Grammatica Celtica," a complete Grammar of the four ancient Celtic dialects—Irish or Gaelic—and the three British dialects, Welsh, Cornish, and Armoric: published 1853. It is a closely printed book of over 1000 pages; and it is all written in Latin, except of course the Celtic examples and quotations. Each of the four dialects is treated of separately.

Zeuss was the founder of Celtic philology. The "Grammatica Celtica" was a revelation to scholars, wholly unexpected; and it gave an impetus to the study, which has been rather increasing than diminishing since his time. He made it plain that a knowledge of the Celtic languages is necessary in order to unravel the early history of the peoples of Western Europe. Since the time of Zeuss, many scholarly works have been written on Celtic philology: but the "Grammatica Celtica" still stands at the head of all.

Ancient Glossaries and Grammars.—In consequence of the gradual change of the Irish language, it became customary for native scholars of past times, skilled in the ancient language, to write glossaries of obsolete words to aid students in reading very ancient manuscripts. Many of these are preserved in our old books. The most noted is "Cormac's Glossary," by Archbishop Cormac Mac Cullenan, king of Cashel, who died A.D. 908. It was translated and annotated by John O'Donovan; and this translation and the Irish text, with most valuable additional notes, have been published by Dr. Whitley Stokes. Other Glossaries are those of Michael O'Clery, chief of the Four Masters; of Duald Mac Firbis, and of O'Davoren. In the Books of Ballymote and Lecan there is a very ancient treatise on Irish Grammar, but it has never been translated.

But with all the aids at our command—glossaries, glosses, translations, and commentaries—there are many Irish pieces in the books named below (p. 208) that have up to the present defied the attempts of the best Irish scholars to translate them satisfactorily, so many old words, phrases, and allusions do they contain whose meanings have been lost. This state of things has been caused chiefly by the wholesale destruction of MSS. mentioned at page 206, *infra*, which left great gaps, and broke the continuity of the Irish language and literature. But the subject is attracting more and more attention as years go by. Great numbers of Continental scholars as well as those of the British Isles are eagerly engaged in studying ancient Irish texts; year by year the difficulties are being overcome; and there is every hope that before long we shall have translations of most or all of these obscure old pieces.

2. *Writing and Writing Materials.*

Scribes.—After the time of St. Patrick, as everything seems to have been written down that was considered worth preserving, manuscripts accumulated in the course of time, which were kept in monasteries and in the houses of hereditary professors of learning: many also in the libraries of private persons. As there were no printed books, readers had to depend for a supply entirely on manuscript copies. To copy a book was justly considered a very meritorious work, and in the highest degree so if it was a part of the Holy Scriptures, or of any other book on sacred or devotional subjects. Scribes or copyists were therefore much honoured. The handwriting of these old documents is remarkable for its beauty, its plainness, and its perfect uniformity, each scribe, however, having his own characteristic form and style.

Vellum.—Two chief materials were used in Ireland for writing on:—Long, thin, smooth rectangular boards or tablets; and vellum or parchment, made from the skins of sheep, goats, or calves, which was the most usual and the most important material. Inscriptions were also carved on stone, both in ordinary Irish letters and in Ogham. The scribes had to make all their own materials—tablets, vellum, ink, and pens..

Ink (Irish *dub* or *dubh*, i.e. 'black': pron. *dhuv*). The ink was made from carbon, without iron or any other mineral, as is shown by delicate chemical analysis. In the more ancient MSS., a thick kind of ink was used, remarkable for its intense blackness and durability: and its excellence is proved by the fact that in most of the very old books the writing is almost or altogether as black as it was when written, more than a thousand years ago. The ink was kept in a little vessel commonly made of part of a cow's horn, and therefore called *adarcin* or *adircin* [ey-arkeen], meaning 'little horn,' from *adarc* [ey-ark], 'a horn.'

Pen.—The pens were made from the quills of geese, swans, crows, and other birds: no metallic pens were used. In some figures of the evangelists drawn in MSS. of the eighth century, the pens with their feathers, and the penknife with which they were cut, are quite plain to be seen.

Wooden Tablets.—The other materials for writing on were long, narrow, smooth, wooden slits, called by various names:—*Taibhli filidh* [tav'ila-filla], 'tablets of the poets'; and *tabhall lorga*, 'tablet staves' (*lorg*, 'a staff'). On these the letters were either written in ink or cut with a knife. The staves were generally tied up in a bundle, so as to be carried conveniently. The use of tablets for writing on was not peculiar to the Irish: for it is well known that, before parchment came into general use, the Romans, the Jews, and other ancient nations inscribed their laws, poems, &c., on wooden tablets.

Fig. 59.

From an illuminated manuscript copy of Giraldus Cambrensis, written about A D. 1200. now in British Museum Underneath is the inscription—"The Scribe writing the Marvellous Kildare Gospels." Photographed from reproduction in Gilbert's Facsim Nat. MSS, and reproduced here from the photograph.

The writing-tablets used by ecclesiastics, which must have been similar to the poets' tablets, were commonly known by the name of *pólaire* (3-syll.), a term used collectively to denote a number of single staves. Sometimes they were written on with ink; but more commonly the surface was covered with wax, which was written on with a metallic style. Waxed tablets were used for temporary purposes, such as taking notes of a sermon, or other such memorandums: when the purpose was served, the wax was smoothed to be written on again. They were employed also by schoolmasters in old times for teaching their scholars the elements of reading. Adamnan, in the seventh century, mentions that he inscribed certain writings at first (temporarily) on waxed tablets, and afterwards on vellum. All literary matter intended to be permanent was written on vellum or parchment. The use of waxed tablets continued till the seventeenth century.

Style.—When writing on a waxed tablet, they used a *graib* or *graif*, i.e. *graphium*, a sharp-pointed style of metal, which, when not in use, was commonly kept fastened in a loop or flap fixed on the sleeve or on the front of the cloak. When St. Patrick was in the act of destroying the idol, Cromm Cruach, his *graif* fell out of his mantle into the heather, where he had some difficulty in finding it afterwards.

3. *Ancient Libraries.*

"**House of Manuscripts.**"—Considering the fame of the Irish universities for learning, and the need of books for students, it is plain that in all the important Irish monasteries there must have been good general libraries, including not only copies of native Irish books, but also works in Irish and Latin on the various branches of learning then known, and copies of the Latin and Greek classics. The Annals of Tigernach, who was abbot of Clonmacnoise, and died in 1088, show that there was a well-furnished library in that great monastery. We often find mention of the *Tech-screptra* ('house of manuscripts'), which was the Irish name of the library.

Book-Satchels.—The books in a library were usually kept, not on shelves, but in satchels, generally of leather, hung on pegs or racks round the walls: each satchel containing one or more manuscript volumes and labelled on the outside. Satchels were very generally employed to carry books about from place to place; commonly slung from the shoulder by one or more straps. Manuscripts that were greatly valued were kept in elaborately wrought and beautifully ornamented leather covers: of which two are still preserved in Ireland, namely, the cover of the Book of Armagh, which is figured in the larger Social History, vol. I., p. 488; and that of the shrine of St. Maidoc.

Destruction and Exportation of Books.—Books abounded in Ireland when the Danes first made their appearance, about the beginning of the ninth century: so that the old Irish writers often speak with pride of "the hosts of the books of Erin." But with the first Danish arrivals began the woful destruction of manuscripts, the records of ancient learning. The animosity of the barbarians was specially directed against books, monasteries, and monuments of religion: and all the manuscripts they could lay hold on they either burned or "drowned"—*i.e.* flung them into the nearest lake or river.

For two centuries the destruction of manuscripts went on: and it ceased only when the Danes were finally crushed at Clontarf in 1014. During all this time the Irish missionaries and scholars who went abroad brought away great numbers of manuscripts merely to save them from destruction. Scores of these venerable volumes are now found in Continental libraries: some no doubt written by Irishmen on the spot, but most brought from Ireland. Books were also often sent as presentations from the monasteries at home to Continental monasteries founded by Irishmen. The consequence of this long-continued exportation of Irish books is that there is now a vastly greater quantity of Irish of the ninth and earlier centuries on the Continent than we have in Ireland.

After the Battle of Clontarf there was a breathing time; and scholars like Mac Kelleher, Mac Gorman, and Mac Criffan (pp. 209, 211, *infra*) set to work to rescue what was left of the old literature, collecting the scattered fragments and copying into new volumes everything that they could find worth preserving. Numbers of such books were compiled, and much of the learning and romance of the old days was reproduced in the eleventh and twelfth centuries. Notwithstanding the Danish devastations, many of the original volumes also—written long before the time of Mac Kelleher—still remained. But next came the Anglo-Norman invasion, which was quite as destructive of native learning and art as the Danish inroads, or more so; and most of the new transcripts, as well as of the old volumes that survived, were scattered and lost. The destruction of manuscripts continued during the perpetual wars that distracted the country, down to comparatively recent times : and many which existed even so late as 200 years ago are now gone. O'Curry, in the first Lecture of his "Manuscript Materials," gives a long list of the "Lost Books of Erin."

4. *Existing Books.*

Volumes of Miscellaneous Matter.—Of the eleventh- and twelfth-century transcript volumes, portions, and only portions, of just two remain—Lebar-na-hUidhre [Lowr-na-Heera], or the Book of the Dun Cow, and Lebar Laigen [Lowr-Lyen], or the Book of Leinster. That these two books are copies from older manuscripts, and not themselves original compositions of the time, there is ample and unquestionable internal evidence. But it must be borne in mind that we have many other books like the two above mentioned, copied after 1100 from very ancient volumes since lost. The Yellow Book of Lecan, for example, contains pieces as old as those in the Book of the Dun Cow—or older—though copied at a much later period.

Most of the books alluded to here and named below consist of miscellaneous matter :—tales, poems, biographies, genealogies, histories, annals, and so forth —all mixed up, with scarcely any attempt at orderly arrangement, and almost always copied from older books. This practice of copying miscellaneous pieces into one great volume was very common. Some of these books were large and important literary monuments, which were kept with affectionate care by their owners, and were celebrated among scholars as great depositories of Celtic learning, and commonly known by special names, such as the *Cuilmen*, the *Saltair of Cashel*, the *Book of Cuana*. The value set on such books may be estimated from the fact that one of them was sometimes given as ransom for a captive chief. I will here notice a few of the most important of those we possess—all vellum; but there are also many important paper manuscripts.

The oldest of all these books of miscellaneous literature is the **Lebar-na-Heera,** or the **Book of the Dun Cow,*** now in the Royal Irish Academy. By "the oldest" is meant that it was transcribed at an earlier time than any other remaining: but some books of later transcription contain pieces quite as old, or older. This book was written by Mailmuri Mac Kelleher, a learned scribe who died in Clonmacnoise in the year 1106. An entry in his own handwriting shows that the book was copied from older books. It is all through heavily glossed between the lines, proving the great antiquity of the pieces, since Mac Kelleher, even in 1100, found it necessary to explain in this manner numerous old words and phrases.

As it now stands it consists of only 134 folio pages —a mere fragment of the original work. It contains sixty-five pieces of various kinds, several of which are imperfect on account of missing leaves. There

---

* Irish name *Lebar-na-h Uidhre*; so called because the original manuscript of that name (which no longer exists) was written on vellum made from the skin of St. Ciaran's pet cow at Clonmacnoise. Irish, *odhar* [o-ar], a 'brown' [cow]; gen. *idhre* or *h-uidhre*.

are a number of romantic tales in prose; a copy of the celebrated *Amra* or Elegy on St. Columkille, composed by Dallan Forgaill about the year 592; an

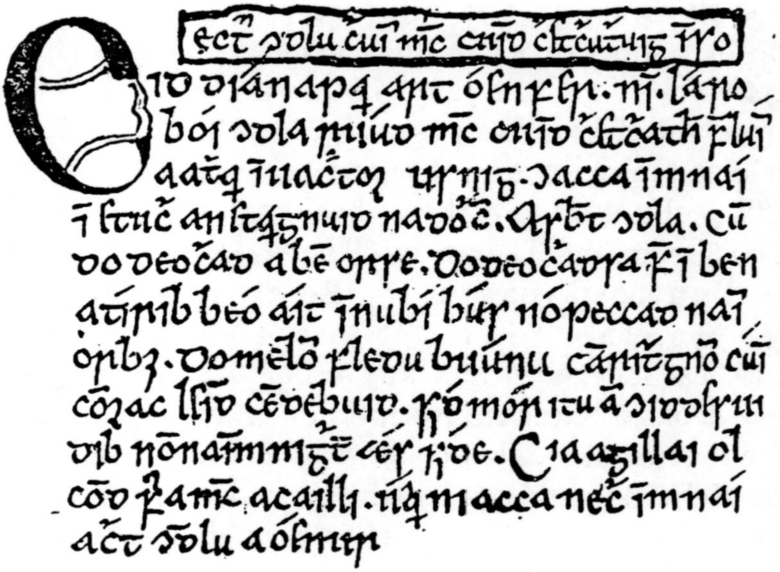

FIG. 60.

Facsimile of part of the Book of the Dun Cow, p 120, col. 1. (Slightly smaller than the original) The beginning of the story of Connla the Comely, or Connla of the Golden Hair. (This story will be found fully translated in Joyce's Old Celtic Romances.) This passage has no glosses.

Translation:—" The adventures of Connla the Comely, son of Conn the Hundred-Fighter, here. Whence the name of Art the Lone one? [Art the son of Conn, who was called 'Art the Lone One,' after his brother Connla had been taken away by the fairy] Not difficult to answer. On a certain day as Connla of the Golden Hair, son of Conn the Hundred-Fighter, stood beside his father on the Hill of Ushnagh, he saw a lady in strange attire coming towards him. Connla spoke: 'Whence hast thou come, O lady?' he says. 'I have come,' replied the lady, 'from the and of the ever-living, a place where there is neither death, nor sin, nor transgression. We have continual feasts: we practise every benevolent work without contention. We dwell in a large *Shee*; and hence we are called the People of the Fairy-Mound.' 'To whom art thou speaking, my boy?' says Conn to his son: for no one saw the lady save Connla only."

imperfect copy of the Voyage of Maildune; and an imperfect copy of the Táin-bo-Quelna, with several of the minor tales connected with it. Among the historical and romantic tales are the Courtship of Emer; the Feast of Bricriu; the Abduction of Prince Connla the Comely by the *shee* or fairies; part of the Destruction of the palace of Da Derga and the Death of Conari, king of Ireland. The language of this book is nearer to the pure language of the Zeussian glosses than that of any other old book of general literature we possess.

The **Book of Leinster,** the next in order of age, now in Trinity College, Dublin, was written not later than the year 1160, by Finn Mac Gorman, bishop of Kildare, and by Aed Mac Criffan, tutor of Dermot Mac Murrogh, king of Leinster. The part of the original book remaining consists of 410 folio pages, and contains nearly 1000 pieces of various kinds, prose and poetry—historical sketches, romantic tales, topographical tracts, genealogies, &c.—a vast collection of ancient Irish lore. Among its contents are a very fine perfect copy of the Táin-bo-Quelna, a History of the origin of the Boru Tribute, a description of Tara, a full copy of the Dinnsenchus or description of the celebrated places of Erin. The Book of Leinster is an immense volume, containing about as much matter as six of Scott's prose novels.

The **Lebar Brecc,** or **Speckled** Book of Mac Egan, is in the Royal Irish Academy. It is a large folio volume, now consisting of 280 pages, but originally containing many more, written in a small, uniform, beautiful hand. The text contains 226 pieces, with numbers of marginal and interlined entries, generally explanatory or illustrative of the text. The book was copied from various older books, most of them now lost. All, both text and notes, with a few exceptions, are on religious subjects: there is a good deal of Latin mixed with the Irish. Among the pieces are the *Feilire* of Aengus the Culdee, Lives of SS. Patrick, Brigit, and Columkille, and a Life of Alexander the Great.

The **Book of Ballymote**, in the Royal Irish Academy, is a large folio volume of 501 pages. It was written by several scribes about the year 1391, at Ballymote in Sligo, from older books, and contains a great number of pieces in prose and verse. Among them is a copy of the ancient Book of Invasions, *i.e.*, a history of the Conquests of Ireland by the several ancient colonists. There are genealogies of almost all the principal Irish families; several historical and romantic tales of the early Irish kings; a history of the most remarkable women of Ireland down to the English invasion; an Irish translation of Nennius' History of the Britons; a copy of the Dinnsenchus; a translation of the Argonautic Expedition, and of the War of Troy.

The **Yellow Book of Lecan** [Leckan], in Trinity College, is a large quarto volume of about 500 pages. It was written at Lecan in the county Sligo, in or about the year 1390, by two of the scholarly family of Mac Firbis—Donagh and Gilla Isa. It contains a great number of pieces in prose and verse, historical, biographical, topographical, &c.; among them the Battle of Moyrath, the Destruction of Bruden Da Derga, an imperfect copy of the Táin-bo-Quelna, and the Voyage of Maildune.

The five books above described have been published in facsimile without translations—but with valuable introductions, and full descriptions of contents—by the Royal Irish Academy, page for page, line for line, letter for letter. Next to the publication of the Grammatica Celtica, the issue of these facsimiles was the greatest stimulus in modern times to the elucidation of ancient Gaelic lore: for scholars in all parts of the world can now study those five old books without coming to Dublin.

The **Book of Lecan,** in the Royal Irish Academy, about 600 vellum pages, was written in 1416, chiefly by Gilla Isa Mór Mac Firbis. The contents resemble in a general way those of the Book of Ballymote.

There are many other books of miscellaneous Gaelic literature in the Royal Irish Academy and in Trinity College, such as the Book of Lismore, the Book of Fermoy, the Book of Hy Many; besides numbers of books without special names. There are also numerous MS. volumes devoted to special subjects, such as Law, Medicine, Astronomy, and so forth, as will be found mentioned elsewhere in this book.

The vast mass of Irish literature sketched in this section is to be found in manuscripts, not in any one library; but scattered over almost all the libraries of Europe. The two most important collections are those in Trinity College and in the Royal Irish Academy, Dublin, where there are manuscripts of various ages, from the sixth or seventh down to the nineteenth century. In the Franciscan Monastery of Adam and Eve, Dublin, and in Maynooth College, are a number of valuable manuscripts; and there are also many important Irish manuscripts in the British

Museum in London; in the Bodleian Library at Oxford; and in the Advocates' Library in Edinburgh; besides the numerous MSS. in Continental libraries.

Classification of Subject-Matter.—Irish literature, so far as it has been preserved, may be classed as follows:—

    I. Ecclesiastical and Religious writings.
    II. Annals, History, and Genealogy.
    III. Tales—Historical and Romantic.
    IV. Law, Medicine, and Science.
    V. Translations or versions from other languages—Latin, Greek, French, &c.

Translations.—As to this last class: it is enough to say here that there is an immense amount of translation into Irish, of romance, history, science, biography, medicine, and sacred subjects, from Latin, French, Spanish, and other languages. That such a mass of translation exists in Irish manuscripts shows—if there was need to show—the lively literary curiosity and the intense love of knowledge of every kind of the ancient Irish scholars. Apart from their literary aspect, these translations are of the highest value to students of the Irish language, as enabling them to determine the meaning of many obsolete Gaelic words and phrases.

5. *Irish Poetry and Prosody.*

As a large part of Irish literature has been handed down to us in the form of verse, it will be proper to say something here about Irish Poetry and its laws.

In very early times, not only poetry proper, but histories, biographies, laws, genealogies, and such like, were often written in verse as an aid to the memory. Among all peoples there were—as there are still—certain laws or rules, commonly known as Prosody, which poets had to observe in the construction of their verse: of which the main object was harmony of numbers. The classification and the laws of Irish versification were probably the most complicated that were ever invented: indicating on the part of the ancient Irish people, both learned and unlearned, a delicate appreciation of harmonious combinations of sounds.

That the old writers of verse were able to comply with their numerous difficult prosodial rules we have positive proof in our manuscripts; and the result is marvellous. No poetry of any European language, ancient or modern, could compare with that of Irish for richness of melody. Well might Dr. Atkinson exclaim (in his Lecture on "Irish Metric"):—"I believe Irish verse to have been about the most perfectly harmonious combination of sounds that the world has ever known. I know of nothing in the world's literature like it."

Of each principal kind or measure of verse there were many divisions and subdivisions, comprising altogether several hundred different metrical varieties, all instantly distinguishable by the trained ears of poet and audience.

Some of the greatest Celtic scholars that ever lived—among them Zeuss and Nigra—maintain that rhyme, now so common in all European languages, originated with the old Irish poets, and that from the Irish language it was adopted into Latin, from which it gradually penetrated to other languages, till it finally spread over all Europe. One thing is quite certain, that rhyme—as we have already said—was brought to far greater perfection in Irish than in any other language.

The great majority of the ancient Irish poetical pieces—poetry in the true sense of the word—are still hidden away in manuscripts scattered through the libraries of all Europe. The few that have been brought to light show that many of the ancient Irish poets were inspired with true poetical genius: but sufficient materials are not yet available to enable us to pass a general judgment on the character of early Irish poetry. Most of these pieces are characterised by one prevailing note—a close observation and an intense love of nature in all its aspects. This characteristic of the Irish people will be treated of in a section of chapter xxvi. Among the remains of later times—from the fifteenth century down—we have many pieces of great beauty—odes, ballads, elegies, songs, &c.

In modern Irish poetry the old prosodial rules are almost wholly disregarded. The rhymes are assonantal, and very frequent: they occur not only at the ends of the lines but within them—sometimes once, sometimes twice; and not unfrequently the same rhyme runs through several stanzas. In other respects modern Irish poetry generally follows the metrical construction of English verse.

Sculpture on Window: Cathedral Church, Glendalough   Beranger, 1779.
(From Petrie's Round Towers)

CHAPTER IX.

ECCLESIASTICAL AND RELIGIOUS WRITINGS.

COPIES of the Gospels or of other portions of Scripture, that were either written or owned by eminent saints of the early Irish Church, were treasured with great veneration by succeeding generations; and it became a common practice to enclose them, for better preservation, in ornamental boxes or shrines. Many shrines with their precious contents are still preserved: they are generally of exquisite workmanship in gold, silver, or other metals, precious stones, and enamel. Books of this kind are the oldest we possess.

The **Domnach Airgid**, or 'Silver Shrine,' which is in the National Museum, Dublin, is a box containing a Latin copy of the Gospels written on vellum. It was once thought that the enclosed book was the identical copy of the Gospels presented by St. Patrick to St. Mac Carthenn of Clogher; but recent investigations go to show that it is not so old as the time of the great apostle.

The **Book of Kells** is the most remarkable book of this class, though not the oldest. A description of it will be found farther on, in the chapter on Irish Art.

The **Cathach** [Caha] or **Battle-Book** of the O'Donnells. This is a copy of the Psalms, enclosed in a beautifully wrought case of gilt silver, enamel, and precious stones, which is now preserved in the National Museum in Dublin. The O'Donnells of Tirconnell always brought it with them to battle, hoping by means of it to obtain victory (p. 65, above). In Trinity College, Dublin, are two beautiful shrines enclosing two illuminated Gospel manuscripts, the **Book of Dimma**, and the **Book of St. Moling**, both written in the seventh or eighth century.

The **Book of Armagh**, now in Trinity College, for beauty of execution stands only second to the Book of Kells, and occasionally exceeds it in fineness and richness of ornamentation. The learned and accomplished scribe of this book was Ferdomnach of Armagh, who finished it in 807, and died in 845. It is chiefly in Latin, with a good deal of Old Irish interspersed. It opens with a Life of St. Patrick. Following this are a number of notes of the Life and acts of the saint, compiled by Bishop Tirechan, who himself received them from his master Bishop Ultan, of the seventh century; a complete copy of the New Testament; and a Life of St. Martin of Tours. Perhaps the most interesting part of the whole manuscript is what is now commonly known as St. Patrick's Confession, in which the saint gives a brief account, in simple Latin, of his captivity, his escape from slavery, his return to Ireland, the hardships and dangers he encountered, and the final success of his mission. It appears that Ferdomnach had before him a book in the very handwriting of the great apostle, from which he copied the Confession. This venerable book is now about to be published. Other Latin-Irish books of this class still preserved are mentioned below in the chapter on Art.

We have a vast body of original ecclesiastical and religious writings. Among them are the **Lives of a great many of the most distinguished Irish saints**, mostly in Irish, some few in Latin, some on vellum, some on paper, of various ages, from the seventh century down to the eighteenth. Of these the best-known is the "Tripartite Life of St. Patrick," so called because it is divided into three Parts. It is in Irish, mixed here and there with words and sentences in Latin. It was written, so far as can be judged, in the ninth or tenth century, on the authority of, and partly copied from, older books. It has been lately printed in two volumes, with translations and elaborate and valuable introduction and notes, by Dr. Stokes.

Besides the Irish Lives of St. Columkille, there is one in Latin, written by Adamnan, who died in the year 703. He was a native of Donegal, and ninth abbot of Iona; and his memoir has been pronounced by the learned Scotch writer Pinkerton—who is not given to praise Irish things—to be "the most complete piece of such biography that all Europe can boast of, not only at so early a period, but even through the whole Middle Ages." It has been published by the Rev. Dr. William Reeves, who, in his Introduction and Notes, supplies historical, local, and biographical information drawn from every conceivable source.

In the year 1645 the Rev. John Colgan, a Franciscan friar, a native of Donegal, published at Louvain, where he then resided in the Irish monastery of that city, a large volume entitled "Acta Sanctorum Hiberniæ," the 'Lives of the Saints of Ireland,' all in Latin, translated by himself from ancient Irish manuscripts. In 1647 he published another volume, also in Latin, devoted to Saints Patrick, Brigit, and Columkille, and consisting almost entirely of translations of all the old Irish Lives of these three saints that he could find. Both volumes are elaborately annotated by the learned editor; and text and notes—all in Latin—contain a vast amount of biographical, historical, topographical, and legendary information.

Another class of Irish ecclesiastical writings are the Calendars, or **Martyrologies,** or **Festilogies**— Irish, **Féilire** [fail′ira], a festival list. The *Féilire* is a catalogue of saints, arranged according to their festival days, with usually a few facts about each, briefly stated, but with no detailed memoirs. One of these, commonly known as the Martyrology of Donegal, was compiled by Michael O'Clery, the chief of the Four Masters. It has been published with translation by Drs. O'Donovan, Todd, and Reeves. Another—the most elaborate and important of all— is the Féilire or Calendar of Aengus the Culdee, who wrote it about the year 800. The body of the poem consists of 365 quatrain stanzas, one for each day in the year, each stanza commemorating one or more saints—chiefly but not exclusively Irish—whose festivals occur on the particular day. But there are also prefaces and a great collection of glosses and commentaries, all in Irish, interspersed with the text;

Fig. 61.

Church and (imperfect) Round Tower of Dysert-Aengus, one mile west of Croom in Limerick, where St Aengus the Culdee founded a church about A.D. 800. (From Mrs. Hall's Ireland.)

and all written by various persons who lived after the time of Aengus. The whole *Féilire*, with Prefaces, Glosses, and Commentaries, has been translated and edited, with learned notes, by Dr. Whitley Stokes. The **Saltair na Rann**, *i.e.* the 'Psalter of the Quatrains,' consists of 162 short Irish poems on sacred subjects. The whole collection has been published by Dr. Whitley Stokes, with glossary of words, but without translation.

The **Book of Hymns** is one of the manuscripts in Trinity College, Dublin, copied at some time not later than the ninth or tenth century. It consists of a number of hymns—some in Latin, some in Irish—composed by the primitive saints of Ireland—St. Sechnall, St. Ultan, St. Cummain Fada, St. Columba, and others—with Prefaces, Glosses, and Commentaries, mostly in Irish, by ancient copyists and editors. It has been published in two editions; one by the Rev. Dr. Todd; the other by the Rev. Dr. Bernard, F.T.C.D., and Dr. Robert Atkinson.

Another ecclesiastical relic belonging to Ireland should be mentioned—the Antiphonary, or Hymn Book, of St. Comgall's monastery of Bangor, in the County Down, written in this monastery about A.D. 680. In order to save it from certain destruction by the Danes, it was brought to the Continent, probably by the learned monk Dungal, already mentioned (page 194). After lying hidden and neglected for a thousand years, it was found at last in Bobbio; and it has since been several times published.

There are manuscripts on various other ecclesiastical subjects scattered through libraries—canons and rules of monastic life, prayers and litanies, hymns, sermons, explanations of the Christian mysteries, commentaries on the Scriptures, &c.—many very ancient. Of the numerous modern writings of this class, I will specify only two, written in classical modern Irish about the year 1630 by the Rev. Geoffrey Keating:—the "Key-shield of the

Mass" and the "Three Shafts of Death." This last has been edited with a Glossary, but without translation, by Dr. Robert Atkinson.

These are only a few of the existing Irish ecclesiastical works: there are many others in the libraries of Great Britain and the Continent.

Writers of sacred history sometimes illustrated their narratives with rude pen-and-ink sketches of

FIG. 62.

Noah's Ark: reduced from the larger sketch on a fly-leaf of the Book of Ballymote. (From Kilk. Archæol. Journ.)

Biblical subjects, of which an example is given here—a quaint figure of Noah's Ark drawn on a fly-leaf of the Book of Ballymote in the fourteenth century.

Sculpture on a Capital · Priest's House, Glendalough: Beranger 1779.
(From Petrie's Round Towers.)

CHAPTER X.

ANNALS, HISTORIES, AND GENEALOGIES.

SECTION 1. *How the Annals were compiled.*

AMONG the various classes of persons who devoted themselves to literature in ancient Ireland, there were special **Annalists**, who made it their business to record, with the utmost accuracy, all remarkable events simply and briefly, without any ornament of language, without exaggeration, and without fictitious embellishment. The extreme care they took that their statements should be truthful is shown by the manner in which they compiled their books. As a general rule they admitted nothing into their records except either what occurred during their lifetime, and which may be said to have come under their own personal knowledge, or what they found recorded in the compilations of previous annalists, who had themselves followed the same plan. These men took nothing on hearsay: and in this manner successive annalists carried on a continued chronicle from age to age, thus giving the whole series the force of contemporary testimony.*

We have still preserved to us many books of native Annals, the most important of which will be briefly described in this chapter. Most of the ancient manuscripts whose entries are copied into the books of Annals we now possess have been lost; but that the entries were so copied is rendered quite certain by various expressions found in the present existing Annals, as well as by the known history of several of the compilations.

The Irish Annals deal with the affairs of Ireland—generally but not exclusively. Many of them record events occurring in other parts of the world; and it was a common practice to begin the work with a brief general history, after which the Annalist takes up the affairs of Ireland.

2. *Tests of Accuracy.*

Physical Phenomena.—There are many tests of the accuracy of our records, of which I will here notice three classes: physical phenomena, such as eclipses and comets: the testimony of foreign writers: and the consistency of the records among themselves. Whenever it happens that we are enabled to apply tests belonging to any one of these three classes— and it happens very frequently—the result is almost invariably a vindication of the accuracy of the records.

---

* Of course it is not claimed for the Irish Annals that they are absolutely free from error. In the early parts there is much legendary matter; and some errors have crept in among the records belonging to the historical period.

The Irish Annals record about twenty-five eclipses and comets at the several years from A.D. 496 to 1066. The dates of all these are found, according to modern scientific calculation and the records of other countries, to be correct. This shows conclusively that the original records were made by eye-witnesses, and not by calculation in subsequent times: for any such calculation would be sure—on account of errors in the methods then used — to give an incorrect result.

A well-known entry in the Irish account of the Battle of Clontarf, fought A.D. 1014, comes under the tests of natural phenomena. The author of the account, who wrote soon after the battle, states that it was fought on Good Friday, the 23rd of April, 1014; and that it began at sunrise, *when the tide was full in.* To test the truth of this, the Rev. Dr. Todd, of Trinity College, Dublin, asked the Rev. Samuel Haughton, a great science scholar, to calculate the time of high water in Dublin Bay on the 23rd April, 1014. After a laborious calculation, Dr. Haughton found that the tide was at its height that morning at half-past five o'clock, just as the sun was coming over the horizon: a striking confirmation of the truth of this part of the narrative. It shows, too, that the account was written by, or taken down from, an eye-witness of the battle.

Testimony of Foreign Writers.—Whenever events occurring in Ireland in the Middle Ages are mentioned by British or Continental writers they are always—or nearly always—in agreement with the native records. Irish bardic history relates in much detail how the Picts landed on the coast of Leinster in the reign of Eremon, the first Milesian king of Ireland, many centuries before the Christian era. After some time they sailed to Scotland to conquer a territory for themselves: but before embarking they asked Eremon to give them Irish women for wives, which he did, but only on this condition, that the right of succession to the kingship should be vested in the female progeny rather than in the male. And so the Picts settled in Scotland with their wives. Now all this is confirmed by the Venerable Bede, who says that the Picts obtained wives from the Scots (*i.e.* the Irish) on condition that when any difficulty arose they should choose a king from the female royal line rather than from the male; "which custom," continues Bede, "has been observed among them to this day." We have already seen (p. 37, *supra*) that the Irish accounts of the colony led by Carbery Riada to Scotland in the third century of the Christian era have been confirmed by the Venerable Bede..

All the Irish Annals record a great defeat of the Danes near Killarney in the year 812. This account is fully borne out by an authority totally unconnected with Ireland, the well-known Book of Annals, written by Eginhard (the tutor of Charlemagne), who was living at this very time. Under A.D. 812 he writes:—"The fleet of the Northmen, having invaded Hibernia, the island of the Scots, after a battle had been fought with the Scots, and after no small number of the Norsemen had been slain, they basely took to flight and returned home." Several other examples of a similar kind might be quoted.

Consistency of the Records among themselves. Testimonies under this heading might be almost indefinitely multiplied. References by Irishmen to Irish affairs are found in numerous volumes scattered over all Europe:—Annalistic entries, direct statements in tales and biographies, marginal notes, incidental references to persons, places, and customs, and so forth, written by various men at various times; which, when compared one with another, and with the home records, hardly ever exhibit a disagreement.

The more the ancient historical records of Ireland are examined and tested, the more their truthfulness is made manifest. Their uniform agreement among themselves, and their accuracy, as tried by the ordeals of astronomical calculation and of foreign writers' testimony, have drawn forth the acknowledgments of the greatest Irish scholars and archæologists that ever lived. These men knew what they were writing about; and it is instructive, and indeed something of a warning to us, to mark the sober and respectful tone in which they speak of Irish records, occasionally varied by an outburst of admiration as some unexpected proof turns up of the faithfulness of the old Irish writers and the triumphant manner in which they come through all ordeals of criticism.

3. *Principal Books of Annals.*

The following are the principal books of Irish Annals remaining. The **Synchronisms of Flann,** who was a layman, *Ferleginn* or chief professor of the school of Monasterboice; died in **1056.** He compares the chronology of Ireland with that of other countries, and gives the names of the monarchs that reigned in the principal ancient kingdoms and empires of the world, with the Irish kings who reigned contemporaneously. Copies of this tract are preserved in the Books of Lecan and Ballymote.

The **Annals of Tighernach** [Teerna]. Tighernach O'Breen, the compiler of these annals, one of the greatest scholars of his time, was abbot of the two monasteries of Clonmacnoise and Roscommon. He was acquainted with the chief historical writers of the world known in his day, compares them, and quotes from them; and he made use of Flann's Synchronisms, and of most other ancient Irish historical writings of importance. His work is written in Irish mixed a good deal with Latin; it has lately been translated by Dr. Stokes. He states that authentic Irish history begins at the foundation of Emania, and that all preceding accounts are uncertain. Tighernach died in 1088.

The **Annals of Innisfallen** were compiled about the year 1215 by some scholars of the monastery of Innisfallen, in the Lower Lake of Killarney.

The **Annals of Ulster** were written in the little island of Senait Mac Manus, now called Belle Isle, in Upper Lough Erne. The original compiler was Cathal [Cahal] Maguire, who died of small-pox in 1498. They have lately been translated and published.

The **Annals of Lough Ce** [Key] were copied in 1588 for Bryan Mac Dermot, who had his residence on an island in Lough Key, in Roscommon. They have been translated and edited in two volumes.

The **Annals of Connaught** from 1224 to 1562.

The **Chronicon Scotorum** (Chronicle of the Scots or Irish), down to A.D. 1135, was compiled about 1650 by the great Irish antiquary Duald Mac Firbis. These annals have been printed with translation.

The **Annals of Boyle**, from the earliest time to 1253, are written in Irish mixed with Latin; and the entries throughout are very meagre.

The **Annals of Clonmacnoise** from the earliest period to 1408. The original Irish of these is lost; but we have an English translation by Connell Mac Geoghegan of Westmeath, which he completed in 1627.

The **Annals of the Four Masters**, also called the Annals of Donegal, are the most important of all. They were compiled in the Franciscan monastery of Donegal, by three of the O'Clerys, Michael, Conary, and Cucogry, and by Ferfesa O'Mulconry, who are now commonly known as the Four Masters. They began in 1632, and completed the work in 1636. "The Annals of the Four Masters" was translated with most elaborate and learned annotations by Dr. John O'Donovan; and it was published—Irish text, translation, and notes—in seven large volumes.

A book of annals called the **Psalter of Cashel** was compiled by Cormac Mac Cullenan, but this has been lost. He also wrote "Cormac's Glossary," an explanation of many old Irish words. This work has been translated and printed: see p. 201, above.

The Annals noticed so far are all in the Irish language, occasionally mixed with Latin: but besides these there are Annals of Ireland wholly in Latin; such as those of Clyn, Dowling, Pembridge, Multyfarnham, &c., most of which have been published.

CHAP. X.] ANNALS, HISTORIES, AND GENEALOGIES. 231

4. *Histories : Genealogies : Dinnsenchus.*

Histories.—None of the Irish writers of old times conceived the plan of writing a general history of Ireland. The first history of the whole country was

Fig. 63.

Tubbrid Church, the burial-place of the Rev. Geoffrey Keating, as it appeared in 1845. (From Mrs. Hall's Ireland.) The exact spot in this graveyard where he is interred is not known but he is commemorated in a Latin inscription on a tablet over the door of the church (seen in the illustration).

the **Forus Feasa ar Erinn,** or History of Ireland, from the most ancient times to the Anglo-Norman invasion, written by Dr. Geoffrey Keating of Tubbrid in Tipperary, a Catholic priest : died 1644. Keating was deeply versed in the ancient language and literature of Ireland; and his history, though containing much that is legendary, is very interesting and valuable.

Genealogies.—The genealogies of the principal families were most faithfully preserved in ancient Ireland. Each king and chief had in his household a **Shanachy** or historian, whose duty it was to keep a written record of all the ancestors and of the several branches of the family.

Many of the ancient genealogies are preserved in the Books of Leinster, Lecan, Ballymote, &c. But the most important collection of all is the great Book of Genealogies compiled in the years 1650 to 1666 in the College of St. Nicholas in Galway, by Duald Mac Firbis.

In this place may be mentioned the **Dinnsenchus** [Din-Shan′ahus], a topographical tract giving the legendary history and the etymology of the names of remarkable hills, mounds, caves, carns, cromlechs, raths, duns, plains, lakes, rivers, fords, islands, and so forth. The stories are mostly fictitious—invented to suit the really existing names: nevertheless this tract is of the utmost value for elucidating the topography and antiquities of the country. Copies of it are found in several of the old Irish books of miscellaneous literature, as already mentioned.

Another very important tract—one about the names of remarkable Irish persons, called **Cóir Anmann** ('Fitness of Names'), corresponding with the Dinnsenchus for place-names, has been published with translation by Dr. Stokes.

Sculpture on Window: Cathedral Church, Glendalough: Beranger, 1779.
(From Petrie's Round Towers)

CHAPTER XI.

HISTORICAL AND ROMANTIC TALES.

SECTION 1. *Classes, Lists, and Numbers.*

EVEN from the most remote times, beyond the ken of history, the Irish people, like those of other countries, had stories, which, before the introduction of the art of writing, were transmitted orally, and modified, improved, and enlarged as time went on, by successive shanachies, or 'storytellers.' They began to be written down when writing became general: and a careful examination of their structure, and of the language in which they are written, has led to the conclusion that the main tales assumed their present forms in the seventh, eighth, and ninth centuries; while the originals from which they sprang are much older. Once they began to be written down, a great body of romantic and historical written literature rapidly accumulated, consisting chiefly of prose tales. Of many of the tales we have, in the Book of the Dun Cow, and the Book of Leinster, copies made in the eleventh and twelfth centuries; and there are numerous others in manuscripts copied by various scribes from that period to the present century, many of them from original volumes older than the Book of the Dun Cow.

In the Book of Leinster there is a very interesting List of the classes to which the ancient historical tales belong, with a number of individual tales named under each class as examples, numbering altogether 187. This List is as follows (with a few additions from other sources):—1. Battles: 2. *Imrama*, Navigations, or Voyages: 3. Tragedies: 4. Adventures: 5. Cattle-raids: 6. Hostings or Military Expeditions: 7. Courtships: 8. Elopements: 9. Caves or Hidings (*i.e.* adventures of persons hiding for some reason in caves or other remote places): 10. Destructions (of palaces, &c.): 11. Sieges or Encampments: 12. Feasts: 13. Slaughters: 14. Pursuits: 15. Visions: 16. Exiles or Banishments: 17. Lake Eruptions.

We have in our old books stories belonging to every one of these classes. The whole number now existing in MSS. is close on 600: of which about 150 have been published and translated. But outside these, great numbers have been lost: destroyed during the Danish and Anglo-Norman wars.

2. *Chronological Cycles of the Tales.*

Most of the Irish Tales fall under four main cycles of History and Legend, which, in all the Irish poetical and romantic literature, were kept quite distinct.

1. The Mythological Cycle, the stories of which are concerned with the mythical colonies preceding the Milesians, especially the Dedannans. The heroes of the Tales belonging to this cycle, who are assigned to periods long before the Christian era, are gods, namely, the gods of the pagan Irish.

2. The Cycle of Concobar mac Nessa and his Red Branch Knights, who flourished in the first century.

3. The Cycle of the Fena of Erin, belonging to a period two centuries later than those of the Red Branch.

4. Stories founded on events that happened after the dispersal of the Fena (in the end of the third century, p. 45, *supra*), such as the Battle of Moyrath (A.D. 637), most of the Visions, &c.

The stories of the Red Branch Knights form the finest part of our ancient Romantic Literature. The most celebrated of all these is the **Táin-bo-Cuailnge** [Quelnĕ], the epic of Ireland. *Medb* [Maive], queen of Connaught, who resided in her palace of Croghan, set out with her army for Ulster on a plundering expedition, attended by all the great heroes of Connaught, and by an Ulster contingent who had enlisted in her service. The invading army entered that part of Ulster called *Cuailnge* or Cooley, the principality of the hero Cuculainn, the north part of the present county Louth, including the Carlingford peninsula. At this time the Ulstermen were under a spell of feebleness, all but Cuculainn, who had to defend single-handed the several fords and passes, in a series of single combats, against Maive's best champions. She succeeded in this first raid, and brought away a great brown bull—which was the chief motive of the expedition—with flocks and herds beyond number. At length the Ulstermen, having been freed from the spell, attacked and routed the Connaught army. The battles, single combats, and other incidents of this war, form the subject of the *Táin*, which consists of one main epic story with about thirty shorter tales grouped round it. It has lately been translated into English by Miss L. Winifred Faraday, and into German by the great Celtic scholar Windisch. For the chief Red Branch heroes, see p. 39, above.

Of the Cycle of Finn and the Fena of Erin we have a vast collection of stories. The chief heroes under Finn have been already mentioned (p. 43). The Tales of the Fena, though not so old as those of the Red Branch Knights, are still of great antiquity: for some of them are found in the Book of the Dun Cow and in the Book of Leinster, copied from older volumes.

3. *General Character of the Tales.*

Some of the tales are historical, *i.e.* founded on historical events—history embellished with some fiction; while others are altogether fictitious—pure creations of the imagination. From this great body of stories it would be easy to select a large number, powerful in conception and execution, high and dignified in tone and feeling, all inculcating truthfulness and manliness, many of them worthy to rank with the best literature of their kind in any language. The stories of the Sons of Usna, the

Children of Lir, the Fingal Ronain, the Voyage of Maeldune, Da Derga's Hostel, the Boroma, and the Fairy Palace of the Quicken Trees—all of which have been published with translations—are only a few instances in point.

As to the general moral tone of the ancient Irish tales, it is to be observed that in all early literatures, Irish among the rest, there is much plain speaking of a character that would now be considered coarse, and would not be tolerated in our present social and domestic life. But on the score of morality and purity the Irish tales can compare favourably with the corresponding literature of other countries; and they are much freer from objectionable matter than the works of many of those early English and Continental authors which are now regarded as classics.

In this respect "The Colloquy of the Ancient Men" may be taken as a typical example. It consists of a series of short stories, of which the great Irish scholar Dr. Whitley Stokes says:—" The tales are generally told with sobriety and directness: they evince genuine feeling for natural beauty, a passion for music, a moral purity, singular in a mediæval collection of stories, a noble love of manliness and honour." On the same point Professor Kuno Meyer justly remarks:—" The literature of no nation is free from occasional grossness; and considering the great antiquity of Irish literature, and the primitive life which it reflects, what will strike an impartial observer most is not its license or coarseness, but rather the purity, loftiness, and tenderness which pervade it."

4. *Story-telling and Recitation.*

The tales were brought into direct touch with the people, not by reading—for there were few books outside libraries, and few people were able to read them—but by recitation: and the Irish of all classes, like the Greeks, were excessively fond of hearing tales and poetry recited. There were professional shanachies and poets whose duty it was to know by heart numerous old tales, poems, and historical pieces, and to recite them, at festive gatherings, for the entertainment of the chiefs and their guests: and every intelligent person was supposed to know a reasonable number of them, so as to be always ready to take a part in amusing and instructing his company. The tales of those times correspond with the novels and historical romances of our own day, and served a purpose somewhat similar. Indeed they served a much higher purpose than the generality of our novels; for in conjunction with poetry they were the chief agency in education—education in the best sense of the word—a real healthful informing exercise for the intellect. They conveyed a knowledge of history and geography, and they inculcated truthful and honourable conduct. Moreover, this education was universal; for though few could read, the knowledge and recitation of poetry and stories reached the whole body of the people. This ancient institution of story-telling held its ground both in Ireland and Scotland down to a period within living memory.

Sculpture on a Capita of the Church of the Monastery, Glendalough. Beranger, 1779.
(From Petrie's Round Towers.)

CHAPTER XII.

ART.

SECTION 1. *Penwork and Illumination.*

IRELAND art was practised chiefly in four different branches:—Ornamentation and Illumination of Manuscript-books: Metal-work: Stone-carving: and Building. In Leather-work also the Irish artists attained to great skill, as we may see in several beautiful specimens of book-binding still preserved. Some branches of art were cultivated—as we shall see—in pagan Ireland; but art in general reached its highest perfection in the period between the end of the ninth and the beginning of the twelfth century.

The special style of pen ornamentation, which in its most advanced stage is quite characteristic of the Celtic people of Ireland, was developed in the course of centuries by successive generations of artists who brought it to marvellous perfection. Its most marked characteristic is interlaced work formed by bands and ribbons, which are curved and twisted and interwoven in the most intricate way, something like basket-work infinitely varied in pattern. These are intermingled and alternated with zigzags, waves, spirals, and lozenges; while here and there among the curves are seen the faces or forms of dragons, serpents, or other strange-looking animals, their tails or ears or tongues not unfrequently elongated and woven till they become merged and lost in the general design; and sometimes human faces, or full figures of men or of angels. But vegetable forms are very rare. This ornamentation was commonly used in the capital letters, which are generally very large: one splendid capital of the Book of Kells covers a whole page. The pattern is often so minute and complicated as to require the aid of a magnifying glass to examine it. The penwork is throughout illuminated in brilliant colours, in preparing the materials of which the scribes were as skilful as in making their ink: for in some of the old books the colours, especially the red, are even now very little faded after the lapse of so many centuries.

We have many books ornamented in this style. The Book of Kells, a vellum manuscript of the Four Gospels in Latin, written in the seventh or eighth century, is the most beautifully written book in existence. Miss Stokes, who has examined it with great care, thus speaks of it:—" No effort hitherto made to transcribe any one page of this book has the perfection of execution and rich harmony of colour which belongs to this wonderful book." Professor J. O. Westwood, of Oxford, who examined

[Fac-simile of one page of the Book of Mac Durnan, exactly as it left the hand of the Irish scribe, A.D. 850. The words, which are much contracted, are the beginning of the Gospel of Saint Mark, in Latin. For further reference to this frontispiece, see pp. 14, 493. —From Westwood's *Fac.-sim. of Ang.-Sax and Irish MSS*.]

FIG. 64.—Outlines of the illuminated page from the Book of Mac Durnan.

*Latin words with contra*ctions *as they stand in the page.*—Initium Avangeli dūi nr̄i īhu chri ii di sicut scrip ē̄ in esaia ꝓfeta Ecce mitto anguelum meum

Latin words fully written out.—Initium Aevangelii domini nostri ihesu christi filii dei sicut riptum est in esaia profeta Ecce mitto anguelum meum

Translation.—The beginning of the Gospel of our Lord Jesus Christ Son of God as it is written Esaia the prophet Behold I send my angel

the best specimens of ancient penwork all over Europe, speaks even more strongly:—"It is the most astonishing book of the Four Gospels which exists in the world. . . . I know pretty well all the libraries in Europe where such books as this occur, but there is no such book in any of them; . . . there is nothing like it in all the books which were written for Charlemagne and his immediate successors."

The Book of Durrow and the Book of Armagh, both in Trinity College, Dublin; the Book of Mac Durnan, now in the Archbishop's Library, Lambeth; the Stowe Missal in the Royal Irish Academy; and the Garland of Howth in Trinity College—all written by Irishmen in the seventh, eighth, and ninth centuries—are splendidly ornamented and illuminated: and of the Book of Armagh, some portions of the penwork surpass even the finest parts of the Book of Kells.

Giraldus Cambrensis, when in Ireland in 1185, saw a copy of the Four Gospels in St. Brigit's nunnery in Kildare, which so astonished him that he has recorded—in a special and separate chapter of his book—a legend that it was written under the direction of an angel.

This beautiful art originated in the East—in Byzantium after the fall of the first empire—and was brought to Ireland—no doubt by Irish monks, or by natives of Central Europe who came to Ireland to study—in the early ages of Christianity. But as first introduced it was very simple. Though the Irish did not originate it, they made it, as it were, their own after adopting it, and cultivated it to greater

FIG. 65.

The beginning of the Gospel of St. John, from an Irish manuscript Gospel Book now in Bavaria. (In the original MS, this is illuminated in colour.)

perfection than was ever dreamed of in Byzantium or Italy. Combining the Byzantine interlacings with the familiar pagan designs at home, they produced a variety of patterns, and developed new and intricate forms of marvellous beauty and symmetry. Accordingly it is now known by the name *Opus Hibernicum*, 'Irish Work.' Irish manuscript books, ornamented in this manner and richly illuminated, are found, not only in Ireland, but in numerous libraries all over Great Britain and the Continent. (See illustration, last page.)

In pagan times the Irish practised a sort of ornamentation consisting of zigzags, lozenges, circles both single and in concentric groups, spirals of both single and double lines, and other such patterns, many very beautiful, which may be seen on bronze and gold ornaments preserved in museums, and on sepulchral stone monuments, such as those at New Grange and Loughcrew. But in all this pre-Christian ornamentation there is not the least trace of interlaced work.

2. *Gold, Silver, and Enamel, as Working Materials.*

Gold and Silver.—It is certain that gold and silver mines were worked in this country from the most remote antiquity, and that gold was found anciently in much greater abundance than it has been in recent times. According to the bardic annals, the monarch Tigernmas [Tiernmas] was the first that smelted gold in Ireland, and with it covered drinking-goblets and brooches; the mines were situated in the *Foithre* [fira], or woody districts, east of the Liffey; and the artificer was *Uchadan*, who lived in that part of the country. In the same district gold is found to this day. But other parts of the country produced gold also, as, for instance, the district of O'Gonneloe near Killaloe, and the neighbourhood of the Moyola river in Derry. There were gold districts also in Antrim, Tyrone, Dublin, Wexford, and Kildare. The general truthfulness of the old Irish traditions and records is fully borne out by the great quantities of golden ornaments found in every part of the country, of which numerous specimens may be seen in the National Museum, Dublin.

As in the case of gold, we have also very ancient legends about silver; and it was, and is, found in many parts of Ireland.

Enamel and Enamel Work.—On many of the specimens of metal-work preserved in the National Museum may be seen enamel patterns worked with exquisite skill, showing that the Irish artists were thorough masters of this branch of art. Their enamel was a sort of whitish or yellowish transparent glass as a foundation, coloured with different metallic oxides. It was fused on to the surface of the heated metal, where it adhered, and was worked while soft into various patterns. The art of enamelling was common to the Celtic people of Great Britain and Ireland, in pre-Christian as well as in Christian times; and beautiful specimens have been found in both countries, some obviously Christian, and others, as their designs and other characteristics show, belonging to remote pagan ages. It was taken up and improved by the Christian artists, who used it in metal-work with the interlaced ornamentation, similar to the penwork described above (p. 240). A few years ago a great block of *cruan* or red enamel weighing 10lb., formed of glass coloured with red oxide of copper—being the raw material intended for future work—was found under one of the raths at Tara, and is now in the National Museum. The enamel work of Christian artists is seen in perfection in the Cross of Cong, the Ardagh Chalice, and the Tara Brooch.

3. *Artistic Metal Work.*

The pagan Irish, like the ancient Britons, practised from time immemorial—long before the introduction of Christianity—the art of working in bronze, silver, gold, and enamel; an art which had become highly developed in Ireland by the time St. Patrick and his fellow-missionaries arrived. Some of the antique Irish articles made in pagan times show great mastery over metals, and admirable skill in design and execution. This primitive art was continued into Christian times, and was brought to its highest perfection in the tenth and eleventh centuries. Artistic metal work continued to flourish to about the end of the twelfth century, but gradually declined after that, owing to the general disorganisation of society consequent on the Anglo-Norman invasion, and to the want of encouragement. The ornamental designs of metal work executed by Christian artists were generally similar to those used in manuscripts, and the execution was distinguished by the same exquisite skill and masterly precision. The three most remarkable as well as the most beautiful and most elaborately ornamented objects in the National Museum are the **Ardagh Chalice**, the **Tara Brooch**, and the **Cross of Cong**, all made by Christian artists. But there are others little, if at all, inferior to these in workmanship.

The Ardagh Chalice, which is seven inches high and $9\frac{1}{2}$ inches in diameter at top, was found a few

Fig. 66.

The Ardagh Chalice. (From Miss Stokes's Early Christian Art in Ireland.) Underneath the ornamental band, near the top, and extending all round the circumference, there is an inscription giving the names of the twelve Apostles: but the letters are too delicate to be shown in this illustration.

years ago buried in the ground under a stone in an old *lis* at Ardagh in the county Limerick. It is elaborately ornamented with designs in metal and enamel; and, judging from its shape and from its admirable workmanship, it was probably made some short time before the tenth century.

FIG. 67.

The Tara Brooch: front view. (Pin cut short here to save space.) (From Miss Stokes's Early Christian Art in Ireland.) The plates with the ornamental designs have been knocked off seven of the little panels.

The Tara brooch was found in 1850 by a child on the strand near Drogheda. It is ornamented all over with amber, glass, and enamel, and with the characteristic Irish filigree or interlaced work in metal. From its style of workmanship it seems obviously contemporaneous with the Ardagh chalice. No drawing can give any adequate idea of the extraordinary delicacy and beauty of the work on this brooch, which is perhaps the finest specimen of ancient metal-work remaining in any country.

The Cross of Cong, which is 2 feet 6 inches high, is all covered over with elaborate ornamentation of pure Celtic design; and a series of inscriptions in the Irish language along the sides give its full history. It was made by order of Turlogh O'Conor, king of Connaught, for the church of Tuam, then governed by Archbishop Muredach O'Duffy. The accomplished artist, who finished his work in 1123, and who deserves to be remembered to all time, was Mailisa Mac Braddan O'Hechan.

4. *Stone-Carving.*

Artistic stone-carving is chiefly exhibited in the great stone crosses, of which about fifty-five still remain in various parts of Ireland. Their dates extend over a period from the tenth to the thirteenth century, inclusive. All are ornamented with the *Opus Hibernicum*, already described. Most of the high crosses contain groups of figures representing various subjects of sacred history, such as the Crucifixion, the fall of man, Noah in the ark, the sacrifice of Isaac, the fight of David and Goliath, the arrest of our Lord, Eve presenting the apple to Adam, the journey to Egypt, &c.

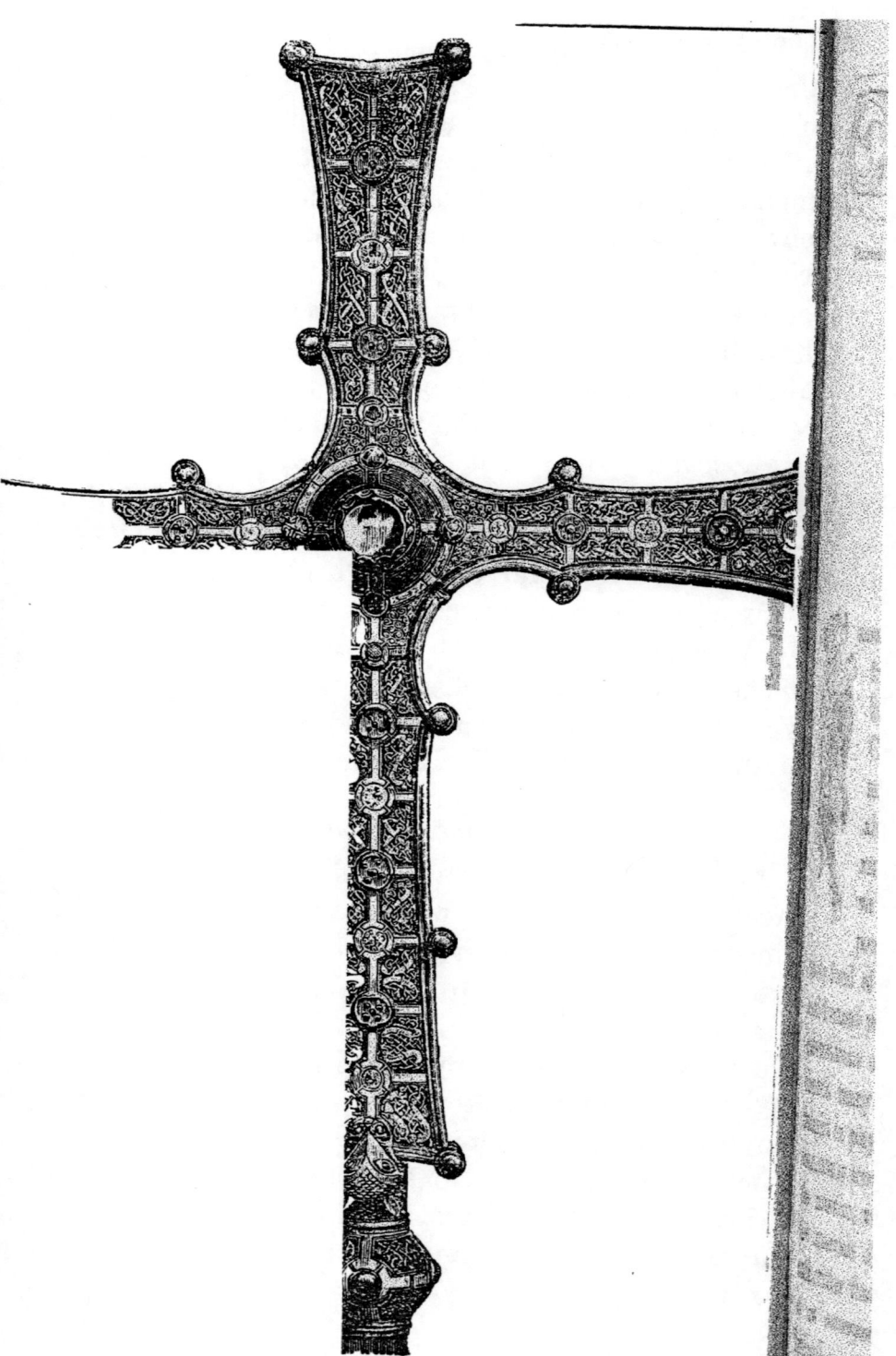

Ornament on leather case of Book of Armagh. (From Petrie's Round Towers.)

CHAPTER XIII.

MUSIC.

SECTION 1. *History.*

IRISH Musicians were celebrated for their skill from the very earliest ages. Our native literature—whether referring to pagan or Christian times—abounds in references to music and to skilful musicians, who are always spoken of in terms of the utmost respect. Everywhere through the Records we find evidences that the ancient Irish people, both high and low, were passionately fond of music: it entered into their daily life, and formed part of their amusements, meetings, and celebrations of every kind. In the early ages of the church many of the Irish ecclesiastics took great delight in playing on the harp; and for this purpose commonly brought a small harp with them when on the mission, which beguiled many a weary hour in the intervals of hard work. It appears from several authorities that the practice of playing on the harp *as an accompaniment to the voice* was common in Ireland as early as the fifth or sixth century.

During the long period when learning flourished in Ireland, Irish professors and teachers of music would seem to have been as much in request in foreign countries as those of literature and philosophy. In the middle of the seventh century, Gertrude, daughter of Pepin, mayor of the palace, abbess of Nivelle in Belgium, engaged SS. Foillan and Ultan, brothers of the Irish saint Fursa of Peronne, to instruct her nuns in psalmody. In the latter half of the ninth century the cloister schools of St. Gall were conducted by an Irishman, Maengal or Marcellus, a man deeply versed in sacred and human literature, including music. Under his teaching the music school there attained its highest fame.

In early times the Irish harpers were constantly employed to instruct the Welsh bards—a practice that continued down to the eleventh century: and in 1078, a Welsh king, Gryffith ap Conan, brought to Wales a number of skilled Irish musicians, who, in conference with the native bards, reformed the instrumental music of the Welsh. Ireland was also long the school for Scottish harpers, as it was for those of Wales · "Till within the memory of persons still living"—says Mr. Jameson, a Scotch writer—"the school for Highland poetry and music was Ireland, and thither professional men were sent to be accomplished in these arts." Such facts as these sufficiently explain why so many Irish airs have become naturalised in Scotland.

Giraldus Cambrensis, who seldom had a good word for anything Irish, heard the Irish harpers in 1185, and gives his experience as follows:—"They are incomparably more skilful than any other nation I have ever seen. They enter into a movement and conclude it in so delicate a manner and tinkle the little strings so sportively under the deeper tones of the bass strings—that the perfection of their art appears in the concealment of art."

For centuries after the time of Giraldus music continued to be cultivated uninterruptedly, and there was an unbroken succession of great professional harpers. Drayton (1613) has the following stanza in his " Polyolbion ":—

> " The Irish I admire
> And still cleave to that lyre,
>   As our Muse's mother ;
> And think till I expire,
>   Apollo's such another."

But the great harpers of those very old times are all lost to history. The oldest harper of great eminence whom we are able to identify is Rory Dall (blind) O'Cahan, who, although a musician from taste and choice, was really one of the chiefs of the Antrim family of O'Cahan. He was the composer of many fine airs, some of which we still possess. He visited Scotland with a retinue of gentlemen about the year 1600, where he died after a short residence; and many of his airs are still favourites among the Scotch people, who claim them—and sometimes even the author himself—as their own. Thomas O'Connallon was born in the county Sligo early in the seventeenth century. He seems to have been incomparably the greatest harper of his day, and composed many exquisite airs. A much better-known personage was Turlough O'Carolan or Carolan: born at Nobber, county Meath, about 1670 : died in 1738. He became blind in his youth from an attack of smallpox, after which he began to learn the harp; and ultimately he became the greatest Irish musical composer of modern times; but his musical compositions are, generally, less typically Irish than those of his predecessors. Like the bards of old, he was a poet as well as a musician. He always travelled about with a pair of horses, one for himself and the other for his servant who carried his harp; and he was received and welcomed everywhere by the gentry, Protestant as well as Catholic.

2. *Musical Instruments.*

The **Harp** is mentioned in the earliest Irish literature; it is constantly mixed up with our oldest legends and historical romances; and it was in use from the remotest pagan times. It was called *crott* or *cruit*; but *cláirsech* is now the name in general use. Several harps are sculptured on the high crosses, one of which is depicted on next page and another at p. 257, farther on, from which we can form a good idea of their shape and size in old times. From all these, and from several incidental expressions found in the literature, we can see that the harps of the ninth, tenth, and eleventh centuries were of medium size or rather small, the average height being about 30 inches: and some were not much more than half that height. Probably those of the early centuries were of much the same size—from 16 to

36 inches. The specimens of harps belonging to later ages—including "Brian Boru's harp" noticed below—are all small—still about thirty inches. But in more recent times it has been the fashion to make them larger.

The ordinary harp of the fifteenth and sixteenth centuries—as we know by many specimens remaining—had generally thirty strings, comprehending a little more than four octaves. Several harps of the old pattern are still preserved in museums in Dublin and elsewhere, the most interesting of which is the one now popularly known as Brian Boru's harp in Trinity College, Dublin. This is the oldest harp in Ireland—probably the oldest in existence. Yet it did not belong to Brian Boru; though it is likely as old as the thirteenth century. It is thirty-two inches high; it had thirty strings: and the ornamentation and general workmanship are very beautiful.

FIG. 69.

Harper on west face of High Cross of Castledermot, of about the end of tenth century. (From Miss Stokes's High Crosses of Castledermot and Durrow.)

The Irish had a small stringed instrument called a **Timpan**, which had only a few strings—from three to eight. The body was a small flat drum or *tympanum* (whence the name) with a short neck added; the strings were stretched across the flat face and along the neck, and were tuned and regulated by pins or keys and a bridge, something like the modern guitar, or banjo, but with the neck much shorter. It was played with a bow, or with both a bow and plectrum, or with the finger-nail; and the strings were probably stopped with the fingers of the left hand, like those of a violin.

The harp—as well as the timpan—was furnished with brass strings. The tuning-key had a wooden handle tipped with steel, like the modern piano-key. Both harp and timpan, when not in use, were kept in a case, commonly of otter-skins.

In very early ages a professional harper was honoured beyond all other musicians. In the eighteenth century, almost everyone among the high and middle classes played the harp.

The **bagpipes** were known in Ireland from the earliest times: the form used was something like that now commonly known as the Highland pipes — slung from the shoulder, the bag inflated by the mouth. The other form—resting on the lap, the bag inflated by a bellows — which is much the finer instrument, is of modern invention. The bagpipes were in very general use, especially among the lower classes.

Fig. 70.

Irish Piper playing at the head of a band marching to battle. (From Derrick's Image of Ireland, 1578.)

The **simple pipe**—as we might expect—was much in use, blown by the mouth at the end; the note being produced either by a whistle as in the modern flageolet, or by a reed as in the clarionet.

We find it often sculptured on the high crosses, as shown in fig. 71, which will give a good idea of shape and size.

FIG. 71.

Harp- and Pipe-players. Figure on Durrow High Cross. (This is a pipe, not a trumpet.) (From Miss Stokes's High Crosses of Castledermot and Durrow.) Belongs to about the tenth century.

The Irish had curved bronze **trumpets** and **horns**, of various shapes and sizes, which, judging from the great numbers found buried in clay and bogs, must have been in very general use. They occur indeed in far greater numbers in Ireland than in any other country. The fact that many are often found hoarded together would indicate their military use. In the National Museum in Dublin there is a collection of twenty-six trumpets, varying in length from about 18 inches to 8 feet; most of them of finished and beautiful workmanship.

258   RELIGION, LEARNING, AND ART.   [PART II.

Among the household of every king and chief there was a band of trumpeters, who were assigned their proper places at feasts and meetings. Trumpets were used for various purposes:—in war (p. 68, above); in hunting; for signals during meetings and banquets; as a mark of honour on the arrival

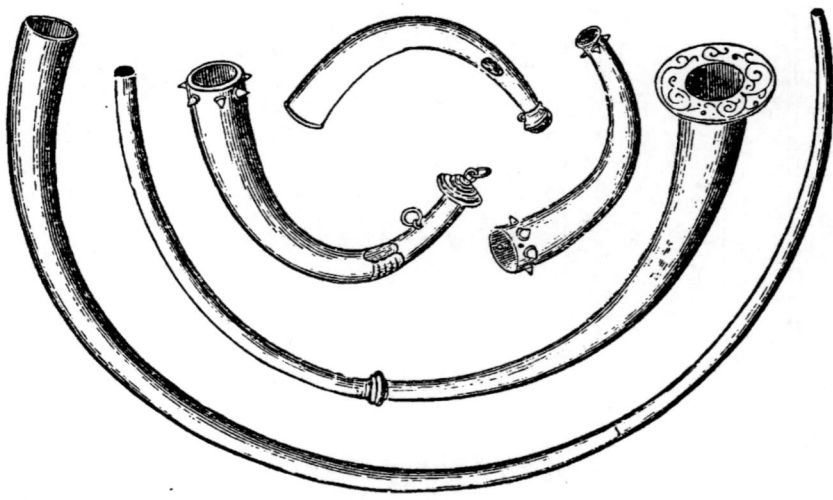

FIG. 72.

Group of Irish Trumpets, now in National Museum, Dublin. The two at bottom, hammered bronze: the larger, 8½ feet long; the smaller, 6 feet, with circular ornamented plate at end, shown in fig. 73. Each of these formed of two pieces, most skilfully riveted along the whole length. The three smaller ones at top made in one piece by casting. (From Wilde's Catalogue.)

of distinguished visitors; and such like. For war purposes, trumpeters—as already noticed—had different calls for directing movements.

The ancient Irish were very fond of a *craebh-ciuil* [crave-cule], or 'musical branch,' a little branch on which were suspended a number of diminutive bells, which produced a sweet tinkling when shaken:

a custom found also in early times on the Continent. The musical branch figures much in Irish romantic literature.

Fig. 73.

Ornamental bronze Plate at end of Trumpet.
(From Wilde's Catalogue)

3. *Characteristics; Classes; Styles.*

There was not in Ireland, any more than elsewhere, anything like modern developments of music. There were no such sustained and elaborate compositions as operas, oratorios, or sonatas. The music of ancient Ireland consisted wholly of **short airs**, each with two strains or parts—seldom more. But these, though simple in comparison with modern music, were constructed with such exquisite art that of a large proportion of them it may be truly said no modern composer can produce airs of a similar kind to equal them.

The ancient Irish used **harmony**, though of a very simple kind compared with that used at present: and they had several names for it. This appears from many passages in old Irish writings; as well as from Giraldus's mention—in the passage quoted at p. 253—of the little strings tinkling under the deeper tones of the bass strings.

The Irish musicians had three **styles**, the effects of which the old Irish romance-writers describe with much exaggeration, as the Greeks describe the effects produced by the harp of Orpheus. Of all three we have numerous well-marked examples, descending to the present day. The **Gen-traige** [gan-tree], which incited to merriment and laughter, is represented by the lively dance-tunes and other such spirited pieces. The **Gol-traige** [gol-tree] expressed sorrow: represented by the *keens* or death-tunes, many of which are still preserved. The **Súan-traige** [suan-tree] produced sleep. This style is seen in our lullabies or nurse-tunes, of which we have numerous beautiful specimens.

The Irish had also what may be called **occupation-tunes**. The young girls accompanied their spinning with songs—both air and words made to suit the occupation. Special airs and songs were used during working-time by smiths, by weavers, and by boatmen: and we have still a "Smith's Song," the notes of which imitate the sound of the hammers on the anvil, like Handel's "Harmonious Blacksmith." At milking-time the girls were in the habit of chanting a particular sort of air, in a low, gentle voice. These milking-songs were slow and plaintive, something like the nurse-tunes, and had the effect of soothing the cows and of making them submit more gently to be milked. This practice was common down to fifty or sixty years ago: and I remember seeing cows grow restless when the song was interrupted, and become again quiet and placid when it was resumed. The old practice also prevailed in Scotland, and probably has not yet died out there. Referring to our own time, a distinguished Scotch writer, Mr. Alexander Carmichael, says:— " The cows become accustomed to these lilts, and will not give their milk without them, nor, occasionally, without their favourite airs being sung to them ": and so generally is this recognised that— as he tells us—girls with good voices get higher wages than those that cannot sing.

While ploughmen were at their work, they whistled a peculiar wild, slow, and sad strain, which had as powerful an effect in soothing the horses at their hard work as the milking-songs had on the cows. Plough-whistles also were quite usual down to 1847, and often when a mere boy, did I listen enraptured to the exquisite whistling of Phil Gleeson on a calm spring-day behind his plough. There were, besides, hymn-tunes: and young people used simple airs for all sorts of games and sports. In most cases, words suitable to the several occasions were sung with lullabies, laments, and occupation-tunes. Like the kindred Scotch, each tribe had a war-march which inspirited them when advancing to battle. Specimens of all these may be found in the collections of Bunting, Petrie, Joyce, and others. We have evidence that occupation-tunes were in use at a very early time.

4. *Modern Collections of ancient Irish Music.*

In early times they had no means of writing down music; and musical compositions were preserved in the memory and handed down by tradition from generation to generation; but in the absence of written record many were lost. It was only in the seventeenth or eighteenth century that people began to collect Irish airs from singers and players, and to write them down. There are now several collections of ancient Irish music, of which the chief are those by Bunting, Petrie, Joyce, and Horncastle; a large collection in a Dublin periodical called "The Citizen"; and a volume of Carolan's airs published by his son.

The man who did most in modern times to draw attention to Irish music was Thomas Moore. He composed his exquisite songs to old Irish airs; and songs and airs were published in successive numbers or volumes, beginning in 1807. They at once became popular, not only in the British Islands, but on the Continent and in America; and Irish music was thenceforward studied and admired where it would have never been heard of but for Moore. The whole collection of songs and airs—well known as "Moore's Melodies"—is now published in one small, cheap volume.

We know the authors of many of the airs composed within the last 200 years: but these form the smallest portion of the whole body of Irish music. All the rest have come down from old times, scattered fragments of exquisite beauty, that remind us of the refined musical culture of our forefathers. To this last class belong such well-known airs as Savourneen Dheelish, There came to the Beach, Shule Aroon, Molly Asthore, The Boyne Water, Garryowen, Patrick's Day, Eileen Aroon, Langolee (Dear Harp of my Country), The Groves of Blarney (The Last Rose of Summer), &c., &c. To illustrate what is here said, I may mention that of about 120 Irish airs in all " Moore's Melodies," we know the authors of less than a dozen: as to the rest, nothing is known either of the persons who composed them or of the times of their composition.

As the Scotch of the west of Scotland were descendants of Irish colonists, preserving the same language and traditions, and as the people of the two countries kept up intimate intercourse with each other for many centuries, the national music of Scotland is, as might be expected, of much the same general character as that of Ireland. This close connexion and constant intercourse continued till the end of the eighteenth century; and it was a common practice among Irish harpers, even from the earliest times, to travel through Scotland. Accordingly, as already mentioned, much of our Irish music was brought to Scotland, and became naturalised there; and a very large number of airs now claimed by Scotland are really Irish, of which the well-known air Eileen Aroon or Robin Adair is an example.

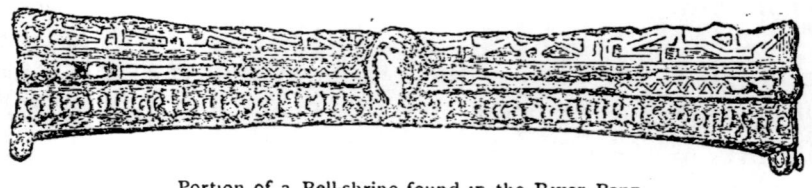

Portion of a Bell-shrine found in the River Bann.
(From Miss Stokes's Christian Inscriptions.)

CHAPTER XIV.

MEDICINE AND MEDICAL DOCTORS.

Section 1. *Medical Doctors.*

MEDICINE and surgery were carefully studied in Ireland from the very earliest times. There was a distinct professional class of physicians who underwent a regular course of education and practical training, and whose qualifications and privileges were universally recognised. Those intended for the profession were usually educated by being apprenticed to a physician of standing, in whose house they lived during their pupilage, and by whom they were instructed. This profession, like others in ancient Ireland, became in great measure hereditary in certain families.

The Irish, like the Greeks and other ancient nations, had their great mythical physicians, of whom the most distinguished was the Dedannan leech-god Diancecht [Dianket]. His name signifies 'vehement power,' and marvellous stories are related of his healing skill; similar to those of some old Greek physicians. He is mentioned in certain Irish Glosses and Incantations for health, written in the eighth century: so that at that early time he was regarded as a god, belonging to a period looked back to, even then, as the dim twilight of antiquity.

He had a son Midach and a daughter Airmeda, both of whom in some respects excelled himself; and in one of the old tales we are told that he grew at last so jealous of Midach that he killed him. And after a time there grew up from the young physician's grave 365 herbs from the 365 joints and sinews and members of his body, each herb with mighty virtue to cure diseases of the part it grew from. His sister Airmeda plucked up the herbs, and carefully sorting them, wrapped them up in her mantle. But the jealous old Diancecht came and mixed them all up, so that now no leech has complete knowledge of their distinctive qualities "unless"—adds the story—"the Holy Spirit should teach him."

Medical doctors figure conspicuously in the Tales of the Red Branch Knights. A whole medical corps, under one head physician, accompanied each army during the war of the Táin. Each leech of the company carried, slung from his waist, a bag—called a *lés* [lace]—full of medicaments; and at the end of the day's fighting, whether between numbers or individuals, they came forward and applied their salves.

Though the profession continued uninterruptedly from the most distant ages, the first notice of an individual physician we find in the annals of

Christian times occurs under A.D. 860, where the death is recorded of Maelodar O'Tinnri, "the best physician in Ireland": but from that period downwards the annals record a succession of eminent physicians, whose reputation, like that of the Irish scholars of other professions, reached the Continent. In the beginning of the seventeenth century, when medicine had been successfully studied in Ireland for more than a thousand years, Van Helmont of Brussels, a distinguished physician and writer on medical subjects, gave a brief but very correct account of the Irish physicians of his time, their books, and their remedies, and praised them for their skill. He says:—

"The Irish nobility have in every family a domestic physician, who has a tract of land free for his remuneration, and who is appointed, not on account of the amount of learning he brings away in his head from colleges, but because he can cure disorders. These doctors obtain their medical knowledge chiefly from books belonging to particular families left them by their ancestors, in which are laid down the symptoms of the several diseases, with the remedies annexed; which remedies are the productions of their own country. Accordingly the Irish are better managed in sickness than the Italians, who have a physician in every village."

From the earliest times reached by our records the kings and great Irish families had physicians attached to their households, whose office was, as in other professions, hereditary. The O'Callanans were physicians to the Mac Carthys of Desmond; the O'Cassidys, of whom individuals of eminence are recorded, to the Maguires of Fermanagh; the O'Lees, to the O'Flahertys of Connaught; and the

O'Hickeys, to the O'Briens of Thomond, to the O'Kennedys of Ormond, and to the Macnamaras of Clare.

The O'Shiels were physicians to the Mac Mahons of Oriel, and to the Mac Coghlans of Delvin, in the present King's County: and their hereditary estate, which is near the village of Ferbane, is still called Ballyshiel, 'O'Shiel's town.' Colgan states that in his time—seventeenth century—the O'Shiels were widely spread through Ireland, and were celebrated for their skill in natural science and medicine. Only quite recently—in 1889—Dr. Shiel, an eminent physician of Ballyshannon, left by his will a large fortune to found a hospital for the poor in that town. So that even still the hereditary genius of the family continues to exercise its benign influence.

The amount of remuneration of a family leech depended on his own eminence and on the status of the king or chief in whose household he lived. The stipend usually consisted of a tract of land and a residence in the neighbourhood, held free of all rent and tribute, together with certain allowances and perquisites: and the physician might practise for fee outside his patron's household. Five hundred acres of land was a usual allowance: and some of these estates—now ordinary townlands—retain the family names to this day. The household physician to a king—who should always be an *ollave-leech*, that is, one who had attained the highest rank in the profession (p. 185, *supra*)—held a very dignified position, and indeed lived like a prince, with a household and dependents of his own. He was always among the king's immediate retinue, and was entitled to a distinguished place at table.

Speaking generally, the best physicians were those attached to noble households. Those unattached lived by their fees; the amounts for the several operations or attendances being defined by the Brehon Laws. A qualified physician—as we have said—kept pupils or graduates who lived in his house and accompanied him in his visitations to learn his methods. We have already seen (p. 88) that a man who inflicted a wound had, on conviction, to pay a certain eric-fine to the wounded person. A leech who, through carelessness, or neglect, or gross want of skill, failed to cure a wound, had to pay the same fine to the patient as if he had inflicted the wound with his own hand; and if he had received his fee, he should return it.

It is worthy of remark that in our legendary history female physicians are often mentioned: and so we see that in ancient Ireland the idea was abroad which is so extensively coming into practice in our own day.

2. *Medical Manuscripts.*

The physicians of ancient Ireland, like those of other countries, derived a large part of their special learning from books, which in those times were all manuscripts. The members of each medical family had generally their own special book, which was handed down reverently from father to son, and which, at long intervals, when it had become damaged and illegible through age, was carefully transcribed into a new volume. Several of these venerable leech-books are still preserved, as mentioned farther on.

But besides these special books belonging to particular families, there were many others, which were copied and multiplied from time to time; so that the chief medical families had libraries containing such medical knowledge as was then available. There are still preserved in various libraries a great number of Irish medical MSS., forming a collection of medical literature in Irish, probably the largest in existence in any one tongue.

The manner in which these books were generally compiled and the motives of the compilers may be gathered from the following translation of a prefatory statement in Irish by the writer of a medical manuscript of the year 1352, now in the Royal Irish Academy,—a statement breathing a noble spirit, worthy of the best traditions of the faculty :—

"May the merciful God have mercy on us all. I have here collected practical rules from several works, for the honour of God, for the benefit of the Irish people, for the instruction of my pupils, and for the love of my friends and of my kindred. I have translated them into Gaelic from Latin books containing the lore of the great leeches of Greece and Rome. These are things gentle, sweet, profitable, and of little evil, things which have been often tested by us and by our instructors. I pray God to bless those doctors who will use this book; and I lay it on their souls as an injunction, that they extract not sparingly from it; and more especially that they do their duty devotedly in cases where they receive no pay [on account of the poverty of the patients]. I implore every doctor, that before he begins his treatment he remember God, the father of health, to the end that his work may be finished prosperously. Moreover, let him not be in mortal sin, and let him implore the patient to be also free from grievous sin. Let him offer up a secret prayer for the sick person, and implore the Heavenly Father, the physician and balm-giver for all mankind, to prosper the work he is entering upon."

The Book of the O'Lees in the Royal Irish Academy is a large-sized vellum manuscript, written in 1443, partly in Latin and partly in Irish. It is a complete system of medicine, treating of most of the diseases then known. The Book of the O'Hickeys, now in the Royal Irish Academy, commonly known as the "Lily of Medicine," is a translation into Irish of a Latin work, originally written by Bernard Gordon—a Continental physician—in 1303. The Book of the O'Shiels, now also in the Royal Irish Academy, which was transcribed in 1657, from some manuscript of unknown date, contains a system of medical science still more complete and scientific than even the Book of the O'Lees. There are many other medical manuscript books belonging to particular families.

3. *Diseases.*

All the chief diseases and epidemics we are now acquainted with were known and studied by the Irish physicians, and called by Irish names. In early times great plagues were of frequent occurrence all over the world; and Ireland was not exempt. The victims of a plague were commonly buried in one spot, which was fenced round and preserved as in a manner sacred. In Cormac's Glossary it is stated that the place of such wholesale interment was called *tamhlacht*, i.e. 'plague-grave,' from *tamh*, a plague, and *lacht*, a monument or memorial over the dead. *Tamhlacht*, which is still a living word, has given name to the village of Tallaght near Dublin, where the Parthalonian colony, who all died of a plague in one week, were interred. On the side of Tallaght hill are to be seen to this day a number of pagan graves and burial mounds. Within historic times, the most remarkable and destructive of all the ancient plagues was the *Blefed*, or *Buide-Connaill* [boy-connell] or yellow plague, which swept through Ireland twice, in the sixth and seventh centuries, and which, we know from outer sources, desolated all Europe about the same time. The Irish records abound in notices of its ravages.

The idea that a plague could not travel over sea farther than nine waves was very general, both in pagan and Christian times. During the prevalence of the yellow plague, St. Colman of Cloyne, with his terrified companions, fled to an island somewhere near Cork, so as to put a distance of nine waves between them and the mainland.

Some cutaneous disease, very virulent and infectious, known by names—such as *lobor*, *clam*, and *trosc*—that indicate a belief that it was leprosy, existed in Ireland from a very early date: but experts of our day doubt if it was true leprosy. Whatever it was, it would seem to have been a well-recognised disease in the fifth century; and after that time our literature, especially the Lives of the Saints, abounds with notices of the disease.

The annals record several outbreaks of smallpox and many individual deaths from it. It was known by two names, both still in use in different parts of the country:—*bolgach* or 'pustule disease' (*bolg*, 'a bag or pustule'), and *galar-brecc*, the 'speckled disease.'

Consumption was but too well known, then as now: a usual name for it was *serg*, i.e. 'withering' or 'decaying.' In Cormac's Glossary a person in consumption is called by an Irish name signifying 'without fat.'

'Gout in the hand,' is explained in Irish by *crupan na lám*, 'cramp or spasm of the hands': and ophthalmia is *galar súla*, 'disease of the eye.' This word *crupán* [cruppaun], 'a spasm or seizure,' is still used in parts of Ireland to denote a paralytic affection in cattle: it was also applied to convulsions. In the Tripartite Life and other old documents, colic is designated by *tregat*, which is still a spoken word. One of the early kings of Ireland was called Aed Uaridnech (A.D. 603 to 611), or 'Aed of the shivering disease,' no doubt ague. Palsy was known by the descriptive name *crith-lám* [crih-lauv], trembling of the hands,' from *crith*, 'shaking,' and *lám* or *lámh*, 'a hand.'

St. Camin of Inis-Caltra died in 653 of *teine-buirr*, 'fire of swelling'—St. Antony's fire or erysipelas— which withered away all his body. In one of Zeuss's eighth-century glosses, cancer is designated by two Irish words, *tuthle* and *ailse*, the latter of which is still in use in the same sense: and elsewhere in the same glosses another native word for the same disease occurs, *úrphasiu*. Diarrhœa was called in Irish *buinnech*, i.e. 'flux,' from *buinne*, 'a wave or stream.' These are only a few examples of Irish names of diseases.

4. *Treatment.*

Hospitals.—The idea of a hospital, or a house of some kind for the treatment of the sick or wounded, was familiar in Ireland from remote pagan times. In some of the tales of the Táin we read that in the time of the Red Branch Knights there was a hospital for the wounded at Emain called *Bróinbherg* [Broneverrig], the 'house of sorrow.' But coming to historic times, we know that there were hospitals all over the country, many of them in connexion with monasteries. Some were for sick persons in general; some were special, as, for instance, leper-houses. Monastic hospitals and leper-houses are very often mentioned in the annals. These were charitable institutions, supported by, and under the direction and management of, the monastic authorities.

But there were secular hospitals for the common use of the people of the *tuath* or district. These came under the direct cognisance of the Brehon Law, which laid down certain general regulations for their management. Patients who were in a position to do so were expected to pay for food, medicine, and the attendance of a physician. In all cases cleanliness and ventilation seem to have been well attended to; for it was expressly prescribed in the law that any house in which sick persons were treated should be free from dirt, should have four open doors, and should have a stream of water running across it through the middle of the floor. These regulations —rough and ready as they were, though in the right direction—applied also to a house or private hospital kept by a doctor for the treatment of his patients. The regulation about the four open doors and the stream of water may be said to have anticipated by a thousand years the present open-air treatment for consumption.

If a person wounded another or injured him bodily in any way, without justification, he was obliged by the Brehon Law to pay for " Sick maintenance," *i.e.* the cost of maintaining the wounded man in a hospital, either wholly or partly, according to the circumstances of the case, till recovery or death; which payment included the fees of the physician, and one or more attendants according to the rank of the injured person. Moreover, it was the duty of the aggressor to see that the patient was properly treated:—that there were the usual four doors and a stream of water; that the bed was properly furnished; that the physician's orders were strictly carried out—for example, the patient was not to be put into a bed forbidden by the doctor, or given prohibited food; and " dogs and fools and talkative noisy people" were to be kept away from him lest he might be worried. If the wounder neglected this duty, he was liable to penalty. Leper hospitals were established in various parts of Ireland, generally in connexion with monasteries, so that they became very general, and are often noticed in the annals.

Trefining or **Trepanning**. — In the Battle of Moyrath, fought A.D. 637, a young Irish chief named Cennfaelad [Kenfaila] had his skull fractured by a blow of a sword, after which he was a year under cure at the celebrated school of Tomregan in the present County Cavan. The injured portion of the skull and a portion of the brain were removed, which so cleared his intellect and improved his memory that on his recovery he became a great scholar and a great jurist, whose name—"Kennfaela the Learned"—is to this day well known in Irish literature. He was the author of the "Primer of the Poets," a work still in existence. Certain Legal Commentaries which have been recently published, forming part of the Book of Acaill, have also been attributed to him; and he was subsequently the founder of a famous school at Derryloran in Tyrone.

The old Irish writer of the Tale accounts for the sudden improvement in Kennfaela's memory by saying that his *brain of forgetfulness* was removed. It would be hardly scientific to reject all this as mere fable. What really happens in such cases is this. Injuries of the head are often followed by loss of memory, or by some other mental disturbance, which in modern times is cured, and the mind restored to its former healthful action—but nothing beyond—by a successful operation on skull and brain. The effects of such cures, which are sufficiently marvellous, have been exaggerated even in our own day; and in modern medical literature physicians of some standing have left highly-coloured accounts of sudden wonderful improvements of intellect following injuries of the head after cure. Kennfaela's case comes well within historic times: and the old Irish writer's account seems merely an exaggeration of what was a successful cure. We must bear in mind that the mere existence in Irish literature of this story, and of some others like it, shows that this critical operation—trefining—was well known and recognised, not only among the faculty but among the general public. In those fighting times, too, the cases must have been sufficiently numerous to afford surgeons good practice.

Stitching Wounds.—The art of closing up wounds by stitching was known to the old Irish surgeons. In the story of the death of King Concobar mac Nessa we are told that the surgeons stitched up the wound in his head with thread of gold, because his hair was golden colour.

Cupping and Probing.—Cupping was commonly practised by the Irish physicians, who for this purpose carried about with them a sort of horn called a *gipne* or *gibne*, as doctors now always carry a stethoscope. An actual case of cupping is mentioned in one old tale, where the female leech Bebinn had the venom drawn from an old unhealed wound on Cailte's leg, by means of two *fedans* or tubes; by which the wound was healed. It is stated in the text that these were "the *fedans* of Modarn's daughter Binn," a former lady-doctor, from which we may infer that they were something more than simple tubes—that they were of some special construction cunningly designed for the operation. We find a parallel case among the Homeric Greeks, where the physician Machaon healed an arrow-wound on Menelaus by sucking out the noxious blood and applying salves. The lady-physician Bebinn also treated Cailte for general indisposition by administering five successive emetics at proper intervals, of which the effects of each are fully described in the old text. Bebinn prepared the draughts by steeping certain herbs in water: each draught was different from all the others, and acted differently; and the treatment restored the patient to health. A probe (*fraig*) was another instrument regarded, like the cupping-horn, as requisite for a physician.

Sleeping-Draught.—In one of the oldest of the Irish Tales it is stated that the warrior lady Scathach gave Cuculainn a sleeping-draught to keep him from going to battle: it was strong enough to put an ordinary person to sleep for twenty-four hours: but Cuculainn woke up after one hour. This shows that at the early period when this story was written—seventh or eighth century—the Irish had a knowledge of sleeping-potions, and knew how to regulate their strength.

Materia Medica.—I have stated that some of the medical manuscripts contain descriptions of the medical properties of herbs. But besides these there are regular treatises on materia medica consisting of long lists of herbs and a few mineral substances, such as copperas and alum, with a description of their medical qualities, their application to various diseases, and the modes of preparing and administering them, the Latin names being given, and also the Irish names in case of native products. The herbs are classified according to the old system, into "moist and dry," "hot and cold."

The Irish doctors had the reputation—outside Ireland—of being specially skilled in medicinal botany.

Vapour Bath and Sweating-House.—We know that the Turkish bath is of recent introduction in these countries. But the hot-air or vapour bath was well known in Ireland, and was used as a cure for rheumatism down to a few years ago. It was probably in use from old times; and the masonry of the Inishmurray sweating-house, represented opposite, has all the appearance—as Mr. Wakeman remarks—of being as old as any of the other primitive buildings in the island. The structures in which these baths were given are known by the name of *Tigh 'n alluis* [Teenollish], ' sweating-house ' (*allus*, ' sweat'). They are still well known in the northern parts of Ireland—small houses, entirely of stone, from five to seven feet long inside, with a low little door through which one must creep : always placed remote from habitations : and near by is commonly a pool or tank of water four or five feet deep. They were used in this way. A great fire of turf was kindled inside till the house became heated like an oven ; after which the embers and ashes were swept out, and water was splashed on the stones, which produced a thick warm vapour. Then the person, wrapping himself in a blanket, crept in and sat down on a bench of sods, after which the door was closed up. He remained there an hour or so till he was in a profuse perspiration : and then creeping out, plunged right into the cold water, after emerging from which he was well rubbed till he became warm. After several baths at intervals of some days he commonly got cured. Persons are still living who used these baths or saw them used.

In the descriptions of the various curative applications given in old Irish medical books there is an odd mixture of sound knowledge and superstition, common in those times, not only among Irish physicians, but among those of all countries. Magic, charms, and astrological observations, as aids in

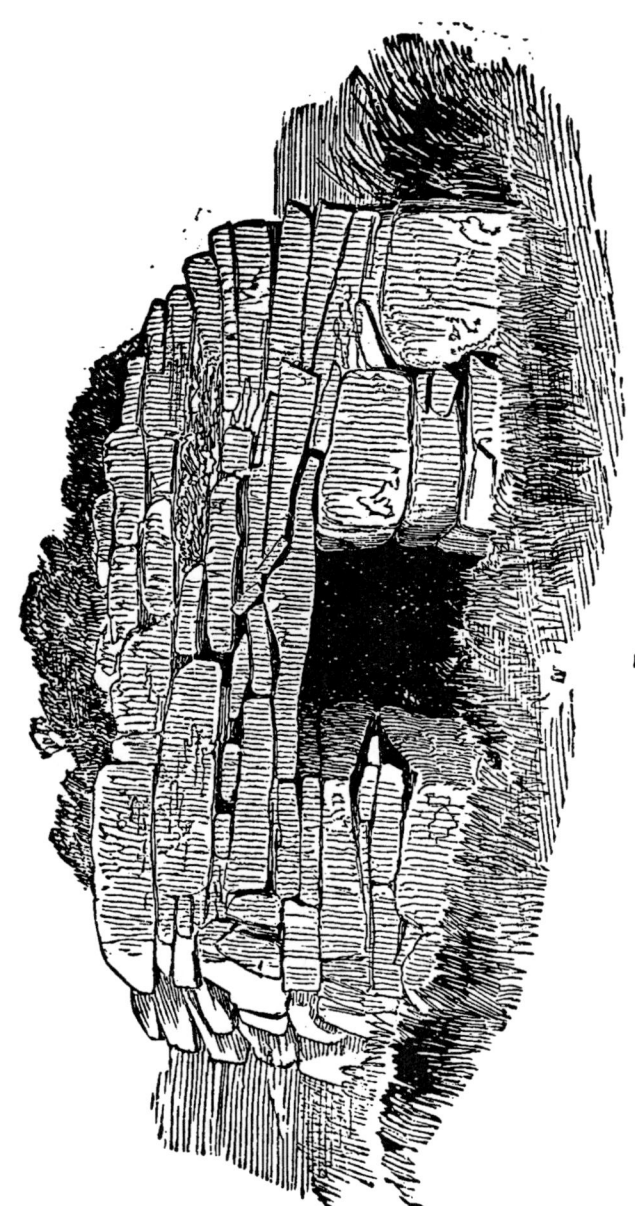

Fig. 74.

Sweating-house on Inishmurray. Interior measurements: 5½ feet long, 4 feet wide, and 5 feet high. (From Kilk. Archæol. Journ.)

medical treatment, were universal among physicians in England down to the seventeenth century.

Popular Herb-Knowledge.—The peasantry were skilled in the curative qualities of herbs and in preparing and applying them to wounds and local diseases; and their skill has in a measure descended to the peasantry of the present day. There were "herb-doctors," of whom the most intelligent, deriving their knowledge chiefly from Irish manuscripts, had considerable skill and did a good practice. But these were not recognised among the profession: they were amateurs without any technical qualification; and they were liable to certain disabilities and dangers from which the regular physicians were free, like quack-doctors of the present day. From the peasantry of two centuries ago, Threlkeld and others who wrote on Irish botany obtained a large part of the useful information they have given us in their books. Popular cures were generally mixed up with much fairy superstition, which may perhaps be taken as indicating their great antiquity and pagan origin.

Poison.—How to poison with deadly herbs was known. The satirist Cridenbél died by swallowing something put into his food by the Dagda, whom the people then accused of murdering him. After Coffagh the Slender of Brega had murdered his brother Laery Lorc, king of Ireland, he had Laery's son Ailill murdered also by paying a fellow to poison him.

PART III.

SOCIAL AND DOMESTIC LIFE.

Ornament, with Inscription, on the cover of the Misach, an ancient reliquary belonging to Inishowen. (From Miss Stokes's Christian Inscriptions.)

CHAPTER XV

THE FAMILY.

Section 1. *Marriage.*

In ancient Ireland it was a very general custom, as it was in Wales, and in Greece in the time of Homer, that when a couple got married the man was bound to bring the marriage portion or dowry, not the woman. Instances of this custom are mentioned everywhere in our literature. The dowry consisted of gold, silver, or brass; or of cattle, clothes, horses, horse-bridles, land, &c.

In Ireland, as among all the Aryan nations, the original conception was that the man purchased his affianced wife from the father or other guardian, and the dowry he brought in was the bride-price. It was usually paid over by the bridegroom to the father of the bride. The bride-price often consisted of a yearly payment from the husband after marriage: and we find it laid down in the Brehon Law that the woman's father was entitled to the whole of the first year's payment, to two-thirds of the second year's, to one-half of the third: and so on, diminishing to the twenty-first, when the claim ceased. In each case, what was left belonged to the wife. Any goods or valuables brought in by the bride on her wedding-day, continued to belong to her as her own special property after the marriage. Sometimes the friends of the young couple made a collection for them, which was called *Tinól* (i.e. 'collection': pron. tinnole), of which two-thirds belonged by law to the man, and one-third to the woman. Our present custom of making a young married couple presents is not unlike the old Irish *tinnole*. A tribute had to be paid—at least in some cases—to the king, on the marriage of every maiden of his people.

The general custom was to have only one wife: but there were exceptions, for in very early times we sometimes find a king or chief with two. That chastity and modesty were prized we know from many passages, such as that in the Life of St. Finnchua, in which he leaves blessings to the Leinstermen, among others "chastity in their queens and in their wives, and modesty in their maidens."

2. *Position of Women and Children.*

In ancient Ireland free women (as distinguished from slaves) held a good position: and it may be said that as to social rights and property they were in most respects quite on a level with men. Husband and wife continued to own the respective shares they brought in at marriage, such as land, flocks, household goods, &c., the man retaining his part and the woman hers, each quite independently of the other. Of this custom we find illustrations everywhere; and there are many records of married women taking legal proceedings on their own account against outsiders, quite independently of the husband, in defence of their special property.

But notwithstanding this separate ownership, as both portions were worked more or less in conjunction, and naturally increased from year to year, it was generally impossible—even if so desired—to keep them distinct, so that a part at least of the entire possessions might be looked upon as joint property: and for this state of things the law provided. It is from the Brehon Law we get the clearest exposition of the rights of women regarding property. The respective privileges of the couple after marriage depended very much on the amount of property they brought in. If their properties were equal at marriage, " the wife "—says the Senchus Mór—" is called the wife of equal rank "; and she was recognised as in all respects, in regard to property, on an equality with her husband.

That the husband and wife were on terms of equality as to property is made still more clear from the provisions laid down to meet the case of separation. If the couple separated by mutual consent, the woman took away with her all she had brought on the marriage day; while the man retained what he had contributed. Supposing the joint property had gone on increasing during married life: then at separation the couple divided the whole in proportion to the original contributions. Husband and wife stood on equal terms in a brehon's court, so that if the husband gave evidence against his wife, she was entitled to give evidence against him. But a father could give evidence against his daughter, whether married or single, and she was not permitted to rebut it by her evidence.

The testimonies hitherto brought forward are mostly legal and historical. But the general popular conception of the position of married women may be also gathered from the old romantic tales and legends, including those of the Dinnsenchus, in which women hold as high a place as men. We read of great female physicians, some of whom are mentioned in last chapter; and of distinguished female brehons or lawyers, such as Brigh Brugaid, whose decisions were followed as precedents for centuries after her death.

3. *Fosterage.*

One of the leading features of Irish social life was fosterage (Irish, *altrum*), which prevailed from the remotest period. It was practised by persons of all classes, but more especially by those in the higher ranks. The most usual type of fosterage was this:— A man sent his child to be reared and educated in the home and with the family of another member of the tribe, who then became foster-father, and his children the foster-brothers and foster-sisters of the child.

There were **two** kinds of fosterage—**for affection** and **for payment**. In the first there was no fee: in the second the fee varied according to rank. The fosterage fee sometimes consisted of land, but more generally of cattle. For the son of the lowest order of chief, the fee was three cows; and from that upwards to the son of a king, for whom the fee was from eighteen to thirty cows. For girls, as giving more trouble, requiring more care, and as being less able to help the foster-parents in after-life, it was something higher than for boys. The child, during fosterage, was treated in all respects like the children of the house: he worked at some appropriate employment or discharged some suitable function for the benefit of the foster-father: and he had to be educated in a way that suited his station in life: as has been already described. In cases where children were left without parents or guardians, and required protection, the law required that they should be placed in fosterage under suitable persons, at the expense of the tribe.

Fosterage was the closest of all ties between families. The relationship was regarded as something sacred. The foster-children were often more attached to the foster-parents and foster-brothers than to the members of their own family: and cases have occurred where a man has voluntarily laid down his life to save the life of his foster-father or foster-brother. The custom of fosterage existed in Ireland—though in a modified form—even so late as the seventeenth or eighteenth century; and it was formerly common among the Welsh, the Anglo-Saxons, and the Scandinavians.

Gossipred.—When a man stood sponsor for a child at baptism, he became the child's godfather, and gossip to the parents. Gossipred was regarded —as it is still—as a sort of religious relationship between families, and created mutual obligations of regard and friendship.

After the Anglo-Norman invasion the people of the English colony, from the great lords down, often sent their children to be fostered by the Irish: and, as might be expected, these young persons grew up speaking the Irish language, and thoroughly Irish in every way. Mainly for this reason the two customs of fosterage and gossipred were bitterly denounced by early English writers, most of whom were anxious to keep the two races apart: and we know that the Government passed several stringent laws forbidding them under the penalty of high treason: but these laws were generally disregarded. Gossipred in a modified form exists to this day all over the empire.

4. *Family-Names.*

Hereditary family-names became general in Ireland about the time of Brian Boru, viz. at the end of the tenth and the beginning of the eleventh century: and some authorities assert that they were adopted in obedience to an ordinance of that monarch. The manner of forming the names was very simple. Each person had one proper name of his own. In addition to this, all the members of a family, and of their descendants, took as a common surname the name of their father, with *Mac* (son) prefixed, or of their grandfather or some more remote ancestor, with *Ua* or *O* (grandson or descendant) prefixed. Thus the O'Neills are so called from their ancestor *Niall* Glunduff, king of Ireland (A.D. 916), and 'John O'Neill' means John the descendant of *Niall*.

Composed from the Book of Kells.

CHAPTER XVI.

THE HOUSE.

SECTION 1. *Construction, Shape, and Size.*

BEFORE the introduction of Christianity, buildings in Ireland, whether domestic, military, or sepulchral, were generally round or oval. The quadrangular shape, which was used in the churches in the time of St. Patrick, came very slowly into use, and round structures finally disappeared only in the fourteenth or fifteenth century. But the round shape was not universal, even in the most ancient period. The great Banqueting-Hall of Tara was quadrangular, as we see by its ruins at the present day; and in case of many of the ordinary good-sized dwelling-houses, the walls were straight and parallel. Some of the old lisses or forts still to be seen are of this shape: and even where the surrounding rampart was round, the wooden houses it enclosed were often quadrangular.

The common Irish word for a house is *tech*, Lat. *tectum*. A dwelling in general is denoted by *arus*; a homestead by *baile*, now generally anglicised *bally*, but used in a more extended sense to denote a townland. The word *brug* or *brugh* [broo] was also applied to a large dwelling.

It has sometimes been stated that there were no towns or cities in ancient Ireland: but this statement is misleading. There were many centres of population, though they were never surrounded by walls; and the dwellings were detached and scattered a good deal—not closely packed as in modern towns. In our old writings, both native and Anglo-Irish, we have many records of towns and cities. Then we know that some of the large monasteries had two or three thousand students, which implies a total population much larger. Some of the provisions of the Brehon Law show that numbers of lis-dwellings must have been clustered together.

The dwelling-houses, as well indeed as the early churches, were nearly always of wood, as that material was much the most easily procured. The custom of building in wood was so general in Ireland that it was considered a characteristic of the Irish—*more Scottorum*, " after the manner of the Scots "—as Bede expresses it. Yet we know that the Britons, Saxons, and Franks also very generally built in wood. Wooden houses, highly ornamented, continued in use in Dublin, Drogheda, and other towns, down to the last century.

But although wood building was general in Ireland before the twelfth century, it was not universal: for some stone churches were erected from the time of the introduction of Christianity: beehive-shaped houses, as well as cahers and cashels (see below), were built of stone, without mortar, from pre-historic times: and the remains of these primitive structures —churches, houses, and cahers—are still to be seen in many parts of Ireland. In all these mortarless buildings, the stones, though in their natural state—not hammered or chiselled into shape—are fitted to each other with great skill and accuracy : or, as Petrie expresses it, " with wonderful art."

FIG. 75.

Trim Castle, originally built by Hugh de Lacy the Elder, end of twelfth century; but afterwards rebuilt One of the Anglo-Norman strongholds referred to farther on. (From Cromwell's Tours. Drawn by Petrie.)

The dwelling-houses were almost always constructed of wickerwork. The wall (*fraig*) was formed of long stout poles placed in a circle, if the house was to be round, standing pretty near each other, with their ends fixed deep in the ground, the spaces between closed in with rods and twigs neatly and firmly interwoven; generally of hazel. The poles were peeled and polished smooth. The whole surface of the wickerwork was plastered on the outside, and made brilliantly white with lime, or occasionally striped in various colours; leaving the white poles exposed to view.

When the house was to be four-sided, the poles were set in two parallel rows, filled in with wickerwork. The height of the wall depended on the size of the house. In small houses it was low, so that often the thatch was within reach of the hand: in large dwellings it was usually high. The walls of the Banqueting-Hall at Tara were at least 45 feet high. In the large houses there were often two stories. When there was more than one apartment in a house, each had a separate wall and roof: except, of course, where one apartment was over another. Building in wickerwork was common to the Celtic people of Ireland, Scotland, and Britain. It is very often referred to in Irish writings of all kinds. In the Highlands of Scotland wattled or wicker houses were used, even among high-class people, down to the end of the eighteenth century; and it is probable that they continued in use in Ireland to as late a period.

In many superior houses, and in churches, a better plan of building was adopted, by forming the wall with sawed planks instead of wickerwork. In the houses of the higher classes the doorposts and other special parts of the dwelling and furniture were often made of yew, carved, and ornamented with gold, silver, bronze, and gems. We know this from the old records; and still more convincing evidence is afforded by the Brehon Law, which prescribes fines for scratching or otherwise disfiguring the posts or lintels of doors, the heads or posts of beds, or the ornamental parts of other furniture.

The roof of the circular house was of a conical shape, brought to a point, with an opening in the centre for the smoke. It was of wickerwork or hurdles supported by rafters sloping upwards from the tops of the wall-poles all round, to the centre at the very top. The roof of the quadrangular houses was much like that of the common run of houses of the present day. If the house was large, the conical roof of those of circular form was supported by a tall, strong pole standing on the centre of the floor; in case the house was quadrangular, there was a row of such supporting poles, or two rows if the structure was very large. Straw was used for roof-covering from the earliest times, and its use has continued to the present day: but rushes and reeds were also very common. Whatever the material, the covering was in all cases put on with some degree of art and neatness, such as we see in the work of the skilled straw-thatchers of the present day.

A better class of roof than any of the preceding was what is called in Irish *slinn*, namely thin boards of oak, laid and fastened so as to overlap, as in modern slated or tiled roofs. Sometimes, anticipating modern usage, they employed materials superior to any of the preceding. The Annals of Ulster record that in the year 1008, the oratory of Armagh was roofed with lead.

The thatch of ladies' greenans (see p. 300, *infra*) was sometimes covered with birds' plumage, so arranged as to form bright stripes of brown, reddish purple, and other colours: and sometimes the hoods of chariots were similarly roofed.

There were windows in the *fraig* or wall, and often a skylight in the roof. Glass was known among various ancient nations from the most remote period: the Celts of Britain were well acquainted with it: and from constant references to it in our oldest writings, it is obvious that it was well known to the ancient

Fig. 76.

Fig. 77.

Fig. 78.

Glass and porcelain ornaments, full size, now in the National Museum. In figs 76 and 77 the coloured ornaments form part of the substance, and were worked into shape, with great skill, while the whole mass was softened by heat. Fig 76, of clear glass, with yellow spiral ornament Fig 77, pin-head of fine light-red porcelain, decorated with wavy stripes, some white, some yellow: found with part of bronze pin attached, as shown in figure.

There are in the Museum many ornaments of coloured glass, with variously coloured patterns of enamel on the surface, of which the most beautiful is shown, full size, in fig 78. It is a flat circular disk, half-inch thick, the body of dark blue glass, with a wavy pattern of white enamel, like an open flower, on the surface. (All from Wilde's Catalogue)

Irish. Beads and other small ornamental objects of glass, variously coloured, are constantly found in Irish pre-Christian graves and crannoges. All the objects of this kind wherever found in Ireland were formed while the material was heated to softness.

Moreover, the manufacture of these little articles was an art requiring long training and much delicate manipulative skill, for most of them are made of different-coloured glass or porcelain—blue, white, yellow, pale red, &c.—blended and moulded and beautifully striated in the manner shown imperfectly in the black-and-white figures on the opposite page. They were used for ornamentation, very often forming the heads of pins, but sometimes made into rings, or strung together for beads.

Glass drinking-vessels were known to the Irish at least as early as the sixth century; and they are frequently mentioned in the most ancient of the tales. Add to all this that the remains of a regular glass factory have been found in the county Wicklow, where great quantities of lumps of glass, chiefly of the three colours, blue, green, and white, have been —and can still be—dug up.

Glass was used in England for church windows in the seventh century; and it had been long previously in use for this purpose on the Continent: so we may conclude that the knowledge of the use of glass for windows found its way into Ireland from Gaul, Italy, and England, through missionaries and merchants. At all events glass windows are mentioned in many of the ancient Irish tales, which shows that this use of glass was familiarly known to the original writers.

There was one large door leading to the principal apartment of the dwelling-house, with smaller doors, opening externally, for the other rooms. Generally the several rooms did not communicate with each other internally. In the outer *lis* or rampart surrounding the homestead (for which see farther on), there was a single large door. The common Irish word for door was, and is, *dorus*: a single leaf of a door was *comla*. The knocker was a small log of wood called *bas-chrann*, i.e. 'hand-wood,' which lay in a niche by the door. It is everywhere mentioned in the old tales that visitors knocked with the *bas-*

Fig. 79.

Carrickfergus Castle: one of the Anglo-Norman strongholds referred to in this chapter. (From the Dub. Pen. Journ., I. 113)

chrann. In rich people's houses there was a special doorkeeper to answer knocks and admit visitors. At the bottom of the door was a *táirsech* or threshold. The jamb was called *ursa*: the lintel was *for-dorus* (i.e. 'on the door'). On the outside of the large door of the *lis* was a porch called *aurdúine* (lit. 'front part of the *dún*'). Cormac's Glossary explains *aurdúine* as a structure "at the doors of the *dúns*, which is made by the artisans"—implying ornamentation. The *lis* door was always closed at night.

The door was secured on the inside either by a bolt or by a lock. We have the best evidence to show that locks were used in Ireland in very early times. Mention is made of the *aradh* [ara] or ladder, which must have been in constant use.

Fig. 80.

King John's Castle in Limerick. Erected in the beginning of 13th century by one of the Anglo-Norman chiefs. Some authorities state that it was built by the order of King John. One of the Anglo-Norman castles referred to farther on. (From Mrs. Hall's Ireland.)

The houses were generally small, according to our idea of size. But then we must remember that, like the people of other ancient nations, the Irish had very little furniture. In the main room there was probably nothing—besides the couches—but a sufficient number of small movable seats and a large table of some sort, or perhaps a number of small tables. Moreover the standard of living was in all countries low and rude compared with what we are now accustomed to—a fact that ought to be borne in mind by the reader of the account given here of the domestic arrangements in ancient Irish houses. In England, even so late as the time of Holinshed—sixteenth century—hardly any houses had chimneys. A big fire of logs was kindled against the wall of the principal room, the smoke from which escaped through an orifice in the roof right overhead. Here the meat was cooked, and here the family dined. In very few houses were there beds or bedrooms; and the general way of sleeping was on a pallet of straw covered with a sheet, under coverlets of various coarse materials, with a log of wood for a pillow: while the manner of eating, which is noticed farther on, was correspondingly rude. All this is described for England by a trustworthy English writer named Roberts.

We know that many of the great houses were very large. The present remains of the Banqueting-Hall of Tara measure 759 feet long and 46 feet wide: and Petrie states that it must have been originally much wider. We are told that the measurement of the hall of Emain was "fifteen feet and nine score" (195 feet): which refers to a square shape.

We may form some idea of the better class of dwellings from an enumeration, in one of the law books, of the various buildings in the homestead of a well-to-do farmer of the class *bo-aire*, who rented land from a chief, and whose property was chiefly in

CHAP. XVI.] THE HOUSE. 299

cattle. His dwelling consisted of (at least) seven different houses, each, as already observed, with a separate wall, door, and roof:—1. Dwelling-house, at least 27 feet in diameter: 2. Kitchen or cooking-

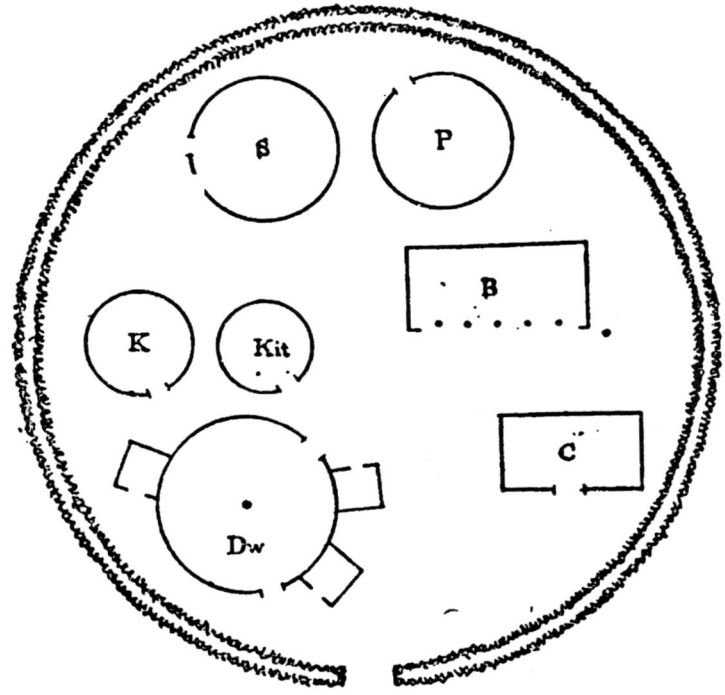

FIG. 81.

Conjectural plan of homestead of a well-to-do farmer of the *bo-aire* class, constructed from descriptions given in Brehon Laws. "Dw," family dwelling-house: of wickerwork, 27 feet in diameter (at least), with three outside sleeping-rooms (which might be either round or rectangular): "Kit," kitchen: "K," kiln (chiefly for corn-drying): "B," barn: "C," calf-nouse: "P," pig-house: "S," sheep-house. Whole group surrounded by a circular rath, with one entrance. The cows and horses were kept outside this enclosure.

house, at the back of the dwelling-house: 3. A kiln for drying corn: 4. A barn in which corn was stored: 5. A sheep-house: 6. A calf-house: 7. A pig-sty. These were all in one group close together; and each generally, though not always, consisted of the usual round-shaped wicker-house with conical roof: the whole group being surrounded by the *lis* or *rath*, described farther on. In all houses of the more comfortable class, the kitchen was separate from the dwelling-house and placed at the back: and there was a separate pantry for provisions. The barn was oblong and had one side quite open, with the roof supported at that side on posts.

The women had a separate apartment or a separate house in the sunniest and pleasantest part of the homestead. This was called a *grianan* [greenan], which signifies a summer-house: a diminutive derivative from *grian*, 'the sun.' The women's greenan is constantly mentioned in Irish writings. In Croghan the greenan was placed over the *for dorus* or lintel, as much as to say it was placed in front over the common sitting-room: and probably it occupied some such position in most houses. In great houses there was one apartment called "the House of conversation," answering to the modern "drawing-room," where the family often sat, especially to receive visitors.

2. *Interior Arrangements and Sleeping Accommodation.*

It will be shown farther on that in large houses there were separate sleeping-rooms. But among the ordinary run of comfortable, well-to-do people, including many of the upper classes, the family commonly lived, ate, and slept in the one principal apartment, as was the case in the houses of the Anglo-Saxons, the English, the Germans, and the Scandinavians of the same period. In the better class of houses in Ireland there were, ranged along the wall, little compartments or cubicles, each containing a bed, or sometimes more, for one or more persons, with its head to the wall. The wooden partitions enclosing the beds were not carried up to the roof; they were probably about eight or nine feet high, so that the several compartments were open at top. A little

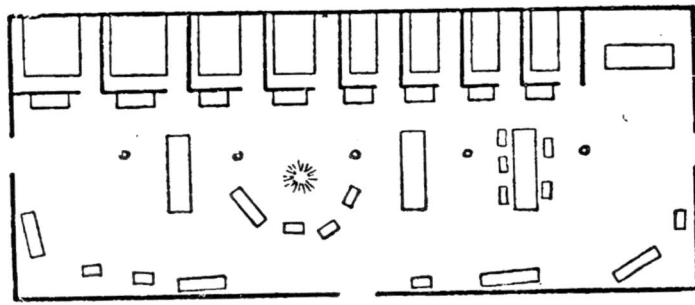

FIG. 82.

Conjectural plan of a good-class house, where the family lived, ate, and slept in the one large apartment: constructed from descriptions in Tales and Brehon Laws. (House here made quadrangular, but might be round or oval) Eight *imdas* or sleeping-places, each with one bed: some beds for one person, some for two, some for three. Four low, small tables and a number of seats are shown, all movable. Seats at ends of cubicles outside are fixed. Five supporting posts, (shown by little circles) · five near middle. Openings or windows in walls not marked here; neither are the doors in doorways of house and *imdas*.

compartment of this kind, whether open or closed overhead, was called an *imda*. The primary meaning of *imda* is a 'bed'; but by a natural extension of meaning the word is often used to denote the whole compartment or cubicle with its bedstead.

At the foot of each *imda* outside, and projecting into the main room, there was a low fixed seat, often stuffed with some soft material, for use during the day. Besides these there were on the floor of the main apartment a number of detached movable day-couches or seats—all low—with one or more low tables of some sort.

The preceding description of the disposition of the beds applies to the better class of houses. The lower classes of people probably slept, like those of Wales and Scotland of those times, on beds or pallets ranged along the wall with little or no attempt to screen one from another. Giraldus describes the Welsh as sleeping in this manner with their heads to the circular wall and their feet towards the fire.

The fire was in or near the middle, and the people sat or reclined by day all round it; while the smoke escaped through an opening in the roof: a custom which, as Scott records, existed in Scotland down to 200 years ago. In England also, down to the time of Elizabeth, before coal was brought into domestic use, and when wood was the general fuel, the fire was lighted—as in Ireland and Scotland—in the centre of the single big room or hall, or up against one of the walls, the smoke escaping through a hole in the roof.

The bedstead within the *imda*, in the best class of houses, consisted of four pillars connected by rails, with a canopy overhead, and curtains running by rings on copper rods. Such a bed was designated a 'protected,' enclosed, or testered bed: and this designation occurs so often that such beds must have been pretty common. Near the foot of the bed and within the *imda* there was a rack with pins or hooks for hanging clothes or other articles on. The commonest name for a bed was *lepad*, which, in the form *leabadh* [labba], is the term in use at the present day. This word was also used to denote a couch for day use, which had generally a little table beside it for food and drink.

As distinct from the *imda* and bedstead, the bed-tick or mattress was called *dergud* [dergu]. The word *colcaid* [culkee] was sometimes applied to a bed-tick, and also to a quilt, blanket, or other covering. The bed-coverings were brought out by day to be aired and sunned. White linen sheets were used, and in grand houses they were often embroidered with figures.

Beds of the best class were stuffed with feathers. Straw was often used, subjected to some sort of previous preparation. Beds were sometimes made of rushes—as in Wales—especially in cases of emergency or for temporary use. When Cuculainn and Ferdiad had finished their day's fighting, their attendants prepared beds of fresh rushes for them. When the Fena of Erin were out on their hunting excursions, they put up hunting-booths each evening, after which—to use the words of Keating:—" Each man constructed his bed of the brushwood of the forest, moss, and fresh rushes. The brushwood was laid next the ground; over that was laid the moss; and the fresh rushes were spread over all: which three materials are designated in old books 'the three bed-materials of the Fena.'" The people often used beds of hides stuffed with some soft material: or perhaps they simply spread the skin on the top of straw or rushes. The Senchus Mór mentions "a poor sick man lying on the hides." A pillow was used for the head, often made of feathers in a case of wild-deer skin. The most common word for a pillow was *adart* [eye-art], which is used to this day by speakers of Irish.

FIG. 83.

Castle of Athlone: erected by John de Grey, Lord Justiciary, or Governor, of Ireland, 1210-1213 One of the Anglo-Norman castles referred to below. (From Mrs Hall's Ireland)

Often two and sometimes three persons slept in the same bed. It was a mark of distinction to set apart a bed for one. Maildune and his men came to a certain house in which were a number of bed-couches, one intended for Maildune alone, and each of the others for three of his people. One of the complaints of the unreasonable demands of the poets who were on a visit to Guaire [Goory], king of Connaught, was that they insisted on a separate bed for each.

In great homesteads there were sleeping-houses or apartments distinct and separate both from the sitting- or banquet-room and from one another, each probably circular and having a conical roof of its own: often called *tech-leptha*, i.e. 'bed-house.' "We have distinct statements in our ancient records"—says O'Curry —"that different members of the same family had distinct houses (and not mere apartments) within the same *rath, dún, lis,* or *caher*: that the lord or master had a sleeping-house, his wife a sleeping-house, his sons and daughters, if he had such, separate sleeping-houses, and so on, besides places of reception for strangers and visitors." But this applies to the great houses belonging to people of rank. And even in many high-class houses it was usual to put two or three in the same room, with a bed for each.

It was a common practice in the better class of houses to strew the floor with rushes: and when distinguished visitors were expected, the old rushes were removed and fresh ones supplied. The use of rushes for this purpose was so well understood that there was a special knife for cutting them; and such a knife is enumerated among the household articles in the house of a brewy. Sometimes the floor was covered with soft, green-leaved birch-branches, with rushes strewn over them. We know that this custom of covering the floor with rushes also prevailed in England, where it was continued down to the time of Elizabeth. It was expected that the kitchen of a bo-aire chief should be kept strewn with fresh straw, which one would think a dangerous practice.

3. *Outer Premises and Defence.*

The homesteads had to be fenced in to protect them from robbers and wild animals. This was usually done by digging a deep circular trench, the clay from which was thrown up on the inside. This was shaped and faced; and thus was formed, all round, a high mound or dyke with a trench outside, and having one opening for a door or gate. Whenever water was at hand, the trench was flooded as an additional security: and there was a bridge opposite the opening, which was raised, or closed in some way, at night. The houses of the Gauls were fenced round in a similar manner. Houses built and fortified in the way here described continued in use in Ireland till the thirteenth or fourteenth century.

These old circular forts are found in every part of Ireland, but more in the south and west than elsewhere; many of them still very perfect—but of course the timber houses are all gone. Almost all are believed in popular superstition to be the haunts of fairies. They are now known by various names— *lis, rath, brugh, múr, dún, moat, caiseal* [cashel], and *cathair* [caher]: the cashels, múrs, and cahers being usually built of stone without mortar. These are generally the very names found in the oldest manuscripts. The forts vary in size from 40 or 50 feet in diameter, through all intermediate stages up to 1500 feet: the size of the homestead depending on the rank or means of the owner. Very often the flat middle space is raised to a higher level than the surrounding land, and sometimes there is a great mound in the centre, with a flat top, as seen in the illustration, on which the strong wooden house of the chief stood. Forts of this exact type are still to be seen in England, Wales, and Scotland, as well as in various parts of the Continent; but they are most numerous in Ireland. Round the very large forts there are often three or more great circumvallations, sometimes as many as seven. The "moat or fort of Kilfinnane," here figured, has three.

Fig. 84.

The great "Moat of Kilfinnane," Co Limerick, believed to be one of the seats of the kings of Munster. Total diameter 320 feet. (From a drawing by the author, 1854.)

A *dún*, sometimes also called *dind*, *dinn*, and *dingna*, was the residence of a *Ri* [ree] or king: according to law it should have at least two surrounding walls with water between. Round the great forts of kings or chiefs were grouped the timber dwellings of the *fudirs* and other dependents who were not of the immediate household, forming a sort of village.

In most of the forts, both large and small, whether with flat areas or with raised mounds, there are underground chambers, commonly beehive-shaped, which were probably used as storehouses, and in case of sudden attack as places of refuge for women and children. In the ancient literature there are many references to them as places of refuge. The Irish did not then know the use of mortar, or how to build an arch, any more than the ancient Greeks; and these chambers are of dry-stone work, built with much rude skill, the dome being formed by the projection of one stone beyond another, till the top was closed in by a single flag.

Where stone was abundant the surrounding rampart was often built of dry masonry, the stones being

FIG. 85.

Staigue Fort in Kerry Of stones without mortar External diameter 114 feet wall 13 feet thick at bottom, 5 feet at top. (From Wood-Martin's Pagan Ireland, and that from Wilde's Catalogue.)

fitted with great exactness. In some of these structures the stones are very large, and then the style of building is termed cyclopean. Many great stone fortresses of the kind described here, usually called caher, Irish *cathair*, still remain near the coasts of Sligo, Galway, Clare, and Kerry, and a few in Antrim and Donegal: two characteristic examples are Greenan-Ely, the ancient palace of the kings of the northern Hy Neill, in Donegal, and Staigue Fort near Sneem in Kerry. The most magnificent fortress of this kind in all Ireland is Dun Aengus on a perpendicular cliff right over the Atlantic Ocean on the south coast of Great Aran Island.

At the most accessible side of some of these stone cahers, or all round if necessary, were placed a number of large standing stones firmly fixed in the ground, in no order—quite irregular—and a few feet apart. This was a very effectual precaution against

Fig. 86.

Dun-Aengus on Great Island of Aran, on the edge of a cliff overhanging the sea: circular caher: without mortar: standing-stones intended to prevent a rush of a body of enemies. (From Wilde's Lough Corrib.)

a sudden rush of a body of assailants. Beside some of the existing cabers these stones, or large numbers of them, still remain in their places (as shown in fig. 86).

The cashel was a strong stone wall round a king's house, or round a monastery; of uncemented stones in pagan times, but often built with mortar when in connexion with monasteries. The caher was distinguished from the cashel by being generally more massive in structure, with much thicker walls. The cahers are almost confined to the south and west of Ireland. Buildings like our cahers are also found on the Continent.

That the wooden dwelling-houses were erected within the enclosing *lis*, or *rath*, is abundantly evident from the records. Queen Maive Lederg (not Queen Maive of Croghan) is recorded to have built the rath near Tara, now called from her, Rath-Maive· "and she built a choice house within that rath" There were often several dwelling-houses within one large rath: inside the great rath at Emain there were at least three large houses, with others smaller: the Rath-na-Righ at Tara had several houses within it: and in the romantic story of Cormac in Fairyland, we are told that he saw "a very large kingly *dún* which had four houses within it."

The rampart enclosing a homestead was usually planted on top with bushes or trees, or with a close thick hedge, for shelter and security: or there was a strong palisade on it. Lisses and raths such as we see through the country are generally round or oval: but they are occasionally quadrangular. Vitrified forts, *i.e.* having the clay, gravel, or stone of the rampart converted into a coarse glassy substance through the agency of enormous fires, are found in various parts of Ireland as well as in Scotland: and similar forts are still to be seen in several parts of the Continent.

Immediately outside the outer door of the rath was an ornamental lawn or green called *aurla, urla,* or *erla,* which was regarded as forming part of the homestead: "then queen Maive went out through the door of the *liss* into the *aurla,* and three times fifty maidens along with her" Beside the *dún* or *lis,* but beyond and distinct from the *aurla,* was a large level sward or green called a *faithche* [faha], which was chiefly used for athletic exercises and games of various kinds. Some idea of its size may be formed from the statement in the law that the *faithche* of a brewy extends as far as the voice of a bell (*i.e.* of the small bell of those times) or the crowing of a cock can be heard. The higher the rank of the chief the larger the *faithche*. The haggard for grain-stacks, which was always near the homestead, was called

FIG. 87.

Carlow Castle in 1845: believed to have been erected by Hugh de Lacy, who was appointed Governor of Ireland in 1179 One of the Anglo-Norman castles referred to at p. 313, below. (From Mrs. Hall's Ireland)

ithlann, from *ith*, ' corn.' At a little distance from the dwelling it was usual to enclose an area with a strong rampart, into which the cattle were driven for safety by night. This was what was called a *badhun* [bawn], *i.e.* 'cow-keep,' from *ba*, pl. of *bo*, ' a cow,' and *dún*. This custom continued down to a late time.

The outer defence, whether of clay, or stone, or timber, that surrounded the homestead was generally whitened with lime—a practice often referred to in old Irish literature. The great ramparts of Tara must have shone brilliantly over the surrounding plain: for it is called "White-sided Tara," in some old Irish writings.

Fig. 88.

Dundrun Castle, near Newcastle, County Down. Built at end of 12th century by John de Courcy, on the very site of the old Irish fortress called Dun Rury, which covered the summit of the rock. The great earthworks belonging to the original *dún* still remain at the base of the rock at one side, but are not seen in this figure (From Kilk. Archæol Journ.)

In modern times, when the native knowledge of Irish history and antiquities had greatly degenerated, and the light of our own day had not yet dawned, many writers attributed the ancient Irish raths and duns to the Danes, so that it became the fashion to call them "Danish raths or forts": but this idea has been long since exploded.

The Anglo-Normans built stone castles in Ireland according to their fashion: and not unfrequently they selected the very site, or the very vicinity, of the old Irish fortresses: for an Anglo-Norman had at least as keen an eye for a good military position as an old Irish warrior. Accordingly the circumvallations of the ancient native forts still remain round the ruins of many of the Anglo-Norman castles. It is to be observed that the Irish began to abandon their earthen forts and build stone castles—many of them round like the older earthen forts and cahers—shortly before the arrival of the Anglo-Normans in 1169: but this was probably in imitation of their warlike neighbours.

Crannoges.—For greater security, dwellings were often constructed on artificial islands made with stakes, trees, and bushes, covered with earth and stones in shallow lakes, or on small, flat natural islands if they answered. These were called by the name *crannóg* [crannoge], a word derived from *crann*, 'a tree,' as they were constructed almost entirely of wood. Communication with the shore was carried on by means of a small boat, commonly dug out of one tree-trunk. Usually one family only, with their attendants, lived on a crannoge island: but sometimes several families, each having a separate wooden house. Where a lake was well suited for it—pretty large and shallow—several islands were formed, each with one or more families, so as to form a kind of little crannoge village.

Crannoge dwellings were in use from the most remote prehistoric times; they are very often noticed, both by native Irish and by English writers, and they continued down to the time of Elizabeth. Great numbers of crannoges have of late years been explored, and the articles found in them show that they were occupied by many generations of residents. In most of them rude "dug-out" boats have been found, many specimens of which are preserved in the National Museum, Dublin, and elsewhere. Lake-dwellings similar to the Irish crannoges were in use in early times all over Europe, and explorers have examined many of them, especially in Switzerland.

4. *Domestic Vessels.*

The material in most general use for vessels was wood; but there were vessels of gold, silver, bronze, and brass, all of which, however, were expensive. Occasionally, we read of iron being used. There were also vessels of stone: but these were not much in use. Drinking-goblets of glass have been already noticed; and leather vessels for holding liquids will be described in chap. xxii., sect. 5.

FIG. 89.

Stone Drinking-cup, 4¾ in. wide across the bowl. Found, buried deep, in the bed of the Shannon. (Wilde's Catalogue.)

For making wooden vessels beech was oftenest employed: but the best were made of yew. A large proportion of the timber vessels used were made of staves bound by hoops, like those in use at present, indicating skill and accuracy in planing and jointing. In a certain old Irish list of yew-tree vessels, several are mentioned as having grown so old that *the hoops at last fell off*.

A large open hooped tub or vat, with two handles or ears like those of the present day, was called by several names, the most common of which was *dabach* [dauvagh]. Another name for a tub or trough was *lothar* [lōher]: grains left after brewing, used for feeding pigs, were often kept in a *lothar*.

FIG. 90.

Bronze Drinking-vessel in the National Museum: 7¾ inches wide: hammered out and shaped with great skill from one single thin flat piece of metal. Found in a crannoge in County Roscommon. (From Wilde's Catalogue.)

A moderately-sized tub with two handles, called a *drolmach*, was used by women for bringing water. This word is still in use and pronounced *drowlagh*. The people used a sort of pitcher or hand-vessel called a *cilorn* [keelorn], having a *stuag* or circular handle in its side, from which it was also called *stuagach*, i.e. 'circle-handled.'

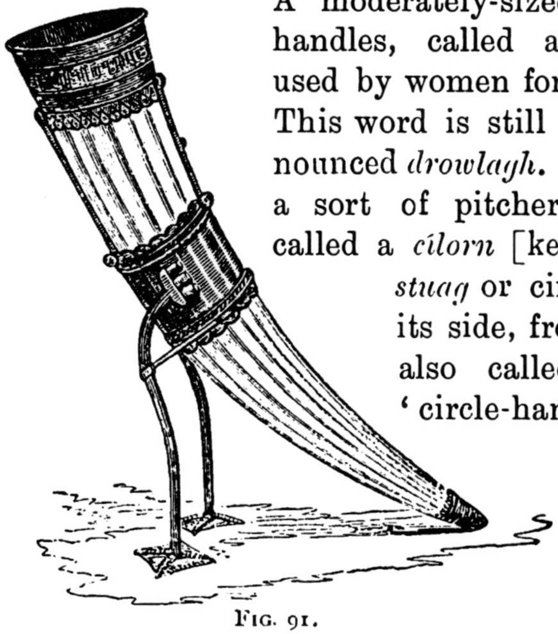

A *corn* [curn] or horn was a drinking-vessel, usually made from a bullock's horn, hollowed out and often highly ornamented with

FIG. 91.

The "Kavanagh Horn," a *Corn*, 22 inches along the convex or under side. On a brass plate round the top is this inscription:—"TIGERNANUS O LAUAN ME FECIT DEO GRACIAS. I. II S.", which gives the name of the artist, Tiernan O'Lavan. This is not a very old specimen. (From Wilde's Catalogue.)

metal-work and gems. Drinking-*corns* were made at

home from cows' or bullocks' horns; but very large ones were imported and much valued. These *corns* were sometimes given as a part of the stipend due from one king to another, as we find by many entries

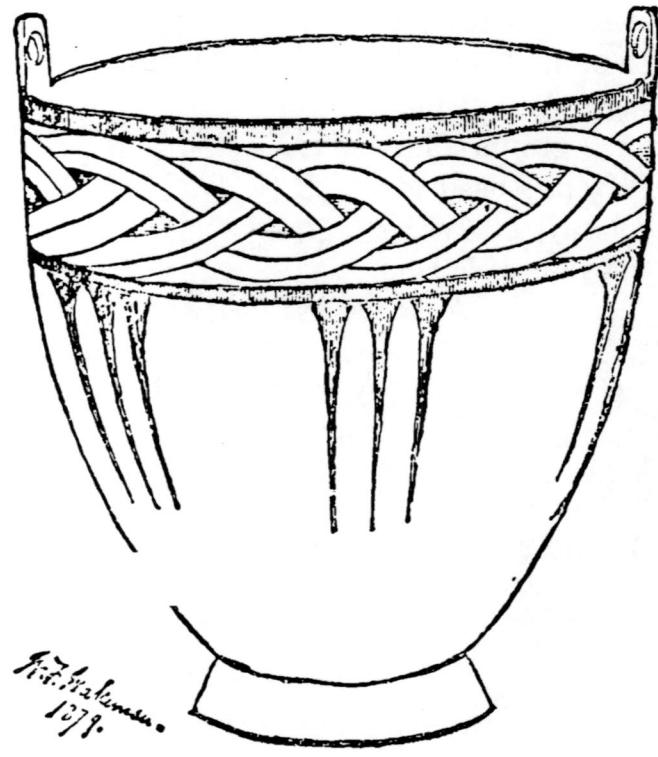

FIG. 92.

Ancient Irish vessel, 15 inches high: made out of a single piece of oak. The carving on the side is the *Opus Hibernicum* or interlaced work. The whole outer surface was originally painted in a kind of dark enamel, portions of which still remain. (From Kilk Archæol Journ)

in the Book of Rights, where they are often called *curved corns* from their shape. Sometimes they were brightly coloured.

The *escra* was a drinking-goblet: Cormac's Glossary says it was a copper vessel for distributing water;

but it was sometimes made of silver. The sons of O'Corra, in the course of their voyage, landed on an island, where a lady came towards them having in one hand a copper *cilorn* full of food like cheese, and in the other a silver *escra*. The word *lestar* was applied to vessels of various kinds, among others to drinking-vessels: it was often used as a generic term for vessels of all kinds, including ships. The beautiful *lestar* represented in figure 92 was found some years ago, five feet deep in a bog.

Fig. 93.

Grotesque figure of a nan drinking, fron the Book of Kells 7th or 8th century. (From Wilde's Catalogue)

The simple word *cua*, and its derivatives *cuad* and *cuach*, all mean 'a cup.' *Cuach*, which is the common term for 'cup,' is retained in Scotland to this day, and used as an English word in the forms of *quaigh* and *cogue*, for a drinking-cup. *Ian*, gen. *ena*, means 'a vessel': it is often applied to a small drinking-mug.

The usual drinking-vessel among the common people, especially at meals and drinking-bouts, was a *mether* (so called from the drink called *mead*), made of wood, with two or four handles: it circulated from hand to hand, each passing it to his neighbour after taking a drink. Many of these *methers* are preserved in museums, of which two are figured next page. People drank from the corners. A sort of hamper or vessel called a *rúsc* [roosk] made of bark-strips on a wicker-work frame, was much used in farmhouses.

FIG. 94.

FIG. 95.

Wooden Methers (From Wilde's Catalogue.)

A churn was known by several names—among others *cuinneóg* [quinnoge], which is the present name. The form of churn used among the ancient Irish was that in which the cream or milk is agitated by a dash worked with the hand. For bringing home milk from the milking-place, Adamnan mentions a wooden vessel of such a make that it could be strapped on the back. The lid was kept in its place by a wooden cross-bar (called *gercenn*) which ran through two holes at opposite sides near the rim.

FIG 96.

Pail or bucket, made out of one piece of red deal. 1 foot long Cover made of yew, pressed into shape when softened Now in the National Museum. (From Wilde's Catalogue.)

In the Tripartite Life, the cup that St. Patrick was drinking out of at Tara, when the druid attempted to poison him, is called *ardig*, which is a common old word for a drinking-goblet. A *ballán* seems to have been a simple, cheap, wooden drinking-cup in very general use: in one place, Cormac's Glossary defines it as "a poor man's vessel." Keating applies it to a drinking-cup; and it was sometimes also applied to a milk-pail. In Connaught it is used to designate round holes in rocks usually filled with water: which use modern antiquarians have borrowed, and they now apply "ballaun" to those small cup-like hollows, generally artificial, often found in rocks, and almost always containing water.

Escann is described in Cormac's Glossary as a vessel for distributing water, derived from *esc*, 'water,' and "*cann*, the name of a vessel." This last phrase is interesting as showing the existence in ancient Gaelic of a term for a drinking-vessel identical with the English word *can*. The word *cernin* [kerneen] is given in Cormac's Glossary as meaning *miass*, i.e. a dish on which food is placed at table. *Cernin* is a diminutive of the simple word *cern* or *cearn*, which is used to denote a dish of any kind, for measuring commodities, such as grain. The word *miass* or *mias*, given above from Cormac's Glossary, is very commonly used for a platter or dinner dish. *Coire*, 'a caldron'; *cusal*; *criol*; and some other terms, as well as the vessels they denote, will be dealt with elsewhere in this book.

FIG. 97.

Earthenware glazed pitcher, 13 inches high. Found in a crannoge in County Down. (From Wilde's Catalogue.)

Earthen vessels of various shapes and sizes were in constant use. They were made either on a potter's wheel, or on a mould, or on both. This appears from a curious commentary on the Latin text of a passage in the Psalms, written in the Irish language by an Irishman, in the eighth or ninth century, contained in a manuscript now in Milan. This old writer, evidently taking his illustration from his native country, explains "a potter's wheel" as "a round wheel on which the potters make the vessels, or a round piece of wood about which they [the vessels] are while being made." The "round piece of wood" was the block or mould on which they were first formed roughly, to be afterwards perfected on the wheel.

It will be seen from what precedes that there was in old times in Ireland quite as great a variety of vessels of all kinds, with distinct names, as there is among the people of the present day.

5. *Royal Residences.*

Almost all the ancient residences of the over-kings of Ireland, as well as those of the provincial and minor kings, are known at the present day; and in most of them the circular ramparts and mounds are still to be seen, more or less dilapidated after the long lapse of time. As there were many kings of the several grades, and as each was obliged to have three suitable houses (p. 24, above), the royal residences were numerous; of which the most important will be noticed here. In addition to these, several of the great strongholds described at pp. 39 to 42, *supra*, were royal residences.

Tara.—The remains of Tara stand on the summit and down the sides of a gently-sloping, round, grassy hill, rising 500 feet over the sea, or about 200 over the surrounding plain, situated six miles south-east of Navan, in Meath, and two miles from the Midland Railway station of Kilmessan. It was in ancient times universally regarded as the capital of all Ireland; so that in building palaces elsewhere it was usual to construct their principal houses and halls in imitation of those of Tara. It was the residence of the supreme kings of Ireland from prehistoric times, down to the sixth century, when it was deserted in the time of King Dermot, the son of Fergus Kervall, on account of St. Ruadan's curse. Although it has been abandoned to decay and ruin for thirteen centuries, it still presents striking vestiges of its ancient importance.

Preserved in the Book of Leinster and other ancient manuscripts there are two detailed Irish descriptions of Tara, written by two distinguished scholars, one in the tenth century by Kineth O'Hartigan, and the other in the eleventh by Cuan O'Lochain. Both these learned men examined the remains personally, and described them as they saw them, after four or five centuries of ruin, giving the names, positions, and bearings of the several features with great exactness. More than sixty years ago Dr. Petrie and Dr. O'Donovan made a most careful detailed examination of the hill and its monuments; and with the aid of those two old topographical treatises they were able, without much difficulty, to identify most of the chief forts and other remains, and to restore their ancient names. The following

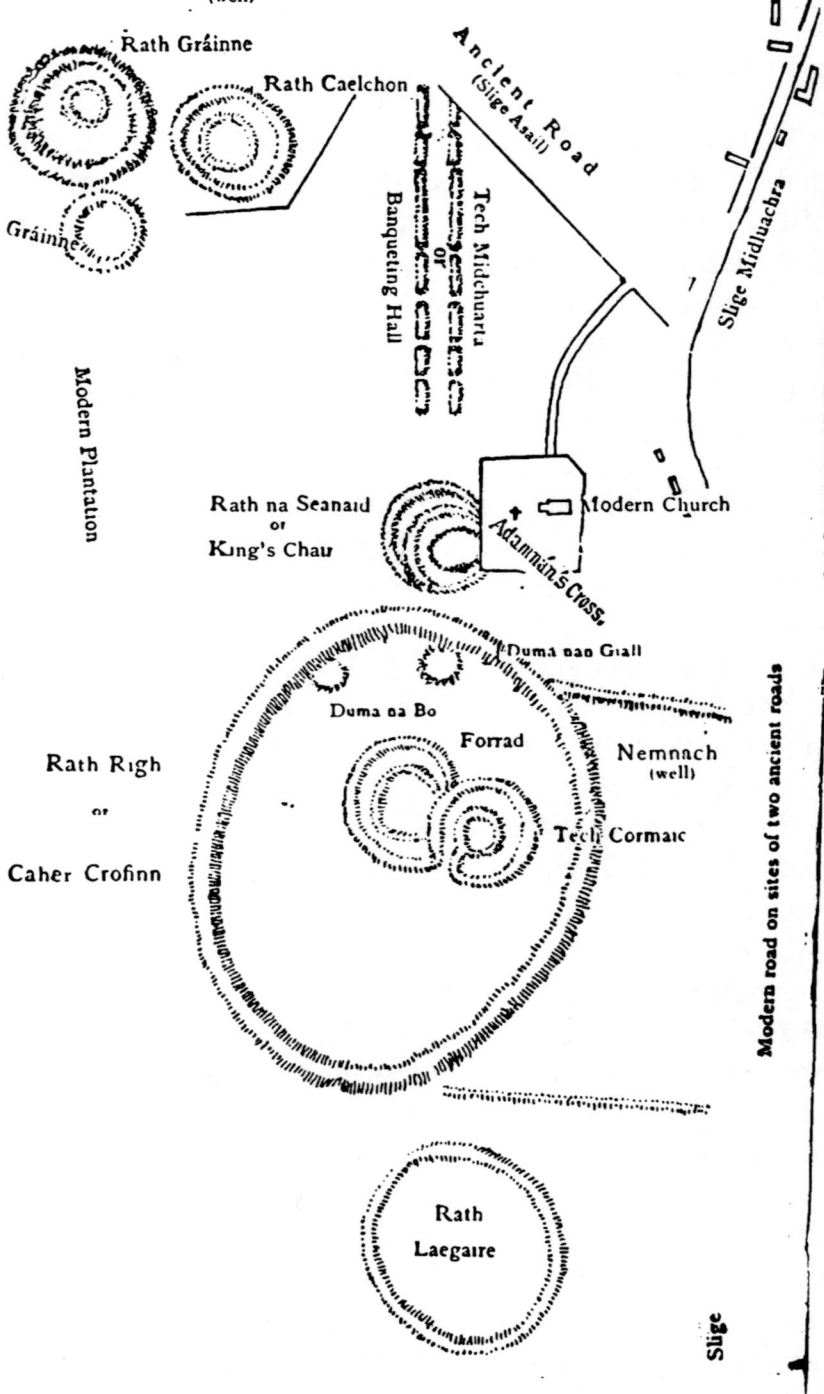

Fig. 98.

Tara, as it exists at the present day. (From the two Plans given by Petrie in his Essay on

are the most important features still existing, and they are all perfectly easy to recognise by any one who walks over the hill with the plan given here in his hand. It is to be borne in mind that the forts now to be seen were the ramparts or defences surrounding and protecting the houses. The houses themselves, as has been already explained (p. 306), were of wood, and have, of course, all disappeared.

The principal fortification is *Rath Rígh* [Rath-Ree], the 'Fort of the kings,' also called *Caher Crofinn*, an oval occupying the summit and southern slope of the hill, measuring 853 feet in its long diameter. The circumvallation can still be traced all round; and consisted originally of two walls or parapets with a deep ditch between. This seems to have been the original fort erected by the first occupiers of the hill, and the most ancient of all the monuments of Tara.

Within the enclosure of Rath Rígh are two large mounds, the *Forrad* [Forra] and *Tech Cormaic*, beside each other, and having portions of their ramparts in common. The Forrad has two outer rings or ramparts and two ditches: its extreme outer diameter is nearly 300 feet. The name "Forrad" signifies 'a place of public meeting,' and also 'a judgment-seat,' cognate with Latin *forum*; so that it seems obvious that this is the structure referred to by the writer of the ancient Norse work called "Kongs Skuggsjo" or 'mirror for kings.' This old writer, in his description of Tara, says:—"And in what was considered the highest point of the city the king had a fair and well-built castle, and in that castle he had a hall fair and spacious, and in that hall he was wont to sit in judgment."

On the top of the Forrad there now stands a remarkable pillar-stone six feet high (with six feet more in the earth), which Petrie believed was the *Lia Fáil*, the inauguration stone of the Irish over-kings, the

Fig. 99.

The Mound called the Forrad, at Tara (From Mrs Hall's Ireland)

stone that *roared* when a king of the true Milesian race stood on it (see p. 20); but recent inquiries have thrown grave doubts on the accuracy of this opinion.

Tech Cormaic ('Cormac's house') was so called from the illustrious King Cormac mac Art, who reigned A.D. 254 to 277. It is a circular rath consisting of a well-marked outer ring or circumvallation, with a ditch between it and the inner space; the extreme external diameter being 244 feet. We may probably assign its erection to King Cormac, which fixes its age.

Duma nan Giall or the 'mound of the hostages,' situated just inside the ring of Rath Rígh, is a circular earthen mound, 13 feet high, 66 feet in diameter at the base, with a flat top, 25 feet in diameter. The timber house in which the hostages lived, as already mentioned (pp. 22, 23), stood on the flat top.

A little to the west of the Mound of the Hostages stands another mound called *Duma na Bo* (the 'mound of the cow'), about 40 feet in diameter and 6 feet high. It was also called *Glas Temrach* (the 'Glas of Tara'), which would seem to indicate that the celebrated legendary cow called Glas Gavlin, which belonged to the Dedannan smith Goibniu, was believed to have been buried under this mound.

About 100 paces from Rath Rígh on the northeast is the well called *Nemnach* ('bright' or 'sparkling'), so celebrated in the legend of Cormac's mill—the first mill erected in Ireland, for which see chap. xxi., below. A little stream called *Nith* ('shining') formerly ran from it, which at some distance from the source turned the mill. The well is now nearly dried up; but it could be easily renewed.

Rath na Scanaid (the 'rath of the synods': pron. Rath-na-Shanny), now popularly called "the King's Chair," has been partly encroached upon by the wall of the modern church: the two ramparts that surrounded it are still well-marked features. Within the large enclosure are two mounds, 106 and 33 feet in diameter respectively. Three Christian synods are recorded as having been held here, from which it had its name. Near the Rath of the Synods, and within the enclosure of the modern church, stood *Adamnan's Cross*, of which the shaft still remains, with a human figure rudely sculptured in relief on it.

On the northern slope of the hill are the remains of the Banqueting-Hall, the only structure in Tara not round or oval. It consists of two parallel mounds, the remnants of the side walls of the old Hall, which, as it now stands, is 759 feet long by 46 feet wide; but it was originally both longer and broader. It is described in the old documents as having twelve (or fourteen) doors: and this description is fully corroborated by the present appearance of the ruin, in which six door-openings are clearly marked in each side wall. Probably there was also a door at each end: but all traces of these are gone.

The whole site of the Hall was occupied by a great timber building, 45 feet high or more, ornamented, carved, and painted in colours. Within this the Féis or Convention of Tara held its meetings, which will be found described in chap. xxv., sect. 1, farther on. Here also were held the banquets from which the Hall was named *Tech Midchuarta* [Meecoorta], the 'mead-circling house'; and there was an elaborate subdivision of the inner space, with the compartments railed or partitioned off, to accommodate the guests according to rank and dignity. For, as will be seen in next chapter, they were very particular in seating the great company in the exact order of dignity and priority. From this Hall, moreover, the banqueting-halls of other great houses commonly received the name of *Tech Midchuarta*.

Rath Caelchon was so called from a Munster chief named Caelchon, who was contemporary with Cormac mac Art, third century. He died in Tara, and was interred in a *leacht* or carn, beside which was raised the rath in commemoration of him. The rath is 220 feet in diameter; and the very carn of stones heaped over the grave still remains on the north-east margin of the rath.

Rath Gráinnĕ is a high, well-marked rath, 258 feet in diameter. It received its name from the lady Gráinnĕ [Graunya: 2 syll.], daughter of King Cormac mac Art, and betrothed wife of Finn mac Cumail. She eloped with Dermot O'Dyna, and the whole episode is told in detail in the historic romance called "The Pursuit of Dermot and Gráinne"* This mound, and also the smaller mound beside it on the south called the *Fothad* [Foha] *of Rath Gráinne*, are now much hidden by trees.

A little north-west of the north end of the Banqueting-Hall, and occupying the space north of Rath Grainne and Rath Caelchon, was the *sheskin* or marsh of Tara, which was drained and dried up only a few years before Petrie's time: but the well which supplied it, Tober Finn (Finn's well), still remains.

Rath Laegaire [Rath Laery], situated south of Rath Rígh, was so called from Laegaire, king of Ireland in St. Patrick's time, by whom, no doubt, it was erected. It is about 300 feet in diameter, and was surrounded by two great rings or ramparts, of which one is still very well marked, and the other can be partially traced. Laegaire was buried in the south-east rampart of this rath, fully armed and standing up in the grave, with his face towards the south as if fighting against his enemies, the Leinster men. (See chap. xxvii., sect. 3, farther on.)

West of Rath Rígh was the well called Laegh [Lay], a name signifying 'calf': it is now dried up, though the ground still remains moist. In this well, according to the seventh-century Annotations of Tirechan,

---

* This fine story will be found in Joyce's Old Celtic Romances.

St. Patrick baptised his first convert at Tara, Erc the son of Dego, who afterwards became bishop of Slane, and who is commemorated in the little hermitage still to be seen beside the Boyne (p. 137, above).

The five main *sliges* [slees], or roads, leading from Tara in five different directions through Ireland, will be found described in chap. xxiv., sect. 1. Of these portions of three are still traceable on the hill. The modern road traverses and covers for some distance the sites of two of them, *Slige Dala* and *Slige Midluachra*, as seen on the plan: *Slige Asail* still remains, and is sometimes turned to use.

In one of the ancient poetical accounts quoted by Petrie, it is stated that the houses of the general body of people who lived near Tara were scattered on the slope and over the plain east of the hill.

In connexion with Tara, two other great circular forts ought to be mentioned. A mile south of Rath Righ lies *Rath Maive*, which is very large—673 feet in diameter; it forms a striking object as seen from the hill, and is well worth examining. It was erected, according to one account, by Queen Maive (not Queen Maive of Croghan), wife of Art the solitary, the father of King Cormac mac Art, which would fix the period of its erection as the beginning of the third century. The other fort is *Rathmiles*, 300 feet in diameter, lying one mile north of the Banqueting-Hall: but nothing is known of its history.

After the abandonment of Tara, the kings of Ireland took up their abode where they pleased, each commonly in one of his other residences, within his own province or immediate territory. One of these seats was **Dun-na-Sciath** (the 'Fort of the Shields': pron. Doon-na-Skee), of which the circular fort still remains on the western shore of Lough Ennell in County Westmeath. Another was at Rath, near the western shore of Lough Lene in Westmeath, two miles from the present town of Castlepollard. This residence was occupied for a time by the Danish tyrant Turgesius, so that the fort, which is one of the finest in the country, is now known as **Dun-Torgeis** or Turgesius' fort; while the Old Irish name has been lost.

It has been already stated (p. 15) that Tuathal the Legitimate, king of Ireland in the second century, built four palaces at **Tara, Tailltenn, Ushnagh**, and **Tlachtga**. The fort of Tlachtga still remains on the summit of the Hill of Ward near the village of Athboy in Meath. There were royal residences also at Dunseverick in Antrim, the ancient **Dun-Sobairce**; at **Rathbeagh** on the Nore, where the rath is still to be seen; at **Dun-Aenguis** on Great Aran Island; and on the site of the present Baily Lighthouse at Howth, where several of the defensive fosses of the old palace-fort of **Dun-Criffan** can still be traced.

Emain.—Next to Tara in celebrity was the palace of Emain or Emain-Macha, or, as its name is Latinised, Emania. It was for 600 years the residence of the kings of Ulster, and attained its greatest glory in the first century of the Christian era, during the reign of Concobar (or Conor) mac Nessa, king of Ulster. It was the centre round which clustered the romantic tales of the Red Branch Knights. The most ancient written

Irish traditions assign the foundation of this palace to Macha of the Golden Hair, wife of *Cimbaeth* [Kimbay], king of Ireland three or four centuries before the Christian era. From that period it continued to be the residence of the Ulster kings till A.D. 335, when it was burned and destroyed by three princes—brothers—commonly known as the Three Collas—after which it was abandoned to ruin. The imposing remains of this palace, consisting of a great mound surrounded by an immense circular rampart and fosse half obliterated, the whole structure covering about eleven English acres, lie two miles west of Armagh. Nay, the ruin retains to this day the old name "Emain" slightly disguised; for it is familiarly called "The Navan Fort or Ring," in which "Navan" correctly represents the sound '*n-Emain*, i.e. the original name with the Irish article '*n* prefixed.

When the Red Branch Knights came to the palace each summer to be exercised in feats of arms, they were lodged in a great house near Emain, called the *Craobh-Ruadh* [Creeveroe], commonly Englished the 'Red Branch,' from which the whole body took their name. The name of this house is also preserved: for "Creeveroe" is still the name of a townland near the Navan fort. So far as we can judge from old tales, the Creeveroe seems to have been altogether built of wood, with no earthen rampart round it, which explains why the present townland of Creeveroe contains no large fort like that of Emain.

Ailech or the **Grianan of Ailech.**—Another Ulster palace, quite as important as Emain, was Ailech, the ruins of which are situated in County Donegal, on the summit of a hill 800 feet high, five miles north-west from Derry, commanding a magnificent view of Lough Foyle and Lough Swilly with the surrounding country. It is a circular stone cashel of dry masonry, 77 feet in internal diameter, the wall about 13 feet thick at the base, and on the outside sloping gradually inwards. This central citadel was surrounded at wide intervals by five concentric ramparts, three of which may still be traced, the whole area originally including many acres. According to the old tradition it was founded by the Dedannans, and continued to be a royal residence to the time of its destruction, sometimes of the king of Ulster, and sometimes of the king of Ireland. After the fourth century it was the recognised residence of the northern Hy Neill kings, down to the year 1101, when it was destroyed by the Munster king Murkertagh, in retaliation for the destruction of Kincora by the Ulstermen thirteen years before. After this it was abandoned. For nearly eight centuries it continued in a state of ruin, the wall being almost levelled; but it has lately been rebuilt by Dr. Bernard, of Derry, a man of taste and culture, who, as far as he could, restored it to its original shape. The wall is now about 17 feet high. It still retains—has all along retained—its ancient name, in the form of Greenan-Ely, where *Ely* correctly represents the sound of *Ailigh*, the genitive of *Ailech*.

Cruachan.—The chief palace of the kings of Connaught was *Cruachan* (or, as it is now called, Croghan) from times beyond the reach of history down to the seventh century. It figures in various parts of this book, and is chiefly celebrated as being the residence of Ailill and Maive, king and queen of the province, in the first century of the Christian era. Here they held their court, which is described in the Tales of the Red Branch Knights in a strain of exaggerated magnificence: and from this the warlike queen set forth with her army to ravage Ulster and bring away the great brown bull which was the main object of the expedition.

The remains, which are situated three miles northwest from the village of Tulsk in Roscommon, are not imposing: for the main features have been effaced by cultivation. The principal rath, on which stood the timber palace and the subordinate houses, is merely a flat, green, circular moat about an English acre in extent, elevated considerably above the surrounding land, with hardly a trace of the enclosing circumvallation. There are many other forts all around, so that, in the words of O'Donovan, the whole site may be said to be "the ruins of a town of raths, having the large rath called Rathcroghan placed in the centre": but they are scattered much more widely and at greater distances than those at Tara. Besides the homestead forts there are also, in the surrounding plain, numerous other antiquarian remains, indicating a once busy centre of royalty and active life—cromlechs, caves, pillarstones, and mounds, including the cemetery of Relig-na-ree (about half a mile south of the main rath), which will be described in chapter xxvii.

Ailenn or **Ailend**, now Knockaulin. The most important residences of the kings of Leinster were Ailenn, Dinnrigh, Naas, Liamhain [Leevan], and

Belach-Chonglais or Baltinglass, in all of which the raths still remain. Ailenn is a round hill, now commonly called Knockaulin (*aulin* representing 'Ailenn'), near Kilcullen in Kildare, rising 600 feet over sea-level, and 200 or 300 feet over the Curragh of Kildare which lies adjacent, and over all the plain around. The whole summit of the hill is enclosed by a huge oval embankment, 514 by 440 yards, enclosing an area of 37 statute acres, one of the largest forts, if not the very largest, in Ireland. Within this great enclosure stood the spacious ornamental wooden houses in which, as we learn from our records, the Leinster kings often resided.

Fig. 100.

Dinnree in 1845. (From Mrs Hall's Ireland)

Dinnrigh.—One of the most noted, and probably the oldest, of the Leinster palaces was *Dinnrigh* [Dinnree: the '*dinn* or fortress of kings']. Besides being very often mentioned in the records, it was the scene of a tragedy which is related in detail in the historical story called "The Destruction of Dinnree," contained in the Book of Leinster, which has been edited and translated by Dr. Whitley Stokes. Some two centuries and a half before the Christian era, Cobhthach [Coffa] the Slender murdered the king of Ireland—his own brother—and also the king's son Ailill, and usurped the throne. But Ailill's son, Lavra the Mariner, who fled to the Continent, returned after some years with a party of Gauls, and landed at Wexford, where he was joined by large contingents of the men of Leinster and Munster, who hated the usurper. Marching quickly and silently by night to Dinnree, where the king then happened to be holding court, he surrounded the palace, and, setting fire to the houses while the company were engaged in feasting, he burned all—palace, king, and courtiers—to ashes. The fine old fort still exists in good preservation. It is situated on a high bank over the River Barrow on the west side, half a mile south of Leighlinbridge, and is now commonly known by the name of "Ballyknockan Moat." The moat or mound—figured in the illustration, last page—is 237 feet in diameter at the base; the circular plateau on the top, on which stood the timber houses, is 135 feet in diameter, and 69 over the River Barrow.

Naas.—In old times Naas was a place of great celebrity, where the Leinster tribes held some of their periodical *aenachs* or fair-meetings, from which it got the name of *Nás-Laigen* [Naas-Lyen], *i.e.* the 'assembly-place of Leinster,' corresponding exactly with the name of Nenagh in Tipperary. There were here two royal houses, the forts of which still remain. One is an ordinary circular, flat rath, now called the South Moat, situated near the southern end of the town. The other, called the North Moat, is a high, flat-topped mound on which the citadel once stood, but which is now occupied by an ugly modern house. Naas continued to be a residence of the Leinster kings till the tenth century.

Fig. 101.

North Moat, Naas. remains of ancient palace House on top modern.
(From a drawing by the author, 1857.)

Belach Chonglais.—Another of the Leinster palaces was at Baltinglass in the county Wicklow, whose old name was *Belach-Chonglais* (Cuglas's road).

powerful king who defeated and slew Aed mac Ainmirech, king of Ireland, in the Battle of Dunbolg, A.D. 598. On the hill rising over the town are two great raths or forts, the remains of the old residences. One, now called Rathcoran, is on the very summit, 1256 feet over sea-level. It is an oval, about a quarter of a mile in its longer diameter, having two ramparts, and containing about twenty-five statute acres. The other and smaller fort, now called Rathnagree, is on the northern slope of the hill: it has also two ramparts, and covers about seven acres.

Liamhain.—The name of *Liamhain* or *Dun-Liamhna* [Dun-lavna] is still preserved in that of Dunlavin, a small village in the county Wicklow. The mound of this residence is still to be seen a mile south of the village: but it has lost its old name and is now called "Tornant Moat." (Tornant, 'nettle-mound': ominous of ruin.)

FIG. 102.

Carbury Castle, County Kildare   (From a photograph.)

Side-Nechtain.—The hill of Carbury in Kildare has a dim legendary history as a royal residence. It was anciently called *Side-Nechtain* [Shee-Nechtan], *i.e.* 'Nechtan's Shee or fairy-hill': showing that it was the site of one of those elf-mounds described at p. 106, *supra*. This Nechtan, according to the old documents, was king of Leinster, and also a poet. But the place contained a residence of a less shadowy kind: for on the north-west slope there are still two remarkable and very perfect military raths or forts. Near the base of the hill is Trinity Well, the source of the Boyne, the enchanted well that in old time burst up and overwhelmed Boand, Nechtan's queen. But in subsequent times the Christian missionaries—as in case of many another well (p. 164, above)—removed its heathenish character and associations, and dedicated it to the Holy Trinity. The Anglo-Norman De Berminghams, who took possession of the district, having an eye to something more substantial than Dedannan fairy palaces, took advantage of the selection of their immediate Milesian predecessors and built a splendid castle not far from the old Irish fortresses, near the summit, the ruins of which are now conspicuous for leagues round the hill.

Cashel was one of the most renowned seats of the North Munster kings, though not the oldest as a royal residence. Its chief feature is the well-known lofty isolated Rock overlooking the surrounding plain—the magnificent Golden Vale, as it is called, from its fertility. Just before the arrival of St. Patrick, Corc, king of Munster, took possession of the whole place, and on the summit of the rock built a stronghold, which then became the chief residence of the Munster kings, and continued so till the beginning of the twelfth century. In 1101

King Murkertagh O'Brien dedicated the whole place to the church, and handed it over to the ecclesiastical authorities, since which time it figures chiefly in ecclesiastical history. Then began to be erected those splendid buildings which remain to this day; so that the "Rock of Cashel" is now well known as containing the most imposing group of ecclesiastical ruins in the United Kingdom.

FIG. 103.

Rock of Cashel (top of Round Tower appears to the right).
(From Brewer's Beauties of Ireland Drawn by Petrie.)

Grianan Lachtna.—One of the ancestral residences of the Dalcassian kings of Thomond or North Munster was Greenan-Lachtna, the fine old fort of which is still to be seen occupying a noble site on the south slope of Craglea in Clare, over the western shore of Lough Derg, two miles north of Killaloe.

Kincora.—But when Brian Boru ascended the throne, he came to live at Kincora, where the remains of the palace have all disappeared, inasmuch as the site is now occupied by the town of Killaloe. The O'Briens, as kings of Thomond, continued to reside at Kincora for two centuries after the Battle of Clontarf: but about 1214 they removed their residence to **Clonroad** near Ennis. One of the outlying forts, a very fine one, still remains, however, beside the Shannon, a mile north of Killaloe, and is now known by the name of Beal Boru.

Fig. 104.

Caher Castle: on the site of the old palace. (From Mrs. Hall's Ireland.)

Caher.—Another of the Munster palaces, was on a little rocky island in the river Suir at the town of

Caher in Tipperary. It was originally called *Duniasgach* [eesga], the 'fish-abounding dun,' from the earthen *dun* that constituted the original fortress-palace. This was succeeded by a circular stone caher, which gave the place its present name. The castle was built by the Anglo-Normans on the site of the caher.

Still another of these Munster palaces was **Dungcláire** [Doonglara], the fort of which is still in good preservation, standing at the northern base of the mountain of Slievereagh near Kilfinnane, two miles nearly north-west from Ballylanders, on the left of the road as you go from this village to Knocklong. It covers about four statute acres, and is now called Doonglara, or more often Lis-Doonglara.

Brugh-righ.—Bruree in the county Limerick, situated beside the river Maigue, was from remote times one of the seats of the kings of South Munster, as its Irish name *Brugh-righ* indicates, signifying the 'House of Kings.' The illustrious King Ailill Olom, ancestor of many of the chief Munster families, lived there in the second century: and it continued to be occupied by the Munster kings till long after the Anglo-Norman Invasion. The Anglo-Norman chiefs also adopted it as a place of residence, as they did many others of the old Irish kingly seats: and the ruins of two of their fine castles remain. There are still to be seen, along the river, several of the old circular forts, the most interesting of which is the one now universally known in the neighbourhood by the name of Lissoleem, inasmuch as it preserves the very name of

King Ailill Olom, whose timber house was situated within its enclosure. It is situated on the western bank of the river, a mile below the village, in the townland of Lower Lotteragh, in the angle formed by the Maigue and a little stream joining it from the west. It is a circular fort with three ramparts, having the reputation—like most other raths—of being haunted by fairies: and, as it is very lonely and much overgrown with bushes, it is as fit a home for fairies as could well be imagined.

This king's name, Ailill Olom, signifies 'Ailill Bare-Ear,' so called because one of his ears was cut off in a struggle. *Olom* is accented on the second syllable, and is compounded of *o*, 'an ear,' and *lom*, 'bare': in the name "Ailill Olom" it is in the nominative case: "Ailill Bare-Ear" (not "of the Bare-Ear"): like the English names William Longsword, Richard Strongbow. But when placed after "Lis," it takes—as it should take —the genitive form, "Oluim": and "*Lis-Oluim*," which is exactly represented in sound by "Lissoleem," signifies 'Olom's *lis* or residence.' Many examples of the preservation of very old personal and other names in our existing topographical nomenclature are given in my "Irish Names of Places"; and this case of Lissoleem—which has not been noticed before —is fully as interesting as any of them.

Temair-Luachra.—In the time of the Red Branch Knights and of the Munster Degads (p. 42, above), and from immemorial ages previously, the chief royal residence of South Munster was Teamair- or Tara-Luachra, the fort of which in all probability still exists, though it has not been identified. Mr. W.

M. Hennessy, in his Introduction to the Mesca Ulad, has brought together the several notices bearing on its position. It was well known in the time of Elizabeth; and anyone acquainted with the country, who would take the trouble to walk over the exact locality indicated, and make inquiry among the old people, would be able, as I believe, to light on and identify the very fort.

Knockgraffon.—Another noted Munster palace was *Cnoc-Rafonn*, now called Knockgraffon, three miles north of Caher in Tipperary, where the great mound, 60 or 70 feet high, still remains, with the ruins of an English castle beside it. Here resided, in the third century, Fiacha Muillethan [Feeha-Mullehan], king of Munster, who, when the great King Cormac mac Art invaded Munster in an attempt to levy tribute, defeated him at Knocklong and routed his army: an event which forms the subject of the historical tale called "The Siege of Knocklong."

The fort is now as noted for fairies as it was in times of old for royalty: and one of the best-known modern fairy stories in connexion with it will be found in Crofton Croker's "Fairy Legends of Ireland" namely, "The Legend of Knockgrafton." This Irish legend has been turned into English verse, but with much interpolation, by Thomas Parnell in his ballad, "A Fairy Tale"

Composed from the Book of Kells.

CHAPTER XVII.

FOOD, FUEL, AND LIGHT: PUBLIC HOSTELS.

SECTION 1. *Meals in General.*

DINNER, the principal meal of the day, was called in Irish, *prainn*, probably a loan-word from the Latin *prandium*. Hence the refectory of a monastery was called *praintech*, literally 'dinner-house.' Dinner was taken late in the evening both among the laity and in monasteries. It was usual to have a light meal between breakfast and dinner, corresponding with the modern luncheon. It was called *etrud*, meaning 'middle-meal.' There was a custom among the laity, as well as in the monastic communities, to have better food on Sundays and church festivals than on other days.

Among the higher classes great care was taken to seat family and guests at table in the order of rank: any departure from the established usage was sure to be resented by the person who was put lower than he should be; and sometimes resulted in serious quarrels or wars.

The king was always attended at banquets by his

subordinate kings, and by other lords and chiefs. Those on the immediate right and left of the king had to sit at a respectful distance. At the feasts of Tara, Tailltenn, and Ushnagh, it was the privilege of the king of Oriell to sit next the king of Ireland, but he sat at such a distance that his sword just reached the high king's hand: and to him also belonged the honour of presenting every third drinking-horn brought to the king. According to Kineth O'Hartigan, while King Cormac mac Art sat at dinner, fifty military guards remained standing beside him.

The banquet-hall of Tara was a long building, with tables arranged along both side-walls. Immediately over the tables were a number of hooks in the wall at regular intervals to hang the shields on. One side of the hall was more dignified than the other; and the tables here were for the lords of territories: those at the other side were for the military captains. Just before the beginning of the feast all persons left the hall except three·—A *Shanachie* or historian: a marshal to regulate the order: and a trumpeter whose duty it was to sound his trumpet just three times. The king and his subordinate kings having first taken their places at the head of the table, the professional ollaves sat down next them. Then the trumpeter blew the first blast, at which the shield-bearers of the lords of territories (for every chief and king had his shield-bearer or squire) came round the door and gave their masters' shields to the marshal, who, under the direction of the Shanachie, hung them on the hooks according to ranks, from the highest to the lowest: and at the second blast the shields of the military commanders were disposed of in like manner. At the third blast the guests all walked in leisurely, each taking his seat under his own shield (which was marked with his special cognisance: see p. 60, *supra*). In this manner all unseemly disputes or jostling for places were avoided. No man sat opposite another, as only one side of each row of tables was occupied, namely, the side next the wall. Moreover, in order to avoid crowding, the shields were hung at such a distance, that when the guests were seated " no man of them would touch another." Similar arrangements were adopted at the banquets of all other royal residences. This rigid adherence to order of priority at table continued in Ireland and Scotland down to a recent period, as Scott often mentions in his novels; and it continues still in a modified and less strict form everywhere.

At all state banquets particular joints were reserved for certain chiefs, officials, and professional men, according to rank. Here is the statement of the commentator on the Senchus Mór:—"A thigh [*laarg*] for a king and a poet: a chine [*croichet*] for a literary sage: a leg [*colptha*] for a young lord: heads for charioteers: a haunch [*les*] for queens." A similar custom existed among the ancient Gauls and also among the Greeks. A remnant of this old custom lingered on in Scotland and Ireland down to a period within our own memory.

In the time of the Red Branch Knights, it was the custom to assign the choicest joint or animal of the whole banquet to the hero who was acknowledged by general consent to have performed the bravest and greatest exploit. This piece was called *curath-mir*, i.e. ' the hero's morsel or share' (*mir*). There were often keen contentions among the Red Branch heroes, and sometimes fights with bloodshed, for this coveted joint or piece: and some of the best stories of the Táin hinge on contests of this kind. This usage, which prevailed among the continental Celts in general, and which also existed among the Greeks, continued in Ireland to comparatively late times.

Tables were, as we have seen, used at the great feasts. But at ordinary meals, high tables, such as we have now, do not seem to have been in general use. There were small low tables, such as that in

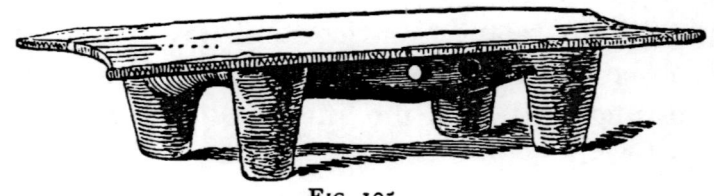

FIG. 105.

Small Table: 28 inches long, 16 inches broad, and 5 inches high: found in a bog, 5 feet under the surface. (From Wilde's Catalogue.)

the illustration, each used no doubt for two or more persons, who sat or reclined on low couches or seats of some kind at meals. Often there was a little table laid beside each person, on which his food was placed—the meat on a platter. According to Giraldus, his countrymen, the Welsh, had no tables at all at their meals: and very probably this was the case in the general run of the houses of the Irish peasantry.

Forks are a late invention: of old the fingers were used at eating. In Ireland, as in England and other countries in those times, each person held his knife in the right hand, and used the fingers of the left instead of a fork. Sometimes—as at banquets, and among very high-class people—the carvers cut off great pieces from the joint, which they brought round and put on the platters. But more commonly each person went to the joint, and using his left-hand fingers to catch hold, cut off a piece for himself and brought it to his own platter. Even so late as the sixteenth century this was the custom in England, according to Roberts, who says that dinner was served without knives or forks, but each had his own clasp-knife, and going to the dish, cut off a piece for himself: and he gives this illustrative verse by Alexander Barclay (sixteenth century):—

> " If the dish be pleasant, either flesche or fische,
> Ten hands at once swarm in the dishe."

When dinner was over—says Roberts, speaking of the English—they removed the grease from their knives by plunging the blade several times into the clay floor. The Greeks and Romans had no forks at meals: they used the fingers only, and were supplied with water to wash their hands after eating.

As early as the eighth or ninth century the Irish of the higher classes used napkins at table, for which they had a native word, *lámbrat*, i.e. 'hand-napkin' (*lám*, ' hand': *brat*, ' a cloth'). This custom is frequently mentioned in the Irish MSS. of those ages, quoted by Zeuss. I suppose the chief use they made of the napkin was to wipe the left-hand fingers; which was badly needed. They sometimes used dried hides as tablecloths. It was the custom, both in monastic communities and in secular life, to take off the shoes or sandals when sitting down to dinner; which was generally done by an attendant. Tho

Romans we know had the same custom; and we may infer that the Irish, like them, reclined during meals on couches on which the feet also rested.

2. *Drink*.

In old times people were quite as fond of intoxicating drinks at dinners and banquets as they are now: and we are constantly told in the tales that when the cups went round, the company became exhilarated and right merry. They sometimes drank more than was good for them too: yet drunkenness was looked upon as reprehensible. At their feasts they often accompanied their carousing with music and singing. Maildune and his men, visiting a certain island, saw the people feasting and drinking, and " heard their ale-music."

Besides plain water and milk, the chief drinks were ale, mead or metheglin, and wine. Giraldus Cambrensis remarks that Ireland never had vineyards: but that there was plenty of wine supplied by foreign commerce; and he mentions Poitou in France especially as supplying vast quantities in exchange for hides. This account is corroborated by the native records, from which we learn that wine was imported in very early ages, and it is frequently mentioned as an accompaniment at banquets.

Of all the intoxicating drinks ale was the most general, not only in Ireland, but among all the peoples of northern Europe: and the more intoxicating it was the more esteemed. Irish ale was well known from the earliest period, even on the Continent, as we see from the statement of Dioscorides in the first century: —" The Britons and the Hiberi or Irish, instead of wine, use a liquor called *courmi* or *curmi*, m barley." This author caught up correctly the a

FIG. 106.

Bronze Strainer, found in a crannoge. Cup shaped, 4½ inches wide and 1½ inch deep. Observe the holes form curve-patterns. (From the Journ. Roy. Soc. Antiqq. Irel.)

Irish name for ale, which was *cuirm* or *coirm*. present word for ale is *linn* or *leann*:- and altho this, too, was one of the words for ale in old time was often used to denote drink in general. The manufacture of ale was understood everywhere; and the whole process is given in detail in the Senchus Mór, and in the commentaries and glosses on it. The grain chiefly used was barley; and what grew on rich land was most valued for the purpose: but it was also often made from rye, as well as from wheat and oats. The corn, of whatever kind, was first converted into malt: Irish *brac* or *braich*; by steeping in water and afterwards drying. The dried malt kept for any length of time, and was often given in payment of rent or tribute.

When the ale was to be prepared, the ground malt was made into mash with water, which was fermented, boiled, strained, &c., till the process was finished. Ale was often made in private houses for family use: for everywhere among the people there were amateur experts who understood the process. But there were houses also set apart for this purpose, where a professional brewer carried on the business. When people felt indisposed or out of sorts, it was usual to give them a draught of ale to refresh or revive them, as we now give a cup of tea or a glass of wine.

Mead or metheglin (Irish *mid*, pron. mee) was made chiefly from honey: it was a drink in much request, and was considered a delicacy, so that a visitor on arrival was often treated to a cup of mead. It was slightly intoxicating. Mead continued to be made in many parts of Ireland till very recently.

Whiskey is a comparatively modern innovation. The first notice of it in the Irish annals appears to be at A.D. 1405, where there is the ominous record that

Richard Mac Rannal, chief of Muinter Eolais, died from an overdose of *uisge beatha* [iskĕ-baha] or whiskey.

3. *Cooking.*

In great houses there were professional cooks, who, while engaged in their work, wore a linen apron round them from the hips down, and a flat linen cap on the head; but among ordinary families the women did the cooking.

Meat and fish were cooked by roasting, boiling, or broiling. A spit (*bir*)—made of iron—was an article in general use, and was regarded as an important household implement. But the spits commonly used in roasting, as well as the skewers for trussing up the joint, were pointed hazel-rods, peeled and made smooth and white. Meat, and even fish, while roasting, were often basted with honey or with a mixture of honey and salt. Meat and fish were often broiled on a gridiron, or something in the nature of a gridiron.

When bodies of men marched through the country, either during war or on hunting excursions, they cooked their meat in a large way. Keating and other writers give the following description of how the Fena of Erin cooked—a plan which is often referred to in the ancient tales, and which was no doubt generally followed, not only by the Fena but by all large parties camping out. The attendants roasted one part on hazel spits before immense fires of wood, and baked the rest on hot stones in a pit dug in the earth. The stones were heated in the fires. At the bottom of the pit the men placed a layer of these hot stones:

then a layer of meat-joints wrapped in sedge or in hay or straw ropes to keep them from being burned: next another layer of hot stones: down on that more meat: and so on till the whole was disposed of, when it was covered up; and in this manner it was effectively cooked. The remains of many of these cooking-pits are still to be seen in various parts of the country, and are easily recognised by the charred wood and blackened stones; and sometimes the very pits are to be seen. To this day they are called by an Irish name signifying 'the cooking places of the Fena."

FIG. 107.

Ancient Bronze Caldron · 12 inches deep · now in National Museum formed of separate pieces, beautifully riveted, the head of each rivet forming a conical stud or button, like the rivets of the gold gorgets and of some of the bronze trumpets. (From Wilde's Catalogue.)

In the house of every chief and of every brewy there was at least one bronze caldron for boiling meat. Its usual name was *coire* or *caire* [2 syll.] · but it was sometimes called *aighean*, or more correctly, *adhan* [ey-an], which is now its usual name in Scotland. It was highly valued as a most important article in the household; and it was looked upon as the special property of the chief or head of the house—much in the same way as his sword and shield. Everywhere we meet with passages reminding us of the great value set on these caldrons. One of them was regarded as a fit present for a king. The caldron of a chief or of a brewy was supposed to be kept in continual use, so that food might be always ready for guests whenever they happened to arrive. Many bronze caldrons have been found from time to time, and are now preserved in the National Museum, Dublin — several of beautiful workmanship, like those in figs. 107, 108. Caldrons appear to have been always made

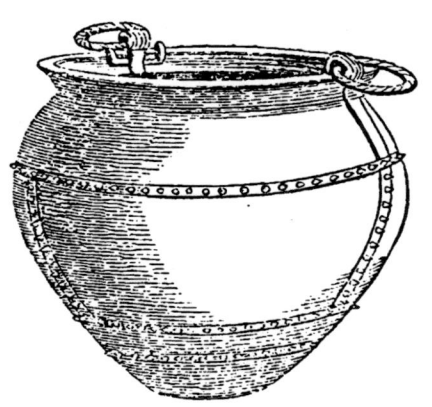

FIG. 108.

Ancient Irish bronze caldron, 12½ inches deep, formed of plates beautifully riveted together. Shows marks and signs of long use over a fire. (From Wilde's Catalogue.)

of brass or bronze—most often the latter. Those hitherto found are all of that material. Caldrons were manufactured at home: but some at least, and those among the most valuable, were imported.

Accompanying every caldron was an *ael* or flesh-fork, for lifting out pieces of meat. On one occasion, soon before the Battle of Dunbolg, A.D. 598, St. Maidoc of Ferns brought to Branduff, king of Leinster, a present of a three-pronged fleshfork (*ael-trébend*), a caldron, a shield, and a sword: an odd combination, quite characteristic of the times. But in early ages kitchen utensils were everywhere regarded as important. The inventory of the jewels of the English King Edward III. gives a list of this king's frying-pans, gridirons, spits, &c. There is a curious provision in the Brehon Law that if any accident occurred to a bystander by the lifting of the joint out of the boiling caldron, the attendant was liable for damages unless he gave the warning· "Take care : here goes the *ael* into the caldron !"

4. *Flesh-meat and its accompaniments.*

The flesh of wild and domestic animals, boiled or roast or broiled, much as at the present day, formed one of the staple food-materials in old times in Ireland as in other countries.

Pork (*muicc-fheóil,* i.e. 'pig-flesh,' pron. *muckole*) was a favourite among all classes, as it was among the Greeks and Romans. Pork was also made into bacon as at present by being salted and hung up on the wall over the fire. Old bacon was considered good for chest disease.

Beef, or, as it was called in Irish, *mairt-fheóil* (i.e. 'ox-flesh': pron. *morthole*), was much in use. The animal seems to have been generally killed with a spear. The flesh of fattened calves, either boiled or roast, was considered a dainty food. Mutton—in Irish *caer-fheóil* or *muilt-fheóil* ('sheep-flesh,' 'wether-flesh': pron. *kairole* and *multhole*)—was perhaps in more request than beef.

Venison was in great favour: everywhere in the tales we read of hunters chasing deer and feasting on the flesh. It was sometimes called *fiadh-fheóil*, 'deer-flesh' [pron. *fee-ole*]: and also *milradh* [milra]. Goats were quite as common in old times as now, and their flesh was as much used, as well as their milk.

Some of the animals mentioned in the records as supplying food are no longer used for this purpose: such, for instance, as badgers: but badgers were eaten in Ireland until very lately. Seals were valued chiefly for their skins, and partly also for their flesh as food, but they are now seldom eaten. Corned meat was everywhere in use. A number of whole pigs salted commonly formed part of the tribute paid to a superior king or chief.

Besides the main joints boiled or roast, we find mention of various preparations of the flesh of animals, mixed up with many ingredients. A pottage or hash formed of meat chopped up small, mixed with vegetables, was called *craibechan* [craiv'a-han]. We find it stated in an Irish document that Esau sold his birthright to Jacob for a *craibechan*. In the "Vision of Mac Conglinne" is mentioned as a dainty food "sprouty *craibechan* with purple-berries": "sprouty," *i.e.* mixed with vegetable sprouts. The "purple-berries" were probably the quicken-berries or rowan-berries added to give a flavour. There are several other terms used to designate meat-preparations of this kind, each of which, no doubt, pointed to some special mode of preparation: but the distinction—if it ever existed—is now lost. Simple broth or meat-juice without any mixture of minced-meat was a favourite with the Irish, and also among the Scottish Highlanders.

Sausages or puddings were a favourite dish, made much the same as at the present day, by filling the intestines of a pig, cow, or sheep with minced-meat and blood. They were known by the terms *indrechtan* and *maróc*. Puddings and sausages got a boil after making, so as to half cook them, and were then put aside till wanted: when about to be brought to table they were fried and served hot as at the present day.

In the "Vision of Mac Conglinne" is mentioned, as good food, the *dressan* of an old wether. The word is a diminutive of *dress* or *driss*, which is familiarly applied to things of a branchy nature, such as a bramble or the smaller intestines: and as applied to an article of food is still in use in Cork in the form of *drisheen*, which has the Irish diminutive *in* instead of the *án* of Mac Conglinne. The name *drisheen* is now used in Cork as an English word, to denote a sort of pudding made of the narrow intestines of a sheep, filled with blood that has been cleared of the red colouring matter, and mixed with meal and some other ingredients. So far as I know, this viand and its name are peculiar to Cork, where *drisheen* is considered suitable for persons of weak or delicate digestion.

Lard (Irish *blonog*) was much used as an *annlann* or condiment, and entered into cooking in various forms. We also find mention of *olar*, 'rich gravy'; and of *inmar*, 'dripping,' both used as a condiment or relish.

Most of the birds used for food at the present day were eaten in old times: and frequent allusions to birds as food are found in ancient Irish writings.

Giraldus Cambrensis says that the Irish loathed the flesh of the heron; but that Henry II. induced those kings and chiefs he entertained in Dublin at Christmas, 1171, to taste it. They do not seem to have much relished it: for ever since that time the Irish people have let the herons alone. Eggs were extensively used: goose-eggs, if we are to judge from their frequent mention, were a favourite. In a legendary account of bishop Erc of Slane, we are told that he kept a flock of geese to lay eggs for him. At the banquet of Dun-nan-gedh, some of these eggs were on the table, cold; and Congal, going in to view the feast, ate a part of one. And when the company sat down, a goose-egg [cold] on a silver dish was placed before each chief. From all this we may infer that eggs were generally boiled hard and eaten cold.

All the fish used for food at the present day were eaten in Ireland in old times, so that there is no need to go into details. Only it may be remarked that salmon was then the favourite; and we meet with constant reference to it as superior to all other fish. The salmon of the "salmon-full Boyne," of Lough Neagh, and of the Barrow, were much prized. The subject of fishing will be treated of in chapter xxv., sect. 6.

Any viand eaten with the principal part of the meal as an accompaniment or condiment, or *kitchen*, as it is called in Ireland and Scotland—anything taken as a relish with more solid food—was designated *annlann*, equivalent to the Latin *obsonium*. The Brehon Laws specify the annlanns with much particularity:—butter, salt bacon, lard, salt, meat of any kind (when used in small quantities and not the principal part of the meal), honey, kale, onions, and other vegetables, &c.

Salt—Irish *sal, salann*—was used for domestic purposes much the same as at the present day. It was not so easily made or procured then as now, so that the supply was limited, and people kept it carefully, avoiding waste. In rich people's houses it was kept in small sacks. The Senchus Mór mentions salt as one of the important articles in the house of a brewy, on which the glossator remarks that it is " an article of necessity at all times, a thing which everyone desires." It was kept in lumps or in coarse grains; and at dinner each person was served with as much as he needed. In the sixteenth century in England—as we are told by Roberts—each guest at dinner was given a little lump of salt, which he ground into powder with the bottom of his glass or drinking-goblet: and something of the same plan may have been followed in Ireland. English salt was largely imported, and was considered the best.

In 1300, salt was exported from Ireland, as we know from the fact that it was one of the commodities sent to Scotland to supply the army of Edward I. The salt must have been manufactured either from sea-water, or from rock-salt taken from the earth, or more likely from both. For we know that there are plenty of salt deposits in Ulster: but of salt mines, or of the mode of preparing the salt, the ancient literature—so far as I know—contains no details.

5. *Milk and its products.*

There are several ancient Irish words for milk, three of which are *ass*, *loim*, and *melg*: this last evidently cognate with Latin *mulgeo* and with English *milk*. The most general word in modern use is *bainne* [bon-yă], which is also an ancient word. The milk chiefly used in ancient Ireland was that of cows; but goats' and sheep's milk was also in much request. Milk was used in a variety of ways, as at the present day. For drinking, the choice condition was as new milk (*lemnacht* or *lemlacht*): and cream was sometimes added as a luxury. But skimmed milk, *i.e.* milk slightly sour, and commonly thick, from which the cream had been skimmed off, was considered a good drink. This was called *draumce* and also *bláthach* [draumkĕ, blawhagh], which last word is the name used at the present day. Thick milk was improved by mixing new milk with it, as I have often seen done in our own day.

Fig. 109.

Ancient butter-print: 5½ inches in diameter: in the National Museum. (From Wilde's Catal.)

The people made butter (Irish *im* or *imm*) in the usual way, in a small churn. Butter of any kind was considered a superior sort of condiment. Salt butter, called *gruiten*, was regarded as very inferior to fresh butter. A lump of butter shaped according to fancy was called a *mescan*, which word is still in very general use even among the English-speaking people, who pronounce it *miscaun* or *miscan*.

In later times it was customary to sink butter deep down in bogs, closed up in casks or wrapped up in cloths, to give it a flavour, or, as some think, as a mode of preserving it. Among the food of the Irish, Dineley (A.D. 1675) mentions butter "mixed with store of a kind of garlick, and buried for some time in a bog to make a provision of an high taste for Lent." Sir William Petty also mentions butter made rancid by keeping in bogs; and other authorities to the same effect might be quoted. Whether this custom existed in ancient times I am unable to say; but at any rate its prevalence, even at this late period, is a sufficient explanation of the fact that butter is now very often found in vessels of various shapes and sizes, deeply embedded in bogs; sometimes in firkins not very different from those now in use. Several specimens of this "bog butter," as it is commonly called, are to be seen in the National Museum.

FIG. 110.

Firkin of Bog-butter 26 inches high made from a single piece of sallow In the National Museum (From Wilde's Catalogue)

Curds—called in Irish *gruth* [gruh]—formed one important article of diet. Milk was converted into curds and whey by calves' rennet: and the curd was made into cheese of various sorts, which was greatly valued as an article of food. Cheese was denoted by several different words, of which the most common were *caise* [cawsha], and *maethail* [maihil]: but this last word was often applied to dried curd. Cheese was made from curd as now, by pressing in a mould, from which it was turned out in firm shapes. Curds were much used in an intermediate stage, not quite turned into cheese, but sufficiently pressed to squeeze out all the whey, so as to form a mass moderately firm and capable of keeping for a long time. This soft material, half curd, half cheese, was often called *milsen*. Cheese pressed tightly in a mould, and turned out very hard, was called *tanag*. Masses of cheese have been found in bogs, of which some specimens may be seen in the National Museum.

Whey—Irish *medg* [maig]—was made use of; but it was considered a poor drink. New milk from a cow that had just calved, now called *beestings*, was in Old Irish called *nús*, a word still in use. This milk was not fit for drinking; but it was turned into curds and whey by merely heating, and in this form it was used as food. But more often the curd was made into thin pancakes. It was evidently valued—as it is at the present day—for old authorities say that one of the blessings brought on the country by Cormac mac Art's benign reign, was that the cows after calving had their udders full of *nús* or beestings.

6. *Corn and its preparations.*

It will be seen in chapter xix., sect. 2, of this book, that all the various kinds of grain cultivated at the present day were in use in ancient Ireland. Corn was ground and sifted into coarse and fine, *i.e.* into meal and flour, which were commonly kept in chests. The staple food of the great mass of the people was porridge or, as it is now called in Ireland, stirabout, made of meal (Irish *min*), generally oatmeal. It was eaten with honey, butter, or milk, as an *annlann* or condiment. The common Irish word for stirabout was, and still is, *leite*, gen. *leitenn* [letthĕ, letthen]; but in the Brehon Laws and elsewhere it is often called *gruss*. The Senchus Mór annotator, laying down the regulations for the food of children in fosterage, mentions three kinds of *leite* or stirabout: — of oatmeal, wheatmeal, and barleymeal: that made from oatmeal being the most general. Wheatmeal stirabout was considered the best: that of barleymeal was inferior to the others. For the rich classes, stirabout was often made on new milk: if sheep's milk, so much the better, as this was looked upon as a delicacy: it was eaten with honey, fres hbutter, or new milk. For the poorer classes stirabout was made on water or buttermilk, and eaten with sour milk or salt butter.

All the various kinds of meal and flour were baked into cakes or loaves of different shapes. The usual word for a cake was *bairgen*, now pronounced *borreen*: hence *borreen-brack*, 'speckled cake' (speckled with currants and raisins), eaten on November eve, now often written *barn-brack*. Flour was usually mixed with water to make dough: but bread made of flour and milk was also much in use. Honey was often kneaded up with cakes as a delicacy: and occasionally the roe of a salmon was similarly used. Wheaten bread was considered the best, as at present: barley-bread was poor. Yeast, or barm, or leaven was used both in baking and in brewing.

The several utensils used in making and baking bread are set forth in the Senchus Mór; and baking and the implements employed therein are always spoken of as specially pertaining to women. The woman had a *criathar* [crïher] or sieve for separating the fine part of the flour from the coarse, which was done on each particular occasion just before baking. Having made the flour into dough (Irish *taos*), she worked it into cakes on a *losat* [losset] or kneading-trough, a shallow wooden trough, such as we see used for making cakes at the present day.

7. *Honey.*

Before entering on the consideration of honey as food, it will be proper to make a few observations on the management of bees by the ancient Irish. From the earliest times Ireland was noted for its abundance of honey. Giraldus expresses the curious opinion that honey would be still more abundant all over Ireland if the bee-swarms were not checked by the bitter and poisonous yews with which the woods abounded.

The management of bees was universally understood; and every comfortable householder kept hives in his garden. Wild bees, too, swarmed everywhere —much more plentifully than at present, on account of the extent of woodland. Before cane-sugar came into general use—sixteenth century—the bee industry was considered so important that a special section of the Brehon Laws is devoted to it. The Irish name for a bee is *bech*: a swarm is called *saithe* [saeha]. The hive was known by various names, but the term now universally in use is *corcóg*. Hives stocked with bees were sometimes given as part of a tribute to a king.

The Brehon Law tract on "Bee-judgments," of which the printed Irish text occupies twenty pages, enters into much detail concerning the rights of the various parties concerned, to swarms, hives, nests, and honey: of which a few examples are given here. If a man found a swarm in the *faithche* [faha], or green surrounding and belonging to a house: one-fourth of the produce to the end of a year was due to the finder, the remaining three-fourths to the owner of the house. If he found them *in a tree* growing in a *faithche* or green: one-half produce for a year to the finder: the rest to the owner. If they were found in land which was not a green: one-third to the finder and two-thirds to the owner of the land. If found in waste land not belonging to an individual, but the common property of the tribe, bees and honey belonged to the finder, except one-ninth to the chief of the tribe. As the bees owned by an individual gathered their honey from the surrounding district, the owners of the four adjacent farms were entitled to a certain small proportion of the honey: and after the third year each was entitled to a swarm. If bees belonging to one man swarmed on the land of another, the produce was divided in certain proportions between the two. It is mentioned in "Bee-judgments" that a sheet was sometimes spread out that a swarm might alight and rest on it: as is often done now. At the time of gathering the honey the bees were smothered.

A mixture of milk and honey was sometimes drunk; a mixture of lard and honey was usual as a condiment. Honey was sometimes brought to table pure, and sometimes in the comb. Often at meals each person had placed before him on the table a little dish, sometimes of silver, filled with honey; and each morsel whether of meat, fish, or bread was dipped into it before being conveyed to the mouth. Stirabout was very generally eaten in the same way with honey as a delicacy. Honey was used to baste meat while roasting, as well as salmon while broiling. In one of the old tales we read that Ailill and Maive, king and queen of Connaught, had a salmon broiled for the young chief, Fraech, which was basted with honey that had been " well made by their daughter, the Princess Findabair ": from which again we learn that the highest persons sometimes employed themselves in preparing honey. It has been already stated that honey was the chief ingredient in mead; and it is probable that it was used in greater quantity in this way than in any other.

8. *Vegetables and Fruit.*

Table vegetables of various kinds were cultivated in an enclosure called *lúbgort* [loo-ort], *i.e.* 'herb-garden' or kitchen-garden: from *lúb*, 'an herb,' and *gort*, a fenced-in cultivated plot. The manner in which the kitchen-garden is mentioned in literature of all kinds shows that it was a common appanage to a homestead.

Cabbage of some kind was an important food-herb among the early Irish, so that it is often mentioned in old authorities. Its Irish name was *braisech* [brasshagh], borrowed probably from the Latin *brassica*. Among the vegetables cultivated in kitchen-gardens and used at table were leeks and onions. "Mac Conglinne's Vision" mentions the leek by one of its Irish names *lus*, and the onion by the name *cainnenn*. *Lus* is now the general word for leek, and was often used in this special sense in old writings: but *lus* primarily means an herb in general. A leek had a more specific name, *folt-chep* (*folt*, 'hair'; "hair-onion" : *chep* or *cep*, corresponding with Lat. *cepa*, ' an onion '). Garlic appears to have been a pretty common condiment, and the same word *cainnenn* was often applied to it. Wild garlic, called in Irish *creamh* [crav or craff] was often used as a pot-herb, but I find no evidence that it was cultivated. The facts that it is often mentioned in Irish literature, and that it has given names to many places, show that it was a well-recognised plant and pretty generally used.

Tap-rooted plants were designated by the general term *meacon* [mackan], with qualifying terms to denote the different kinds: but *meacon* used by itself means a parsnip or a carrot. Both these vegetables were cultivated in kitchen-gardens, and are often mentioned in old writings. Good watercress (*biror*) was prized and eaten raw as a salad or *annlann*, as at present. It is often spoken of in connexion with brooklime, which is called *fothlacht* [fullaght], and which was also eaten. Poor people sometimes ate a pottage made of the tender tops of nettles, as I have seen them do in my own day in time of scarcity : but they mixed a little oatmeal with it when they could get it. The sea-plant called in Irish *duilesc*, and in English *dillesk, dulse, dulsk*, or *dilse*, growing on sea-rocks, was formerly much used as an article of food, that is, as an accompaniment. According to the Brehon Law, seaside arable land was enhanced in value by having rocks on its sea-border producing this plant, and there was a penalty for consuming the *dillesk* belonging to another without leave. Dillesk is still used; and you may see it in Dublin hawked about in baskets by women : it is dry, and people eat it in small quantities raw, like salad.

Though there is not much direct mention in old Irish literature of the management of fruit-trees, various detached passages show that they were much valued and carefully cultivated. The apple (*ubhall*, pron. ooal) appears to have been as much cultivated and used in old times as at the present. Apples, when gathered, were hoarded up to preserve them as long as possible : they were generally eaten uncooked.

The hazel-nut was much used for food. This is plainly indicated by the high value set on both tree and fruit, of which we meet with innumerable instances in tales, poems, and other old records, in such expressions as "Cruachan of the fair hazels": "Derry-na-nath, on which fair-nutted hazels are constantly found." Abundance of hazel-nuts was a mark of a prosperous and plenteous season. Among the blessings a good king brought on the land was plenty of hazel-nuts :—" O'Berga [the chief] for whom the hazels stoop" [with the weight of their fruit]: " Each hazel is rich from [the worthiness of] the hero." From such references and quotations it may be inferred that hazel-nuts were regarded as an important article of human food.

The sloe-tree or blackthorn was called *droigheann* [dree-an], which generally takes a diminutive form *droigheannan* [dreenan]: hence *dreenan-donn* (*donn*, 'brown') is a common name for the blackthorn, even among English-speaking people. The sloe is called *áirne* [awrna]. That sloes were used as food, or as an *annlann* or condiment, and that the sloe bush was cultivated, is evident from the manner in which both are mentioned in Irish literature. Strawberries (sing. *sub*, pl. *suba* : pron. *soo*, *sooa*) are often mentioned as dainties.

We are told in the Book of Rights that one of the prerogatives of the king of Erin was to have the heath-fruit (*fraechmes*) of Slieve Golry in Longford brought to him. The *fraechmes* was no doubt the whortleberry (called *whorts* or *hurts* in Munster), as is indicated by the fact that the whortleberry is now called *fraechóg* and *fraechán*, two diminutives of the same word *fraech*, heath. Most Dublin people have seen women with baskets of "fraughans," as they call them, for sale, picked on the neighbouring mountains; and they are now made into jam. The passage referred to shows that fraughans were eaten in old times even by kings. Beechmast and oakmast were greatly valued for feeding pigs, which were kept in droves among the woods. The general name for mast was *mes* or *mess*. On one occasion the *badb* [bauv] or war-witch, predicting evils for Ireland, included among them " woods without masts."

9. *Fuel and Light.*

Fuel.—As the country abounded in forests, thickets, and brakes, the most common fuel for domestic use was wood. Firewood or "firebote" was called *connadh* [conna]. A bundle of firewood was called a *brossna,* a word found in the oldest authorities and used to this day all over Ireland, even by the English-speaking people, as meaning a bundle of withered branches, or of heath, for fuel.

Peat or turf was much used as fuel. The Senchus Mór speaks of the cutting of turf from a bank (*port*) and carting it home when dry; and mentions a penalty for stealing it. It is recorded in the Annals that Ragallach, king of Connaught in the middle of the seventh century, having exasperated some men who were cutting turf in a bog, they fell on him and killed him with their sharp *ruams* or turf-spades. The whole bog was the "commons" property of the *finè* or group of related families : but a single turf-bank might belong for the time to an individual. The word *ruam,* used above, was a general word for any spade. At the present day the sharp spade used in cutting turf is designated by the special name of *sleaghan* [pron. *slaan,* the *aa* long like the *a* in *star*]. This word is a diminutive of *sleagh* [*sla*], a 'spear.'

Metal-workers used wood charcoal; for neither plain wood nor peat afforded sufficient heat to melt or weld. Charcoal made from birch afforded the highest degree of heat then available ; and was used for fusing the metals known at that time. Allusions to the use of charcoal—which in Irish is designated *gual* or *cual*—are met with in all sorts of Irish literature. The remains of some of the old pits in which charcoal was made are still recognisable. I know one in which the soil is mixed up and quite black with quantities of charcoal-fragments and dust. We do not know if pit-coal was used in Ireland in very early times.

Flint and steel with tinder were used for striking and kindling fire. The whole kindling-gear—flint, steel, and tinder—was carried in the girdle-pocket, so as to be ready to hand; and accordingly, fire struck in this way was called *teine-creasa* [tinnĕ-crassa], ' fire of the *crios*, or girdle.'

Tinder was, and is, commonly called *sponc* [spunk], which is obviously the same as the Latin *spongia*, English *sponge*. Spunk or tinder was sometimes made from the dried leaves of the coltsfoot, so that this plant is now always called *sponc*: but in recent times it was more usually made of coarse brown paper steeped in a solution of nitre and dried.

Light.—In the better class of houses dipped candles were commonly used. The usual Irish word for a candle is *cainnel*, which seems borrowed from the Latin *candela*: but there is also an old native word for it—*innlis*. There are numerous references to candles in ancient Irish authorities. The Senchus Mór mentions candles of " eight fists " (about forty inches) in length, made by [repeated] dipping of peeled rushes in melted tallow or meat grease: from which we learn that the wicks of candles were sometimes made of peeled rushes: but other kinds of wicks were used.

As bees were so abundant, beeswax (Irish *céir*,

pron. cair), as might be expected, was turned to account. Beeswax candles were in use at some early period in the houses of the rich; and beeswax, "found in square masses, and also in the form of candles, has been discovered under circumstances which leave no doubt as to the great antiquity of such articles" Several specimens of this ancient wax are in the National Museum, Dublin.

Although, in very early times, candles were sometimes held in the hands of slaves, they were more commonly placed on candlesticks. The ancient Irish word for a candlestick is *caindelbra*, modern Irish *coinnleoir* [conlore], both of which are modified forms of the Latin *candelabra*. The Senchus Mór notices a *caindelbra* as a usual article in a house. The ancient Latin Hymn of Secundinus makes mention of a light placed on a *candelabrum*: and in the description of the Banqueting-House of Tara in the Book of Leinster it is stated that there were seven *caindelbra* in it.

It was usual to keep a *ríchainnell* [reehannel], or 'king-candle' (*rí*, 'a king'), or royal candle, of enormous size, with a great bushy wick, burning at night in presence of a king: in the palace it was placed high over his head; during war it blazed outside his tent-door; and on night-marches it was borne before him. This custom is mentioned very often in the records. The Four Masters, in the passage already quoted, p. 27, *supra*, describe the "king-candle" kept burning at night before Shane O'Neill's tent (A.D. 1557) as "a huge torch thicker than a man's body": a passage which shows moreover that this custom continued till the sixteenth century.

The poorer classes commonly used a rush-light, *i.e.* a single rush peeled (leaving one little film of rind the whole length to keep it together) and soaked in grease, but not formed into a candle by repeated dippings. It gave a poor light and burned down very quickly; and it was known by two names, *adann* and *itharna* [ey-an : ih′arna].

Oil lamps of various kinds were used; and we find them frequently mentioned in the oldest records under two names—*lespaire* [les-pe-rĕ] and *laucharnn* or *locharnn*. *Luacharnn* occurs several times in the eighth-century Glosses of Zeuss, as the equivalent of *lampas* and *lucerna*, which shows the remote time in which lamps and lanterns were used in Ireland. Some were made of bronze: some of clay. A rude unglazed earthenware lamp, shallow, and with a snout to support a wick, was found some time ago among prehistoric remains near Portstewart.

10. *Free Public Hostels.*

This seems a proper place to give some information regarding the provision made for lodging and entertaining travellers and officials. Hospitality and generosity were virtues highly esteemed in ancient Ireland; in the old Christian writings indeed they are everywhere praised and inculcated as religious duties; and in the secular literature they are equally prominent. The higher the rank of the person the more was expected from him, and a king should be lavish without limit.

If by any accident a person found himself **unable** to discharge the due rites of hospitality, it was supposed that his face became suffused with a *ruice* [ruckĕ] or blush—a blush of honourable shame. The brewy, or head of a hostel, took care to have " the snout of a rooting hog"—meaning he had plenty of pork—" to prevent his face-blush." If anyone through the fault of another ran short of provisions when visitors came, so that he had reason to feel ashamed of his scanty table, the defaulter had to pay him as compensation what was called a "blush-fine" As illustrating what was expected of the higher ranks, the Brehon Law lays down that " the chieftain grades are bound to entertain [a guest] without asking any questions "—*i.e.* questions as to his name, or business, or where he was bound for, and the like. Once the guest had partaken of food in a house, his host was bound to abstain from offering him any violence or disrespect under any circumstances. Bede's testimony as to the hospitality of the Irish has been already quoted.

This universal admiration for hospitality found its outward expression in the establishment, all over the country, of public hostels for the free lodging and entertainment of all who chose to claim them. At the head of each was an officer called a *brugh-fer* or *brugaid* [broo-fer, brewy], a public hospitaller or hosteller, who was held in high honour. He was bound to keep an open house for the reception of certain functionaries—king, bishop, poet, judge, &c. —who were privileged to claim for themselves and their attendants free entertainment when on their circuits: and also for the reception of strangers. He had a tract of land and other large allowances to defray the expenses of his house; and he should have at least one hundred of each kind of cattle, one hundred labourers, and corresponding provision for feeding and lodging guests.

In order to be at all times ready to receive visitors, a brewy was bound to have three kinds of meat cooked and ready to be served up to all who came; three kinds of raw meat ready for cooking; besides animals ready for killing. In one of the law tracts a brewy is quaintly described as "a man of three snouts":—viz. the snout of a live hog rooting in the fields to prevent the blushes of his face; the snout of a dead hog on the hooks cooking; and the pointed snout of a plough: meaning that he had plenty of live animals and of meat cooked and uncooked, with a plough and all other tillage appliances. He was also "a man of three sacks":—for he had always in his house a sack of malt for brewing ale; a sack of salt for curing cattle-joints; and a sack of charcoal for the irons; this last referring to the continual use of iron-shod agricultural implements calling for frequent repair and renewal. We are told also that his kitchen-fire should be kept perpetually alight, and that his caldron should never be taken off the fire, and should always be kept full of joints boiling for guests. There should be a number of open roads leading to the house of a brewy, so that it might be readily accessible: and on each road a man should be stationed to make sure that no traveller should pass by without calling to be entertained; besides which a light was to be kept burning on the *faithche* [faha] or lawn at night to guide travellers from a distance. The brewy was a magistrate, and was empowered to deliver judgment on certain cases that were brought before him to his house. We have already seen (p. 19) that a court was held in his house for the election of the chief of the tribe. Keating says that there were ninety *brugaids* in Connaught, ninety in Ulster, ninety-three in Leinster, and a hundred and thirty in Munster, all with open houses; and though it is not necessary to accept these numbers as strictly accurate, they indicate at least that the houses of hospitality were very numerous. The house of a brewy answered all the purposes of the modern hotel or inn, but with the important distinction, that guests were lodged and entertained with bed and board, free of charge.

There was another sort of public victualler called *biatach* or *biadhtach* [beetagh], who was also bound to entertain travellers, and the chief's soldiers whenever they came that way. In order to enable the *biatagh* to dispense hospitality, he held a tract of arable land free of rent, called a ballybetagh, equal to about 1000 of our present English acres, with a much larger extent of waste land. The distinction between a brewy and a betagh is not very clear, and at any rate there was probably little substantial difference between them.

The Irish missionaries carried this fine custom to the Continent in early ages, as they did many others; for we are told, on the best authority, that before the ninth century they established hostels, chiefly for the use of pilgrims on their way to Rome, some in Germany, but most in France, as lying in the direct route to the Eternal City.

Conposed from the Book of Kells.

CHAPTER XVIII.

DRESS AND PERSONAL ADORNMENT.

SECTION 1. *The Person and the Toilet.*

Marks of Aristocracy.—An oval face, broad above and narrow below, golden hair, fair skin, white, delicate, and well-formed hands, with slender tapering fingers: these were considered by the ancient Irish as marking the type of beauty and aristocracy. Among the higher classes the finger-nails were kept carefully cut and rounded: and beautiful nails are often mentioned with commendation. It was considered shameful for a man of position to have rough unkempt nails. Crimson-coloured finger-nails were greatly admired. In the Táin a young lady is described as having, among other marks of beauty, "regular, circular, crimson nails"; and ladies sometimes dyed them this colour. Deirdre, uttering a lament for the sons of Usna, says:—" I sleep no more, and I shall not crimson my nails: no joy shall ever again come upon my mind."

Ladies often dyed the eyebrows black with the juice of some sort of berry. We have already seen (p. 148) that the Irish missionary monks sometimes painted or dyed their eyelids black. An entry in Cormac's Glossary plainly indicates that the blush of the cheeks was sometimes heightened by a colouring matter obtained from a plant named *ruam*. The *ruam* was the alder: but the sprigs and berries of the elder tree were applied to the same purpose. Among Greek and Roman ladies the practice was very general of painting the cheeks, eyebrows, and other parts of the face.

The Hair.—Both men and women wore the hair long, and commonly flowing down on the back and shoulders—a custom noticed by Cambrensis. The hair was combed daily after a bath. The heroes of the Fena of Erin, before sitting down to their dinner after a hard day's hunting, always took a bath and carefully combed their long hair.

Among the higher classes in very early times great care was bestowed on the hair; its regulation constituted quite an art; and it was dressed up in several ways. Very often the long hair of men, as well as of women, was elaborately curled. Conall Cernach's hair, as described in the story of Da Derga, flowed down his back, and was done up in "hooks and plaits and swordlets." The accuracy of this and other similar descriptions is fully borne out by the most unquestionable authority of all, namely, the figures in the early illuminated manuscripts and on the shrines and high crosses of later ages. In nearly all the figures of the Book of Kells, for example (seventh or eighth century), the hair is combed and dressed with the utmost care, so beautifully adjusted indeed that it could have been done only by skilled professional hairdressers, and must have occupied much time. Whether in case of men or women, it hangs down both behind and at the sides, and is commonly divided the whole way, as well as all over the head, into slender fillets or locks, which sometimes hang

Fig. 111.

Bronze figures of ecclesiastics on the Shrine of St. Maidoc about the thirteenth century. (From Miss Stokes's Early Christian Art.)

down to the eyes in front. In the seventh and eighth centuries this elaborate arrangement of the hair must have been universal among the higher classes: for the artist who drew the figures in the Book of Kells has represented the hair of nearly all of them dressed and curled in the manner described. The two figures given here, both ecclesiastics from the shrine of

CHAP. XVIII.] DRESS AND PERSONAL ADORNMENT. 379

St. Maidoc, thirteenth century, show how men had the hair and beard dressed, which is seen still better in the figure of the Evangelist at page 387, below. I do not find mentioned anywhere that the Irish dyed their hair, as was the custom among the Greeks and Romans.

For women, very long hair has been in Ireland always considered a mark of beauty. This admiration has come down to the present; for you constantly find mentioned in the Irish popular songs of our own day, a maiden "with golden hair that swept the dew off the grass"—or some such expression.

FIG. 112.

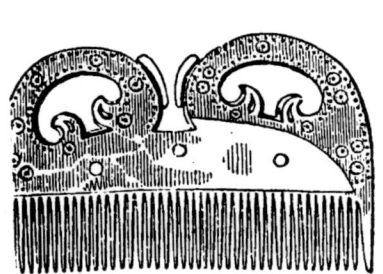

FIG. 113.

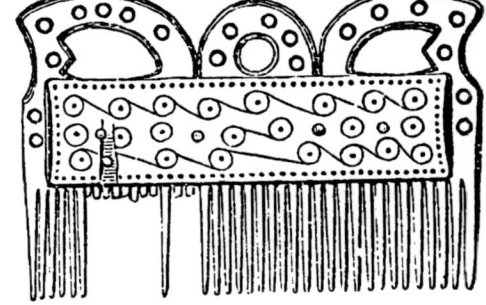

FIG. 114.

Ancient Irish ornamented Combs, of bone, now in the National Museum. Figure 112 is 10 inches long. (From Wilde's Catalogue.)

Combs.—From what precedes it will be understood that combs were in general use with men as well as with women: and many specimens—some made of bone, some of horn—some plain, some ornamented — have been found in lisses, crannoges, and such like places. The comb—Irish *cir* [keer]—is, as we might expect, often mentioned in ancient Irish writings.

The Beard.—The men were as particular about the beard as about the hair. The common Irish names for the beard were *ulcha* and *féasóg* [faissoge], of which the last is still in use. The fashion of wearing the beard varied. Sometimes it was considered becoming to have it long and forked, and gradually narrowed to two points below. Sometimes—as shown in many ancient figures—it falls down in a single mass; while in a few it is cut rectangularly not unlike Assyrian beards. Nearly all have a mustache, in most cases curled up and pointed at the ends as we often see now. In some there is a mustache without a beard: and a few others have the whole face bare. In many the beard is carefully divided into slender twisted fillets, as described above, for the hair. Kings and chiefs had barbers in their service to attend to all this. The beard that grew on the upper lip, when the lower part of the face was shaved, was called *crombéol* ('stoopmouth'), pron. crommail, what we now designate a mustache. That the ancient Irish

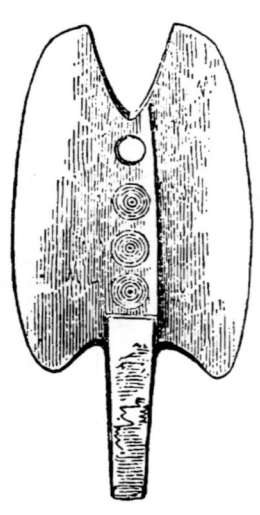

Fig 115.

Bronze cutting-instrument, believed to be a Razor all one piece, 3½ inches long; two edges very thin, hard, and sharp In National Museum, where there are others like it (From Wilde's Catalogue.)

used a razor (in Irish *alt* or *altan*) is proved by the fact that it is mentioned in our very oldest documents—such, for instance, as Cormac's Glossary and the eighth-century Milan Glosses—and in such a way as shows it to have been a very familiar article.

The Bath.—Bathing was very usual, at least among the upper classes, and baths and the use of baths are constantly mentioned in the old tales and other writings. The bath was a large tub or vat usually called *dabach* [dauvagh]. In the better class of lay houses a bath was considered a necessary article. There was a bath for the use of visitors in the guest-house of every monastery; and we are told in the law books that every brewy had in his house a bathing-vessel. Kings and chiefs were in the habit of bathing and anointing themselves with oil and precious sweet-scented herbs. So Ulysses bathes and anoints himself with olive oil after being shipwrecked on the coast of Phæacea. As the people had a full bath some time down late in the day, they did not bathe in the morning, but merely washed their hands; for which purpose they generally went out immediately after rising and dressing, to some well or stream near the house. This practice is constantly referred to. In both washing and bathing they used soap (*sleic*, pron. slake).

Small Toilet Articles.—Mirrors of polished metal must have been common from very early times, for they are often mentioned; generally by one or the other of the two names, *scathán* [skahan] and *scadarc* [sky-ark]. The great antiquity of the article is shown by its mention in the Zeuss Glosses, where the old form *scaterc* is derived from *scáth-derc*, 'shadow-seeing,' or a 'shadow see-er.' From *scáth* [skaw], 'a shadow,' is also derived the other name *scathán*, which is merely a diminutive form. Small articles of the toilet, and especially combs, were kept by women in a little bag which they carried about with them, called a *ciorbholg* [keerwolg], *i.e.* 'comb-bag' (*cior*, 'a comb,' and *bolg*, 'a bag').

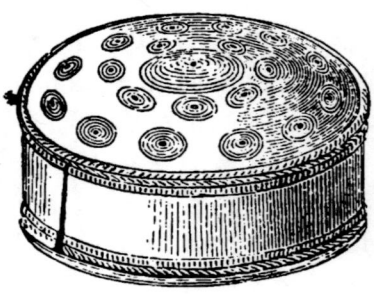

FIG. 116.

Cold box 2¼ inches across found in a grave. Probably belonging to a lady's toilet. (From Wilde's Catalogue.)

2. *Dress.*

Materials.—Woollen and linen clothes formed the dress of the great mass of the people. Both were produced at home; and elsewhere in this book the mode of manufacturing them will be described. Silk and satin, which were of course imported, were much worn among the higher classes, and we find both constantly noticed in our literature. The flags and banners used with armies were usually made of silk or satin. The ordinary word for silk was *sida* [sheeda]; and for satin, *sról* [srole]. The furs of animals, such as seals, otters, badgers, foxes, &c., were much used for capes and jackets, and for the edgings of various garments, so that skins of all the various kinds were valuable. They formed, too, an important item of everyday traffic, and they were also exported. In 1861, a cape was found in a bog at Derrykeighan in Antrim, six feet beneath the surface, made altogether of otter-skins. "The workmanship of the sewing" —says Mr. Robert Mac Adam, a distinguished Belfast antiquary, who gives an account of it—"is wonderfully beautiful and regular: and the several parts are joined so as not to disturb the fur, so that from the outside it looks as if formed of one piece."

In Scotland the tartan is much used—a sort of cloth, generally of wool, sometimes silk—plaided or cross-barred in various colours; of which both the material and the name originated in Ireland. The original Gaelic name is *tuartan*, as we find it used several times, both in the Senchus Mór, and in the glosses on it, where *tuartan* is defined to be a sort of material "containing cloth of every colour."

Colours.—The ancient Irish loved bright colours. In this respect they resembled many other nations of antiquity—as well indeed as of the present day; and they illustrated Ruskin's saying (speaking of poppies): —" Whenever men are noble they love bright colour, ... and bright colour is given to them in sky, sea, flowers, and living creatures." The Irish love of colour expressed itself in all parts of their raiment: and in chapter xxii., sect. 3, below, it will be shown that they well understood the art of dyeing.

Everywhere in our ancient literature we find dress-colours mentioned. In the Ulster army, as described in the Táin, was one company with various-coloured mantles:—" some with red cloaks; others with light blue cloaks; others with deep blue cloaks; others with green, or blay, or white, or yellow cloaks, bright and fluttering about them: and there is a young red-freckled lad, with a crimson cloak in their midst." Any number of such quotations might be given.

The several articles of dress on one person were usually coloured differently. Even the single outer cloak was often striped, spotted, or chequered in various colours. King Domnall, in the seventh century, on one occasion sent a many-coloured tunic to his foster-son Prince Congal : like Joseph's coat of many colours.

We are told in our legendary history that exact regulations for the wearing of colours by the different ranks of people were made by King Tigernmas [Teernmas] and by his successor, many centuries before the Christian era :—a slave was to be dressed in clothes of one colour ; a peasant or farmer in two ; and so on up to a king and queen and an ollave of any sort: all of whom were privileged to wear six.

At the present day green is universally regarded as the national colour : but this is a very modern innovation, and as a matter of fact the ancient Irish had no national colour.

Classification of Upper Garments.—The upper garments worn by men were of a variety of forms and had many names : besides which, fashions of course changed as time went on, though, as I think, very slowly. Moreover, the several names were often loosely applied, like the English words "coat," "mantle," "frock," &c. ; so that it is often impossible to fix exact limitations. But the articles themselves were somewhat less vague than their names : and, so far as they can be reduced to order, the upper garments of men may be said to have been mainly of four classes :—

1. A large cloak, generally without sleeves, varying in length, but commonly covering the whole person from the shoulders down.

2. A short tight-fitting coat or jacket with sleeves, but with no collar.

3. A cape for the shoulders, commonly, but not always, carrying a hood to cover the head.

4. A sort of petticoat, the same as the present Highland kilt. There was nothing to correspond with our waistcoat.

Sometimes only one of those was used, viz. either the outer mantle or the short frock—with of course in all cases the under and nether clothing; but often two were worn together; sometimes three; and occasionally the whole four.

1. **Loose Upper Garment.**—The long cloak assumed many shapes: sometimes it was a formless mantle down to the knees; but more often it was a loose though shaped cloak reaching to the ankles. This last was so generally worn by men in out-door life that it was considered characteristic of the Irish. It had frequently a fringed or shaggy border, round the neck and down the whole way on both edges, in front; and its material was according to the rank or means of the wearer. Among the higher classes it was of fine cloth edged with silk or satin or other costly material. Sometimes the whole cloak was of silk or satin; and it was commonly dyed in some bright colour, or more often—as we have said—striped or spotted with several colours. In the numerous figures in the Book of Kells (seventh or eighth century) the over-garment is very common: sometimes it is represented full length, but often only as far as the knees or the middle of the thigh.

The large outer garment of whatever material was known by several names, according to shape, of which the most common was *brat* or *bratt*: which appears to have been a general term for any outer garment, and which is still in common use, though somewhat altered in meaning. The word *fallainn* [folling] was

Fig. 117.

Representation of an Angel, showing the long narrow mantle described in text. (From the Book of Kells: Dr. Abbott's Reproductions.)

applied to a loose cloak or mantle, reaching about to the knees: but it has nearly or altogether dropped out of use. A coarse loose wrap, either dyed or in the natural colour of the wool, was called a *lummon*. Women had similar cloaks, called by the same

CHAP. XVIII.] DRESS AND PERSONAL ADORNMENT. 387

names. They often wore a variously-coloured tunic down to the very feet, with many folds and much material—twenty or thirty yards—which was different from the *bratt* and from the hooded cloak mentioned below. Under this was a long gown or kirtle. The long cloak worn by women had often a hood attached at top which commonly hung down on the back over the cloak, but which could be turned up so as to cover the head at any moment when wanted. This still continues in use among the countrywomen.

It is difficult or impossible to embrace all varieties of clothing in any formal classification: and as a matter of fact there was another article of full-covering dress worn in very early times by both men and women, hardly included in any of the preceding descriptions. In the Book of Kells (seventh or eighth century) a large number of the figures, both of men and women, have the usual outside mantle

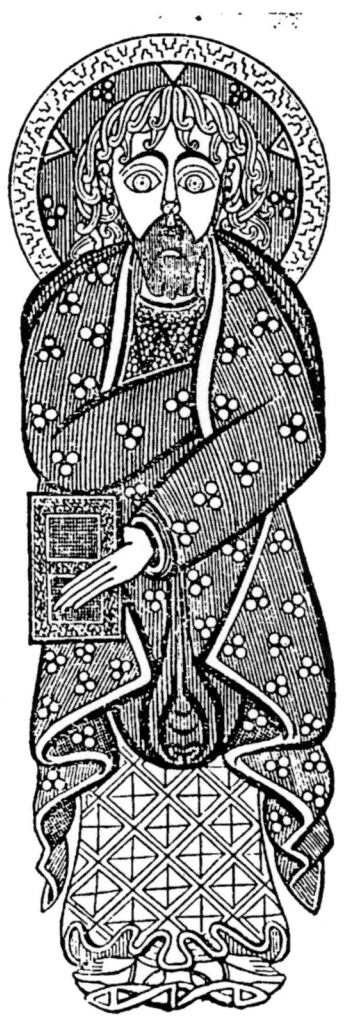

FIG. 118.
Representation of one of the Evangelists, showing long narrow mantle, described in text (From the Book of Kells Dr Abbott's Reproductions)

2 c 2

generally reaching to about the knees, and under it a long narrow garment like a petticoat (but not a kilt), from the shoulders down to the insteps, widening towards the bottom, yet so narrow that it would obviously interfere with the free movement of the feet in quick walking. I do not find this mentioned in the written records anywhere—at least so as to be recognisable; but it is depicted so often in the Book of Kells (figs. 117, 118) that it must have been in general use.

Distinct apparently from the preceding over-mantles was the loose-flowing tunic—worn over all—usually of linen dyed saffron, commonly called *léine* [2 syll.], which was in very general use and worn by men and women in outdoor life. This is noticed by Spenser as prevalent in his time (sixteenth century). It had many folds and plaits and much material—sometimes as much as thirty yards.

The outer covering of the general run of the peasantry was just one loose sleeved coat or mantle, generally of frieze, which covered them down to the ankles; and which they wore winter and summer.

2. Tight-fitting Upper Garments.—The tight-fitting sleeved upper garment was something like the present frock-coat; but it had no collar, and was much shorter, usually reaching to about the middle of the thigh, and often only a little below the hips; with a girdle at the waist. It was often called *inar*, but it had other names. Persons are very often described as wearing this short coat with a *brat* or mantle over it. The short coat is very well represented in the figures given on next page, which, however, belong to a comparatively late time, but serve to show how this garment held on in fashion.

Fig. 119.

Group on ancient engraved book-cover of bone, showing costume: one with cynbals; and all engaged in some kind of dance: 14th or 15th century. (From Wilde's Catalogue.)

3. **Cape and Hood.**—The short cape, with or without a hood, was called *cocholl*, corresponding in shape and name with the Gallo-Roman *cucullus*, English *cowl*: but this English word *cowl* is now often applied to a hood simply. This fashion continued long: Thomas Dineley (in 1675) observed that the men, in parts of Ireland, covered their heads with their cloaks.

4. **The Kilt.**—The Gaelic form of this name is *celt* [kelt], of which "kilt" is a phonetic rendering. The word occurs so seldom, and is used so vaguely, that we might find it difficult to identify the particular article it designates, if the Scotch had not retained both the article itself and its name: for the Highland kilt is the ancient Irish *celt*. The kilt—commonly falling to the knees—is very frequently

met with on the figures of manuscripts, shrines, and crosses, so that it must have been very much worn

Fig 120.

The figures on one face of the shrine of St Mancian (date, eleventh century) They diminish in size to the right to suit shape of panel. (From Kilk. Archæol. Journ.)

both by ecclesiastics and laymen. It appears in **a** very decided form in the eleventh-century illustration given here (fig. 120).

CHAP. XVIII.] DRESS AND PERSONAL ADORNMENT. 391

Fasteners for Upper Garments.—The overgarments were fastened by brooches, pins, buttons, girdles, strings, and loops. Brooches will be treated of in next section. Simple pins were generally ornamented, head, or shank, or both, as seen in the figures given on next page, of which the originals are all in the National Museum, with many others.

Nether Garments.—The ancient Irish wore a trousers which differed in some respects from that worn at the present day. It generally reached from the hips to the ankles, and was so tight-fitting as to show perfectly the shape of the limbs. When terminating at the ankles it was held down by a slender strap passing under the foot, as seen in one of the figures in the Book of Kells. Like other Irish garments it was generally striped or speckled in various colours.

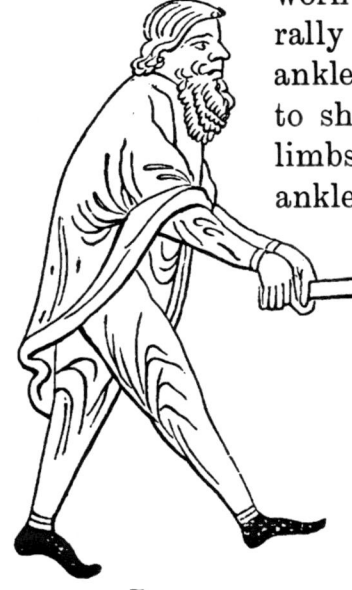

FIG. 121.

Showing the tight trews or trousers, with a *fallainn* or short cloak, dyed olive-green. (From a copy of Giraldus, A.D. 1200 Wilde's Catalogue.)

Leggings (called *ochra*) of cloth or of thin soft leather were worn, probably as an accompaniment to the kilt. They were laced on by strings tipped with *findruine* or white bronze, the bright metallic extremities falling down after lacing, so as to form pendant ornaments. There are many passages in our ancient literature showing that it was pretty usual with those engaged in war to leave

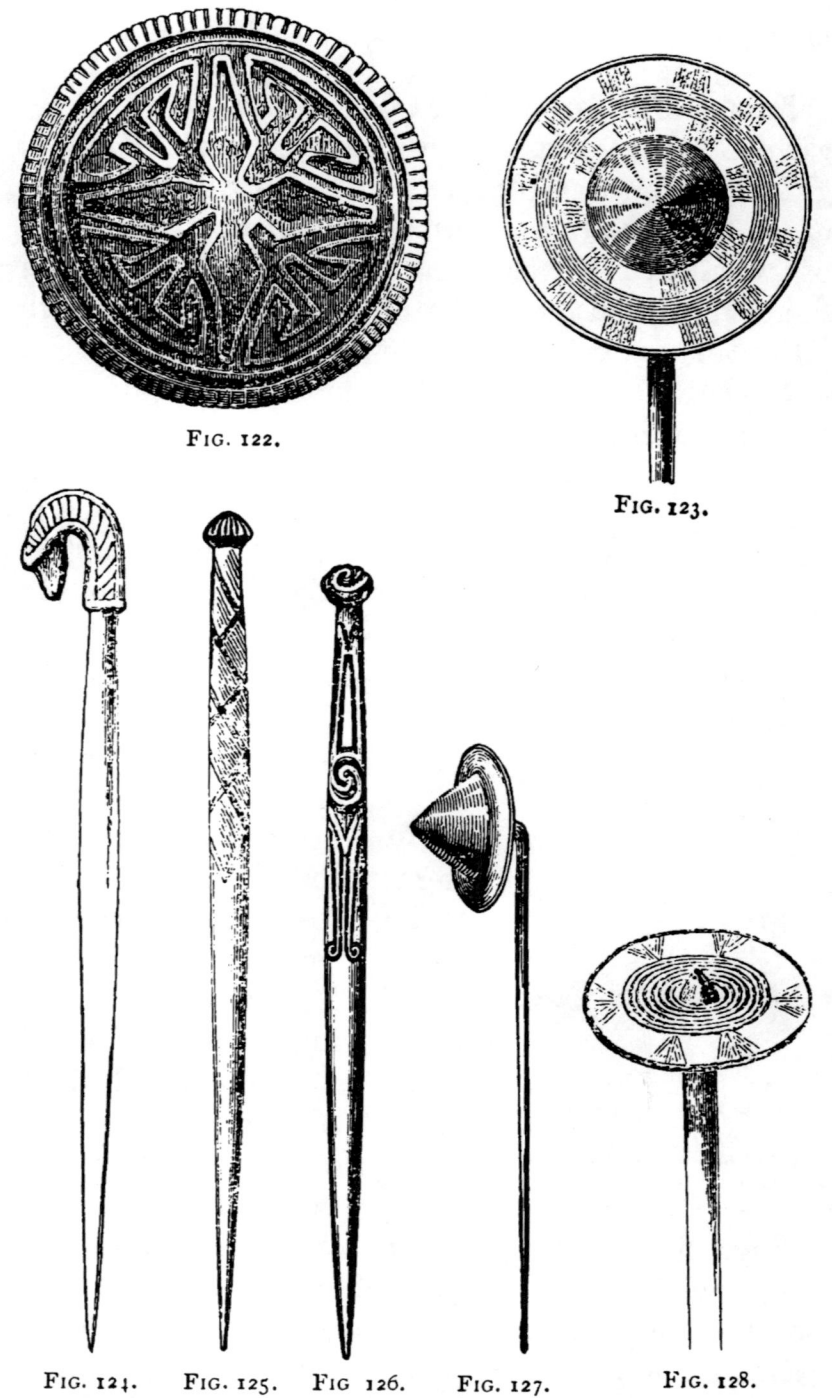

FIG. 122. FIG. 123. FIG. 124. FIG. 125. FIG 126. FIG. 127. FIG. 128.

Bronze button and pins all very ancient Figure 122, a highly-decorated bronze button, enamelled in red and green, with a small metal fastening-loop at back, as on modern buttons. natural size Figures 124, 125, 126, bronze pins, natural size; figure 128, bronze pin, 13½ inches with disk 2¼ inches in diameter. (All from Wilde's Catalogue)

the legs naked: a fashion perpetuated by the Scotch to this day. This fashion is also indicated by such nicknames as Glúnduff ('black-knee'), Glúngel ('white-knee'), &c., which were very common.

As illustrative of all that precedes, a series of costumes of the year 1600 are presented here.

Fig. 129.   Fig. 130.

Fig. 131.   Fig. 132.   Fig. 133.   Fig. 134.

Irish Costumes, A D 1600. (From Speed's map of Ireland: A.D. 1611.) Figures 129 and 130, gentleman and lady of the high classes. Figures 131 and 132, persons of the middle rank. Figures 133 and 134, peasants

Underclothing.—Both men and women wore a garment of fine texture next the skin. This is constantly mentioned in the tales, and, whether for men or women, is denoted by the word *léine* or *léne* [2 syll.], which is now the common Irish word for a shirt. It was usually made of wool or flax: sometimes it was of silk, occasionally of satin, highly ornamented with devices in gold and silver thread, worked with the needle.

Girdles and Garters.—A girdle or belt (Ir. *criss*) was commonly worn round the waist, inside the outer loose mantle; and it was often made in such a way as to serve as a pocket for carrying small articles. Sometimes a *bossan* or purse (also called *sparán*) was hung from it, in which small articles were kept, such as rings. The girdles of chiefs and other high-class people were often elaborately ornamented and very valuable: worth from £40 to £100 of our money. Garters were worn, sometimes for use and sometimes for mere ornament, or to serve both purposes. They were made of various materials according to the rank of the wearer: kings, chiefs, and ollaves of poetry often wore garters of gold.

Gloves.—That gloves were commonly worn is proved by many ancient passages and indirect references. They appear to have been common among all classes—poor as well as rich. One of the good works of charity laid down in the Senchus Mór is "sheltering the miserable," which the gloss explains, "to give them staves and gloves and shoes for God's sake." The evangelist depicted in the Book of Kells (fig. 118, p. 387, above) wears gloves, with the fingers divided as in our present gloves, and having the tops lengthened out beyond the natural fingers. Rich people's gloves were often highly ornamented. As to material: probably gloves were made, as at present, both of cloth and of animal skins and furs. The importance and general use of gloves as an article of dress are to some extent indicated by their frequent mention and by the number of names for them. The common word for a glove was *lamann*, which is still in use.

Head Gear.—The men wore a hat of a conical shape, without a leaf, called a *barréd* [barraid], a native word, of which the first syllable, *barr*, signifies top. Among the peasantry, the men, in their daily life, commonly went bare-headed, wearing the hair long behind so as to hang down on the back, and clipped short in front. Sometimes men, even in military service, when not engaged in actual warfare, went bare-headed in this manner. In the panels of one of the crosses at Clonmacnoise are figures of several soldiers: and while some have conical caps, others are bare-headed. Camden describes Shane O'Neill's galloglasses, as they appeared at the English court in the sixteenth century, as having their heads bare, their long hair curling down on the shoulders and clipped short in front just above the eyes.

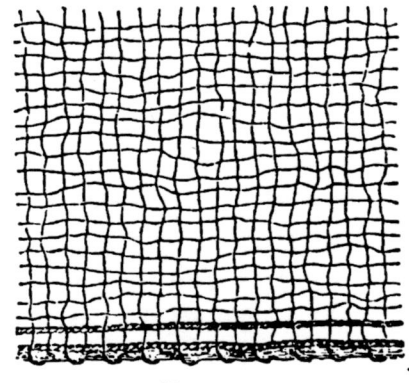

FIG. 135.

Portion of "a light gauzy woollen veil, of most delicate texture" (Wilde) Found on the body of a woman. (From Proc. Roy. Ir. Acad)

Married women usually had the head covered either with a hood (*caille*, pron. cal-lĕ) or with a long web of linen wreathed round the head in several folds. The veil was in constant use among the higher classes, and when not actually worn was usually carried, among other small articles, in a lady's ornamental hand-bag.

Foot-Wear.—The most general term for a shoe was *brōg*, which was applied to a shoe of any kind: it is still the word in common use. The *brōg* was very often made of untanned hide, or only half tanned, free from hair, and retaining softness and pliability like the raw hide. This sort of shoe was also often

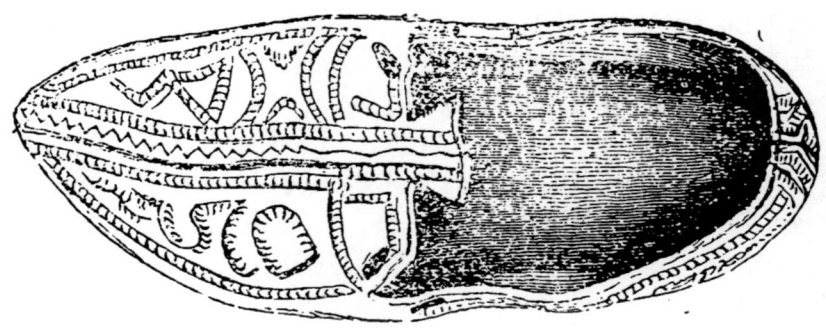

FIG. 136.
Ancient Irish ornamented Shoe, in National Museum.

called *cuarán* or *cuaróg*, from which a brogue-maker was called *cuaránaidhe* [cooraunee]. This shoe had no lift under the heel: the whole was stitched together with thongs cut from the same hide. But there was a more shapely shoe than the *cuaran*, made of fully tanned leather, having serviceable sole and heel, and often highly ornamented. There are several specimens of such shoes in the National Museum, Dublin, of which one is represented here (fig. 136). To this kind of shoe the two terms *ass* (pl. *assa*) and *maelan* were often applied; but these have long

CHAP. XVIII.] DRESS AND PERSONAL ADORNMENT. 397

dropped out of use. Most of the figures depicted in the Book of Kells and on the shrines and high crosses have shoes or sandals, though some have the feet bare. One wears well-shaped narrow-toed shoes seamed down along the instep, something like the shoe represented on last page (fig. 136), but much finer and more shapely. Some have sandals consisting merely of a sole bound on by straps running over the foot: and in all such cases the naked toes are seen. On many of the sandals there are what appear to be little circular rosettes just under or on the ankles, one on each side of the foot—perhaps mere

FIG. 137.

Small portion of panel in Book of Kells, showing sandals under feet, with rosettes. (Dr. Abbott's Reproductions.)

ornaments. They are seen in the figure of the angel, p. 386, *supra*; and more plainly in fig. 137 given here, also from the Book of Kells.

In many of the most ancient Irish tales we often find it mentioned that persons wore *assa* or *maelassa* or shoes made of silver or of *findruine* (white bronze). Such shoes or sandals must have been worn only on special or formal occasions: as they would be so inconvenient as to be practically useless in real everyday life. As confirming this idea of temporary and exceptional use, we have in the National Museum a curious pair of (ordinary leather) shoes—shown in the illustration — connected permanently, so that they could only be used by a person sitting down or standing in one spot.

In whatever way and for whatever purpose the metallic shoes were used, they must have been pretty common, for many have been found in the earth,

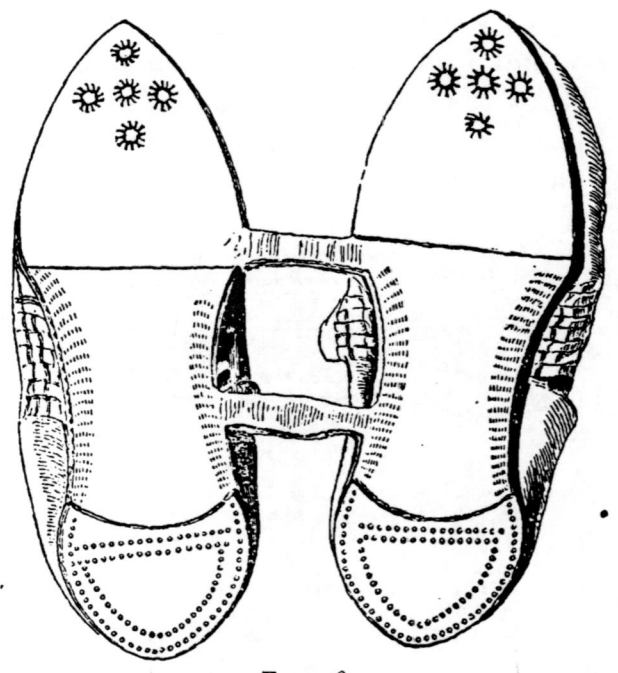

FIG. 138.

Pair of shoes permanently connected by straps. two soles and straps cut out of one piece. Most beautifully made. (From Wilde's Catalogue.)

and some are now preserved in museums. There were tradesmen, too, who made and dealt in them, as is proved by the fact that about the year 1850 more than two dozen ancient bronze shoes were found embedded in the earth in a single hoard near the Giant's Causeway.

The finding of bronze shoes, and in such numbers, is a striking illustration of how the truthfulness of many old Irish records, that might otherwise be considered fabulous, is confirmed by actual existing remains.

3. *Personal Ornaments.*

Legendary Origin.—In ancient Irish tales and other records, referring to both pagan and Christian times, gold and silver ornaments—especially gold—are everywhere mentioned as worn by the upper classes : and these accounts are fully corroborated by the great numbers of objects of both metals found from time to time in various parts of Ireland.

In the National Museum there is a great collection of ancient artistic ornamental objects, some of pure gold, some of silver, and some of mixed metals and precious stones. All, or nearly all—of whatever kind or material—are ornamented in various patterns, some simply, some elaborately. Those decorated with the peculiar patterns known as *opus Hibernicum* or Irish interlaced work were made in Christian times by Christian artists, and are nearly all of mixed metals and precious stónes. Those that have no interlaced work, but only spirals, circles, zigzags, lozenges, parallel lines, &c., are mostly of pagan and pre-Christian origin, many of them dating from a period long antecedent to the Christian era. Nearly all the gold objects, except closed rings and bracelets —and most even of these—belong to this class— made in pagan times by pagan artists. All the articles of gold are placed in one compartment of the Museum, and they form by far the largest collection of the kind in the British Islands : twelve or thirteen times more than that in the British Museum.

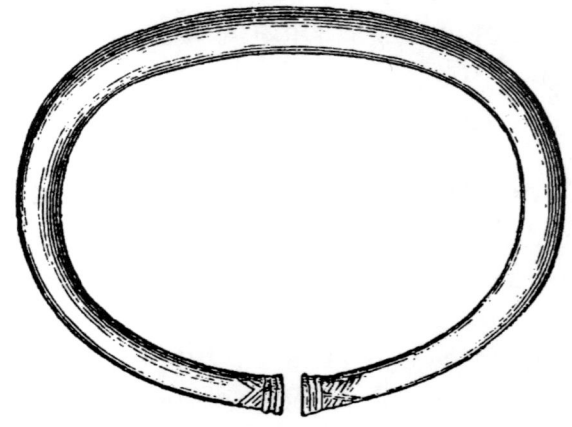

Fig. 139.

Irish Bracelet or Armlet, of solid gold, double size of picture, of beautiful shape and workmanship: weighs 3¾ oz. in National Museum (From Wilde's Catalogue)

Rings and Bracelets.—Among the high classes the custom of wearing rings and bracelets of gold, silver, and *findruine* (white bronze) on the fore-arm,

Fig. 140.

Bronze Bracelet: in National Museum (From Wilde's Catalogue)

wrist, and fingers—including the thumb—was universal, and is mentioned everywhere in ancient Irish literature. The words for a ring, whether for finger or arm, are *fáil*: *fáinne* [faun-yĕ] : *nasc*, which was applied to a ring, bracelet, collar, or tie of any kind: and sometimes *flesc*. The word *id* was applied to a ring, collar, circlet, or chain. Still another name for a ring or bracelet was *bunne* [2 syll.]. These several names were no doubt applied to rings of different makes or sizes: but the distinctions have been in many cases lost.

Both men and women belonging to the highest and richest classes had the arm covered with rings of gold, partly for personal adornment, and partly to have them ready to bestow on poets, musicians, story-tellers, and ollaves of other arts, who acquitted themselves satisfactorily. Circlets of gold, silver, or findruinĕ were also worn round the legs above the ankle. Fully answering to all the entries and descriptions in the records we find in the National Museum in Dublin, and in other Irish museums, gold and silver rings and bracelets of all makes and sizes: some pagan, some Christian.

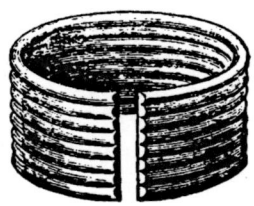

FIG. 141.

Ancient Irish Finger-ring: pure gold. In the National Museum. (From Wilde's Catalogue)

Precious Stones and Necklaces.—Ireland produced gems of many kinds—more or less valuable—which were either worn as personal ornaments by themselves — cut into shape and engraved with patterns—or used by artists in ornamental work. Precious stones are often mentioned in ancient Irish writings. In Kerry were found—and are still found—"Kerry diamonds," amethysts, topazes, emeralds, and sapphires: and several other precious stones, such as garnet, were found native in other

2 D

parts of the country. A pearl was usually designated by the word *séd* [shade]: but this word, as we shall see in chapter xxiii., sect. 4, was also applied to a

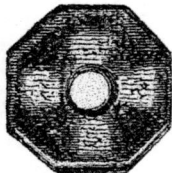  

Fig. 142.   Fig. 143.   Fig. 144.
Beads or Studs of jet: in National Museum. Used as buttons or fasteners, or strung for necklaces. (From Wilde's Catalogue.)

cow regarded as an article of value or exchange; and it was often used to designate a gem or jewel of any kind. *Séd* is still in use in this last sense. Several Irish rivers were formerly celebrated for their pearls; and in many the mussels that produce pearls are found to this day—often with pearls in them.

Of the various ornaments worn on the person, the common necklace was perhaps the earliest in use.

Fig. 145.   Fig. 146.
Gold Beads portions of necklaces natural size
In National Museum (From Wilde's Catalogue.)

Necklaces formed of small shells are common among primitive people all over the world, and they have been found with skeletons under cromlechs in several parts of Ireland, of which specimens may be seen in the National Museum in Dublin, belonging to prehistoric ages. In historic times necklaces formed of expensive gems of various kinds, or of beads of gold, were in use in Ireland; and they are frequently mentioned in the tales and other ancient Irish records.

CHAP. XVIII.] DRESS AND PERSONAL ADORNMENT. 403

Torques or Muntorcs.—Besides the necklaces properly so called, there were various kinds of gold and silver ornaments for wearing round the neck, of which perhaps the best known was the torque, which is repeatedly mentioned in our literature under the names *torc* and *muntorc*. The torque was often formed of a single straight bar of gold, square or triangular, from which the metal had been hollowed out along the flat sides, so as to leave four, or three, ribbons along the corners, after which it was twisted into a spiral, something like a screw with four, or three, threads: and the whole bar bended into a circular shape. But they were formed in other ways, as may be seen by an inspection of those in the National Museum in Dublin. There are in this Museum many

FIG. 147.

Gold Torque: in National Museum 15½ inches in diameter. found in 1810 n a nound at Tara. (Fron Petrie's Tara.)

muntorcs of various shapes and sizes. Some are barely the size of the neck, while others are so large that when worn they extended over the breast almost to the shoulders : and there are all intermediate sizes. One of the largest, found at Tara in the year 1810, is represented here (fig. 147). The one represented in fig. 148 is of unusual make, being formed by twisting a single plate of gold, and having two apples or balls of gold at the ends. The custom of wearing torques, as well as rings and bracelets, was in ancient times very general, not only among the Irish, but among the northern nations, both of

Fig. 148.

Gold Torque, half size of original now in National Museum, found near Clonmacnoise (From Wilde's Catalogue.)

Europe and Asia, especially the Gauls, as all who have read Roman history will remember.

Crescents, Gorgets, or Necklets.—The word *muince* [moon-kĕ] denotes a neck-circlet, from *muin*, the neck. It was used in several different applications; but the necklets that we find constantly mentioned in

CHAP. XVIII.] DRESS AND PERSONAL ADORNMENT. 405

the ancient tales by the name *muince* are to be generally understood as golden gorgets or collars for the neck, worn by both men and women, now often conveniently called " crescents." These golden crescents are of **three** main types. The FIRST is quite

FIG. 149.

Gold Crescent of the first type, one continuous bright plate: 7 inches in outside diameter: weight, 18 dwts. In National Museum. (From Wilde's Catalogue.)

flat, thin, and brightly burnished. Most of those of this kind are ornamented in delicate line patterns, which were produced by fine chisel-edged punches. Crescents of this kind are often called by the name *lunula* or *lunette*. Fig. 149 represents one of those beautiful objects, of which there are now more than thirty in the National Museum.

The SECOND type, and by far the most elaborate, is dish-shaped in general make, convex on one side,

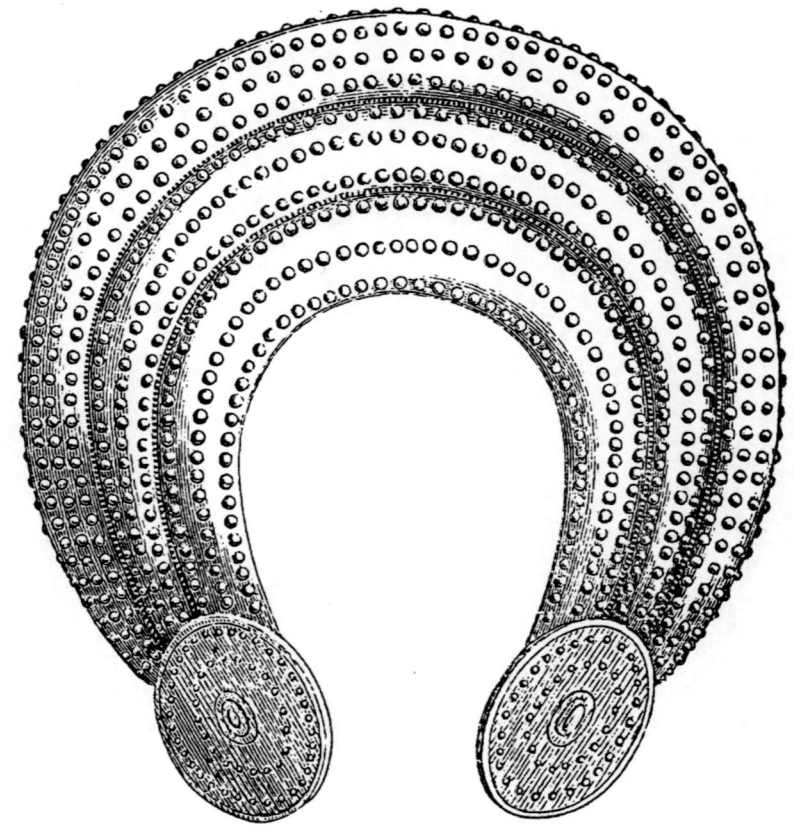

FIG. 150.

Gold Muince, Crescent, or Gorget, of second type: the largest and most beautiful of this kind in the collection. Diameter 11 inches: weight, 16½ oz. Found in County Clare. Now in National Museum. (From Wilde's Catalogue)

concave on the other: covered all over with ornamental designs. The illustrations (figs. 150 and 151) will give a good idea of the general shape, but represent the ornamentation only imperfectly. There

CHAP. XVIII.] DRESS AND PERSONAL ADORNMENT 407

are five specimens of these gorgets in the Museum, all of very thin gold. Both the general convex shape and the designs were produced by hammering with a mallet and punches on a shaped solid mould. The designs are all raised from the surface (with corre-

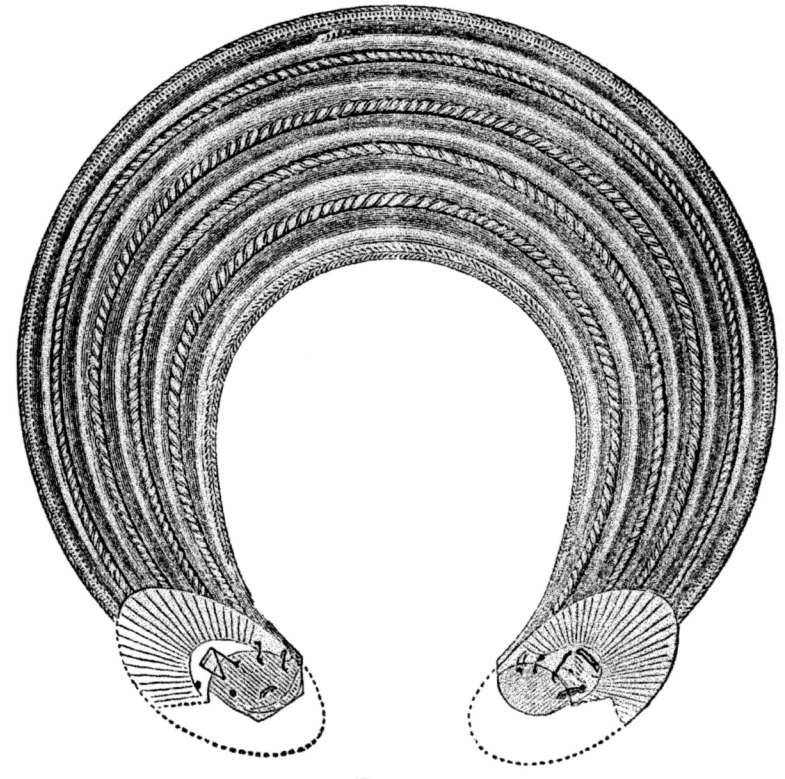

Fig. 151.

Another gold Crescent, of second type: now in National Museum: 11 inches in diameter: weight, 7½ oz. (From Wilde's Catalogue.)

sponding hollows at the back); and in this respect they differ from those of the other two kinds of crescent in which the lines are indented. The patterns and workmanship on these are astonishingly fine, showing extraordinary skill of manipulation : they are indeed so complicated and perfect that it is difficult to understand how they could have been produced by mere handwork with moulds, hammers, and punches. Yet they could have been done in no other way.

The circular bosses at the ends of these gorgets deserve special notice. One of them is shown of half-size in fig. 152. They were made separately from the general body of the crescent, to which they are securely fastened: and the ornamentation on them is of extraordinary delicacy and beauty. Each of the little circular ornaments forming the two rows between centre and edge (19 in the inner row, 28 in the outer) consists of three delicate raised concentric circles, each triple series of circles round a central conical stud or button, with point projecting outwards: and in the centre of the whole boss is a large projecting stud of the same shape surrounded with raised circles: all of pure gold. Each boss consists of two saucer-shaped discs, fastened (not soldered) together all round the edge, with the convex sides outwards so as to enclose a hollow space.

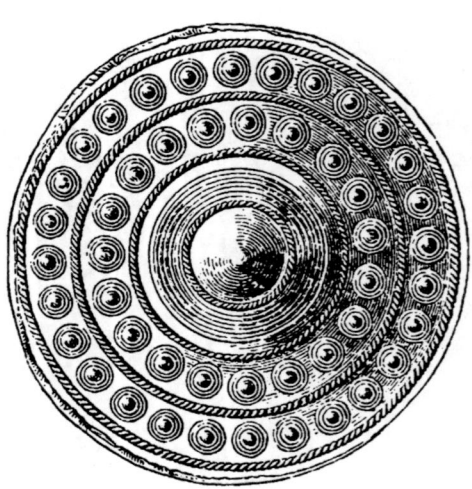

FIG. 152.

One of the gold Bosses (front view) at ends of Crescents of second type described in text Drawn half size. (From Wilde's Catalogue.)

Of the five gorgets of this class in the Museum, Wilde truly observes:—"It may with safety be

CHAP. XVIII.] DRESS AND PERSONAL ADORNMENT. 409

asserted that, both in design and execution, they are undoubtedly the most gorgeous and magnificent specimens of antique gold work which have as yet been discovered in any part of the world." In weight they vary from four to sixteen ounces: and taking material and workmanship into account they must have been of immense value in their time.

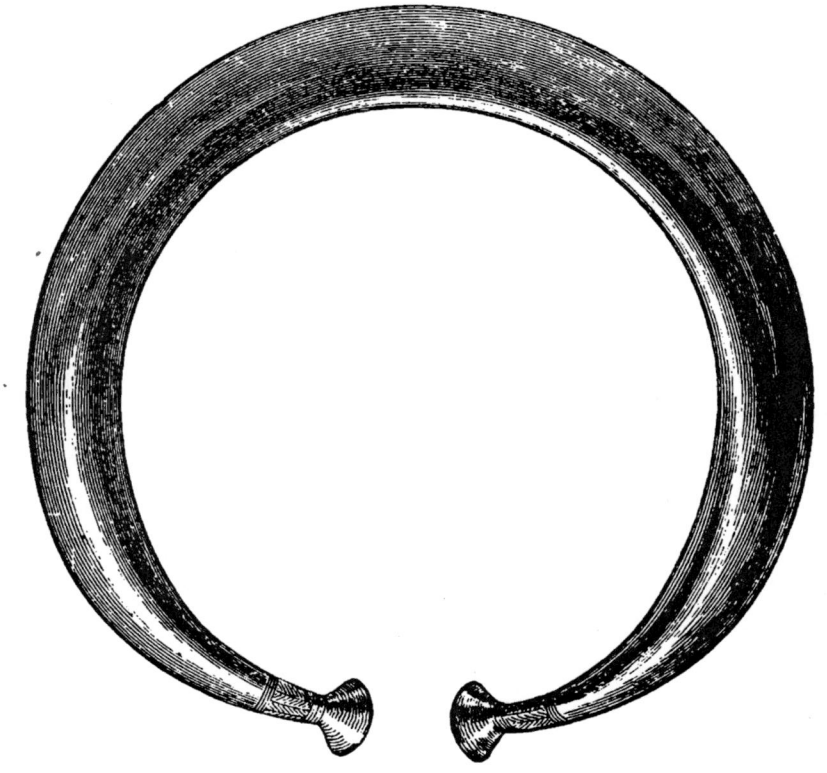

FIG. 153.
Gold Crescent or Necklet of the third type: in National Museum · 7½ inches across on the outside: weight 7 oz. (From Wilde's Catalogue)

The necklets of the THIRD kind, of which the Museum contains five specimens, are of a semi-tubular make, the plate being bended round so as to form, in some specimens, about a half tube, in others less than half. The gold is much thicker than in those of the other two types. The one represented in fig. 153, which is the largest and most perfect of the five, is ornamented at the ends with a punched herring-bone pattern. In an adjacent case of the Museum are five models of the type of these five real ones, of which the originals—all pure gold— were found in Clare in the great hoard mentioned at p. 420, below, paragraph at bottom,

All the *muinces* of the three types were intended, and were very suitable, for the neck. The inside circular-opening is in every case of the right size to fit the neck, and on account of the flexibility of the plates they can be put on and taken off with perfect ease, even though the opening at the ends is only a couple of inches, or less.

All these crescents—of the three types—were worn on the neck with the ends in front, so as to exhibit the ornamented bosses to full advantage. Some have thought that the crescents of the first two types (represented in figs. 149, 150, and 151) were worn on the front of the head as diadems: but this was not, and could not have been, the case: the crescents of the three types were all *muinces* or necklets.

The Do-at and the Muince-do-at.—At each extremity of all the *muinces* or crescents is a disc or boss or button—seen in the illustrations—generally circular, or nearly so: very elaborate in one of the types, simple in the other two. Their primary use was as fasteners, to catch the ornamental string by which the necklet was secured. These terminal appendages were known in ancient Irish records by the name of *at*, a word which means a knob, button,

CHAP. XVIII.] DRESS AND PERSONAL ADORNMENT. 411

or disc—a swelling of any kind. Accordingly these gorgets, of all the three kinds, are designated *muince-do-at*, 'the necklet of the two *ats* or terminal discs.'

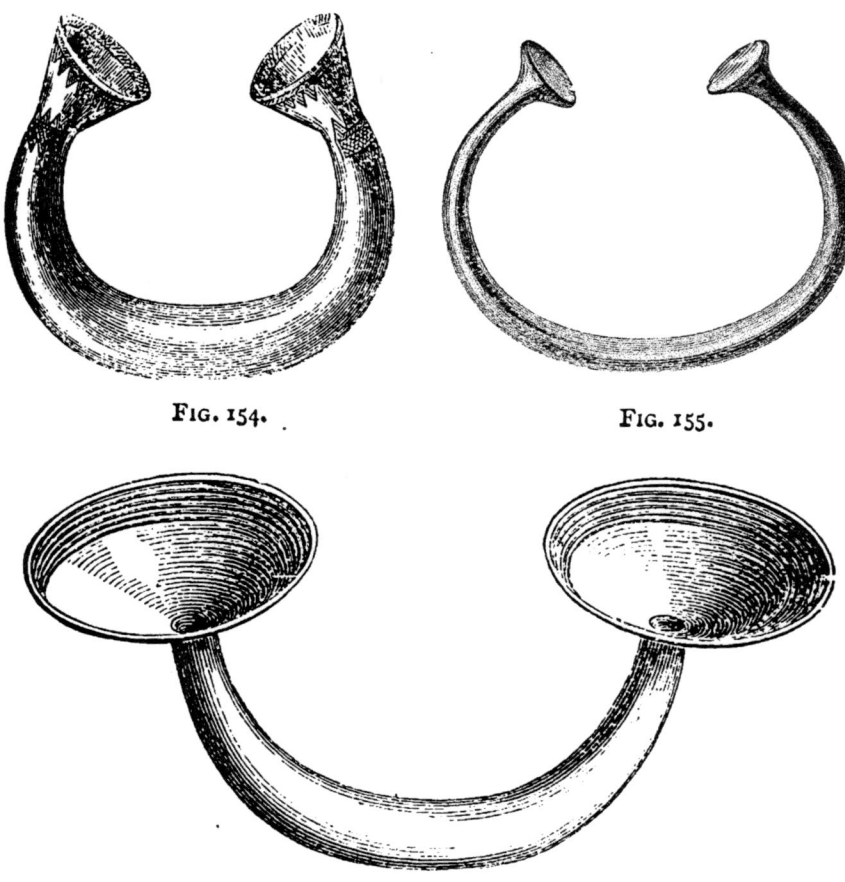

FIG. 154.   FIG. 155.

FIG. 156.

Examples of the gold *Bunne-do-at* or fibula · drawn half size · all in National Museum. Figure 154, hollow; weight, 2¼ oz. Figure 155, solid; over 3½ oz. Figure 156, hollow: 5¼ oz. (From Wilde's Catalogue.)

The Bunne and the Bunne-do-at.—There is a class of gold objects in the National Museum, very numerous—much more numerous than any other gold articles—and of various shapes and sizes, but all agreeing in two points of similarity:—open rings with *ats* or buttons at the two ends, of which figs. 154, 155, and 156 represent typical examples. These are what are called in the old records by the name *Bunnĕ-do-at*, in which *bunne* (or *buinne*) means 'a ring,' and *do* 'two':—*Bunnĕ-do-at*, a ring with two *ats*, terminal knobs, or buttons. The designation *Bunne-do-at* for these rings is exactly similar to *Muince-do-at* for the neck crescents, and applied for the same reason. There are in the Museum about 150 specimens of the Bunne-do-at: they are now commonly called by the name "Fibula." They are of various shapes, as shown in the figures; and are of all sizes, from the diminutive specimens here shown in their natural size to the great bunne-do-at represented in fig. 159, the largest known to exist.

FIG. 157.   FIG. 158.

Two specimens of the very small gold *Bunne-do-at* full size: originals in National Museum. (From Wilde's Catalogue.)

The Bunne-do-at was used as a personal ornament, and also as a mark of affluence—like many valuable articles of the present day—the size and value of course depending on the rank and means of the wearer. These articles were sometimes worn in pairs, one on each breast, and sometimes singly, on one breast: suspended from buttons like that shown at page 392, fig. 122. In one of the old tales certain persons are described as wearing Bunne-do-ats each of thirty *ungas* or ounces of gold (equal 22½ oz. Troy). There is not necessarily any exaggeration in this statement, inasmuch as the Trinity College *bunne-do-at* figured here is much heavier, weighing 33 Troy ounces.

FIG. 159.

Solid gold *Bunne-do-at*, one-third size. Now in the Museum of Trinity College, Dublin : 33 oz. So far as is known, the heaviest of its kind n existence. (From Wilde's Catalogue)

Circular Gold Plates.—Among the gold ornaments in the National Museum are a number of very thin circular plates, with raised ornamental patterns punched from the back, varying in diameter from $1\frac{1}{2}$ inch up to 4 inches. Fig. 160 represents one of these, $3\frac{1}{4}$ inches in diameter, found near Ballina in Mayo. All of them have the two holes at the centre (shown here) for fastening on the dress.

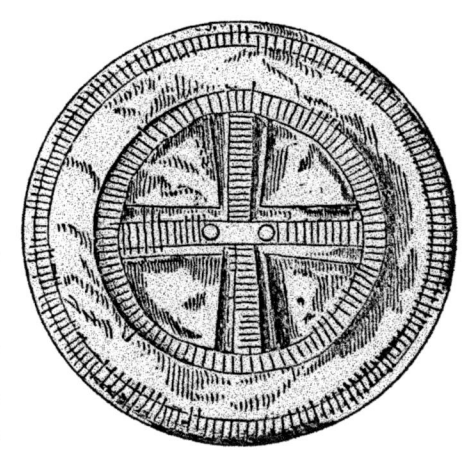

FIG. 160.

Circular gold Plate. One of those in National Museum. (From Wilde's Catalogue.)

Brooches.—The brooch was worn by both men and women, and was the commonest of all articles of jewellery. It was used to fasten the mantle at the throat and was fixed crosswise. Its value—like that of the *bunne-do-at*—depended on the rank and means of the wearer. The poorer people wore a plain one of iron or bronze, with little or no ornamentation; but kings, queens, and other persons of high rank wore brooches made of the precious metals set with gems, and in Christian times elaborately ornamented with the peculiar Irish interlaced work. These must

FIG. 161.

Specially-shaped bronze Brooch: natural size: original in National Museum: pin turning on a hinge one of the most beautiful bronze articles in the Museum, both as to design and workmanship Ornamentation on the ends produced by punching or hammering from behind. Found in a crannoge (From Wilde's Catalogue)

have been immensely expensive. That the descriptions given of brooches in old Irish writings are not exaggerated we have ample proofs in some of those now preserved in our Museums, of which the Tara Brooch figured at p. 248 is the most perfect.

The general run of brooches had the body circular, from two to four inches in diameter, with a pin from six to nine inches long. But some were much smaller, while others again were larger and longer, and reached in fact from shoulder to shoulder. These great brooches are often noticed in the records; and the Brehon Law mentions a fine for injuries caused by the points extending beyond the shoulders. As in many other cases, the records are here corroborated by existing remains; for among the collection of brooches in the National Museum are two specimens 22 and 20 inches long respectively. Brooches were made of other shapes also, of which one is represented opposite.

The usual names for brooches were *delg* (a 'thorn'), *eó* [1 syll.], *cassan* ('having a twisted shape'), *roth* ('a wheel'), and *brethnas*: but there were others.

The Lann, Blade, or Plate.—It was customary to wear a band or ribbon of some kind round the forehead to confine the hair. It was generally of some woven fabric; and it will be mentioned farther on that a charioteer wore a bright yellow *gipne* or fillet in this manner as a distinctive mark. Among the higher and richer classes the band was often a very thin flexible plate, strip, or ribbon, of burnished gold, silver, or findruine. This was what was called a *lann*, i.e. 'blade,' or more commonly *niam-lann*, 'bright-blade.'

The Minn, Diadem, or Crown.— Kings and queens wore a diadem or crown, commonly called *minn*: often designated *minn óir*, 'diadem of gold': which does not mean wholly of gold, but ornamented with gold. The *minn*, however, was not confined to kings and queens, but was worn by men and women belonging to all the higher classes, probably indicating rank according to shape and make, like the coronets of modern nobility. It was not worn in common, but was used on special occasions: a lady usually carried her *minn-óir* in her ornamental work-bag, along with other such valuable or ornamental articles, ready to be used at any moment.

The Irish *minn*, diadem, or crown was very expensive, and elaborately made, its value and shape being in accordance with the rank of the wearer. The body was of some fabric, probably silk or satin, adorned with gold, silver, white bronze, gems, and enamel. It was a cap made to encircle and cover the head, of which a good idea is given by the illustration (fig. 162), a representation of an Irish king, seated in state; copied from the high cross of Durrow, erected about A.D. 1010. The original crown of which this is a representation was about five inches high, quite flat on top, with a slender band all round, above and below, the two bands connected by slender little fillets or bars, about two inches asunder. It covers the whole head like a hat, and there are two bosses over the ears, three or four inches in diameter.

FIG. 162.

Crowned Irish king, seated, with shield, sword, and spear: a dog on each side (From the high cross of Durrow.) Copied here from a drawing by Miss Stokes

The Irish crown varied in shape, however. It is pretty certain that some had rays or fillets standing up detached all round. Crowns of this kind, belonging to the O'Conors, kings of Connaught, as represented in the thirteenth-century fresco-painting in Knockmoy Abbey, are shown at p. 24; and they are also mentioned in our old records. Two small objects now in the National Museum are believed to be portions—rays or fillets—of an old Irish radiated crown. One of them is figured in outline here; but this illustration gives no idea of the extraordinary beauty of the original, which is ornamented all over in richly coloured enamel. Mr. Kemble, a distinguished English antiquarian, says of these two objects:—"For beauty of design and execution they may challenge comparison with any specimen of cast bronze work that it has ever been my fortune to see."

FIG. 163.

Enamelled metallic object in National Museum: believed to be a ray or fillet of a crown half size. (From Miss Stokes.)

Earrings.—Men of the high class wore gold earrings, as we know from Cormac's Glossary and other old Irish authorities. An earring was called *Unasc*, from *u* or *o*, 'the ear,' and *nasc*, 'a clasp or ring.' There were several other names, all of which—as well as *unasc*—mean 'ear-clasp' or 'ear-binder,' from which, and from other evidence besides, we know that the ear was not pierced; but a thin elastic ring was clasped round it; and from the lower extremity of this another little ring was suspended (like that represented in fig. 164).

FIG. 164.
Ancient Irish gold Earring: one of a pair found in Roscommon

Golden Balls for the Hair.—Both men and women sometimes plaited the long hair; and at the end of the plait they fastened a thin, light, hollow ball of gold, which was furnished for the purpose with little apertures at opposite sides. Sometimes these balls were worn singly—probably behind—and sometimes in pairs, one on each side. These are often mentioned in the tales. King *Labraid* is described as having an apple of gold enclosing the end of his hair [behind]: Cuculainn had spheres of gold at his two ears into which his hair was gathered: and a young warrior is seen having two balls of gold on the ends of the two divisions of his hair, each the size of a man's fist. Ladies had several very small spheres—sometimes as many as eight—instead of one or two large ones.

As corroborating the records, there are in the National Museum a number of these golden balls, found from time to time in various parts of Ireland. They are all hollow and light, being formed of extremely thin gold: and each has two small circular holes at opposite sides by means of which the hair was fastened so as to hold the ball suspended. Each is formed of two hemispheres, which are joined with the greatest accuracy by being made to overlap about the sixteenth of an inch, and very delicately soldered—so that it requires the use of a lens to detect the joining. The one figured here is nearly 4 inches in diameter: so that the old story-teller was not wrong in describing some of these balls as "the size of a man's fist."

FIG. 165.

Light hollow gold Ball, worn on the end of the hair: 3¾ inches in diameter. (From Wilde's Catalogue)

Some recent writers have expressed the opinion that these balls—large and small—were used for necklaces—strung together on a string, and ranged according to size: but this opinion is erroneous. At the time they wrote—now fifty years ago—they had not before them the information regarding the use of gold balls for the hair that is now available to us.

The corroboration of the truthfulness of the old records by existing remains has been frequently noticed throughout this book; and this is a very striking example, inasmuch as the custom of wearing gold balls in the hair seems so strange that it might be set down as the invention of story-tellers, if their statements were not supported.

4. Short rough classified List of the Gold Objects in the National Museum, Dublin.

More than 30 crescents of the first type (fig. 149); five of the second (figs. 150, 151); five of the third (fig. 153).

Seven hollow balls for the hair (fig. 165).

Great numbers of bracelets and rings of various shapes and sizes (figs. 139, 140, 141).

A number of long thin bright plates and ribbons (see p. 415).

About 150 of those open rings called *bunne-do-at* (figs. 154, 155, 156, 157, 158, and 159).

About 50 very small open rings without the *ats* or buttons (mentioned at page 477, below).

About a dozen thin circular plates with patterns, all with two holes for fastening (fig. 160).

About two dozen torques of different sizes (figs. 147, 148).

A number of small ornamental beads for necklaces, of various shapes (figs. 142, 143, 144, 145, 146).

An open spiral, $2\frac{1}{2}$ inches long and 1 inch in diameter, with nine spires, formed of one square wire.

Besides these there are a number of small objects not classified.

(The total weight of all these articles is about 590 oz., which is twelve or thirteen times the weight of the collection of gold antiquities, from all England and Scotland, in the British Museum. See pp. 399, 400.)

Models.—In 1854 an immense collection of gold articles were found in a stone cist under a small clay mound near Quin in the County Clare, most of them slender delicate rings of the kind called *bunne-do-at*. In one glass-case of the National Museum there are gilt-brass models of a portion of this find, consisting mainly of about 100 *bunne-do-ats*, and five crescents of the third type.

Sculpture on Ciancel Arch, Monastery Church, Glendalough ; drawn, 1845 (From Petrie's Round Towers)

CHAPTER XIX.

AGRICULTURE AND PASTURAGE.

SECTION 1. *Fences.*

EVER since that remote time when legend and history begin to give us glimpses of the occupations of the inhabitants of this country, we find them engaged in agriculture and pasturage. For both of these purposes open land was necessary; and accordingly, the clearing of plains from wood is recorded in the reigns of many of the early kings as a public service worthy of special notice. But there was always more pasturage than tillage.

Farm Fences.—In very remote times, when the population was small and the land was mostly common property (as pointed out at p. 81, *supra*), there was little need for fences, and the country was mostly open, so far as it was free from forest and bog. But in course of time, as tillage gradually increased, and private property in land became more general, it was more and more necessary to fence off the portions belonging to different individuals. Fences are referred to in our oldest literature: and how important they were considered appears from the number of regulations regarding them in the Brehon Law. The general terms for a fence are *ime, fál,* and *aile* [imme, fawl, aule].

Four kinds of farm-fences are specified in the law:—*First*, a trench with the earth piled up on one side as a high embankment; a kind of fence still used all through Ireland: *Second*, a stone wall of dry masonry, which is still very general in stony districts in the west and south: the *Third* was formed of logs laid horizontally and securely fastened: the *Fourth* consisted of pointed stakes standing six feet above ground, and six or eight inches asunder, bound securely by three bands of interwoven osiers, and having a blackthorn crest on top.

Territorial Boundaries.—Fences such as these were too slight and temporary to serve as boundary-marks between large districts. Various landmarks of a more enduring kind were assigned for them in the law, some natural, some put down artificially. Among these are:—a "stone-mark," *i.e.* a large pillar-stone; a "deer-mark," namely, the hair-marks left by deer or cattle on the trees of a wood, or the hair-marked footpath made by them along a plain; a "water-mark," *i.e.* a river, lake, or well; a "way-mark," *i.e.* a king's road, or a carriage-road, or a cow-road (see chap. xxiv., sect. 1); a "mound-mark," *i.e.* a [great] mound or ditch or foss "or any mound whatever," such as that round the trunk of a tree.

CHAP. XIX.] AGRICULTURE AND PASTURAGE. 423

Pillar-Stones and Ramparts.—That pillar-stones were regarded as an important means of marking boundaries is shown by their frequent mention in the records. We are told in one law-tract that when certain tribe-chiefs had taken possession

Fig. 166.

Specimen of a "Holed-stone." (From Kilk. Archæol Journ.)

of a district, they "erected boundaries or placed pillar-stones there"; and in another, that after land has been enclosed a hole is made in the ground on the boundary, into which is put "the chief's standing-stone, in order that his share there may be known." We have seen that a stone set up to mark a boundary was sometimes called a "stone of worship": corresponding with the pillar-stone god Terminus worshipped by the Romans (see p. 120).

Boundary pillar-stones are found standing all over the country. But pillar-stones were erected for other purposes, of which the most usual was as a monument over a grave (for which see chap. xxvii., sect. 5, *infra*), a practice that prevailed in Christian as well as in pagan times. Battles were often commemorated by pillar-stones as well as by carns and mounds. It has been already mentioned that pillar-stones were sometimes erected as idols. Many of the standing-stones still remaining have a hole through them from which they are commonly called "holed-stones"; but the use of these is a mystery (fig. 166).

Pillar-stones are called by several Irish names :— *coirthe* [curha]; *gall*; *gallan*; and *legann*. As to many or most of the pillar-stones now remaining in the country, it is often hard or impossible to tell, in individual cases, for which of the above-mentioned purposes they were erected.

Many of the great mounds or ramparts also still exist: and there is generally a popular legend that they were rooted by an enormous enchanted black pig. One of the largest of all is that in the valley of the Newry river, which separated the sub-kingdoms of Oriell and Ulidia. Great artificial dividing dykes are found in every part of the world, some historic like the Roman wall in Britain, and some prehistoric. Offa's Dyke dividing England from Wales is a grand example: but the most stupendous artificial dyke in the world is the great wall of China.

2. *Land, Crops, and Tillage.*

Classification of Land.—Land was carefully classified in the Brehon Law for the purpose of fixing prices: there being three divisions of "superior or good arable land," and three of "weak arable land."

Manure (Irish *ottrach*) is very often mentioned in the Laws, showing the importance attached to it. The manure mentioned in the Brehon Law was chiefly stable-manure: and a law-tract mentions also the application of shells to land to improve it. This last tract, following old custom, enumerates eleven different things that add to the value of land, and estimates in *séds* or cows the amount added by each. Of these the most important are:—a wood properly fenced in: a mine of copper or iron: the site of an old mill [with millrace and other accessories, rendering easy the erection of a new mill]: a road [opening up communication]: situation by the sea, by a river, or by a cooling pond for cattle.

Digging for Water.—Various passages both in the Brehon Laws and in general Irish literature show that the ancient Irish understood the art of obtaining water by digging deeply into the ground. It must have been a pretty common practice moreover, for the annalists assign a legendary origin for it, a thing they never did except where the custom was general. The Four Masters say, under A.M. 3991: "It was by this king (Fiacha) that the earth was first dug in Ireland in order that water might be in wells." The Greeks similarly assigned the origin of their custom of digging for water to their old hero Danaus, king of the Argives.

Crops.—Most of the native crops now in use were then known and cultivated: chief among them being corn of various kinds. Corn in general was denoted by the words *arbar* [arvar or arroor] and *ith* [ih]; besides which there was a special name for each kind. We know for a certainty that wheat (Irish *cruithnecht*, pron. crunnat) has been cultivated in this country from the most remote ages; for we find it constantly mentioned in our ancient literature: of which an interesting illustration will be found in the record of the death of the two princes in Mailoran's mill at p. 457, below. So also as to oats (Irish *coirce*, pron. curkh-ya); numerous references to its cultivation and use are found in our most ancient literature.

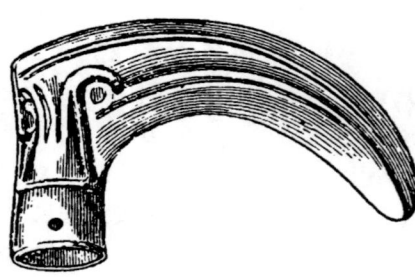

FIG. 167.

Ancient Irish bronze reaping-hook: of beautiful workmanship, 6¼ inches long It was fitted with a handle, which was fastened in the socket with a rivet In the National Museum, Dublin. (Wilde's Catalogue.)

In modern times, before the potato became very general, oats formed one of the principal articles of food of the people, as it did of old. Barley (Irish *eórna* [ōrna]) and rye (Irish *segal*, pron. shaggal) were cultivated, and formed an important part of the food supplies.

Corn was cut with a sickle or reaping-hook, anciently called *serr* or *searr* [shărr]; but the present name is *carrán*. Many specimens of reaping-hooks have been found in Ireland, some of bronze and some of iron, which may be seen in the

National Museum in Dublin. They are all small, and cutting with them must have been slow work. Those of bronze are very ancient—probably beyond the reach of history. The iron ones are hardly so old; but still they have the look of great antiquity. Meadow-grass was cut with a scythe anciently and still called *speal* [spal].

The corn while in sheaves was stacked in a haggard, which was called *ithlann*, 'corn-yard.' The rick (Ir. *cruach*) was commonly covered with thatch, twined or woven with ropes to protect it from wind and rain. The sheaves were threshed with a *súist* or flail, as at present.

Farm Implements.—Most of the common implements employed in farm-work at the present day were used by the ancient Irish, though no doubt they were somewhat different in make. The use of the plough was universal. The old word for it was *arathar* [arraher], but it is now called *céchta* [kaighta], which is also an ancient word. Several of the parts of the plough are mentioned in the old records. The iron coulter or ploughshare was called *socc*, which is the word still used. The plough was generally drawn by oxen: but sometimes by horses. The ploughman had each ox held by a halter, and he also carried a sharp goad (Irish *brot*), "so that"—as the law tract expresses it—"the ox may be mastered."

For breaking clods of clay in a ploughed field farmers used a clod-mallet called *forcca* or *furcha*, which means a mallet of any kind: it had a wooden handle, the head being also made of wood. They used a spade (*rama*) and a shovel (*sluasat*), both fixed on wooden handles and both probably made of iron. In Cormac's Glossary the word for a spade is *fec*, which is still in use even among the English-speaking people of many parts of Ireland, who call a spade *feck* or *fack*. *Rama* and *sluasad* are also retained as living words for spade and shovel: but the former takes the diminutive form *ramhan*, often shortened to *rán*, both pronounced *rawn*. A rake was used, which, as far as we can judge from the description of it given in Cormac's Glossary, must have been much the same as that used at present. It is called in the Glossary *rastal*, which is the present name.

3. *Some Farm-Animals.*

Cows.—From the most remote ages, cows formed one of the principal articles of wealth of the inhabitants of this country; they were in fact the standard of value, as money is at the present day; and prices, wages, and marriage portions were estimated in cows by our ancestors (see chap xxiii., sect. 4, *infra*). The most general Irish word for a cow is *bo*, not only at the present day, but in the oldest manuscripts. A bull is called *tarbh* [tarruv], a word which exists in cognate forms in many languages. *Damh* [dauv], an ox, is evidently cognate with Latin *dama*, a deer. How it came to pass that the same word signifies in Irish an ox, and in Latin a deer, philologists may explain. The chief use of the ox was as a draft and plough animal, for which see "Oxen" in Index. The usual Irish word for a calf is *gamhan* [gowan].

Pigs.—In point of value to the community, pigs came next to cows, and were of more importance to the general run of people than horses. They were kept by almost all, so that they were quite as plentiful and formed as valuable an industry in old times as at present. The usual Irish word for a pig was, and is still, *muc* or *mucc* : a boar was called *torc*. A very young pig was a *banb* or *banbh* [bonniv], a word which is still known in the anglicised form of *bonniv* or *bonny*, or with the diminutive, *bonneen* or *bonniveen*— words used in every part of Ireland for sucking-pigs. It was cheap and easy enough to feed pigs in those days. Forests abounded everywhere, and the animals were simply turned out into the woods and fed on mast and whatever else they could pick up. Wealthy people—chiefs and even kings, as well as rich farmers —kept great herds, which cost little or nothing beyond the pay of a swineherd : and they gave no trouble, for, except in winter, they remained out day and night, needing no sties or pens of any kind, being sufficiently sheltered by the trees and underwood. Woodland was generally a part of the "commons" (p. 83, *supra*), where every member of the sept was free to send his pigs to feed. The special time for fattening was autumn, when mast abounded ; and at the end of the season the fat pigs were slaughtered : those that were left were kept in sties during winter.

When woodland was not convenient, or when for any other reason pigs had to be kept and fattened at home, they were fed on corn or sour milk, and on offal of various kinds : these were managed chiefly by women. The custom of feeding pigs on malt-

grains, now so familiar near breweries, was also practised by the ancient Irish: for we have seen that brewing was then very common. The old Irish race of pigs were long-snouted, thin-spare, muscular, and active: and except when fat they could scour the country like hounds. In the remote forests there were plenty of wild pigs: and we have many references to them in our literature. In the twelfth century Giraldus gives us this testimony:—
" In no part of the world are such vast herds of boars and wild pigs to be found."

Sheep were kept everywhere, as they were of the utmost importance, partly as food, and partly for their wool: and they are constantly mentioned in the Brehon Laws as well as in general Irish literature. The common Irish word for a sheep was, and is, *cáera* [caira].

4. *Herding, Grazing, Milking.*

Herding and Grazing. — There were special keepers of cows, of sheep, of swine: the old word for a cowherd was *bóchaill* or *buachaill* [boohil]; from *bo*, 'a cow': but in modern times the word *buachail* has come to signify 'boy' simply, without any reference to occupation. At the present day a shepherd is called *aedhaire* and *treudaighe* [aira, traidee]. As an aid to herding, bells were sometimes hung round the necks of cows and sheep, and the law laid down a fine for removing the bell. Such bells have continued in use till this day: and in the National Museum may be seen many specimens.

The nature and use of "commons" have been already explained (p. 83). The commons pasture was generally mountain-land, usually at some distance from the lowland homesteads; and it was grazed in common and not fenced in. Each head of a family belonging to the tribe or *finĕ* had the right to send his cattle on it, the number he was entitled to turn out being generally in proportion to the size of his farm. In regulating the right of grazing, animals were classified, a cow being taken as the unit. The legal classification was this:—two geese are equivalent to a sheep; two sheep to one *dairt*, or one-year-old heifer; two *dairts* to one *colpach*, or two-year-old heifer; two *colpachs* to one cow; a cow and a *colpach* equal to one ox. Suppose a man had a right to graze a certain number of cows on the common: he might turn out the exact number of cows, or the equivalent of other animals, any way he pleased, so long as the total did not exceed the amount of his privilege. This custom continued down to recent times.

In the sixteenth and seventeenth centuries it was usual for all the people of a village or townland, after putting down the crops in spring, to migrate to the uplands with their families and cattle, living there in temporary settlements during the summer, and returning to their homes in the beginning of autumn in time to gather in the crops. An upland settlement of this kind was called a *buaile* [booley]: and the custom— which descended from early times—was known as *booleying* by Anglo-Irish writers, several of whom have described it.

Remnants of the old regulations regarding the use of commons land survive in many parts of Ireland to the present day. There are still "commons"—generally mountain-land or lowland moors—attached to village communities, on which several families have a right to graze their cattle according to certain well-defined regulations; and there are bogs where they have a right to cut peat or turf—a right of turbary, as they call it: and if an individual sells or otherwise disposes of his land, these rights always go with it.

Farm Life and Milking.—The people of Ireland, not the farming classes merely, but the general community, were early risers, and went early to bed. The active working-day in the houses of farmers began at sunrise and ended when the cows came to their stalls: and in the houses of chiefs it began when the horse-boy let out the horses in the morning, and ended at bed-time. In milking they used a spancel (Ir. *buarach*) as at present, made, then as now, of a stout rope of twisted hair, about two feet long, with a bit of wood—a sort of long-shaped knob fixed at one end, and a loop at the other end into which the knob was thrust so as to fasten the spancel round the two hind legs of the cow. Women always did the milking, except of course in monasteries, where no women were employed, and the monks had to do all the work of the community. It has been already mentioned that the monks, after the milking, always brought the milk home in a special vessel strapped on their backs, and went first to the abbot that he might bless the milk before use.

Composed from the Book of Kells

CHAPTER XX.

WORKERS IN WOOD, METAL, AND STONE.

Section 1. *Chief Materials.*

imber.—All the chief materials for the work of the various crafts were produced at home. Of wood there was no stint: and there were mines of copper, iron, lead, and possibly of tin, which were worked with intelligence and success.

We know that in early ages Ireland abounded in forests; so that wood as a working material was plentiful everywhere. Even in the time of Giraldus Cambrensis—the end of the twelfth century—when clearances and cultivation had gone on for a thousand years, the greater part of the country was clothed with trees. He says:—" Ireland is well wooded and marshy. The [open] plains are of limited extent compared with the woods." The common Irish word for a tree was, and is still, *crann* : a wood is *coill* or *feadh* [fah]. The Brehon Code, in setting forth the law for illegally felling trees, divides them into four classes, with a special fine for each class.

2·F

Metals.—The metallic weapons and tools preserved in our museums are generally either of bronze (sometimes brass, occasionally copper) or iron. The bronze objects far outnumber those of iron, which is partly explained by the fact that iron rusts and wastes away much more quickly than bronze. It is generally recognised that the three materials—stone, bronze, iron—represent three successive stages of human progress; that is to say, stone in its use as a material for tools and weapons is more ancient than bronze, and bronze than iron. But there was no sudden or well-marked change from one to another: they all overlap. Stone was used in a primitive stage when bronze was not known; but it continued to be used long after the introduction of bronze. So bronze was used for some long period before iron was known; but continued in use long after the discovery of iron. And more than that: all three were used together down into Christian times.

That the ancient Irish were familiar with mines, and with the modes of smelting and of extracting metals of various kinds from the ore, is shown by the frequent notices of mines and mining both in the Laws and in the general literature; and the truth of this documentary testimony is fully confirmed by evidence under our own eyes. Sir Richard Griffith remarks that the numbers of ancient mine excavations still visible in every part of Ireland prove that "an ardent spirit of mining adventure" must have pervaded the country at some remote period; and he gives many instances. Of the detailed smelting processes of the Irish we have very little knowledge. But we know that, whether these arts grew from within or were brought hither by the first immigrants, the Irish miners successfully extracted from their ores all the native metals then known.

In Ireland as elsewhere copper was known before iron. It was almost always used as bronze, which will be treated of farther on. It is certain that iron was known in Ireland at least as early as the first century: probably much earlier. According to tradition, the mines of Slieve-an-ierin (the 'mountain of iron'), east of Lough Allen in the County of Leitrim, were worked by *Goibniu*, the great Dedannan smith: and it is now as celebrated for its iron ore as it was when it got the name, long ages ago.

Tinstone occurs in several parts of Ireland, such as Wicklow, Dublin, and Killarney. But whether tin was mined at home or imported from Cornwall— or both, as is more likely—it was constantly used— mixed with copper—in making bronze: and often, in ornamental work, without any mixture. The ores of lead are found in many parts of Ireland; and the mines were worked too, so that the metal was sufficiently abundant. Zinc, which was chiefly used in making brass, was also found, commonly in connexion with lead. Gold and silver have been already treated of.

2. *Builders.*

From the most remote times there were in Ireland professional architects or builders, as there were smiths, poets, historians, physicians, and druids; and we find them often mentioned in our earliest literature. There were two main branches of the builder's profession:—stone-building and wood-building. An ollave builder was supposed to be master of both, and, in addition to this, to be so far acquainted with many subordinate crafts as to be able to "superintend" them, as the Law expresses it: in other words, to be a thorough judge as to whether the work was properly turned out by the several tradesmen, so as to be able to pass or reject as the works deserved: all which resembles what is expected from architects and builders of the present day.

The most distinguished ollave builder of a district was taken into the direct service of the king, and received from him a yearly stipend of twenty-one cows, answering to a fixed salary of £250 or £300 of the present day: for which he was to oversee and have properly executed all the king's building and other structural works. In addition to this he was permitted to exercise his art for the general public for pay: and as he had a great name, and had plenty of time on hands, he usually made a large income.

By far the most celebrated of all the ancient architects of Ireland was the Gobban Saer, who flourished in the seventh century of our era, and who therefore comes well within historic times. He is mentioned in the Lives of many of the Irish saints as having been employed by them to build churches, oratories, and houses, some of which still retain his name. To this day the peasantry all over Ireland tell numerous stories about him.

3. *Braziers and Founders.*

The word *goba* [gow] is applied to a worker in iron—a smith: *cerd* or *cerdd* [caird], to a worker in brass, gold, and silver—a brazier, goldsmith, or silversmith: *saer* to a carpenter, builder, or mason—a worker in timber or stone. These are the usual applications: but as the arts and trades sometimes overlap, so the words are often applied in somewhat more extended senses.

We have already seen that the ancient Irish were very skilful in metallic art. Metallic compounds were carefully and successfully studied, copper commonly forming one of the ingredients. The most general alloy was bronze, formed of copper and tin: but brass, a compound of copper and zinc, was also

Fig. 168.

Brazier's or Goldsmith's Anvil: natural size; much worn. the little shallow holes were for riveting. (From Wildes Catalogue)

used. The Irish name for copper was *uma* [ooa], which is used also to denote both bronze and brass.

There were two chief kinds of bronze, red and white, or rather reddish and whitish. The red bronze was called *derg-uma* (*derg*, 'red') or *cred-uma*, and the white was called *finn-uma* (*finn*, 'white'), or *findruine* [fin-drině]. *Findruine* was much more expensive than *creduma*, and was kept for the finer kinds of work. The red bronze may be seen in the spear-heads and caldrons in the National Museum, and the *findruine* or white bronze in the ornamental shrines, and other ancient works of art.

Metal-casting is very often referred to in general terms in our literature, showing how familiar it was: and through these incidental references we get now and then a glimpse at the artists' tools and appliances. The workmen used charcoal for their fires, that made from birch-wood, giving the greatest heat then attainable, sufficient — with the help of a flux — to melt all ordinary metals. They used a ladle (Irish, *liach*) to pour out the melted metal.

FIG 169.

Inlaid hook, natural size. Possibly for suspending a sword. The scroll-work indicates Christian times. Now in National Museum. (From Wilde's Catalogue.)

FIG. 170.

Spear-head, now in National Museum, where many equally or more beautiful are preserved. (From Wilde's Catalogue.)

The exquisite skill of the ancient Irish braziers is best proved by the articles they made, of which hundreds are preserved in our Museum. Two illustra-

CHAP. XX.] WORKERS IN WOOD, METAL, AND STONE. 439

tions are given opposite (figs. 169 and 170); a beautiful specimen of enamelled metal-work is described at page 417, *supra*, and shown in fig. 163; and others will be found in various parts of this book, especially in the chapter on Art. The gracefully-shaped spearheads, which, in point of artistic excellence, are fully equal to any of those found in Greece, Rome, or Egypt, were cast in moulds: and we have not only the spear-heads themselves but many of the moulds, usually of stone, proving—if proof

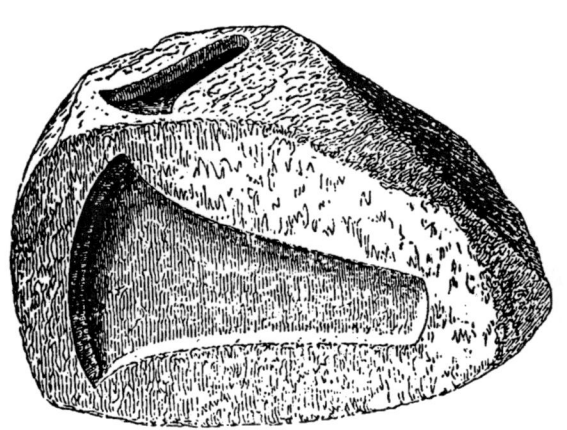

FIG. 171.   FIG. 172.

Stone Moulds. Fig. 171 in Belfast Museum · fig 172 n National Museum, Dublin.
(From Wilde's Catalogue)

was needed—that all these articles were of native manufacture. In one glass case in the National Museum there are more than forty moulds for celts, spear-heads, arrow-heads, &c.: some looking as fresh as if they had been in use yesterday. The old cairds were equally accomplished in making articles of hammered bronze, of which the most characteristic and important are the beautifully-formed caldrons—many of exquisite workmanship—made of a series of bronze plates, hammered into shape and riveted together. Of these, numerous specimens may be seen in the National Museum; and some are figured in this book (see figs. 107, 108, pp. 352, 353; also fig. 90, p. 315, above).

4. *The Blacksmith and his Forge.*

In a state of society when war was regarded as the most noble of all professions, and before the invention of gunpowder, those who manufactured swords and spears were naturally looked upon as very important personages. In Ireland they were held in great estimation; and in the historical and legendary tales, we find smiths entertaining kings, princes, and chiefs, and entertained by them in turn. We know that Vulcan was a Grecian god; and the ancient Irish had their smith-god also, the Dedannan, Goibniu, who figures in many of the old romances.

Cérdcha [cairda] originally meant a workshop in general; but its most usual application was to a forge: and it is still so applied, and pronounced *cartha* (the first syll. long, as in *star*). A forge was in old times regarded as one of the important centres of a district. If, for instance, horses whose owners were not known were impounded for trespass, notice had to be sent to the dun or fortress of the nearest lord, to the principal church, to the fort of the brehon of the place, and to the forge of the smith: and in like manner notice of a waif should be sent to seven leading persons, among them the chief smith of the district. For forges were places well frequented, as they are at the present day, partly by those who came to get work done, and partly by idlers.

The anvil (*inneoin*, pron. innone), which was large and heavy, and shaped something like that now in use, with a long projecting snout on the side, was placed on a block or stock, called *cepp* [kep]. The smith held the red-hot iron in a *tennchair* [tinneher], pincers or tongs, using his own hand-hammer, while a sledger—if needed—struck with a heavy *ord* or sledge, as we see at the present day.

A water-trough was kept in the forge, commonly called *umar*. The smith kept a supply of wood-charcoal in bags, called *cual crainn*, i.e. 'coal of wood.' I do not know if coal from the mine was used: but the distinctive term *cual crainn* would seem to imply that it was: and besides, very ancient coal mines have been found near Ballycastle in Antrim. The smith wore an apron commonly of buckskin, like those smiths wear now.

The Irish name for a smith's bellows is *builgg* [bullig], which is merely the plural form of *bolg*, a bag, like the English *bellows* ('bags'); indicating that, in Ireland as in other countries, the primitive bellows consisted of at least two bags, which of course were made of leather. Why two bags were used is obvious—in order to keep up a continuous blast; each being kept blowing in turn while the other was filling. This word *builgg* the Irish continued to employ for their bellows, even in its most improved form, just as we now call the instruments we have in use 'bellows,' though this word originally meant 'bags,' like the Irish *builgg*.

From several passages in old Irish literature we are in a measure enabled to reconstruct the old Irish smith's bellows, and exhibit the mode of working it. In the flag standing at the back of the fire was a small hole through which the pipe directed the air-current from the bellows. The name given to the bellows in Cormac's Glossary—*di bolg*, 'two bags'—indicates that the bellows in view here had two separate chambers lying side by side. Each of these must have consisted of an upper and an under board with sides of leather· and in the under board of each was a simple clapper-valve as in our present kitchen-bellows. From each chamber extended a pipe, the two pipes uniting into one which was inserted into the hole in the flagstone. The two chambers were placed close to each other, and there must have been a short cross-beam or lever (AA in fig. 173) turning on a centre pivot, with its two ends loosely fastened to the two backward projections of the upper boards. In every forge there was a special bellows-blower, who blew strongly or gently as occasion required, sometimes directed by the smith. The bellows was worked by the naked feet. The bellows-blower stood on top, one foot on each board (at BB), and pressed the two down alternately. As each was

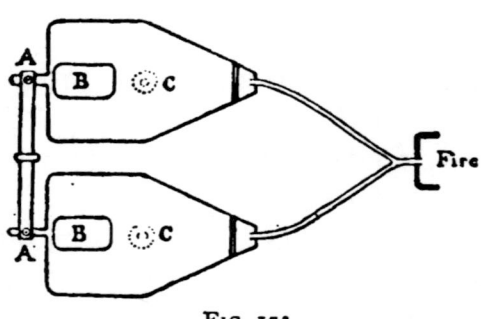

FIG. 173.

Conjectural plan of double or two-chambered orge-bellows The bellows-blower stood with his feet on BB, facing fire. AA, the cross-beam, turning on its centre. CC, clapper-valves in bottom boards The rest of the diagram explains itself

pressed down, and its chamber emptied through the pipe, the other was drawn up by its own end of the cross-beam, and the chamber was filled through the clapper-valve at bottom: and thus the chambers were compressed and expanded in turn so as to keep up a continuous blast. There was a cross-bar fixed firmly above the bellows for the blower to grasp with his hands, so as to steady him and enable him to thrust downwards with his feet when a strong blast was required, like a modern bicyclist when mounting a hill.

The bellows used in private houses was totally different in make and mode of using from the forge-bellows, as well as from our present common kitchen-bellows. It was one of those made to blow by revolving fans inside: and it was made of wood, with leather if needed. Accordingly it was called — not *builgg* — but *séidire* [shaidera], *i.e.* 'blower.' All this we infer from the accurate description given in the Laws. This form of bellows is still occasionally met with, but the body is now made of lacquered tin instead of wood and leather.

The last of the smith's appliances to be noticed is the furnace: and the old Irish authorities enable us to reconstruct this as well as the bellows. At the back of the fire was an upright flag with a little hole for the bellows-pipe. The other three sides, which enclosed and confined the fire, were made of clay specially prepared. When they got burned or worn out they were cleared away and replaced by a new structure. For this purpose a mould was used, with an upright handle like that shown here (fig. 174). The mould was set in its place, and the soft moist clay was worked round three of its sides into proper form with the hands, which was done in a few minutes. Then the mould was carefully lifted up, leaving the new furnace ready for use. The smith always kept a supply of the prepared furnace-clay in bags in his forge.

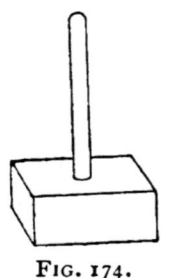

FIG. 174.
Ness, or Mould.

It was necessary to enclose the fire by a furnace; for the fuel in those days was of wood charcoal, which being lighter than our coal, would, if unconfined, be blown about and scattered by the blast of the bellows.

5. *Carpenters, Masons, and other Craftsmen.*

Carpenters.—Woodworkers of whatever kind do not figure near so prominently in the ancient literature as smiths and braziers; yet they must have been more numerous, for there was more work to be done in wood than in metals. One important source of employment for carpenters was the building of houses, which in old times were nearly always of wood: and there were special tradesmen for it.

The yew-tree was formerly very abundant. Its wood was highly valued and used in making a great variety of articles: so that working in yew was regarded as one of the most important of trades. It required great skill and much training and practice: for yew is about the hardest and most difficult to work of all our native timber: and the cutting tools must have been particularly fine in quality. Various domestic vessels were made from it—as we have seen—and it was used for doorposts and lintels and other prominent parts of houses, as well as for the posts, bars, and legs of beds and couches, always carved. In the most ancient of the tales we often find mention of houses ornamented with "carvings of red yew."

Among other tradesmen, there were the *dŭalaidhe* [doolee] or painter. (from *dŭal*, a brush); the *rinnaidhe* [rinnee] or metal engraver (from *rinn*, a sharp point, a sharp-pointed instrument); and the *erscoraidhe* [erscoree] or wood-carver. Carvers were in much request and exercised their art in the highest perfection on yew-wood.

Various Tools.—Besides other tools mentioned elsewhere in connexion with certain special arts and crafts, the following, chiefly used by wood-workers, may be dealt with here. They are often noticed in Irish literature, but more frequently in the Brehon Laws than elsewhere. The old Irish wood- and metal-workers seem indeed to have used quite as many tools as those of the present day.

A saw had two names, *turesc* and *rodhb* [rove], of which *turesc* is still used. There were—as at the present day—several kinds of axes and hatchets variously shaped, and used in different sorts of work, as may be seen by the number of names for them, and the manner in which they are often distinguished. In all forms of axe, the metallic head was fixed on the handle, the same as now, by wedging the wood through the *cro* or opening in the iron or bronze. The common hatchet used in the workshop was called *tuagh* [tooa], which seems to be a general name for a hatchet or axe of any kind. A *biail* [beeal] was a sort of axe often used in clearing wood : a *fidba* [feeva] was like our common billhook. Great numbers of bronze axes are preserved in the National Museum, Dublin. The carpenter's hatchet was probably like some of those figured on p. 56, *supra*.

Fig. 175.
Bronze adze: in National Museum: 4⅞ inches wide along edge. (From Wilde's Catalogue.)

A *tál* [tawl] or adze— *i.e.* an axe having the edge across or at right angles to the line of the handle — was used for special sorts of work; as, for instance, in making wooden shields; and of course in cooperage. It was an exceedingly common tool, and it is constantly mentioned in all sorts of records.

An awl, by whatsoever tradesman used, was called *menad* or *meanadh* [manna], which is still the Irish word all through Ireland. The old Irish carpenters used an auger and called it *taráthar* [tarauher], a name which is still in use. They had compasses which they named *gabulrinn* [gowlrin], a term which is quite descriptive, being compounded of the two words, *gabal*, a fork, and *rinn*, a point: that is to say a fork with two points.

The circles on some of the flat golden gorgets and on some bunne-do-ats (pp. 405, 413, *supra*) were obviously made with a compass: all going to confirm the truthfulness of the records.

The mallet used by carpenters, fence-makers, and other workmen, was generally called *farcha* or *forcha*. A sledge was called *ord*: an ordinary hammer was *lámh-ord* ('hand-sledge'): but sometimes *cas-ord*, now generally made *casúr* [cossoor]. The *cas* in this, which means 'twisted' or 'bended,' probably refers to the 'claw,' so that a *casord* or *casúr* would be a 'claw-hammer.' The word *mailin* was used to designate another kind of hammer, one without a claw: for *mailin* means 'bald' or 'bare': a 'bare or clawless little hammer.'

Carpenters used a *rungenn* or *runcan*, 'a plane': in the Brehon Law, it is stated that the posts of the doors and beds of certain classes of houses were finished off with a moulding-plane. Workers in wood used a sort of press called *cantair*, either for straightening wood or forcing it into certain shapes—after being softened probably by water or steam. The ancient Irish builders used a crane of some kind for lifting heavy articles, which they called *corr aurógbala* [aurógala], 'a crane for lifting.' Here the Irish word corresponding to 'crane' is *corr*, which is still the name of any bird of the crane kind: and it is applied in this passage to the machine, exactly like the English word *crane*, on account of the long beak.

The lathe and other turning-wheels were well known and employed for a variety of purposes. The Brehon Law when setting forth the privileges of various classes of craftsmen has *tornoire* or 'turners' among them, explaining that these are the men "who do turning." A much older authority, an eighth-century Irish glossator, in his remarks on a verse of one of the Psalms, gives an explanation of the potter's wheel. The Irish word for a lathe is *deil* [dell]; and at the present day, speakers, whether using the Irish or English language, call a lathe a *dell*.

Chisels of a variety of shapes and sizes were used by wood-workers of which the following illustrations will give a very good idea the originals—

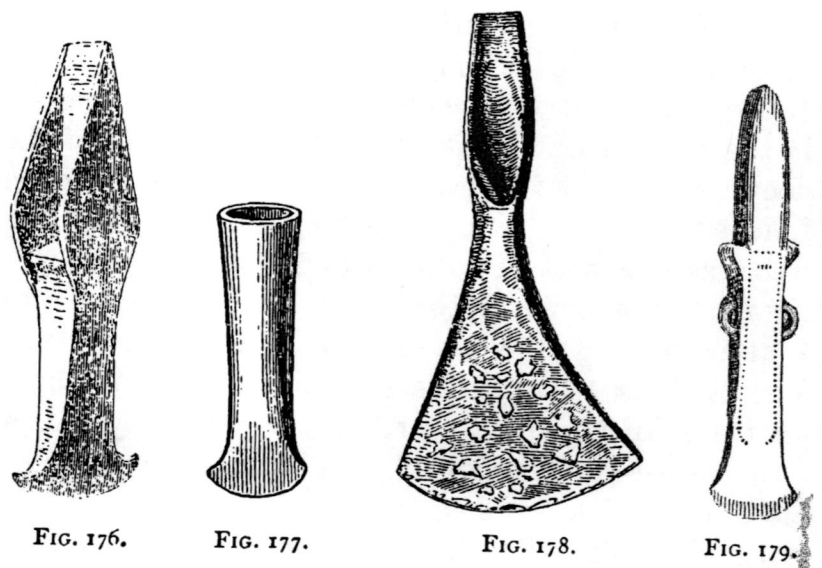

Fig. 176.   Fig. 177.   Fig. 178.   Fig. 179.

Bronze Chisels in National Museum   (From Wilde's Catalogue.)

which are all of bronze—are preserved in the National Museum. A large number of bronze gouges are preserved in the same Museum; but I have not found any special Irish name for a gouge. Among the collection of bronze tools found at Dooros-Heath in King's County (next page) are three gouges with the regularly curved edges, well adapted for excavating and paring wooden bowls and goblets.

and about the same time another was found in Wexford. The bronze of these and of all the other cutting instruments in the King's County collection is excessively hard. It may be observed that bronze can be made almost or altogether as hard as steel by hammering.

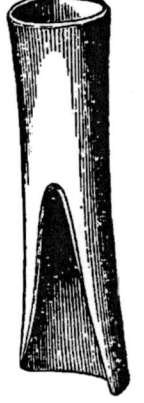

Fig. 180.

Bronze Gouge in Nat Museum. (From Wilde's Catalogue)

Sharpening.—For sharpening edged tools and weapons, the people used a whetstone, which is called in Cormac's Glossary *cotud*, literally meaning 'hard,' and defined " a stone on which iron tools or weapons are ground ": but it is often called *lec*, which is the general name for a flat stone. They had also a circular grindstone which was turned on an axis like those now in use. The grindstone was called *liom-brón* [leev-vrone], 'sharpening millstone,' and also *lic-limad* [lic-leeva], 'stone of grinding'—corresponding exactly with the English name " grinding-stone ": and it was turned round by means of a cranked handle called *ruiti*.

Remains of Ancient Workshops.—It is worthy of remark that the remains of ancient workshops or factories belonging to several trades have been discovered from time to time in different parts of Ireland. About the year 1820 a brazier's workshop was turned up in a place called Dooros-Heath, in the parish of Eglish near Birr in King's County, where great quantities of gold-coloured bronze articles were found—bells, spearheads, celts, trumpets, gouges, and so forth: also whetstones, flat, convex, and concave. That this was a workshop is shown by

2 G

several facts: many of the articles were unfinished or only half made, while some were mended: and there was one lump of unworked bronze—mere material. The remains of a glass factory will be found mentioned at p. 295, *supra*; and an old workshop of a family of goldsmiths has lately been found near Cullen in Tipperary. In parts of Ulster where flints are common, flint workshops are sometimes turned up, with vast numbers of finished and half-finished flint articles. Ancient Gaulish workshops of various crafts have in like manner been lately found in France.

Masons and their work.—A knowledge of the use of lime-mortar and of the arch was introduced by St. Patrick and his foreign missionaries. Before his time the Irish built their stone structures of dry masonry: and not knowing how to construct an arch, they brought their walls to converge in a curve—like the ancient Greeks and other nations of antiquity—by the gradual overlapping of the flat-lying stones. Numerous specimens of their handiwork in this department of ancient art still remain, especially in the south and west, in the beehive-shaped houses and stone cahers, which show much skill in fitting the stones to one another so as to form very close joints. Although the Irish did not employ lime (Irish *aol*: pron. *ail*) in making mortar till the fifth century, it was used as a whitener in pagan times (p. 312, *supra*). They made lime by burning limestone or sea-shells in a limekiln, much as is done at the present day.

Numerous structures erected in Christian times, but before the invasion, with lime-mortar, still re-

CHAP. XX.] WORKERS IN WOOD, METAL, AND STONE. 451

main all over the country, chiefly primitive churches and round towers. It is only necessary to point to

FIG. 181.

Round Tower of Devenish Island, in Lough Erne · 85 feet high. To illustrate what is said here in the text as to beauty of outline and general shape. (From Petrie's Round Towers.)

the round towers to show the admirable skill and the delicate perception of gracefulness of outline

2 G 2

possessed by the ancient Irish builders. A similar remark might be made regarding many of the ancient churches, especially those called Romanesque.

Fig. 182.

Beautiful window of Castledermot Abbey. (From Miss Stokes's High Crosses of Castledermot and Durrow.) To illustrate the statements about the skill of Irish masons.

6. *Protection of Crafts and Social Position of Craftsmen.*

Artificers of all kinds held a good position in society and were taken care of by the Brehon Law. Among the higher classes of craftsmen a builder of an oratory or of ships was entitled to the same compensation for any injury inflicted on him in person, honour, or reputation, as the lowest rank of noble; and similar provisions are set forth in the law for craftsmen of a lower grade. Elsewhere it is stated that the artist who made the articles of adornment of precious metals for the person or household of a king was entitled to compensation for injury equal to half the amount payable to the king himself for a like injury.

As illustrating this phase of society we sometimes find people of very high rank engaging in handicrafts. One of St. Patrick's three smiths was Fortchern, son of Laegaire, king of Ireland. But, on the other hand, a king was never allowed to engage in manual labour of any kind (p. 25, *supra*). Many of the ancient Irish saints were skilled artists. In the time of St. Brigit there was a noted school of metal-workers near her convent, over which presided St. Conleth, first bishop of Kildare, who was himself a most skilful artist. St. Dega of Iniskeen in Louth was a famous artificer. He was chief artist to St. Kieran of Seirkieran, sixth century; and he was a man of many parts, being a *caird* or brazier, a *goba* or smith, and besides, a choice scribe. In the Martyrology of Donegal it is stated that "he made 150 bells, 150 crosiers: and also [leather] cases or covers for sixty Gospel Books," *i.e.* books containing the Four Gospels.

In the household of St. Patrick there were several artists, all of them ecclesiastics, who made church furniture for him. His three smiths were Macecht, who made Patrick's famous bell called 'Sweet-sounding'; Laebhan; and Prince Fortchern, as mentioned above. His three braziers were Assicus, Tairill, and Tasach. In the "Tripartite Life" it is stated that "the holy bishop Assicus was Patrick's coppersmith; and he made altars and quadrangular tables, and quadrangular book-covers in honour of Patrick " We have already seen how highly scribes

Fig. 183.

Doorway of Rahan Church, King's Co., dating from middle of eighth century. Specimen of skilled mason-work to illustrate what is said at pp. 451, 452, *supra*. (From Petrie's Round Towers.

and book-illuminators were held in esteem. Nearly all the *artists* selected by St. Patrick for his household were natives, though there were many foreigners in his train, some of whom he appointed to other functions : a confirmation of what has been already observed, that he found, on his arrival, arts and crafts in an advanced stage of cultivation.

No individual tradesman was permitted to practise till his work had been in the first place examined at a meeting of chiefs and specially-qualified ollaves, held either at Croghan or at Emain, where a number of craftsmen candidates always presented themselves. But besides this there was another precautionary regulation. In each district there was a head-craftsman of each trade, designated *sai-re-cérd* [see-re-caird], *i.e.* ' sage in handicraft.' He presided over all those of his own craft in the district: and a workman who had passed the test of the examiners at Croghan or Emain had further to obtain the approval and sanction of his own head-craftsman before he was permitted to follow his trade in the district. It will be seen from all this that precautions were adopted to secure competency in handicrafts similar to those now adopted in the professions.

Young persons learned trades by apprenticeship, and commonly resided during the term in the houses of their masters. They generally gave a fee : but sometimes they were taught free—or as the law-tract expresses it—" for God's sake." When an apprentice paid a fee, the master was responsible for his misdeeds: otherwise not. The apprentice was bound to do all sorts of menial work—digging, reaping, feeding pigs, &c.—for his master, during apprenticeship.

Ornament on top of Devenish Round Tower. (From Petrie's Round Towers.)

CHAPTER XXI.

CORN MILLS AND QUERNS.

Section 1. *Mills.*

VERY early Irish tradition, transmitted through ancient manuscripts, assigns the erection of the first watermill in Ireland to the illustrious King Cormac mac Art (reigned A.D. 254 to 277). He sent "across the sea" for a mill-wright, who constructed a mill on the stream of Nith, flowing from the well named *Nemnach* ('sparkling') beside Tara. The spot on which this mill was constructed, and where a mill was kept working time out of mind until very recently, was called Lismullin (the 'fort of the mill'): and the place, which is a mile northeast from Tara, retains the same name to this day.

Whatever amount of truth may be in this tradition, we have ample evidence that from a period soon after the advent of St. Patrick, watermills were in very general use all through Ireland, and were an important factor in daily life, both in the monasteries and among the people in general. Each *muilenn* [mullen] or mill was managed by a skilled *muilleóir* [millore] or miller. Mills and millers are mentioned in the oldest Irish literature; and monastic mills are mixed up with the Lives of many of the early Irish saints.

In the year 651 Donogh and Conall, the two sons of Blathmac (one of the joint kings of Ireland— A.D. 656 to 664), were slain by the Leinstermen at "the mill of Mailoran the son of Dima Crón." This event, which created a great sensation at the time, is recorded in Tighernach, as well as in all the other principal Irish Annals. It happened in this way. On a certain occasion Mailoran and his party pursued the princes, who took refuge among the works of the mill beside the *mol* or shaft: but the pursuers opened the sluice and let the water run, so that the mill was set going, and the young men were crushed to death in the works. A contemporary poet composed a poem on this event, in which he apostrophises the mill in the following strikingly vivid stanza:—

"O mill, what hast thou ground? Precious thy wheat!
It is not oats thou hast ground, but the offspring of Kervall [*i.e.* the princes].
The grain which the mill has ground is not oats but blood-red wheat;
With the scions of the great tree (Kervall, their ancestor) Mailoran's mill was fed."

This mill was situated on the little river that runs from Lough Owel to Lough Iron in Westmeath, near the point where the river is now crossed by a bridge; and the place still retains the name of Mullenoran. It is curious that a mill existed there from the time of the death of the princes—and no one can tell how long before—down to the end of the eighteenth century; and there are some old people still living there whose grandfathers saw it in full work.

A *mulenn* or mill is mentioned in the St. Gall glosses of Zeuss—seventh or eighth century—at which time the name *mulenn*, which is used in the Irish passage copied by Zeuss, and which was borrowed from Latin, had become well naturalised in the Irish language. We may then take it for certain that watermills—howsoever derived—were in use in Ireland from the earliest ages of Christianity. Accordingly the statement, which is sometimes made, that mills were introduced into this country by the Danes is quite erroneous, inasmuch as they were known and worked here long before the Danes ever appeared on our shores. But there is as yet no sufficient evidence to prove that they were known in pagan times.

Ancient mill-sites and the remains of old mills have been found in various parts of Ireland buried deep in bog or clay, always beside a stream, many presenting appearances of very remote antiquity. Some are small horizontal-wheel mills, which were common down to recent times; some are the remains of larger mills with vertical overshot wheels. In most of those sites millstones have been found, of various sizes up to three feet in diameter: and there is often a long narrow oaken trough or shoot—generally hollowed out from a single tree-trunk—for conveying the water to the wheel. Parts of the framework surrounding the mill, with the flooring, also remain in some of these old sites, mortised together, but never fastened by nails: the woodwork of all generally of oak.

The mills used in Ireland were of various shapes and sizes, which, as well as the modes of working them and preparing the corn for grinding, will be found fully described in my larger work, "A Social History of Ancient Ireland."

Fig. 184.

Upper stone of a Quern· 18 inches m diameter· in National Museum. (From Wilde's Catalogue)

2. *Querns and Grain-Rubbers.*

A grinding-machine much more primitive and ancient than the water-mill was the quern or hand-mill. It was called in Irish *bro*, gen. *brón* [brone]: and often *cloch-bhrón* [cloch-vrone]: *cloch*, 'a stone':

but both these terms were also applied to a millstone. The upper stone worked on an axis or strong peg fixed in the lower one, and was turned round by one or by two handles. The corn was supplied at the axis-opening in the centre of the upper stone, and according as it was ground between the two stones came out at the edge. Sometimes it was worked by one person, sometimes by two, who pushed the handles from one to the other. In ancient times it was — in Ireland — considered the proper work of women, and especially of the *cumal* or bondmaid, to grind at the quern. Querns were used down to our own day in Ireland and Scotland; and they may still be found at work in some remote localities.

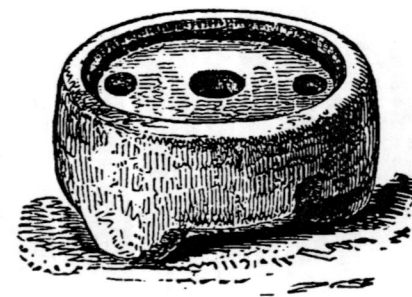

FIG. 185.
Complete pot-shaped Quern: 9 inches in diameter in the National Museum. (From Wilde's Catalogue.)

The almost universal use of querns is proved by their frequent mention in the Brehon Laws and other ancient Irish literature, as well as by the number of them now found in bogs, in or near ancient residences, and especially crannoges. Some of these are very primitive and rude, showing their great antiquity. Quern-grinding was tedious work; for it took about an hour for two women to grind 10 lb. of meal. It is hardly necessary to say that the quern or handmill was in use among all the ancient peoples of Europe, Asia, and Africa: and that it is still employed where water-mills have not found their way.

CHAP. XXI.]   CORN MILLS AND QUERNS.   461

In comparatively modern times mill-owners who ground the corn of the people for pay looked on the use of querns with great dislike, as taking away custom. Quern-grinding by the poorer people was regarded as a sort of poaching; and where the mill belonged to the landlord he usually gave orders to his miller to break all the querns he could find; so that the people had to hide them much as they hide a still nowadays. In Scotland laws were made in the thirteenth century to compel the poor people to abandon querns for water-mills, all in the interests of landlords and other rich persons. It was the same in England: in 1556 the local lord in one of the western English counties issued an order that no tenants should keep querns "because they ought to grind at their lord's mill." But these laws were quite ineffective, for the people still kept their querns.

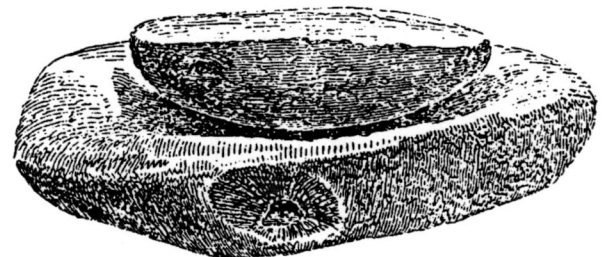

Fig. 186.
Grain-rubber: oval-shaped: 16 inches long.
(From Wilde's Catalogue)

The most ancient grinding-machine of all, and most difficult and laborious to work, was the grain-rubber, about which sufficient information will be derived from the illustration. Several of these may be seen in the National Museum: they are still used among primitive peoples all over the world.

MS ornamentation (From Miss Stokes's Early Christian Architecture.)

CHAPTER XXII.

TRADES AND INDUSTRIES CONNECTED WITH CLOTHING.

SECTION 1. *Wool and Woollen Fabrics.*

hearing and Carding.—The wool—called in Irish *olann*—was taken from the sheep with a shears, which, from the manner in which it is mentioned, must have been much like those used at present. The usual old Irish name is *demess* (meaning 'two edges'—*mess*, 'an edge'), which is still used, in the modern form *deimheas* (pronounced deeas). The shearing appears to have been done by men: but after this the whole work up to the finished cloth was regarded as specially pertaining to women: except fulling, which was often or mostly men's work. After being sorted, the wool was scoured to remove the oiliness: then *teased* or mixed: next combed or carded twice, first roughly, and a second time more carefully and finely. The carding (*cirad*, pron. keera: from *cír*, 'a comb') was done by hand: the woman sitting down while at work, and using a pair of cards, much the

same as those in use for hand-carding now. The second carding turned out the wool in the form of soft little *loes*, locks or rolls (*lo*, 'a lock of wool') fit for spinning, just as wool-carders do at the present day.

Spinning.—In those times spinning was done, in Ireland as elsewhere, by the distaff and spindle; for the spinning-wheel was not invented till the fifteenth or sixteenth century. The wool or flax in preparation for spinning was wound and fastened loosely on a *rock* or distaff called in Irish *cuigéal* [quiggail]. From the distaff the material was drawn off gradually, with the help of the left hand, by the spindle or spinning-stick, which was held in the right hand and manipulated dexterously so as to twist the material into thread, and wind it on the spindle according as spun. The *abras* or thread ready for weaving was rolled up in balls, on which it was wound from the spindles according as these got filled

Weaving.—The thread was woven into cloth in a hand-loom, nearly always by women: and like the rest of the cloth-making process, it was a cottage industry. The complete weaving machinery or loom had two beams: the larger one called *garmain* (and sometimes *gae-mathri*), and the other *lu-garmain* or 'smaller beam' (*lu*, 'small'). The principal beam must have been large: for we find the massive spear of a hero sometimes compared—in Irish tales—to a weaver's beam, like that of Goliath. What were called the "swords" (*claidim*), or weaving-rods, were long laths used during the process of weaving, which were nearly or altogether as long as the beam. The warp was called *dluth* [dluh]: and the weft or woof *innech*. While the woman was weaving she used a *feith-géir* [feh-gair], "which put a smooth face upon her weaving": and which is represented by the sleeking-stick or "rubbing-bone" still used by hand-weavers.

The piece of woven cloth had usually a border or fringe (*corrthar*: pron. curher), which was sometimes woven with the whole piece and formed part of it: and sometimes separately, and afterwards sewed on. In this last case it was woven with a short light *claidem* or lath, altogether apart from the loom, something like the crochet or netting or meshing work of modern times: and weaving ornamental borders or long scarfs in this manner was practised by ladies of the higher ranks as they practised embroidery.

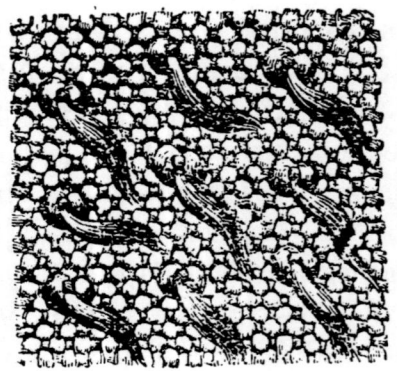

FIG. 187.

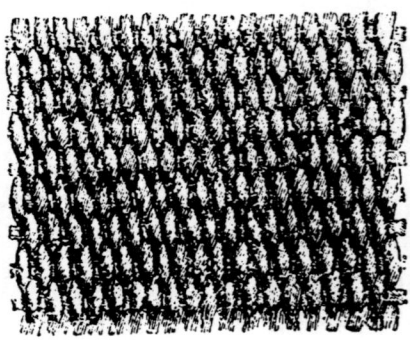

FIG. 188.

Portions of antique woollen clothing found on the body of a woman. (From Proc. Roy. Ir. Academy.)

door, as a signal for the people to bring in their cloth. The custom of tradesmen blowing a horn for such purposes continued to a period almost within our own memory.

2. *Flax and its Preparation.*

The preparation of flax is described in old Irish authorities, especially in the Brehon Law, though not in such detail as that of wool. One of the names of this plant is still preserved in a great number of the European languages, the forms slightly varying, but all derived from the root *lin*. The Greek word is *linon*; Latin, *linum*; English, *linen*; A.-Sax., *lin*; Russ., *lenû*; &c. This shows that it was cultivated by the western Aryan people since before the time of their separation into the various nationalities of Europe.

The Celtic tribes who first set foot on our shores, brought a knowledge of the plant and its cultivation with them; and corresponding to all the names given above, is the Irish *lin* [leen], which is still the word in universal use for flax. Besides the evidence of philology, our own records show that linen was manufactured in Ireland from the earliest historic times. It was a very common article of dress, and was worked up and dyed in a great variety of forms and colours, and exported besides in large quantities to foreign nations. So that the manufacture for which Ulster is famous at the present day, is merely an energetic development of an industry whose history is lost in the twilight of antiquity.

The flax, after pulling, was tied up in sheaves and dried, after which it was put through various stages of preparation like those of the present day. After spinning, the thread was finally wound in balls ready for weaving.

3. *Dyeing.*

Dyestuffs and dyeing in general.—The beautiful illumination of the Book of Kells, the Book of Mac Durnan, and numerous other old manuscripts, proves that the ancient Irish were very skilful in colours: and it will be shown here that the art of dyeing was well understood. The dyestuffs were not imported: they were all produced at home; and were considered of great importance.

The people understood how to produce various shades by the mixture of different colours, and were acquainted with the use of mordants for fixing them. One of these mordants, alum, is a native product, and was probably known in very early times. Dyeing was what we now call a cottage industry, *i.e.* the work was always carried on in the house: as I saw it carried on in the homes of Munster more than half a century ago. In the cultivation of the dye-plant, men might take a part: but the rest of the process was considered the special work of women, so that men seldom assisted. Even the presence of men or boys looking on at the work was considered unlucky. Cloth was dyed in the piece, the wool being left of the natural colour till after weaving and fulling. But woollen cloth was often worn without being dyed at all—just with the shade it brought from the back of the sheep.

Ground Colour.—There were two main stages in the process of dyeing. The first was imparting a ground or foundation colour of reddish brown, which was done by steeping and boiling the cloth with the twigs of the *ruam* or alder. This was what the people called *riming*, from "ruam." After this the cloth was ready for the second stage—imparting the final colour: which was done by boiling it with the special dyestuff.

Black.—The dyestuff for black was a sediment or deposit of an intense black found at the bottom of pools in bogs. It always contained more or less iron, which helped in the dyeing. Boiled with this, the cloth acquired a dull black colour: but if some twigs or chips of oak were added, the colour produced was a glossy jet black, very fixed and permanent.

Crimson.—A crimson or bright-red colour was imparted by a plant anciently called *rud* or *roid*, which required good land, and was cultivated in beds like table-vegetables, requiring great care. There were several stages of preparation; but the final dyestuff was a sort of meal or coarse flour of a reddish colour.

Blue.—To dye the cloth blue, after it had been limed, it was boiled with a dyestuff obtained from woad, called in Irish *glaisin* [glasheen]. This name was also given to the prepared dyestuff, which was in lumps or cakes. As in the case of *roid*, there were several stages in the preparation of the final dyestuff.

Purple was called in Irish *corcur*. In one of the pages of an ancient manuscript now in Turin, is a passage written by an Irish hand in the beginning of the ninth century, which proves that at that early time the Irish were acquainted with the art of dyeing purple by means of a lichen. The knowledge of

2 H 2

dyeing from rock lichen was never lost, but was continued from generation to generation down to recent times; and early in the last century considerable quantities of the lichen dyestuff in the form of balls were sold in the markets of Dingle in Kerry.

The ancient Irish obtained a beautiful purple from small shellfish like cockles; and in some places whole heaps of shells have recently been found, all broken uniformly at one particular point—just the point inside which was situated the elongated little sac containing the purple colouring matter: evidently with the object of extracting the precious little globule. This method of obtaining purple dye continued to be practised in the eastern Irish counties, as well as on the opposite coast of Wales, down to the beginning of the last century. The art continued in Wales, as well as in Ireland, from the earliest times: for the Venerable Bede records that in his day (the eighth century) the Britons (or Welsh) produced a most beautiful purple colour from shellfish. The celebrated Tyrian purple was produced in a similar way.

The purple dyestuff, however obtained, was produced in very small quantities, so that it was extremely scarce; and the colour was excessively expensive in Ireland as elsewhere: on the Continent in old times it was worth thirty or forty times its weight in gold. Partly for this reason, and partly for its beauty, purple was a favourite with kings and great chiefs, so that writers often designate it a royal or imperial colour.

Saffron.—Until recent times linen was dyed saffron with the *cróch* or saffron plant (Lat. *crocus*), which was the simplest of all the dyeing operations.

Popular Knowledge of Dyeing. — The Irish peasantry of the present day, as well as the Highland Scotch, possess considerable knowledge of the stuffs—chiefly obtained from herbs—used in imparting various colours, and are skilled in simple dyeing: knowledge and skill that have descended to them from old times.

4. *Sewing and Embroidery.*

Needle and Thread.—The thread used for sewing was generally of wool. In primitive ages fine filaments of gut were often used. The sewing-thread

FIG. 189.

Two bronze Needles, natural size: in National Museum, Dublin. (From Wilde's Catalogue.)

was kept in the form of a clew, or ball, like that for weaving : and women sewed with a needle furnished with a *cro* or eye as at present. From an early time needles were made of steel, but in primitive ages of bronze. In those days a steel or bronze needle was difficult to make ; so that needles were very expensive. For instance, the price of an embroidering needle was an ounce of silver. The word for a needle was *snáthat* [snawhat], which is still used. Bronze needles are now often found, which, judging from both material and shape, must be of great antiquity.

Dressmaking.—Needlework was most commonly practised in ordinary dressmaking. The old Irish dressmakers were accomplished workers. The sewing on ancient articles of dress found from time to time is generally very neat and uniform, like that on the fur cape mentioned at p. 383, *supra*, which Mr. Mac Adam describes as "wonderfully beautiful and regular."

Embroidery was also practised as a separate art or trade by women. An embroiderer kept for her work, among other materials, thread of various colours, as well as silver thread, and a special needle. The design or pattern to be embroidered—as we find recorded and described in the Senchus Mór—was drawn and stamped beforehand, by a designer, on a piece of leather, which the embroiderer placed lying before her and imitated with her needle. This curious and interesting record indicates the refinement and carefulness of the old Irish embroiderers. The art of stamping designs on leather, for other purposes as well as for embroidery, was carried to great perfection, as we know from the beautiful specimens of book-covers preserved in our museums (see pp. 10, 239).

It was usual for the most eminent of the Irish saints to have one or more embroiderers in their households, whose chief employment was the making and ornamentation of church robes and vestments. St. Patrick kept three constantly at work. Embroidery was practised in Ireland in pre-Christian times, and was a well-recognised art from the earliest period of legend. We know from many ancient authorities that Irish ladies of the highest rank practised needle-work and embroidery as an accomplishment and recreation. For this purpose they spun ornamental thread, which, as well as needles, they constantly carried about in a little ornamental bag.

5. *Tanning and tanned Leather.*

The art of tanning leather was well understood in ancient Ireland. The name for a tanner was *súdaire* [sooděră], which is still a living word. Oak bark was employed, and in connexion with this use was called *coirtech* [curtagh : Lat. *cortex*], as we find the word used in the Laws. By the process of tanning, the hide was thickened and hardened, as at present. Tanned leather was used for various purposes, one of the principal being as material for shoes; but we know that shoes were also made of untanned hide (see p. 396, *supra*). Curraghs or wicker-boats were often covered with leather (see chap. xxiv., sect. 4). A jacket of hard, tough, tanned leather was sometimes worn in battle as a protecting corselet. Bags made of leather, and often of undressed skins, were pretty generally used to hold liquids. There was a sort of leather wallet or bag called a *crioll*, used like a modern travelling-bag, to hold clothes and other soft articles.

The parts of every article made of leather were joined together by stitching with thongs. Those tradesmen in leather-work who stitched with thongs, namely, the leather-bottle maker, the shoemaker, and the leather-wallet maker, worked with a pair of thongs, forming a stitch with each alternately, the workman, while using the free end of one, holding the end of the other between his teeth : exactly like the ancient Egyptian shoemakers as they are depicted in stone and brick records.

Ornament on leather case of Book of Armagh   (From Petrie's Round Towers.)

CHAPTER XXIII.

MEASURES, WEIGHTS, AND MEDIUMS OF EXCHANGE.

Section 1. *Length and Area.*

Like other ancient peoples, the Irish fixed their standards of length-measures, for want of better, mostly, but not exclusively, with reference to parts of the human body. The *troigid* [tro-id] or foot was the length of a man's foot, which was counted equal to twelve *ordlachs*—thumb-measures or inches: so that this *troigid* was practically the same as the present English foot.

The following table of long measures, which is given in the Book of Aicill, may be taken as the one in most general use. The grain, *i.e.* the length of a grain of wheat of average size, was the smallest measure used by the Irish:—

3 grains, ...	1 *ordlach* or inch.
4 inches, ...	1 *bas*, palm, or hand.
3 palms, ...	1 *troighid* or foot.
12 feet, ...	1 *fertach* or rod.
12 rods or *fertachs*,	1 *forrach*.
12 *forrachs* in length by 6 *forrachs* in width	1 *tír-cumaile* (i.e. '*cumal*-land').

According to this table a tír-cumaile contained about 34 English acres; and it was so called because it was considered sufficient to graze a *cumal*, i.e. three cows.

When English ideas and practices began to obtain a footing in Ireland, after the Anglo-Norman Invasion, various other measures of land were adopted, the most general of which was the acre. Land was commonly estimated in acres and ploughlands according to the following table :—

120 acres,	. .	1 *seisrech* [sheshera] or ploughland.
12 ploughlands,	.	1 *baile*, bally, or townland.
30 *bailes*,	. .	1 *tuath* or *tricha*.

Various other length-measures were in use. A *céim* [kaim] or step was 2½ feet. For small measures the *bas* [boss] and the *dorn* [durn] were in constant use. The *bas* or 'palm' was the width of the hand at the roots of the fingers, which was fixed at 4 inches. The *dorn* or 'fist,' with the thumb closed in, was 5 inches: with the thumb extended, 6 inches.

Lengths and distances were often roughly indicated by sound. For example, in connexion with the law of distress, certain distances, called in the Senchus Mór "magh-spaces," were made use of; and the old commentator defines a magh-space to be "as far as the sound of the bell [*i.e.* the small hand-bell of those times] or the crow of the barn-door cock could be heard." The crow of a cock and the sound of a bell, as distance-measures, are very often met with; and the ancient Germans also used them. Other vague modes of estimating lengths were used. The legal size of the *faithche* [faha] or green round a house depended on the rank of the owner; and the unit of measure was the distance a man could cast a spear standing at the house.

2. *Capacity.*

The standard unit of capacity adopted by the Irish was the full of a hen-eggshell of moderate size, which perhaps was as good a standard as could be found at the time. Beginning with this there is a regular table of measures of capacity. Twelve eggshellfuls made a *méisrin* [messhereen], which contained about as much as our present pint.

3. *Weight.*

The smallest weight used was a grain of the best wheat. The following is the table of weight founded on the average grain of wheat:—

8 grains, .	1 *pinginn* or penny of silver.
3 pinginns,	1 *screpall.*
24 screpalls, .	1 *unga* or ounce.

The *unga* or ounce (576 grains of wheat or about 432 grains Troy) was the standard used in weighing metals. The word seems to have been borrowed from the Latin *uncia*: but there was an older native word, *mann*, for the ounce.

From numerous references in the old writings, we learn that the ancient Irish had balances of different kinds and sizes, and with different names. The most usual Irish term for a balance in general, and also for the beam of a balance, was *meadh* [ma], which is the word in use at the present day. A *puincern* [punkern: meaning 'notched beam'] was a sort of steelyard, *i.e.* a balance having a single weight movable along a graduated beam *from notch to notch*, which by its distance from the suspension point indicated the weight of the commodity—identical with our modern steelyard. As bearing upon this point, it is well to observe that an old steelyard of bronze was found in 1864 in a rath near Ballyshannon in Donegal, ornamented and carefully

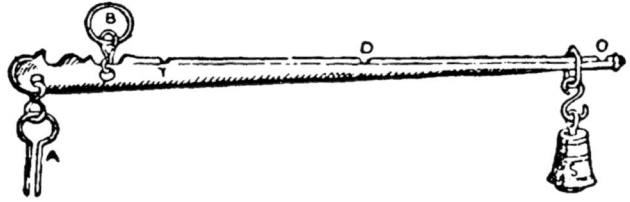

Fig. 190.

Ancient Irish Steelyard. (From Kilk. Archæol. Journ.)

graduated: the material—bronze—indicating great antiquity. But the Irish had also a two-dish balance like those in use at the present day, of which bronze specimens have been found in the earth.

4. *Standards of Value and Mediums of Exchange.*

In early stages of society in Ireland, as in all other countries, buying and selling and other commercial transactions were carried on by means of payment in kind: and there is hardly any description of valuable articles that was not used for this purpose. Payments were made for purchases, tribute, fines, &c., in cows, sacks of corn, salted pigs, butter, mantles, and soforth: the parties determining the values according to the customs of the place. But mixed up with this barter in kind, gold and silver, told out by weight, and—after the middle of the eighth century—silver coins, were used as mediums of exchange.

That the Irish were acquainted with the use of coined money, at least as early as the eighth century, is proved by the records: but whether they coined money for themselves before the tenth century is a

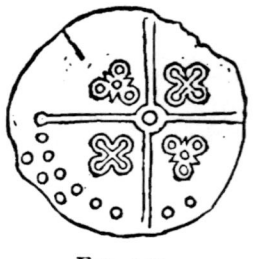 

FIG. 191.   FIG. 192.
Irish bracteate Coins now in National Museum, Dublin.
(From Petrie's Round Towers.)

matter that has not been determined. The coins in circulation among the Irish were the *pinginn* and the *screpall* [skreppal], both of silver. The pinginn weighed 8 grains of wheat, equal to 6 grains Troy: the screpall was equal to 3 pinginns, *i.e.* 18 grains Troy.

Many specimens of the pinginn and of the screpall are preserved in the National Museum. The pinginns are what are called "bracteate" coins, *i.e.* struck only on one side; but the screpalls are impressed on both sides.

From the very beginning of our records gold and silver were used as a medium of exchange, sometimes as ingots, but more commonly in the form of rings, bracelets, and other ornaments. They were weighed by the ounce, which, as we have seen, was equal in weight to 576 grains of wheat, or to 432 grains Troy. In order to facilitate interchange of this kind, gold and silver rings of various forms, as well as other gold and silver ornaments, were generally or always made of definite weights. Notices of this custom are found everywhere in Irish literature. So also Cæsar records that in his time the people of Britain " used brass or iron rings *fixed at a certain weight* as their money." But in Ireland, gold, as being comparatively abundant, was used instead of the inferior metals. The custom of making gold ornaments after a fixed weight seems to have been general among all civilised nations of antiquity.

FIG. 193.

Gold *Bunne* or Ring, full size open, but without the *do-ats*. Used as money. Now in the National Museum (From Wilde's Catalogue)

It may be considered certain that in Ireland the open gold rings called *bunne-do-at* (now often called *fibulæ*: articles, were used as money. But besides those see p. 412, *supra*) as well as other gold ornamental called *bunne-do-at*, there are in the National Museum a great number—fifty or more—of very small open gold rings, from ¼ to ¾ inch in diameter, without the terminal knobs or *ats*: these are *bunnës* simply, not *bunne-do-ats*. From their great numbers, and from their simple, unornamental construction, they have all the appearance of having been used mainly as currency.

A full-grown cow, or ox, was in ancient times a very general standard of value, not only in Ireland, but all over the civilised world: and was considered equal in value to one ounce of gold. In this use—as an article of payment—a cow was in Ireland generally called a *séd* [shade]. Cows or *séds* were very often used both in actual payments and in estimating amounts. Next above the *séd* was the *cumal*, which was originally applied to a bondmaid · but the word came to be used very generally to signify the value of a bondmaid, which was counted as three *séds*, or cows.

A *miach* or sack of corn—generally of oats or barley—which for convenience sake must have been always made of uniform size—was very often used as a standard of value: it is indeed adopted in the Brehon Law as the almost universal standard in estimating fines for trespass, and payments for grazing.

5. *Time.*

The Irish divided their year into quarters. The four quarters were called *Earrach* [arragh], Spring; *Samhradh* [sowra], Summer; *Foghmhar* [fowar], Autumn; *Geimhridh* [gevrĕ], Winter: and they began on the first days of February, May, August, and November, respectively. We have historical testimony that festivals with games—which will be described in chapter xxv.—were celebrated at the beginning of Summer, Autumn, and Winter; but we have no account of any such celebrations at the beginning of Spring. These divisions of the year and the festivities by which they were ushered in originated with the Pagan Irish, and were continued into Christian times.

The 1st February, the beginning of Spring, was called *Oimelc*, signifying 'ewe-milk,' "for that is the time the sheep's milk comes": but this day is now universally known among Irish speakers as *Féil Bhríghde* [Fail Vreeda], 'St. Brigit's festival,' the old Pagan name *Oimelc*, being obsolete for centuries.

The first day of May was the beginning of Summer. It was called *Belltaine* or *Beltene* [beltĭnă], which is the name for the 1st May still always used by speakers of Irish; and it is well known in Scotland, where *Beltane* has quite taken its place as an English word:—

> "Ours is no sapling, chance sown by the fountain,
> Blooming at Beltane, in winter to fade."
>
> *Lady of the Lake.*

The 1st of August, the beginning of Autumn, was, and is still, called *Lugnasad* [Loonasa], from the *nasa* or games instituted by the Dedannan king Lug [Loo] of the Long Arms, which were celebrated at Tailltenn yearly on that day.

Samain or *Samhuin* [sowin], the first of November, was the first day of Winter. This name is still used even among the English-speaking people in Scotland and the north of Ireland, in the form of *sowin* or *sowins*, which is the name of a sort of flummery usually made about the 1st November.

The ancient Irish counted time rather by nights than by days. Thus in the Life of St. Fechin we are told:—"Moses was forty nights on Mount Sinai without drink, without food." In coupling together day and night they always put the night first: in other words, the night belonging to any particular day was the night preceding; so that what they called Sunday night was the same as Saturday night with us.

CHAPTER XXIV.

LOCOMOTION AND COMMERCE.

SECTION 1. *Roads, Bridges, and Causeways.*

Roads.—That the country was well provided with roads we know, partly from our ancient literature, and partly from the general use of chariots. They were not indeed anything like our present hard, smooth roads, but constructed according to the knowledge and needs of the period, sometimes laid with wood and stone, sometimes not, but always open and level enough for car and horse traffic. There were five main roads leading from Tara through the country in different directions: and numerous roads—all with distinct names—are mentioned in the annals. Many of the old roads are still traceable: and some are in use at the present day, but so improved to meet modern requirements as to efface all marks of antiquity.

The ancient Irish classified their roads in regard to size and use into seven kinds, which are named and partly described in an interesting passage in Cormac's Glossary, where he gives the names of the whole seven; but here it will be sufficient to give the terms in most general use. *Conair* and *cai* [kee] are used for a road of any kind. *Slighe* [slee] is a main high road. *Bóthar* [boher] is now the most usual term for a road; and the diminutive *bohereen* or *boreen*, representing the sound of the Irish *bóithrín*, is a familiar Anglo-Irish word for a little road or country lane. The word *bealach* [ballagh] means a pass, commonly with a road or path through it.

The five main roads leading from Tara are mentioned in our oldest authorities, as, for instance, in the story of Bruden Da Derga in the Book of the Dun Cow. They were all called *slige*. 1. *Slige Asail* [slee-assil] ran from Tara due west towards Lough Owel in Westmeath, and thence probably in a north-westerly direction. 2. *Slige Midluachra* [meelooghra] extended northwards towards Slane on the Boyne, through the Moyry Pass north of Dundalk, and round the base of Slieve Fuaid, near the present Newtown-Hamilton in Armagh, to the palace of Emain, and on to Dunseverick on the north coast of Antrim: portions of the present northern highway run along its site. 3. *Slige Cualann* ran south-east through Dublin, across the Liffey by the hurdle-bridge that gave the city the ancient name of *Baile-atha-cliath* (the town of the hurdle-ford: now pron. Blaa-clee): crossed the Dodder near Donnybrook: then southwards still through the old district of Cualann, which it first entered a little north of Dublin, and from which it took its name (the *slige* or road of Cualann), and on by Bray, keeping generally near the coast. Fifty years ago a part of this road was plainly traceable between Dublin and Bray. 4. *Slige Dala*, the south-western road, running from Tara towards and through Ossory in the present Co. Kilkenny. This old name is still applied to the road from Kells to Carrick-on-Suir by Windgap. 5. *Slige Mór* ('great highway') led south-west from Tara till it joined the Esker-Riada* near Clonard, along which it mostly continued till it reached Galway. Portions of this road along the old Esker which raised it high and dry over the bogs are still in use, being traversed by the present main highway.

Besides these five great highways, which are con-constantly referred to, the Annals and other old documents notice numerous individual roads. In the Four Masters we find thirty-seven ancient roads mentioned with the general name *bealach* [ballagh], nearly all with descriptive epithets, like Ballaghmoon near Carlow.

In old times the roads seem to have been very well looked after: and the regulations for making and cleaning them, and keeping them in repair, are set forth with much detail in the Brehon Laws.

Bridges.—The place chosen for the erection of a bridge was very usually where the river had already

---

* Esker-Riada, a long, natural, wavy ridge formed of gravel, running almost across the whole country from Dublin to Galway. It was much celebrated in old times, and divided Ireland into two equal parts, Leth-Conn ('Conn's half') on the north, and Leth-Mow ('Mow's half') on the south. It may be seen marked on the map, running through squares 33, 34, 35, 36. For the origin of the names Leth-Conn and Leth-Mow, see my Short History of Ireland to 1608, page 131.

been crossed by a ford ; for, besides the convenience of retaining the previously existing roads, the point most easily fordable was in general most suitable for a bridge. There is no evidence to show that the Irish built stone bridges before the Anglo-Norman invasion. Bridges were very often built of planks laid across the stream from bank to bank if it was narrow enough, or supported on rests of natural rock or on artificial piers if the river was wide : a kind of bridge occasionally used at the present day. Sometimes bridges were constructed of strong hurdles supported on piles ; like that across the Liffey which gave Dublin its old name. These timber bridges of the several kinds were extremely common, and they are frequently mentioned in old authorities.

Causeways.—In early ages, before the extension of cultivation and drainage, the roads through the country were often interrupted by bogs and morasses, which were made passable by causeways. They were variously constructed: but the materials were generally branches of trees, bushes, earth, and stones, placed in layers, and trampled down till they were sufficiently firm ; and they were called by the Irish name of *tóchar*, now usually anglicised *togher*. These *toghers* were very common all over the country ; our Annals record the construction of many in early ages, and some of these are still traceable.

2. *Chariots and Cars.*

Our literature affords unquestionable evidence that chariots were used in Ireland from the most remote ages, both in private life and in war. They are mentioned constantly, as quite common and familiar, in the ancient records, both legendary and historical, as well as in the Brehon Laws, where many regulations are set forth regarding them. The usual Irish word for a chariot is *carbad*, but there were some other terms.

In the old romances there are several descriptions of Cuculainn's chariot, as well as of those belonging to other chiefs; and in these, and many other authorities, details are given, from all which we can obtain a good general idea of the construction of the vehicle. The body (Irish *cret*) was made of wickerwork, supported by an outer frame of strong wooden bars; and it was frequently ornamented with tin, a practice which also prevailed among the Gauls. The ordinary one- or two-horse chariot had two shafts, which were made of hard wood. In a two-horse chariot there was a pole between the two horses. A one-horse chariot had two shafts but no pole. A two-wheeled chariot, whether with one or two horses, was in very general use. The wheels were spoked and were from three to four and a half feet high, as we see by several delineations of chariots on the high crosses (p. 486, below). They were shod all round, generally with iron. This corresponds with what we know of the ancient British chariots, of which some specimens have lately been found in burial-mounds, with iron rims on the wheels. Some chariots had four wheels; and we know that four-wheeled chariots were also in use among the Gauls. The axle was fixed immovable in the vehicle, and the wheels revolved on it, and were kept in their place by linch-pins.

There was often an awning or hood overhead, commonly of cloth, dyed in some bright colour; but in elaborate chariots, the awning was occasionally covered with the plumage of birds, as ladies sometimes roofed their greenans. Kings, queens, and chieftains of high rank rode in chariots, luxuriously fitted up and ornamented with gold, silver, and feathers. But with all this, the Irish chariot, like those of the Romans and other nations, was a rough springless machine, and made a great deal of noise. They evidently took pride in the noise: and the more distinguished the person riding in a chariot, the greater was supposed to be the creaking and rattle, as is often boastfully remarked by the old Irish writers, "a chariot under a king" being the noisiest of all. A good chariot was worth about twelve cows, representing £150 or £160 of our money. But royal chariots were worth as much as eighty or ninety cows. With rare exceptions, only two persons rode in a chariot, whether in battle or in everyday life: viz. the master (or mistress) and the driver or charioteer: a custom which prevailed also among the Gauls. The two generally sat side by side, the charioteer being on the right. The usual word to designate the principal person in the chariot, the warrior or master, or chariot-chief, was *err*: the charioteer or driver was called *ara*.

On several of the high crosses chariots are carved, as, for instance, on those of Clonmacnoise, Tuam, and Monasterboice. The chariots represented on next page, from one of the Clonmacnoise crosses, have each only one horse and one pair of wheels: but two-horse chariots were more usual, and seem to have been a common vehicle for travelling. The chariot ordinarily used in·battle had two wheels and two horses; but four horses were sometimes used. Chariots were generally drawn by horses, especially those of chiefs and military men. But ordinary persons, and non-military people in general, often employed oxen: St. Patrick's chariot was drawn by two oxen. Besides

FIG. 194.

Ancient Irish Chariots on base of Cross of Clonmacnoise: ninth century.
(From Wood-Martin's Pagan Ireland.)

the chariots hitherto mentioned, both for travelling and for fighting, there was a special war-chariot furnished with scythes and spikes, like those of the Gauls and ancient Britons, which is repeatedly mentioned in the Tales. Farmers and people in general used rough carts, commonly called *carr*, for work of various kinds, and drawn by oxen, but they are hardly noticed in the ancient literature. They had probably solid wheels—such as we know the people used in later times—spoked wheels being expensive.

3. *Horse-Riding.*

Horses were put to the same uses as at present:— riding, drawing chariots, racing; and more rarely ploughing, drawing carts, and as pack-animals: all which uses are mentioned in our old literature. The horse is known by various names. *Ech* signifies any horse of a superior kind: cognate with Latin *equus*, and Greek *hippos*. *Marc*, another word for horse, is explained 'a steed or mare': hence the common word *marcach*, 'a horseman.' *Capall*, meaning a horse of any kind—a term existing in varied forms in several European languages—is the word now used among Irish-speakers. *Gearrán*, a hack-horse, in the modern form *garron*, is in general use at the present day in Ireland among speakers of English to denote a heavily-worked half-broken-down old horse.

From many passages in the Brehon Laws and other old writings it appears that horses were often imported, and that those from Wales and France were specially prized. In the fourteenth, fifteenth, and sixteenth centuries, those Irish horses called *hobbies* were known all over Europe "and held in great esteem for their easy amble: . . . from this kind of horse the Irish light-armed bodies of horse were called hobellers" (Ware).

Giraldus Cambrensis tells us that in his time the Irish used no saddles in riding. Two hundred years later, Mac Murrogh Kavanagh, king of Leinster, had a splendid horse that cost him 400 cows, which he rode with wonderful swiftness without saddle down a hill to meet the Earl of Gloucester; and the custom must have been very general at a still later time, for laws were made to compel the Irish and Anglo-Irish to ride like the English—with saddles. Yet this custom prevailed among the English themselves in early times, as well as among the ancient Britons, Gauls, and Romans. But from the earliest times the higher classes of the Irish used a thick cloth called *dillat*, between them and the horse; which occasionally covered the whole animal, as in fig. 195.

Fig. 195.

Grotesque representation of a horseman given in the Book of Kells. Man's cap yellow; cloak green, with bright red and yellow border; breeches green; leg clothed; foot naked. Dillat yellow. (From Wilde's Catalogue.)

This cloth covering gradually developed into a regular saddle, and the name was retained in the modern form *dialluid* [deelid], which is now the general Irish name for a saddle.

Two kinds of bridle having two different names were in use. The single-rein bridle, called *srian* [sreean] was used in horse-riding. This rein was attached to a nose-band, not at the side, but at the top, and came to the hand of the rider over the animal's forehead, passing right between the eyes and ears, and being held in its place by a loop or ring in the face-band which ran across the horse's forehead and formed part of the bridle-gear. This single rein was used to restrain merely: it could not be used to guide, which as we shall presently see, was done by a horse-rod. The two-rein bridle, called *all* or *fall*, was used with chariot-horses. The charioteer, who sat too far from the horse's head to guide by a horse-rod, had to use double reins, both to guide and to restrain, like those of the present day. The distinction between these two kinds of bridle— single-rein and two-rein— is clearly set forth in the law, and is always observed in the Tales.

FIG. 196.

Grotesque representation of horseman, using horse-rod, given in Book of Kells. (From Wilde's Catalogue.)

The bridle was often elaborately and expensively ornamented. Among the royal tributes of the Book of Rights are "fifty steeds with costly bridles"; and in the old literature we find very often mentioned bridles mounted and adorned with gold, silver, and *cruan* or red enamel. Accordingly, special provisions were laid down in the Brehon Law for compensation to the owner of a bridle in case a borrower did not restore it; from five or six cows up to eighteen or twenty. In corroboration of all these accounts, portions of antique bridles and headstalls have been found from time to time, with enamelled ornamentation of beautiful workmanship, some of them now preserved in the National Museum.

The ancient Irish did not use spurs, but urged on and guided their horses with a rod having a hooked goad at the end, of which we find frequent mention in all sorts of Irish records. Horseriders often used a *sraigell* or whip. Horsemen rode without stirrups: and every man was trained to spring from the ground by an *ech-léim* or 'steed-leap' on to the back of his horse. This ready method of mounting continued to the beginning of the seventeenth century in both Ireland and Scotland :—

> " No foot Fitz-James in stirrup staid,
> No grasp upon the saddle laid,
> But wreathed his left hand in the mane,
> And lightly bounded from the plain."
>
> *Lady of the Lake.*

It was considered necessary that every young man belonging to the upper classes should be taught horse-riding : and so important was this that even the Brehon Law interfered, just as the law of our day requires children to learn reading.

That the ancient Irish protected the horse's hoofs by a shoe of some kind is plainly shown by the records. This shoe is called *cru* in the oldest Irish documents: the term is given with this meaning in modern dictionaries, and *cru* is still the living word for a horseshoe, not only in Irish, but in Scotch Gaelic and Manx. In old times in Ireland, horse-riding as a mode of locomotion in ordinary life was not very general. But nobles commonly rode, and were very proud of their steeds and trappings. Horses were also kept and carefully trained for sporting purposes, chiefly racing, which, as we shall see in next chapter, was a favourite amusement.

The ass hardly figures at all in ancient Irish literature, so that it cannot have been much used.

4. *Communication by Water.*

The boats used by the ancient Irish may be roughly classified as of three kinds:—canoes hollowed out from the trunks of trees; curraghs or wicker-boats; and ordinary vessels—ships or boats—propelled by sails, or oars, or both combined, as occasion required.

The single-piece canoes were very common, especially in connexion with crannoges, where they were used to communicate with shore. Many of these have in late times been found in bogs at the bottom of dried-up lakes and near old crannoges, varying in length from 50 or 60 feet down to six or eight: and numbers of them may be seen in the National Museum in Dublin.

The curragh (Irish form *curach*, connected with Latin *corium*, 'a hide') was the best-known of all the Irish boats. It was made of a wicker-work frame, covered with hides which were stitched together with thongs. Some curraghs had a double hide-covering, some a triple. These boats are constantly mentioned in lay as well as in ecclesiastical literature, and also by Continental writers, the earliest of whom is Solinus in the third century. They are used still round the coasts, but tarred canvas is employed instead of skins. They were propelled by oars or sails according to circumstances.

Many curraghs were so small and light as to be easily carried on a man's back from creek to creek overland, as Giraldus says the Welsh were accustomed to carry their wicker boats: and as people sometimes do to this day in Ireland.

The mode of constructing curraghs has been described by foreign as well as by Irish writers. St. Brendan and his companions, in preparation for their voyage on the Atlantic, " using iron tools [saws, hammers, chisels, &c.], prepared a very light vessel, with wickerwork sides and ribs, after the manner of that country, and covered it with cowhide, tanned in oak-bark, tarring its joints: and they put on board provisions for forty days, with butter enough to dress hides for covering the boat [whenever the covering needed repair], and all utensils necessary for the use of the crew." Curraghs, when intended for long voyages, were made large and strong, furnished with masts and solid decks and seats, and having the hides tanned.

By far the greatest part of the water-communication round the coasts and across the narrow seas, as well as in the lakes and rivers, of Great Britain and Ireland, was carried on in those early days by curraghs, which indeed were used also in other parts of Europe. We know that in the fourth, fifth, and sixth centuries the Irish sent numerous plundering expeditions to Britain, as mentioned at p. 33 *et seq.* These voyages they made in curraghs: and Gildas pictures hordes of them as landing from such vessels. Breccán, grandson of Niall of the Nine Hostages, had a fleet of fifty curraghs trading between Ireland and Scotland, till they were all swallowed up in the terrible whirlpool near Rathlin Island, which thenceforward took the name of *Coire-Bhreccain* [corrie-vreckan], Breccan's caldron or whirlpool.

Many of the ordinary vessels used by the Irish in foreign commerce must have been large; otherwise they could not have traded with Continental ports, as we know they did (p. 495, below). In the Book of Rights it is mentioned that part of the yearly tribute from the king of Cashel to the king of Ireland consisted of " ten ships with beds," as much as to say they were large enough to contain sleeping-berths. There were, and are, several names for a ship, but the most general is *long*.

Ferry-boats were in common use in rivers; and they are often mentioned in the Brehon Laws as subject to strict regulations. They were sometimes owned by individuals, and were sometimes the common property of the people living round the ferry. If a church or monastery happened to be near a river where there was no bridge or ford, the inmates kept a little ferry-boat for their own convenience and for the free use of travellers. Pleasure boating parties were usual in those days as well as now: and young folk were just as inclined to indulge in boisterous merriment; of which it would seem the Brehon Law was in a way conscious; for it prescribes compensation in case the boat was injured during a pleasure excursion.

---

* This whirlpool, which is still well known, but now called Slugnamara ('swallow of the sea'), lies between Rathlin and the coast of Antrim. It was the original Corrievreckan; but its name was borrowed for the dangerous whirlpool between the islands of Scarba and Jura, in Scotland, mentioned in The Lord of the Isles. See Irish Names of Places, vol. II., page 432.

5. Foreign Commerce.

Many passages referring to the communication of Ireland with the outer world in ancient times will be found scattered through this book; but it will be convenient to collect here under one heading a few special notices bearing on the point.

In the native Irish literature, as well as in the writings of English, Anglo-Irish, and foreign authors, there are many statements showing the intercourse and trade of Ireland, both outwards and inwards, with Britain and Continental countries. To begin with early foreign testimony:—The island was known to the Phœnicians, who probably visited it; and Greek writers mention it under the names Iernis and Ierne, and as the Sacred Island inhabited by the Hiberni. Ptolemy, writing in the second century, who is known to have derived his information from Phœnician authorities, has given a description of Ireland much more accurate than that which he has left us of Great Britain. And that the people of Ireland carried on considerable trade with foreign countries in those early ages we know from the statement of Tacitus, that in his time—the end of the first century—the harbours of Ireland were better known to commercial nations than those of Britain. The natural inference from these scattered but pregnant notices is that the country had settled institutions and a certain degree of civilisation—with more or less foreign commerce—as early at least as the beginning of the Christian era.

These accounts, and others from foreign sources that might be cited, are fully confirmed by the native records. There are numerous passages in Irish literature—in the Book of Rights, for instance—in which are mentioned articles of luxury, dress, gold and silver ornaments, swords, shields, slaves, &c., imported from foreign lands. To pass over many other records, we know that in the great triennial fair of Carman there were three principal markets, one of which was " a market of foreigners selling articles of gold and silver," who sold " gold [ornaments] and noble clothes " : so that the fame of this fair found its way to the Continent and attracted foreign merchants with their goods.

This commerce was not confined to the coasts. In the " Life of St. Kieran " it is related that on a certain occasion a cask of wine was brought by merchants to Clonmacnoise from the land of the Franks. The importation of wine is noticed also in the " Life of St. Patrick," and seven centuries later by Giraldus Cambrensis. The various articles mentioned here as brought from foreign lands were imported to supplement the home produce; in which there was nothing more remarkable than our present importation of thousands of articles from foreign countries, all or most of which are also produced at home. The articles anciently imported were paid for in home commodities—skins, wool and woollens, oatmeal, fish, salted hogs, otter and squirrel skins, &c. This trade increased as time went on. But in the seventeenth century laws were made by the English and Anglo-Irish parliaments to destroy Irish trade and commerce: a blow which at once reduced the country to poverty, and from which it has never recovered. (For these laws, see my Child's Hist. of Irel., c. lvi.)

Sculpture on Window: Cathedral Church, Glendalough. Beranger, 1779.
(From Petrie's Round Towers.)

CHAPTER XXV.

PUBLIC ASSEMBLIES, SPORTS, AND PASTIMES.

SECTION 1. *The Great Conventions and Fairs.*

Purposes and Uses.—Public assemblies of different kinds, held periodically, for various purposes and with several designations, formed a marked and important feature of social life in ancient Ireland. Important affairs of various kinds, national or local, were transacted at these meetings. The laws were publicly promulgated or rehearsed to make the people familiar with them. There were councils or courts to consider divers local matters —questions affecting the rights, privileges, and customary usages of the people of the district or province—acts of tyranny or infringement of rights by powerful persons on their weaker neighbours— disputes about property—the levying of fines—the imposition of taxes for the construction or repair of roads—the means of defence to meet a threatened invasion, and soforth. These several functions were discharged by persons specially qualified. In all the fairs there were markets for the sale and purchase of commodities, whether produced at home or imported.

Most of the great meetings, by whatever name known, had their origin in Funeral Games. Tara, Tailltenn, Tlachtga, Ushnagh, Croghan, Emain Macha, and other less prominent meeting-places, are well known as ancient pagan cemeteries, in all of which many illustrious semi-historical personages were interred : and many sepulchral monuments remain in them to this day.

Some meetings were established and convened chiefly for the transaction of serious business: but even at these there were sports in abundance : in others the main object was the celebration of games : but advantage was taken of the occasions to discuss and settle important affairs, as will be described farther on. The word *Fés* or *Féis* [faish], which literally means a feast or celebration, cognate with Latin *festum* and English *feast*, was generally applied to the three great meetings of Tara, Croghan, and Emain. These were not meetings for the general mass of the people, but conventions of delegates who represented the kingdoms and sub-kingdoms, *i.e.* the states in general of all Ireland, who sat and deliberated under the presidency of the supreme monarch.

The **Féis** of Tara, according to the old tradition, was founded by Ollam Fodla [Ollav-Fóla], who was king of Ireland seven or eight centuries before the Christian era. It was originally held, or intended to be held, every third year, at *Samain*, 1st November.

2 K

The provincial kings, the minor kings and chiefs, and the most distinguished representatives of the learned professions—the ollaves of history, law, poetry, medicine, &c.—attended. According to some authorities it lasted for a week, *i.e. Samain* day with three days before and three days after: but others say it lasted for a month.

Each provincial king had a separate house for himself and his retinue during the time; and there was one house for their queens, with private apartments for each, with her attendant ladies. There was still another house called *Rélta na bh-filedh* [Railtha-na-villa], the 'star of the poets,' for the accommodation of the poets and ollaves of all the professions, where also these learned men held their sittings. Every day the king of Ireland feasted the company in the great banqueting-hall—or, as it was called, the Tech Midchuarta or 'mead-circling hall'—which was large enough for a goodly company: for even in its present ruined state it is 759 feet long by 46 feet wide. The results of the deliberations were written by properly qualified ollaves in the national record called the Saltair of Tara. The conventions of Emain and Croghan were largely concerned with industrial affairs, as already stated (p. 455).

The **dál** [dawl] was a meeting convened for some special purpose commonly connected with the tribe or district: a folkmote. A **mórdál** (*mór*, 'great') was a great, or chief, or very important assembly. This last term is often applied to such assemblies as those of Tara, Tailltenn, and Ushnagh.

The **aenach** or fair was an assembly of the people of every grade without distinction: it was the most common kind of large public meeting; and its main object was the celebration of games, athletic exercises, sports, and pastimes of all kinds. The most important of the Aenachs were those of Tailltenn, Tlachtga, and Ushnagh. The Fair of Tailltenn, now Teltown on the Blackwater, midway between Navan and Kells, was attended by people from the whole of Ireland, as well as from Scotland, and was the most celebrated of all for its athletic games and sports: corresponding closely with the Olympic, Isthmian, and other games of Greece. It was held yearly on the 1st of August, and on the days preceding and following. Marriages formed a special feature of this fair. All this is remembered in tradition to the present day: and the people of the place point out the spot where the marriages were performed, which they call "Marriage Hollow." The remains of several immense forts are still to be seen at Teltown, even larger than those at Tara, though not in such good preservation.

The meetings at **Tlachtga** and **Ushnagh**, which have already been mentioned, seem to have been mainly pagan religious celebrations: but games, buying and selling, and conferences on local affairs, were carried on there as at the other assemblies. One of the most noted of all the fairs was **Aenach Colmain** on the Curragh of Kildare, which is noticed at page 509, below, in connexion with races. The memory of one important fair is preserved in the name of **Nenagh** in Tipperary, in which the initial *N* is the Irish article *an*, 'the': N-enagh, 'the fair.' So also Monasteranenagh in Limerick, the 'Monastery of the fair,' where a fair was held long before the monastery was founded.

2. *The Fair of Carman.*

The people of Leinster held a provincial *aenach* at Carman, a place situated probably in South Kildare, once every three years, which began on *Lughnasad* [Loonasa], *i.e.* the 1st of August, and ended on the 6th. Fortunately we have, in the Book of Leinster, the Book of Ballymote, and some other ancient manuscripts, pretty full descriptions—chiefly poems —of this particular *aenach*

There was much formality in the arrangements. While the chief men were sitting in council under the king of Leinster, who presided over all, those belonging to the several sub-kingdoms had special places allotted to them in the council-house or enclosure, which were jealously insisted on. Each day but the last appears to have been given up to the games of some particular tribe or class. One day was set apart for the horse and chariot races of the Ossorians: another was for *roydamnas* or princes only; and there were special games in which only women contended. Some of the deliberative councils were for men only, some for women only, and at some others both men and women attended.

Conspicuous among the entertainments and art-performances was the recitation of poems and romantic tales of all the various kinds mentioned at p. 234, *supra*, like the recitations of the Rhapsodists among the Greeks. For all of these there were sure to be special audiences who listened with delight to the fascinating lore of old times. Music always formed a prominent part of the amusements: and among the musical instruments are mentioned *cruits* or harps; *timpans*; trumpets; wide-mouthed horns; *cuisig* or pipes; and there were plenty of harpers; pipers; fiddlers. There is no mention of dancing either in this or in any other ancient Irish record; and there is good reason to believe that the ancient Irish never danced at all—in our sense of the word.

In another part of the fair the people gave themselves up to uproarious fun, crowded round showmen, jugglers, and clowns with grotesque masks or painted faces, making hideous distortions, all bellowing and roaring out their rough jests to the laughing crowd. There were also performers of horsemanship, who delighted their audiences with feats of activity and skill on horseback, such as we see in modern circuses.

Prizes were awarded to the best performers; and at the close of the proceedings the coveted trophy—always a thing of value, generally a gold ring or some other jewel—was publicly presented by some important person, such as a king, a queen, or a chief.

Special portions of the fair-green were set apart for another very important function—buying and selling. We are told that there were "three [principal] markets: viz. a market of food and clothes: a market of live stock and of horses; while a third was railed off for the use of foreign merchants with gold and silver articles and fine raiment to sell." There was the "slope of the embroidering women," who actually did their work in presence of the spectators. A special space was assigned for cooking, which must have been on an extensive scale to feed such multitudes. On each day of the fair there was a conference of the brehons, chiefs, and leading men in general, to regulate the fiscal and other local affairs of the province for that and the two following years.

When the evening of the last day had come, and all was ended, the men of the entire assembly stood up, at a signal from the president, and made a great clash with their spears, each man striking the handle of the next man's spear with the handle of his own: which was the signal for the crowds to disperse. It always took two years to make the preparations for the holding of this fair. After the introduction of Christianity in the fifth century, the pagan customs were discontinued, and Christian ceremonies were introduced. Each day was ushered in with a religious exercise, and on the next day after the fair there was a grand ceremonial: but beyond this there was little or no change.

The correspondence between these fairs and the Greek celebrations for similar purposes will be obvious to everyone: and it is worth observing that the Carman festival bore a closer resemblance to the Isthmian games, where there were contests in poetry and music, than to those of Olympia, where there were none.

3. *General Regulations for Meetings.*

The accounts that have come down to us show that the ancient Irish were very careful that there should be no quarrelling or fighting, or unseemly disturbance of any kind that might "spoil sport," at the formal *dáls* or *aenachs*, or meetings, for whatever purpose convened. Whatever causes of quarrel may have existed between clans or individuals, whatever grudges may have been nurtured, all had to be repressed during these meetings. There were to be no distraints or other processes for the recovery of debts, so that a debtor, however deeply involved, might enjoy himself here with perfect safety and freedom from arrest. The reader will perceive that all this runs parallel with the "Sacred armistice" proclaimed by the Greeks at their Olympic and Isthmian games, forbidding all quarrelling.

Besides the large fairs or other assemblies, there were smaller meetings for special purposes, such as councils of representative men to deliberate on local matters. These were generally held in the open air on little hills, and were called *airecht*, from *aire* a chief or leading man; for the local king or chief always presided at them. The custom of holding *airechts* was continued down to the end of the sixteenth century. A hill of this kind, set apart for meetings—a convention hill—was designated by the special name *aibinn* or *aiminn* [eevin]. Hills devoted to this important purpose were held in much veneration, and were not to be put to any other use. Great care was taken that they should be kept in proper order: and anyone who stripped sods from the surface or dug into them for any purpose, or put cows to graze on them, was fined.

If the meeting had to be held while the hill happened to be bare of grass, or rough, or dirty, the person having the management of the *dál* should have cloths of some kind spread under the feet of kings, and rushes for the other chief people.

At small meetings held in a building or any other confined space, the president, when he wanted silence, shook what was called "the chain of attention," which was hung with little bells or loose links that gave forth a musical sound. Often the bells were hung on a branch: this was called *craebh sida* [crave shee-a], 'branch of peace.' The musical branch with silver bells figures in many of the romantic tales. Sometimes the president hushed all talk and noise by merely standing up, like the Speaker in the House of Commons.

4. *Some Animals connected with Hunting and Sport.*

The Dog.—Dogs of all kinds were used by the people of Ireland quite as much in ancient times as they are now: but hunting-dogs have, as might be expected, impressed themselves most of all on the literature. By far the most celebrated of the native dogs was the Irish wolf-dog, noted for its size and fierceness. Campion, the English Jesuit, who visited Ireland, and wrote a short history of it in 1571, says:—" They [the Irish] are not without wolves, and greyhounds to hunt them, bigger of bone and limme than a colt." Twelve centuries before his time, a Roman citizen named Flavianus, who had visited Britain, presented seven Irish dogs to his brother Symmachus, a Roman consul, for the games at Rome (A.D. 391)—a gift which Symmachus acknowledges in a letter still extant:—" All Rome," he says, "viewed them with wonder, and thought they must have been brought hither in iron cages." A passage in the Book of Lismore says, "Each of these hounds is as big as an ass." From the fifteenth to the eighteenth century, Irish wolf-dogs were, it might be said, celebrated all over the world, so that they were sent as valuable presents to kings and emperors, princes, grand Turks, noblemen, queens, and highborn ladies, in all the chief cities of Europe, and even in India and Persia. After the final extinction of wolves in Ireland in the early part of the eighteenth century, the need for these great dogs ceased, and the race was let die out.

The word *cu* was generally applied to any fierce dog, this term being qualified by certain epithets to denote dogs of various kinds. A greyhound or hunting-dog, whether a wolf-dog or any other, was commonly called *milchu*. A watch-dog for a house was called *archu*, from *ar* or *air*, to watch. These watch-dogs were kept in every house of any consequence; and they were tied up by day and let loose by night. At the present time the most general name for a dog is *madra* or *mada*, which is also an old word.

It appears from some passages in the Laws, as well as from general Irish literature, that lapdogs were as much in favour in Ireland in old times as they are now: women of all classes, from queens down, kept them. The commonest name for a lapdog was *oircne* [urkĭna], a diminutive of *oirc* [urk], which means, among other things, a little dog. A lapdog was also called *messan*, which is in use among the English-speaking people of Scotland at the present day.

A wicked dog had a muzzle (*srublingi*), and sometimes an eye-cap or covering of leather fastened over his eyes. When a dog was found to be mad, it was hunted down and killed, its body was burned, and

the ashes were thrown into a stream. Here is the quaint language of the Book of Aicill on this point:—
"There is no benefit in proclaiming it [*i.e.* sending round warning of a mad dog] unless it be killed; nor though it be killed, unless it be burned; nor though it be burned, unless its ashes have been cast into a stream."

Wolves.—A common name for a wolf was *cu-allaidh* [coo-allee], *i.e.* 'wild-hound.' Another was *mactíre* [macteera], which literally means 'son of the country,' in allusion to the wild places that were the haunts of these animals. *Faelchu* is now a general name for a wolf. In old times wolves were so numerous in the woods and fastnesses of Ireland as to constitute a formidable danger to the community: so that in Irish writings we meet with frequent notices of their ravages, and of the measures taken to guard against them. In later times, and probably in early ages as well, we know that these animals were hunted down by the great Irish wolf-dog: and they were also caught in traps. As the population and the extent of open cultivated land increased, wolves became less numerous and were held well in check; but during the wars of the reign of Elizabeth, when the country was almost depopulated, they increased enormously and became bolder and fiercer, so that we often find notices of their ravages in the literature of those times.

Deer were plentiful in ancient Ireland, and they are noticed everywhere in the literature, both lay and ecclesiastical. By far the most remarkable of the ancient deer of this country was the gigantic Irish elk, the bones of which are now often found

CHAP. XXV.] ASSEMBLIES, SPORTS, AND PASTIMES. 5

buried deep in clay, sometimes with a thick layer [of]
bog over it. It is well established that this state[ly]
creature lived in the country for some considera[ble]
time contemporaneously with man: but it seer[ms]
probable that it had disappeared before the tir[me]
reached by our oldest writings: so that it is lost [to]
history; and those deer so often spoken of in Iri[sh]

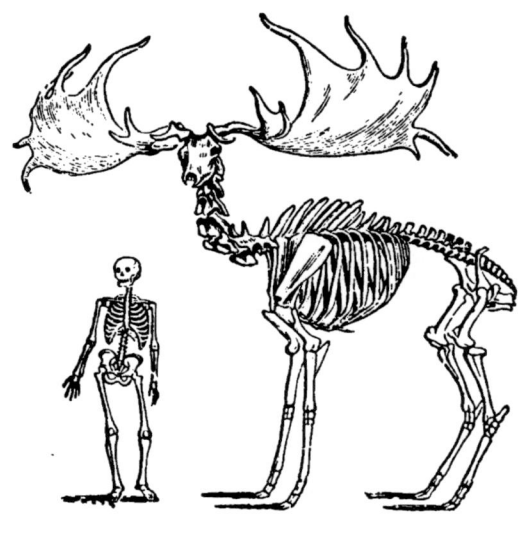

Fig. 197.

Skeleton of Irish Elk in National Museum, Dublin (From plate of Roy. Dub. Soc.) Human skeleton put in for comparison

[l]iterature are not the great Irish elk, but anima[ls]
[l]ike those of the present day. The skeleton of t[he]
[e]lk in the National Museum has antlers extendi[ng]
[t]welve feet from tip to tip: and, as may be se[en]
[f]rom the figure, stands nearly twice the height [of]
[a] man. The most common word for a deer is *fia*[*dh*]
[feea], which originally meant 'wild.'

The Hare would appear to be the smallest animal to which the term *fiadh* ('wild') was applied, if we may judge by the composition of its name *gerr-fhiadh* [gerree']; *i.e.* short or small *fiadh*, from *gcrr*, 'short or deficient.' Sometimes a hare was called *mil-maighe* [meel-mee], 'beast of the plain.'

The Cat.—A cat is called by the same name with slight variations, in nearly all the languages of Europe: in Irish the common name is *catt*. Wild cats were in old times very plentiful: large, wicked, rough-looking creatures, very strong and active and very dangerous; and the race is not yet quite extinct, for wild cats, nearly twice the size of our domestic animals, are still found in some solitary places. It was these animals that gave origin to the legend, very common in ancient Irish story, of a monstrous enchanted wild cat, dwelling in a cave, and a match for the bravest champion. Stories of demon cats have found their way down to modern Irish legend.

Otters.—The otter has several names in Irish, the most usual in old writings being *dobor-chu*, 'water-hound' (from *dobor* or *dobur*, an old word for water). It was also called *madad-* or *madra-uisce*, 'water-dog.' Otters abounded in rivers and lakes, and were hunted, partly for sport and partly for their skins. Otter skins formed an important article of commerce, so that they were sometimes given as payment in kind for rent or tribute.

Of the **badger** it will be enough to say here that it was called in Irish *broc*, and that the chase of the "heavy-sided, low-bellied badger" was a favourite sport among high and low.

5. *Races.*

The old Irish were passionately fond of racing, even more so than those of the present day. Everywhere, in all sorts of Irish literature, we read of races—kings, nobles, and common people attending them at every opportunity. The popularity of the sport affected even the Law: for we find in the Senchus Mór a provision that young sons of kings and chiefs when in fosterage are to be supplied by the foster-fathers with horses in time of races. But perhaps the best illustration of the passionate admiration of people, high and low, for this sport is that it is represented, in some of the old Tales, as one of the delights of the pagan heaven.

The Curragh of Kildare, or, as it was anciently called, the "Curragh of the Liffey," was, as it is still, the most celebrated racecourse in all Ireland: and there are numerous notices of its sports in Annals and Tales. The races were held here in connexion with the yearly fair, which was called *Aenach Colmain* or *Aenach Lifé*, as being on the plain of the Liffey. It was the great fair-meeting of the southern half of Ireland, and especially of the kings of Leinster, when they resided at the palace of Dun-Ailinn (now Knockaulin: see p. 332, above), which was on the edge, and which, being on a flat, detached hill, overlooked the Curragh and its multitudes. Though sports and pastimes of all kinds were carried on there, races constituted the special and most important feature, so that some of the annalists mention the Curragh under the name of "Curragh of the Races." The games here were formally opened by the king, or one of the princes, of Leinster, and lasted for several days: and the great importance attached to them is indicated in the "Will of Cahirmore," in which that king bequeaths to his son Criffan the "leadership of [*i.e.* the privileges of opening and patronising] the games of the province of Leinster."

Numerous references to chariot-racing are met with in Irish literature. During the first three centuries of the Christian era, this sport was universal in Ireland; and it was specially popular among the Red Branch Knights. Horse-racing was also very general, almost as much so indeed as racing with chariots. The Fena of Erin, as we have seen (p. 45, *supra*), did not use chariots, either in battle or in racing; but they were devoted to horse-racing. Foot-racing does not appear to have been much practised by any class.

Coursing with greyhounds was another favourite amusement. On one occasion Irish visitors at a meeting in a distant land were challenged to a coursing match; which came off with victory for the Irish hounds. The greyhounds mentioned in Cormac's Glossary as being always found at *oenachs* or fair-meetings, were for coursing contests, as part of the games carried on at the fair.

6. *Chase and Capture of Wild Animals.*

Some wild animals were chased for sport, some for food, and some merely to extirpate them as being noxious: but it will be convenient to include all here in connexion with sports and pastimes. Everywhere in our literature we meet with notices of hunting, and of various other methods by which wild animals were taken. The hunters led the chase chiefly on foot, with different breeds of hunting-dogs, according to the animals to be chased. The principal kinds of game were deer, wild pigs, badgers, otters, and wolves; and hares and foxes were hunted with beagles for pure amusement. Pig-hunting was a favourite sport.

For the larger and more dangerous game, such as wild boars, wolves, and deer, the hunters employed wolfhounds and other breeds of large dogs; and in the romantic literature we have many a passage describing the dangers of the chase, and the courage, skill, and swiftness of hunters and hounds. The Tales also reflect the immense delight those observant and nature-loving people took in the chase and all its joyous accompaniments.

Most of the details of the manner of trapping deer we learn from the Book of Aicill. They were caught in a deep pit or pitfall, with a trap, and a *bir* or spear fixed firmly in a wooden stock in the bottom, point upwards; the whole gin concealed by a *brathlang* or light covering of sods and brambles. Wild hogs, wolves, and other animals were also caught in traps. Wooden traps for otters are now often found in bogs, with valves, springs, and triggers. The animal, while attempting to force its way through, was caught and held by the edge of the door or valve.

There were traps and nets of several kinds to catch birds. The word *sás* [sauce], which means an engine or gin of any kind, is applied to a bird-trap. A basket-shaped bird-crib, such as is used by boys at the present day, was called *cliabhán* [cleevaun], which is also the word for a child's cradle: a diminutive of *cliabh* [cleeve], a basket. Birds were also caught, as they are still in the Orkneys and Hebrides, by men let down in baskets with ropes over the cliffs round the coasts. Bird-catching was considered of such importance that special laws were laid down to regulate it—" bird-net laws," as they were called.

Fish as an important article of food has been already spoken of. The general Irish word for a fish is *iasc* [eesk], cognate with Latin *piscis* and English *fish*. The people fished with the net and with hook and line, both in the sea and in lakes and rivers. Net-fishing came under the cognisance of the law; it is mentioned in the Senchus Mór; and it appears from the gloss that a fishing-net was called *cochull* and *lin* [leen], both words in use still. Both salmon and eels were often caught with trident spears, or with spears of more than three prongs: and sometimes people followed the primitive plan of transfixing large fish with a single-point spear. Salmon-fishing was the most important of all, and it is oftenest mentioned in the old writings. A salmon is designated by several Irish terms; but *bradan* is now the general name.

FIG. 198.

Iron-pronged Fishing-spear, now in Nat. Mus., Dub. (Drawn from the original.)

Fishing-weirs on rivers were very common. A man who had land adjoining a stream had the right to construct a weir for his own use: but according to law, he could not dam the stream more than one-third across, so that the fish might have freedom to pass up or down to the weirs belonging to others.

7. *Caman or Hurling, and other athletic games.*

Hurling or goaling has been a favourite game among the Irish from the earliest ages; and those who remember the eagerness with which it was practised in many parts of Ireland sixty years ago can well attest that it had not declined in popularity. Down to a recent period it was carried on with great spirit and vigour in the Phœnix Park, Dublin, where the men of Meath contended every year against the men of Kildare. It still continues, though less generally than formerly, to be a favourite pastime; and there is lately a strong movement to revive it.

So far as can be judged from the old literature, it was much the same a thousand years ago as it is now. It was played with a ball (*liathróid*: pronounced leeroad) about four inches in diameter, made of some light elastic material, such as woollen yarn wound round and round, and covered with leather. Each player had a wooden hurley to strike the ball, generally of ash, about three feet long, carefully shaped and smoothed, with the lower end flat and curved. This was called *camán* [commaun], a diminutive from *cam*, 'curved': but in old writings we find another name, *lorg* (*i.e.* 'staff'), also used. The game was called *iomán* [immaun], meaning 'driving' or 'urging': but now commonly *camán*, from the *camán* or hurley. In a regular match the players on each side were equal in number. It was played on a level grassy field, at each end of which was a narrow gap (*berna*) or goal, formed by two poles or bushes, or it might be a gap in the fence. The general name for the winning goal was *báire* [bawrĕ]. The play was commenced by throwing up the ball in the middle of the field: the players struck at it with their hurleys, the two parties in opposite directions towards the gaps; and the game, or part of it, was ended when one party succeeded in driving it through their opponents' gap. It was usual for each party to station one of their most skilful men beside their own gap to intercept the ball in case it should be sent flying direct towards it: this man was said to stand *cúl* [cool], or *cúl-báire*, 'rear-guard': *cúl* meaning 'back.'

Various other athletic exercises were practised, some of them like those we see at the present day.

8. *Chess.*

In ancient Ireland chess-playing was a favourite pastime among the higher classes. Everywhere in the Romantic Tales we read of kings and chiefs amusing themselves with chess; and to be a good player was considered a necessary accomplishment of every man of high position. At banquets and all other festive gatherings this was sure to be one of the leading features of the entertainment. In every chief's house there was accordingly at least one set

[CHAP. XXV.] ASSEMBLIES, SPORTS, AND PASTIMES. 515

of chess appliances for the use of the family and guests: and chess-boards were sometimes given as part of the tributes to kings.

The chessboard, which was divided into black and white squares, was called *fitchell* [fíhel], and this name was also applied to the game itself. The chessmen, when not in use, were kept in a *fer-bolg* or 'man-bag,' which was sometimes of brass or bronze wire woven. The chiefs took great delight in ornamenting their chessboards and men richly and elaborately with the precious metals and gems. The men were distinguished half and half, in some obvious way, to catch the eyes of the two players. Sometimes they were black and white. Many ancient chessmen have been found in bogs, in Lewis and other parts of Scotland: but so far as I know we have only a single specimen belonging to Ireland, which was found about 1817 in a bog in Meath, and which is now in the National Museum, Dublin.

FIG. 199.

Bone Chessman, King, full size, found in a bog in Meath about 1817. Drawn by Petrie.

I have headed this short section with the name Chess," and have all through translated *fitchell* by chess,' in accordance with the usage of O'Donovan,

O'Curry, and Petrie. Dr. Whitley Stokes, on the other hand, uniformly renders it 'draughts.' But, so far as I am aware, there is no internal evidence in Irish literature sufficient to determine with certainty whether the game of *fitchell* was chess or draughts: for the descriptions would apply equally to both.

9. *Jesters, Jugglers, and Gleemen.*

From the most remote times in Ireland, kings kept fools, jesters, and jugglers in their courts, for amusement, like kings of England and other countries in much later times. In the Tales we constantly read of such persons and their sayings and doings. They were often kept in small companies. The most common name for a jester or fool was *drúth* (pron. droo: to be carefully distinguished from *drui*, 'a druid').

Fools when acting as professional clowns were dressed fantastically; and they amused the people something in the same way as the court fools and buffoons of later times—by broad impudent remarks, jests, half witty, half absurd, and odd gestures and grimaces. King Conari's three jesters were such surpassingly funny fellows that, as we are told in the story of Da Derga, no man could refrain from laughing at them, even though the dead body of his father or mother lay stretched out before him. Professional gleemen travelled from place to place, earning a livelihood by amusing the people like travelling showmen of the present day. To these the word *drúth* is sometimes applied, though their more usual name was *crossan*. There was a *drúth* of a different kind from all those noticed above, a hand-juggler—a person who performed sleight-of-hand tricks. Such a person was called a *clessamnach* [classownagh], *i.e.* a 'trick-performer,' from *cless*, a trick. In the Bruden Da Derga, King Conari's *clessamnach* and his trick of throwing up balls and other small articles, catching them one by one as they came down, and throwing them up again, are well described: "He had clasps of gold in his ears (p. 417, *supra*); and wore a speckled white cloak. He had nine [short] swords, nine [small] silvery shields, and nine balls of gold. [Taking up a certain number of them] he flung them up one by one, and not one of them does he let fall to the ground, and there is but one of them at any one time in his hand. Like the buzzing-whirl of bees on a beautiful day was their motion in passing one another."

The crossans or gleemen continued till the sixteenth century; and the poet Spenser describes and denounces them as a mischievous class of people.

People of all the above classes, crossans, drúths, jesters, tumblers, distortionists, and so forth, were looked upon as dishonoured and disreputable. This appears from several passages in the Laws, by which we see they were denied certain civil rights enjoyed by ordinary citizens; and especially from an ordinance of the Senchus Mór, which, classifying banquets into godly, human, and demon banquets, defines demon banquets as those given to evil people, such as satirists, jesters, buffoons, mountebanks, outlaws, heathens, harlots, and bad people in general. And many other passages in Irish literature might be quoted to the same effect.

Sculpture on a Capital · Priest's House, Glendalough : Beranger, 1779.
(From Petrie's Round Towers.)

CHAPTER XXVI.

VARIOUS SOCIAL CUSTOMS AND OBSERVANCES.

SECTION 1. *Salutation.*

SOME of the modes of salutation and of showing respect practised by the ancient Irish indicate much gentleness and refinement of feeling. When a distinguished visitor arrived, it was usual to stand up as a mark of respect. Giving a kiss—or more generally three kisses—on the cheek was a very usual form of respectful and affectionate salutation: it was indeed the most general of all. When St. Columba approached the assembly at Drum-ketta, " King Domnall rose immediately before him, and bade him welcome, and kissed his cheek, and set him down in his own place."

A very pleasing way of showing respect and affection, which we often find noticed, was laying the head gently on the person's bosom. When Erc, King Concobar's grandson, came to him, " he placed his head on the breast of his grandfather." Sometimes persons bent the head and went on one knee to salute a superior.

2. *Pledging, Lending, and Borrowing.*

Although there were no such institutions in ancient Ireland as pawn-offices, pledging articles for a temporary loan was common enough. The practice was such a general feature of society that the Brehon Law took cognisance of it—as our law now takes cognisance of pawn-offices—and stepped in to prevent abuses. Portable articles of any kind—including animals—might be pledged for a loan, or as security for the repayment of a debt; and the law furnishes a long list of pledgable articles. The person holding the pledge might put it to its proper use while in his possession, unless there was express contract against it; but he was not to injure it by rough usage. He was obliged to return it on receiving a day's notice, provided the borrower tendered the sum borrowed, or the debt, with its interest: and if he failed to do so, he was liable to fine. Borrowing or lending, on pledge, was a very common transaction among neighbours; and it was not looked upon as in any sense a thing to be ashamed of, as pawning articles is at the present day.

It may be observed that the existence in ancient Ireland of the practice of pledging and lending for interest, the designation of the several functions by different terms, and the recognition of all by the Brehon Law, may be classed, among numerous other customs and institutions noticed throughout this book, as indicating a very advanced stage of civilisation. At what an early period this stage—of lending for interest—was reached may be seen from the fact that it is mentioned in an Irish gloss of the eighth century.

3. *Provision for Old Age and Destitution.*

Old age was greatly honoured, and provision was made for the maintenance of old persons who were not able to support themselves. When the head of a family became too old to manage his affairs, it was an arrangement sanctioned by the Law that he might retire, and give up both headship and land to his son, on condition of being maintained for the rest of his life. In this case, if he did not choose to live with his son, a separate house was built for him, the dimensions and furniture of which, as well as the dimensions of the little kitchen-garden, are set forth in the law. If the old man had no children, he might make over his property to a stranger on the same condition of due maintenance. Or he might purchase from the neighbouring monastery the right to lodge on the premises and board with the inmates: an arrangement common in England to a late period, where the purchased privilege of boarding and lodging in a monastery was called "Corrody."

As to old persons who had no means, the duty of maintaining them fell primarily of course on the children : or failing children, on the foster-child. A son or daughter who was able to support parents, but who evaded the duty, was punished. If an old person who had no children became destitute, the tribe was bound to take care of him. A usual plan was to send him to live with some family willing to undertake the duty, who had an allowance from the tribe for the cost of support.

In some cases destitute persons dependent on the tribe, who did not choose to live with a strange family, but preferred to have their own little house, received what we now call outdoor relief. There was a special officer called *uaithne* [oohĭnă: lit. a 'pillar'] whose business it was to look after them: or, in the words of the law tract, to "oversee the wretched and the poor," and make sure that they received the proper allowance: like the relieving officer of our present poor laws. He was of course paid for this duty; and it is added that he should bear "attacks on his honour" without his family or himself needing to take any action in the matter—referring to the abuse and insults he was likely to receive from the peevish and querulous class he had in charge.

From the provisions here described it will be seen that the most important features of our modern poor-laws were anticipated in Ireland a thousand years ago.

4. *Love of Nature and of Natural Beauty.*

The poet's adage, "A thing of beauty is a joy for ever," found real and concrete application among the ancient Irish. Their poetry, their tales, and even their proper names, to this day bear testimony to their intense love of nature and their appreciation of natural beauty. Keats, in the opening of

"Endymion," enumerates various natural features and artificial creations as "things of beauty," among others, the sun, the moon, "trees old and new," clear rills, "the mid-forest brake," "all lovely tales that we have heard or read." These and many other features of nature and art, not mentioned by Keats— the boom and dash of the waves, the cry of the sea-birds, the murmur of the wind among the trees, the howling of the storm, the sad desolation of the landscape in winter, the ever-varying beauty of Irish clouds, the cry of the hounds in full career among the glens, the beauty of the native music, tender, sad, or joyous, and soforth in endless variety—all these are noticed and dwelt upon by those observant old Irish writers—especially in their poetry—in words as minutely descriptive and as intensely appreciative as the poetry of Wordsworth.

The singing of birds had a special charm for the old Irish people. Comgan, otherwise called Mac da Cherda (seventh century), standing on the great rath of Cnoc-Rafann (now Knockgraffon in Tipperary: see p. 342, above), which was in his time surrounded with woods, uttered the following verse, as we find it preserved in Cormac's Glossary:

> "This great rath on which I stand,
> Wherein is a little well with a bright silver drinking-cup:
> Sweet was the voice of the wood of blackbirds
> Round this rath of Fiacha son of Moinche."

Among the numerous examples of Metre given in a treatise on Prosody in the Book of Ballymote is the following verse, selected there merely for a grammatical purpose:—

> "The bird that calls within the sallow-tree,
> Beautiful his beak and clear his voice;
> The tip of the bill of the glossy jet-black bird is a lovely yellow;
> The note that the merle warbles is a trilling lay."

It would be hard to find a more striking or a prettier conception of the power of music in the shape of a bird-song, than the account of Blanid's three cows with their three little birds which used to sing to them during milking. These cows were always milked into a caldron, but submitted reluctantly and gave little milk till the birds came to their usual perch—on the cows' ears—and sang for them: then they gave their milk freely till the caldron was filled.*

Many students of our ancient literature have noticed these characteristics. "Another poem"—writes Mr. Alfred Nutt—"strikes a note which remains dominant throughout the entire range of Ossianic Literature: the note of keen and vivid feeling for certain natural conditions. It is a brief description of winter:—

> "'A tale here for you: oxen lowing: winter snowing: summer passed away: wind from the north, high and cold: low the sun and short his course: wildly tossing the wave of the sea. The fern burns deep red. Men wrap themselves closely: the wild goose raises her wonted cry: cold seizes the wing of the bird: 'tis the season of ice: sad my tale.'"

Even the place-names scattered over the country —names that remain in hundreds to this day—bear

---

* See also pp. 260, 261, above, about milking-songs.

testimony to this pleasing feature of the Irish character: for we have numerous places still called by names with such significations as "delightful wood," "silvery stream" "cluster of nuts" (for a hazel wood), "prattling rivulet," "crystal well," "the recess of the bird-warbling," "melodious little hill," "the fragrant bush-cluster," and soforth in endless variety.*

5. *Something further about Animals.*

There are not, and never have been, any venomous reptiles in Ireland. There are small lizards, five or six inches long, commonly called in Irish, *art-* or *arc-luachra*, 'lizard of the rushes,' but they are quite harmless. According to Giraldus, the first frog ever seen in Ireland was found in his own time in a meadow near Waterford: but recently our naturalists have discovered a native frog, or rather a small species of toad, in a remote district in Kerry.

But though we have no great reptiles in nature, we are amply compensated by legends, according to which there lives at the bottom of many of the Irish lakes a monstrous serpent or dragon, usually called *piast* or *béist*, i.e. 'beast,' from Latin *bestia*; and sometimes *nathir*, i.e. 'serpent.' The legend is as prevalent to-day as it was a thousand years ago: and very many lakes have now, as the people say, a frightful monster, with a great hairy mane, at the bottom.

---

* For the originals of all the above names, and for numerous others of a like kind, see Irish Names of Places, vol. II, chap. iv., on "Poetical and Fancy Names."

But we had a much more gigantic and much more deadly sea-monster than any of these—the *Rosualt*—a mighty animal that cut a great figure in Irish tales of the olden time. When the Rosualt was alive —which was in the time of St. Columkille—he was able to vomit in three different ways three years in succession. One year he turned up his tail, and with his head buried deep down, he spewed the contents of his stomach into the water, in consequence of which all the fish died in that part of the sea, and currachs and ships were wrecked and swamped. Next year he sank his tail into the water, and, rearing his head high up in the air, belched out such noisome fumes that all the birds fell dead. In the third year he turned his head shoreward and vomited towards the land, causing a pestilential vapour to creep over the country, that killed men and four-footed animals.

6. *Animals as Pets.*

Many passages, both in the Brehon Laws and in Irish literature in general, show that tenderness for animals was a characteristic of the Irish people. It appears from the Senchus Mór that when cattle were taken to be impounded, if the journey was long, they had to be fed at stations along the way: and while in pound they should be provided with sufficient food and water.

The custom of keeping pet animals was very general; and many kinds were tamed that no one would think of keeping as pets now. We read of lap-dogs, foxes, wolves, deer, badgers, hawks, ravens, crows, cranes, cats, sheep, and even pigs, kept as pets. Pet cranes were very common and are often noticed: the Brehon Law mentions fines for trespasses committed by them. St. Columkille had one which followed him about everywhere like a dog while he was at home in Iona. St. Brendan of Clonfert had a pet *préchán* or crow. St. Colman of Templeshanbo in Wexford kept a flock of ducks on a pond near the church, which were so tame that they came and went at his call.

Such animals were so common, and were mixed up so much with the domestic life of the people, that they are often mentioned in the Brehon Laws. Many of the Irish saints were fond of animal pets; and this amiable trait has supplied numerous legends to our literature. St. Patrick himself, according to Muirchu's seventh-century narrative, showed them a good example of tenderness for animals. When the chief Dárĕ gave the saint a piece of ground at Armagh, they both went to look at it: and on their arrival they found there a doe with its little fawn. Some of St. Patrick's people made towards it to kill it: but he prevented them; and taking up the little animal gently on his shoulder, he brought it and laid it down in another field some distance to the north of Armagh, the mother following him the whole way like a pet sheep.

7. *The Cardinal Points.*

A single point of the compass was called *áird*, which is still used in Scotland in the form of *airt*: " Of a' the airts the wind can blaw, I dearly like the west" (Burns). The four cardinal points were severally designated by the Irish in the same way as by the ancient Hebrews and by the Indians; for they got names which expressed their position with regard to a person standing with his face to the east.

The original Irish word for the east is *oir* [ur]; which however is often written *soir* and *thoir* [sur, hur]. Our ancient literature affords ample proof that these words were used from the earliest times to signify both the front and the east, and the same double application continues in use at the present day. *Iar* [eer] signifies the hinder part, and also the west. *Deas* [dass] means literally the right-hand side; and it is also the word for the south, as the right hand lies towards the south when the face is turned to the east. The word is used in both senses at the present day; and this was the case in the very earliest ages. It is often written *teas* [tass]. *Tuath, tuaith* [thooa], means properly the left hand; and as *deas* is applied to the south, so this word is used to signify the north.

8. *The Wind.*

In some old Irish descriptions of the universe, a curious belief is recorded, that the wind blowing from each quarter has a special colour. God made "four chief winds and four subordinate winds, and four other subordinate winds, so that there are twelve winds." The four chief winds blow from north, south, east, and west, and between each two points of these there are two subordinate winds.

"God also made the colours of the winds, so that the colours of all those winds are different from each other." The old writer then enters into details; and the whole fancy is shown very clearly in the diagram.

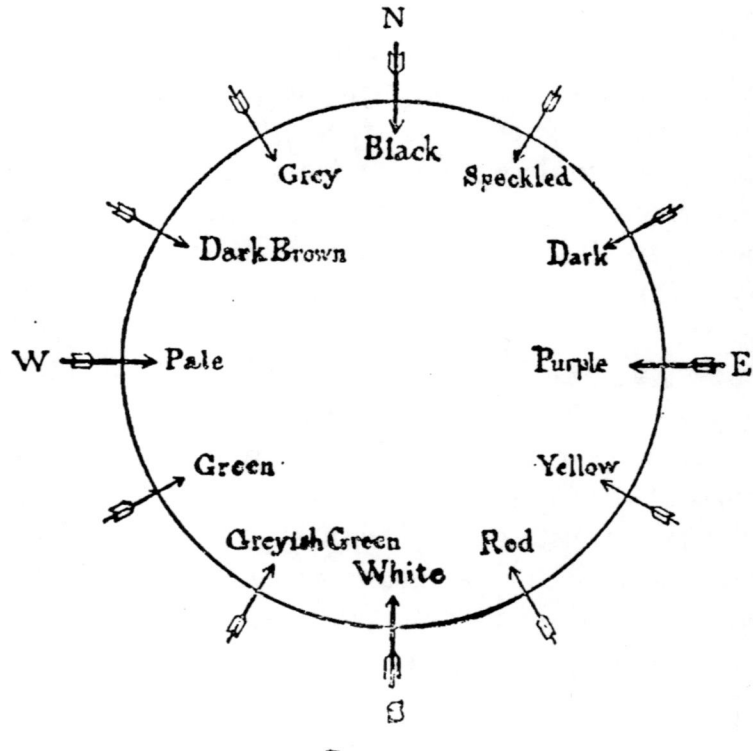

Fig. 200.

The colours of the twelve winds constructed from the description in the Saltair na Rann.

9. *The Sea.*

The sea was called *muir* (gen. *mara*); *'fairrge* [farriga]; and more rarely *lér* or *léar*. If a man brought in a valuable article floating on the sea, nine waves or more out from land, he had a right to it, no matter to whom it belonged, and whether the owner gave permission or not. But if it was less than nine waves out, the owner's permission was necessary (*i.e.* permission to rescue and keep it); and the man who rescued it without this permission could not claim it as his own.

The Three *Tonns* or Waves of Erin are much celebrated in Irish romantic literature. They were *Tonn Cleena* in Glandore harbour in Cork (see p. 111, above); *Tonn Tuaithe* [tooha] outside the mouth of the Bann in Derry; and *Tonn Rudraidhe* [Rury] in Dundrum Bay off the County Down. In stormy weather, when the wind blows in certain directions, the sea at these places, as it tumbles over the sandbanks, or among the caves and fissures of the rocks, utters an unusually loud and solemn roar, which excited the imagination of our ancestors. They believed that these sounds had a supernatural origin, that they gave warning of the deadly danger, or foreboded the approaching death, of kings or chieftains, or bewailed a king's or a great chief's death. Sometimes when a king was sore pressed in battle and in deadly peril, the Three Waves roared in response to the moan of his shield (see p. 62, *supra*). The Welsh people had a similar legend: when the young Welsh hero Dylan was killed, "he was lamented by the Wave of Erin, the Wave of Man, the Wave of the North, and the Wave of Britain of the comely hosts." Though the three Irish Waves named above were the most celebrated, there were several other noted *Tonns* round the coast. Scotland also had its voiceful waves, as our old books record.

10. *Bishop Ultan and the Orphans.*

St. Ultan, bishop of Ardbraccan in Meath, seventh century, is commemorated in the Calendars under the 4th September, and his death is recorded in most of the Annals. In the Feilire [Failera] of Aengus, he is mentioned as " the great sinless prince in whom the little ones are flourishing: the children play greatly round Ultan of Ardbraccan." The annotation explains this in words that give us a glimpse of the havoc wrought by the Yellow Plague —which attacked adults more than children—and of the piteous scenes of human suffering witnessed during its continuance. Everywhere through the country numbers of little children, whose mothers and fathers had been carried off, were left helpless and starving. Ultan collected all the orphan babes he could find, and brought them to his monastery. He procured a great number of cows' teats, and filling them with milk, he put them into the children's mouths with his own hands, and thus contrived to feed the little creatures; so that in the words of the annotation, " the infants were playing around him." In one of the accounts, we are told that he often had as many as 150, so that his noble labour of love—even with help—must have kept his hands pretty busy. It would be difficult to find an instance where charity is presented in greater beauty and tenderness than it is in this simple record of the good bishop Ultan.

As curiously illustrative of this record, it is worthy of mention that, at the present day in Russia, it is a very general custom for those peasant women who do not suckle their own children, to feed them with a rude feeding-bottle, called by a name equivalent to the English word "hornie," namely a cow's horn hollowed out, and having a little opening at the smaller end, on which is tied a cow's teat. When the "hornie" is filled with milk, the teat is put into the infant's mouth, who in this manner feeds itself.

CHAPTER XXVII.

DEATH AND BURIAL.

Section 1. *Wills.*

Many passages in our ancient literature show that the custom of making wills at the approach of death existed among the Irish people from so early a period that we are not able to trace its beginning. Private property was disposed of in this way quite without restriction, though not with such strict legal formalities as are required at the present day. The ancient Irish designated a will by three terms:—*Edoct* or *udhacht* [ooaght], which is the word used at present; *timne*; and *cennaite* [kennitĕ: 3-syll.].

There was, in the law, a merciful provision, called "The rights of a corpse," to save the family of a dead man from destitution in case he died in debt, namely:—"Every dead body has in its own right a cow, and a horse, and a garment, and the furniture of his bed; nor shall any of these be paid in satisfaction of his debts; because they are, as it were, the special property of his body." Of course this reserved property passed to the family, and could not be claimed by a creditor or any other outsider.

2. *Funeral Obsequies.*

There were several words for death:—*és, ég, cro*; all now obsolete, except perhaps *ég*: the word at present in use is *bás* [hauss], which is also an old word.

The pagan Irish, like many other ancient nations, celebrated the obsequies of distinguished persons by funeral games, as already mentioned (p. 497, *supra*): and in some cases the games, once instituted, continued to be carried on periodically at the burial-place, far into Christian times. On the death of ordinary persons there was simply a funeral feast, chiefly for guests, whether among pagans or Christians.

On the death of a Christian a bell was rung. The body was watched or waked for one or more nights. In case of eminent persons the watch was kept up long: St. Patrick was waked for twelve nights; Brian Boru for the same length of time in Armagh in 1014; St. Senan for eight nights; St. Columba for three at Iona. Among the pagan Irish, seven nights and days was the usual time for great persons. In Christian obsequies lights were kept burning the whole time: during St. Patrick's twelve-night wake, the old Irish writers tell us that night was made like day with the blaze of torches.

The mourners raised their voices when weeping, like the Egyptians, Jews, and Greeks of old; a practice mentioned in the most ancient writings, and continued in Ireland to the present day. This wailing was called *caoi* or *caoine* [kee, keena], commonly anglicised *keen* or *keening*—weeping aloud. The lamentation was often accompanied by words expressive of sorrow and of praise of the dead, sometimes in verse, and often extempore. This custom has also come down to modern times. A regular elegy, composed and recited at the time of death, was usually called *Nuall-guba* ('lamentation of sorrow': pron. Nool-gooa); but often *Amra*, a word usually understood as 'a eulogistic elegy.' Dallan Forgall's *Amra* for St. Columbkille has long been celebrated, and is one of the most difficult pieces of Irish in existence.

Among the Irish pagans it was the custom—which probably continued to Christian times—to wash the body. This Irish custom corresponded with that of the Greeks, who washed the bodies of their dead as part of the funeral obsequies: and the same custom prevailed among the Phœnicians and Romans.

The corpse was wrapped in a *recholl*, i.e. a shroud or winding-sheet: also called *esléne* [3-syll.], which is derived from *es*, death, and *léne*, a shirt: 'death-shirt.' When about to be buried, the body was placed on a *fuat* or bier, which was borne to the grave, sometimes by men; but if the distance was considerable, on a car, generally drawn by oxen.

St. Patrick's body was placed on a little car, which was drawn from Saul to the grave at Dun-leth-glass, now Downpatrick, by oxen. In pagan times the body was sometimes brought to the grave wrapped up in a covering of green bushy branches, commonly of birch, which, in some cases at least, was buried with the body. No doubt this branchy covering was intended to protect the body from the clay, like our wooden coffins. The pagan Irish had always a *fé* [fay] or rod, of aspen, with an ogham inscription scored on it, lying in their cemeteries for measuring the bodies and the graves. This *fé* was regarded with the utmost horror, and no one would, on any consideration, take it in his hand or touch it, except of course the person whose business it was to measure.

We know from Cæsar that it was the custom among the Gauls, when celebrating funeral obsequies, to burn, with the body of the chief, his slaves, clients, and favourite animals. But this custom did not reach Ireland. Among the Irish pagans, however, cattle were sometimes sacrificed on such occasions: they were not buried with the corpse, but merely killed and eaten at the funeral feast.

3. *Modes of Burial.*

In ancient Ireland the dead were buried in a variety of ways. One mode was to place the body lying flat in the grave as at present, usually with the feet to the east; and another was to put it standing up, fully armed, as described below. Occasionally it was placed in a sitting posture. Still another mode was to burn the body, and deposit the ashes and fragments of bones in an ornamented urn, generally of baked clay, but sometimes of stone. All four prevailed in pagan times but the first only was sanctioned and continued by Christianity. Of the first two modes of interment — lying flat and standing up — we have ample historical record. But as to the last — cremation — I can find in the whole range of Irish literature only one direct allusion to it, and even that not in the native Irish writings. Yet we know that cremation was extensively practised in pagan Ireland; for urns containing ashes and burnt bones are found in graves in every part of the country.

FIG. 201.

Cinerary Urn, of stone, a very rare and beautiful specimen: 8¾ in. high: now in National Museum. (From Wilde's Catalogue.)

FIG. 202.

Cinerary Urn, of baked clay · 6½ in high: now in the National Museum. (From Wilde's Catalogue.)

Cremation and ordinary burial were practised contemporaneously, as we know from the well-ascertained fact, that in the same cromlech or grave complete skeletons have been found along with urns containing ashes and burnt bones. This is what we should expect; for cremation was a troublesome and expensive process, and could not have been practised by poor people, most of whom must have buried the body without burning.

Occasionally the bodies of kings and chieftains were buried in a standing posture, arrayed in full battle costume, with the face turned towards the territories of their enemies. Of this custom we have several very curious historical records. In the Book of the Dun Cow it is related that King Laegaire [Laery] was killed " by the sun and wind " in a war against the Lagenians; and " his body was afterwards brought from the south, and interred, with his arms of valour, in the south-east of the external rampart of the royal *Rath Laegaire* at *Temur* (Tara), with the face turned southwards upon the Lagenians [as it were] fighting with them, for he was the enemy of the Lagenians in his lifetime." The battle of Culliu was fought on a spot which was subsequently overflowed by Lough Corrib, where Mannanan mac Lir fell: and the Dinnsenchus says:—" He was killed in that battle and buried standing up in that place."

The truthfulness of these records is borne out by the actual discovery of skeletons standing up in graves. In 1848 a tumulus called Croghan Erin in the County Meath was opened, and a skeleton was found under it standing up. About the year 1834, a skeleton was found standing erect in a carn near Belmullet, County Mayo.

The pagan Irish believed that while the body of their king remained in this position, it exercised a malign influence on their enemies, who were thereby always defeated in battle—a superstition that also prevailed among the ancient Britons.*

4. *Cemeteries.*

In pagan times the Irish had royal cemeteries in various parts of the country for the interment of kings and chiefs with their families and relatives. Of these I will notice three—Brugh, Croghan, and Tailltenn.

The cemetery of **Brugh**—the burial-place of the Dedannans—lies on the northern bank of the Boyne, a little below Slane, extending along the river for nearly three miles. It is one of the most remarkable pagan cemeteries in Europe, consisting of about twenty barrows or burial-moulds of various sizes, containing chambers or artificial caves, with shallow saucer-shaped sarcophagi. The three principal mounds are those of New Grange, Knowth, and Dowth, which are the largest sepulchral mounds in Ireland. There are numerous pillar-stones: and many of the great stones forming the sides and roofs of the caves are carved with curious ornamental designs of various patterns—circles, spirals, lozenges, and soforth. The term *brugh* (pron. broo) has several meanings, one of which is a 'great house or mansion' (p. 290, above): and it was applied to this cemetery because the principal mound, that now called

---

* For much more on this point, see my Irish Names of Places, vol. I., p. 330; and the larger Social History, II., 552.

New Grange, was supposed to have been the fairy palace of the Dedannan chief and magician, Aengus Mac-in-Og (see p. 108, *supra*). To this day the name is preserved: for a place beside New Grange mound is now called Broo or Bro.

FIG. 203.

New Grange. About 70 feet high, but once much higher. base occupies more than an acre. Formed of loosely-piled stones, with a surface of clay, covered with grass. It was surrounded at base by a circle of great pillar-stones, about a dozen of which remain. Beehive-shaped chamber in centre, 20 feet in diameter, and 19 feet high, with three recesses, in one of which is a shallow sarcophagus A passage, 60 feet long, leads to exterior: sides of both chamber and passage formed of enormous stones, covered with carvings like those seen on fig. 205, farther on This sepulchre closely resembles some of the ancient Greek tombs. (From Wakeman's Handbook of Irish Antiquities)

The cemetery of **Croghan** is called in old documents *relig na Ríg* [Rellig-na-ree], or the 'burial-place of the kings.' It is half a mile south of Croghan, the seat of the kings of Connaught (for which see p. 331, *supra*), and is still well recognisable, with numerous sepulchral monuments. It covers about two acres, and is surrounded by a dry wall, now all in ruins. A little to the north-west of this main cemetery is a natural cave of considerable extent, still much celebrated in popular legend. This is the very cavern—the "Hell-Gate of Ireland" already mentioned—from which in old times, on every Samain Eve, issued the malignant bird-flocks on their baleful flight, to blight crops and kill animals with their poisonous breath. The great Queen Maive lived at Croghan, and was interred in this cemetery; and to the present day, all over the district, there are vivid traditions about her.

Tailltenn as a palace, and as the scene of a great annual fair, has been already noticed. The cemetery was situated near the palace, but has been long obliterated; and no wonder, seeing that the whole site, including raths, sporting-greens, beds of artificial ponds, cemetery, &c., has been for generations under cultivation: so that, with the exception of one large rath, the ramparts and fences have nearly disappeared.

Besides the great royal cemeteries noticed in the records, the pagan people had their own local burying-places in every part of the country, of which the remains are still to be seen in several places, containing the usual mounds and kistvaens. The history of many of these is quite lost. By far the most remarkable and extensive cemetery of this last class in all Ireland is that on the ridge of the Loughcrew hills near Oldcastle in Meath. It consists of a wonderful collection of great mounds, carns, cromlechs, sepulchral chambers, inscribed stones, and stone saucer-shaped sarcophagi, all of the same general character as those of Brugh. It must have been a noted cemetery; yet not a word about it is to be found in our old books.

By far the greatest number of interments in pagan times were, not in cemeteries, but in detached spots, where individuals or families were interred. Such detached graves are now found in every part of Ireland. Sometimes they are within the enclosure of raths and cashels. After the introduction of Christianity in the fifth century, the people gradually forsook their pagan burial-places : and the dead were buried with Christian rites in the consecrated cemeteries attached to the little primitive churches. *Reilig,* Old Irish *relec,* means a cemetery or graveyard, and it was applied to a pagan as well as to a Christian cemetery. We have already seen (p. 270) that the cemetery in which the victims of a plague were interred was called *Tamhlacht.*

5. *Sepulchral Monuments.*

The monuments constructed round and over the dead in Ireland were of various kinds, very much depending on the rank of the person buried : and they were known by several names. Some were in cemeteries, some—belonging to pagan times— detached. Many of the forms of monuments used by the pagan Irish were continued in Christian times.

Carn and Duma.—In our ancient literature, both lay and ecclesiastical, there are many notices of the erection of carns over graves. The Irish word *carn* simply means 'a heap.' We have records of the building of carns in documents of the seventh century; but they were also erected in times long before the Christian era. In or near the centre of almost every carn, a beehive-shaped chamber of dry masonry was formed, communicating with the exterior by a long narrow passage. The body or urn was placed in the chamber: in some chambers, rude shallow stone coffins shaped like a saucer have been found. In old pagan times people had a fancy to bury on the tops of hills; and the summits of very many hills in Ireland are crowned with carns, under every one of which—in a stone coffin—reposes some person renowned in the olden time. They are sometimes very large, and

FIG. 204.

Duma or burial mound, beside the Boyne, near Clonard· very conspicuous from the railway, on the left as you go westward. Circumference, 433 feet; height, 50 feet. (From Wilde's Boyne and Blackwater.)

form conspicuous objects when viewed from the neighbouring plains. A monumental heap or carn is often called a *lecht* or *leacht*. Sometimes entire skeletons have been found under carns and *lechts*, sometimes cinerary urns, and sometimes both together, showing that these monuments were used with both modes of burial (see pp. 535, 536, *supra*).

The *duma* or mound—often called *tuaim*—was made of clay, or of a mixture of clay and small pebbles, having usually, at the present time, a smooth carpet of grass growing on it. While carns were often placed on hills, the *dumas* were always in the lowlands. The *duma*, like the carn, has a cist or chamber in the

FIG. 205.

Sepulchral chamber with shallow sarcophagus: in the interior of one of the Loughcrew carns. Observe the characteristic pagan carvings. (From Colonel Wood-Martin's Pagan Ireland.)

centre, in which the urn or body was placed: sometimes there is a passage to the outside, sometimes not. Numerous mounds of this class still remain all over the country: they may be generally distinguished from the mounds of *duns* by the absence of circum-

CHAP. XXVII.] DEATH AND BURIAL. 543

vallations. Very often round a *duma* there was a circle of pillar-stones, some of which remain in position to the present day. But stone circles simply, or stone enclosures of other shapes, with a level space within, are often found. These always mark a place of interment, being placed round a grave. One is represented here (fig. 206).

FIG. 206.

Bird's-eye view of sepulchral stone enclosure Between 90 and 100 feet long, by about 30 feet wide. (From Wilde's Catalogue)

Comrar, Kistvaen, Cromlech.—The stone coffin, chest, or cist in which a body was interred, or in which one or more urns were placed, was called in Irish a *comrar*, a word which means 'a protecting cover, shrine, or box of any kind.' It corresponds with the modern Irish *comhra* [cora], which is now the usual word for a coffin : and also with English *coffer* and *coffin*.

When a *comrar* is over ground and formed of very large stones, it is now commonly called a *cromlech* or *dolmen*, both words of late introduction, and neither of Irish origin : when underground and formed of smaller flagstones, it is generally called a *kistvaen*,

Fig. 207.

Great Cromlech at Kilternan. (From Wakeman's Handbook of Irish Antiquities)

meaning 'stonechest,' a Welsh word. Many of the kistvaens, and also some of the cromlechs, were made much larger than was needed for the reception of a single body : in these were interred several persons, probably all members of the same family. The bodies of those who fell in battle were often interred in kistvaens and cromlechs, of which numbers are now found on ancient battlefields.

A cromlech is formed of one great flat stone lying on the tops of several large standing stones, thus enclosing a rude chamber in which one or more bodies or urns were placed. These cromlechs are very numerous in all parts of Ireland, and various theories were formerly in fashion to account for their origin; of which the most common was that they were "Druids' altars," and used for offering sacrifices. It is now, however, well known that they are tombs,

FIG. 208.

Phœnix Park Cromlech *found under a *duma* or burial-mound. Covering stone, 6½ feet long (From Proceedings Roy. Ir Acad.)

which is proved by the fact that under many of them have been found cinerary urns, calcined bones, and sometimes entire skeletons.

Sepulchral monuments of the same class are found all over Europe, and even in India. Some cromlechs are formed of stones so large that to this day it remains a puzzle how they were heaved up to their places by people devoid of powerful mechanical appliances. The covering stone of the cromlech at Kilternan, on the summit of a hill between Dublin and Bray, which is figured on page 544, and which is one of the largest of its kind in Ireland, is 23½ feet long, 17 feet broad, and 6½ feet thick. It is lifted so high that a man can stand straight up under its higher end.

Sometimes regularly formed cromlechs—usually small—are found under *dumas* or mounds; like that shown in fig. 208, which still stands in its original place in the Phœnix Park, Dublin. It was found in the year 1838 under a large earthen tumulus which was cleared away: several urns were dug out of the mound; and under the cromlech lay two human skeletons. But, generally speaking, cromlechs, that is to say, *comrars* formed of a few massive stones, were erected in the open air, and were not covered up.

Pillar-Stones.—The various purposes for which pillar-stones were erected have been already stated (page 424). Here we have to do only with their sepulchral use. All through the tales we find mention of the head-stone or pillar-stone, called by the names *lie* or *lec* and *coirthe* [curha], placed over a grave. A usual formula to describe the burial of a person is:—His funeral rites were performed, his grave was dug, and his stone erected, with his name inscribed in Ogham. In accordance with these accounts, sepulchral pillar-stones are found all over Ireland, some inscribed with Ogham, some not: the inscription, as already stated, usually telling the name of the person, with the name of his father, and often a few other brief particulars. Perhaps the most remarkable and interesting pillar-stone in all Ireland belonging to pagan times is that erected over the body of King Dathi in the cemetery of Croghan;

but it bears no inscription. In later ages the pagan pillar-stone developed into the ordinary headstone with a Christian inscription.

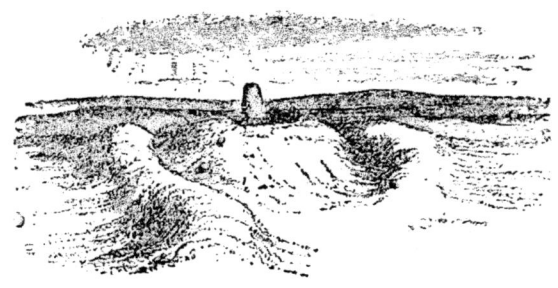

Fig. 209.

King Dathi's Pillar-stone. (From Proc. Roy. Ir. Acad.)

Tombs with Christian Inscriptions.—After the establishment of Christianity it became customary to erect a tomb over the grave, having a flat slab on top, especially in the cemeteries of monasteries, with an inscription, generally in Irish, but sometimes in Latin. In many cases the monument was a simple inscribed pillar-stone; so that some of the headstones that are mentioned under the last heading would fall also under this.

A most interesting Christian inscribed pillar-stone, probably the oldest in Ireland, is the headstone of Lugnaed or Lugna [Loona], standing about two and a half feet over ground, near the very ancient little church of Templepatrick on the island of Inchagoill in Lough Corrib, of which Dr. Petrie has given a full account in his "Round Towers." It is figured on next page from his accurate illustration in the same book.

FIG. 210.—Lugnaed's headstone.

According to the ancient narratives of the Life of St. Patrick, his sister Liemania had seven sons, all of whom accompanied the saint to Ireland, and were settled by him in Connaught in the neighbourhood of Lough Mask. The youngest was Lugna, Patrick's pilot. Petrie and O'Donovan concur in reading the inscription LIE LUGNAEDON MACC LMENUEH, "The stone of Lugnaedon [or Lugnaed] son of Limenueh"; and they identify this Lugnaed with Lugnaed, the son of St. Patrick's sister, which indeed—according to their reading — they could not avoid doing, inasmuch as —besides the local associations—he is the only saint of the name in all Irish Ecclesiastical history.

The connexion of this stone with Lugnaed has lately been questioned by some, on a partial and very narrow view of the whole evidence available to us. But I think I have shown, in another place,* that Petrie and O'Donovan were right, and that this venerable little headstone was really inscribed and erected to commemorate Lugnaed the son of Liemania.

This monument may be classed among those remarkable corroborations of the accuracy of Irish historical records, of which so many examples have been given throughout this book.

The Cross.—From the very earliest period of Christianity in Ireland, it was customary to erect a cross over the grave of a Christian; of which so many notices occur, both in the Lives of the Saints and elsewhere, that it is unnecessary to give references.

FIG. 211.

Monument (lying flat) of Richard de Clare, usually called Strongbow, and his wife Eva, daughter of Dermot Mac Murrogh, king of Leinster, in Christchurch Cathedral, Dublin (From Mrs. Hall's Ireland.)

Effigies.—The custom of carving effigies on tombs was introduced by the Anglo-Normans, and was

---

* Journ. of the Roy. Soc. of Antiqq. of Ireland, 1906, opening paper.

adopted by the native Irish. But as this subject does not fall within the scope of the present book, it will be sufficient to give here two illustrations, one representing the monumental effigy of an Anglo-Norman lord, the other that of an Irish provincial king: both as they appear at the present day.

FIG. 212.

Tomb of Felim O'Conor, king of Connaught, in Roscommon Abbey; died, 1265. The two figures at bottom, showing only the heads, are galloglasses, of which there are eight. The rubbish has been recently cleared away, so that all can now be seen. Two of these fine figures are fully depicted at p. 68, above. (From Kilk. Archæol. Journ.)

Ornament, with Inscription, on the cover of the Misach, an ancient reliquary belonging to Inishowen. (From Miss Stokes's Christian Inscriptions.)

INDEX.

N.B.—The numbers in parentheses after names of places denote the squares of the map where the names are to be found.

ABBEY KNOCKMOY, 24, 160, 417.
Achilles, 54, 107.
Acta Sanctorum Hiberniæ, 220.
Adam and Eve Monastery, Dublin, 213.
Adamnan, 182, 183, 219, 318.
—— his cross, 325.
Administration of justice, 86.
Adoption, 81.
Advocates and pleaders, 91.
Advocates' Library, Edinburgh, 214.
Adze, 446.
Achinn or Achill, the fairy queen, 104, 110, 111.
Aed mac Ainmirech, k. of Irel., 189, 335.
—— mac Criffan, 211.
—— Ruadh, father of Queen Macha, 109, 110.
—— Uaridneach, k. of Ireland, 272.
Aenach or Oenach, a fair: see Fairs.
—— Colmain or A. Life, 499, 509.
Aeneas, 103.
Aeneid, the, 103.
Aengus: see Angus.
—— Mac-in-Og, 108.
—— the Culdee, 177, 220, 221. See Félire and Litany
Age of moon, 196.
Aghaboe in Queen's Co. (30), 194.
Aghagower in Mayo, 164.
Agriculture, 142, 421 and following.
Ague, 272.
Aidan, Bishop, founder of Lindisfarne, 145, 146.
Ailech palace, now Greenan-Ely, (6), 308; described, 330.
Ailenn, palace, 332; described, 333.
Aileran the wise, 176.

Ailill, k. of Connaught, 332, 365.
—— son of Laery Lorc, 280, 334.
—— Olom, k. of Munster, 340, 341.
Aill-na-meeran at Ushnagh, 14.
Aine, the fairy queen, 110.
Aire, a chief, 77, 78, 503.
Aire-echta, a king's champion, 46.
Airmeda, the doctress, 265.
Aithech, a farmer, a peasant, 79, 84.
Alba, gen. Alban, old name of Scotland, 38. In Irish records, the name is sometimes applied to the whole of Britain (as at 33).
Alcuin, 176.
Alder tree, 377.
Aldfrid, k. of Northumbria, 177.
Aldhelm, bishop of Sherborne, 177, 178.
Ale, 348, 349, 350.
Alexander the Great, Life of, 212.
Allen, Hill of, 44, 45.
Alloys, metallic, 437.
Alphabet, 173, 183.
Alps, the, 36.
Altars, pagan, 95, 123.
Alum, 277.
Ambush in fighting, 66.
Amethysts, 401.
Amra of St. Columkille, 210.
Amulets, 123.
Amusements of people, 6; chap. xxv.
Ana or Anann, the goddess, 109.
Anchorites: see Hermits.
Angel, from Book of Kells, 386.
Anglesey, 35.
Anglo-Normans, 62, 67, 69, 71, 84, 159, 160, 191, 207, 234, 246, 288, 313, 340.

INDEX.

Anglo-Saxons, 48, 145, 174, 287, 300.
Angus, son of Erc, 37.
Animals as pets, 525.
—— connected with sport, 504.
Annalists, the Irish, 224.
Annals, 224, 225.
—— faithfulness and accuracy of, 225, 228.
—— principal books of, 228 to 230.
Antiphonary of Bangor, 222.
Antrim, Co. (7, 8), 38, 245.
Anvils, 441.
Apostles, the Twelve, of Erin, 139 and note.
Apples, 367.
Apprenticeship, 455.
Aran Islands (32), 177, 308.
Arch, construction of, 450.
Archery taught, 184.
Architects: see Builders.
Ardagh in Limerick, 246, 247, 249.
—— chalice, 246.
Ardan, s. of Usna, 39.
Ardoilen, off the Galway coast, 153.
Ard-ri, the supreme king, 15, 17.
Argonautic Expedition, translation of, 212.
Aristocracy, marks of, 376.
Ark, Noah's, 223.
—— of the Covenant, 65.
Armagh (17), 128, 168, 293, 526.
Armistice at fairs, 502, 503.
Armoric: see Breton.
Armour, 58.
Arms, 49 to 62, 121.
Arrows and arrow-heads, 50.
Art and artistic work, 9; chap. xii.
Art the Solitary, k. of Ireland, 328.
Artistic metal-work, 246.
Artisans: see Crafts and Craftsmen.
Ass, the, 491.
Assaroe at Ballyshannon, 109.
Assicus, St. Patrick's brazier, 453.
Assonance, 216.
Astronomy, 192 to 196.
Asylum, 158.
—— Military Asylums, 47.
Athboy, 15, 329.
Athelstan, King, 89.
Athene, 103.
Athlone Castle, 304.
Atkinson, Dr. Robert, 215, 222.
Auger, 446.
Augustin, an Irish monk in Carthage, 150, 193.
Augustine, St., of Canterbury, 145, 146.
Authority of kings, 22.
Avenger of blood, 46.
Awls, 446.

Axe, or hatchet, 445, 446: battleaxe. 56.
Axletree, 484.

BAAL, the Phoenician god, 121.
Bacon and Pork, 354, 355.
Badb or Bodb, the war-fury, 112, 113, 368.
Badgers, 508, 511; as food, 355.
—— skins of, 382.
Baetan, an Irish monk in Carthage, 150.
Bagpipes, 256.
Baile (bally), a homestead, a townland, 289, 290.
Baile-atha-cliath, Dublin, 481.
Baily Lighthouse at Howth, 329.
Baking, 362, 363.
Balaam, Balak, 97.
Balances, 11, 474, 475.
Ballaghmoon in Kildare, 482.
Ballaun, a drinking-vessel, a cup-like hollow in a stone, 318, 319.
Ballintober Abbey in Mayo, 160.
Balls of gold for the hair, 418, 419: balls for goaling, 513.
Ballybetagh, 375.
Ballyknockan fort, the ancient Dinnree (46), 334.
Ballymagauran in Cavan, 118.
Ballymote (21), Book of, 212, 223.
Ballyshannon (9, 10), 109, 110.
Ballyshiel in King's County, 267.
Balor of the mighty blows, 130.
Baltinglass (40), 333, 335.
Bananach, a female goblin, 114.
Banba, the Dedannan queen, 117.
Bangor in Co. Down (12), 151, 175, 222.
Bann, River (7), 42.
Banners, 64.
Banqueting Hall at Tara, 289, 292, 298, 344, 371, 498: described, 325, 326.
Banquets to men of learning, 191.
Banshee, a fairy-woman, a woman from the fairy-hills, 110, 111.
Baptismal font of Clonard, 138.
Barbers and hairdressers, 377, 380.
Barclay, Alex., the poet, 347.
Bardic Schools, 180.
Barley, 426.
Barm or yeast, 362.
Barn, 299, 300.
Barrow, the river, 357.
Baths and bathing, 377.
—— described, 381.
Battle-axe, 56.
Battle-goblins, 112.
Bawn, a cattle enclosure, 311.

INDEX. 553

Bavaria, 163, 243.
Beads for necklaces, 294, 402.
Beal Boru near Killaloe, 339.
Beard, the, 380.
Bebinn, the female doctor, 276.
Bective Abbey in Meath, 160.
Bede, the Venerable, 37, 133, 145, 146, 178, 227, 468.
Beds and bedsteads, 301 to 305.
Beechmast, 368, 429.
Beet, 354.
Bees, 363, 364, 365.
Beestings, 361.
Beeswax, 370, 371.
Bél, an Irish idol so called, 120, 121.
Belfast, (12), 20.
Bell of Cummascach mac Ailello, 168.
—— of St. Patrick, or Bell of the Will, 165, 166, 167: see Bells.
Belle Isle in Lough Erne, 229.
Bellows, 441 to 443.
Bells, 165, 258, 430, 453.
Belltaine, May Day, 120, 123, 479.
Benedict, St., 146.
Bennaid, the female brewy, 92.
Bérla Féine, the Old Irish language, 74, 198.
Bernard, the Rev. Dr., 222.
—— Dr., of Derry, 331.
Biatach, a public victualler, 375.
Bible, 143, 150, 202, 218.
Billhook, 446.
Binn, the female physician, 276.
Bird nets and traps, 511, 512.
Birds as food, 356.
—— divination from voices of, 98.
—— feathers of, for roofs, 293, 485.
—— singing, 522, 523.
Bishops, 139.
Black dye and dyestuff, 467.
Blacksmith and his forge, 440 to 444. See Smiths.
Blackthorn, 368.
Blanid's three cows, 523.
Blemish in a king not allowable, 18.
Blinding as punishment, 90.
Blue in dyeing, 467.
Blush of shame and blush-fine, 373.
Bo-aire, a class of chief, 78, 79.
Boand, the lady, 337.
Boats, 491 to 493.
Bobbio in Italy, 222.
Bocanach, a male goblin, 114.
Bodb Derg, the fairy-king, 106, 108.
Bodleian Library at Oxford, 214.
Body-fine, compensation for homicide, 89.
Bog-butter, 360.
Bogs, 3, 369, 432.

Bohereen or boreen, a little road, 481.
Bonnaght, a soldier serving for pay, 47.
Bookbinding, 10, 453, 470.
Book of Acaill, 73, 275.
—— of Armagh, 198, 242.
—— of Armagh described, 218.
—— of Ballymote, 212, 223.
—— of Cuana, 209.
—— of Dimma, 218.
—— of Durrow, 242.
—— of Fermoy, 213.
—— of Genealogies, 232.
—— of Hy Many, 213.
—— of Hymns, 222.
—— of Invasions, 212.
—— of Kells, 143, 218, 240, 242, 377, 378.
—— of Lecan, 213.
—— of Lecan, Yellow, 212.
—— of Leinster, 208, 211.
—— of Lismore, 213.
—— of Mac Durnan, 241, 242.
—— of Rights, 489, 493, 495.
—— of St. Moling, 218.
—— of the Dun Cow, 198, 208, 209, 210, 211.
—— of the O'Hickeys, 270.
—— of the O'Lees, 270.
—— of the O'Shiels, 270.
Book-satchels, 206.
Books, destruction of, 206.
—— in pagan times, 169, 171, 172.
—— of law, 73.
—— of medicine, 268, 269, 270.
—— of mixed subjects, 208.
Booleying and booleys, 431, 432.
Borreen brack or bairn brack, a speckled cake, 362.
Borrowing and lending, 519
Boru or Boroma tribute, 124, 211, 237.
Boundaries between territories, 422.
Bow and arrow, 50.
Boycott in ancient times, 88.
Boyle in Roscommon (21), 230.
Boyne, the river (29), 13, 357.
Bracelets: see Rings.
Bracteate coins, 476.
Bran, son of Febal, 107, 108, 126.
Branch of peace, 504.
Branduff, k. of Leinster, 335, 353.
Brasiers and founders, 437.
Brass, 434, 435, 437.
Bray in Wicklow, 181.
Bread, 362, 363.
Breccan, grandson of Niall 9II., 402.
Breeches, 301, 488.
Brehon, a judge, 71, 89, 90.
—— Laws, 11, 25, chap. iv., 268.

Brendan, St, of Clonfert, the Navigator, 492, 526.
Breton or Armoric language, 197, 198, 199, 200.
Brewers, 350.
Brewy, a keeper of a house of public hospitality, 19, 92, 305, 311, 353, 358, 381.
—— described, 373.
Brian Boru, 26, 30, 288.
"Brian Boru's harp," 255.
Bricriu, of the venom tongue, 39.
Bride, purchased for bride-price, 283, 284.
Bridges, 4, 482, 483.
Bridles, 488, 489.
Brigh Brugaid, the female lawyer, 286.
Brigit, the pagan goddesses of that name, 109.
Brigit, St., of Kildare, 144, 154, 220, 453.
Bristol, 80.
Britain, 33, 34, 95, 135, 144, 146, 149, 172, 177, 245, 292, 477, 492: see England.
British or Britannic languages, 197.
—— Museum, 213, 214, 400.
Britons, 33, 37, 135, 177, 290, 348, 468.
Bróinbherg, the hospital of Emain, 273.
Bronze, 434, 435, 437, 439, 440, 448, 449.
Broo or Bro at New Grange, 538.
Brooches, 391, 413, 414, 415.
Brooklime, 366.
Broth, 355.
Bruden Da Choga, 113.
—— Da Derga: see Da Derga.
Brugh, a great house, 306.
—— on the Boyne, 108.
Bruree (44), royal residence, 340, 341.
Buffoons and jesters, 501, 516, 517.
Builders, 435, 436.
Building, 289 to 300; 435, 436, 444.
Buildings and other material church requisites, 155 to 168.
Bunne-do-at, a sort of open ring, 411, 412, 413, 477.
Bunting and his music, 262.
Burial, modes of, 534.
—— mounds, 538, 539 to 545.
Burning the dead: see Cremation.
Burns, Robert, 527.
Butlers (the family), 69.
Butter, 359, 360, 492.
Buttevant Abbey, 160.
Buttons, 391, 392, 402.
Byzantium, 242, 244.

Castledermot church window, 452.
—— high cross of, 255.
Castles, 291, 296, 297, 304, 311, 312, 313.
Castletown Moat, 39, 40.
Cat, the, 508.
Catalogue of Irish saints, 135 and following pages; 153.
Cathach, or "battler," a consecrated relic, 64.
—— of the O'Donnells, 65, 218.
Cathbad the druid, 100.
Cattle as a standard of value, 477.
Causeways, 483.
Cavalry, 67.
Cavan, Co. (22, 23), 16.
Céile, a free rent-paying tenant, 79, 84, 85.
Celestine, Pope, 133.
Celt, a sort of axe, 32, 57.
Celtar, a cloak of invisibility, 103.
Celtic languages, 197, 198.
Celts, the, 32, 64, 95, 122, 125, 245, 292, 294, 465.
Cemeteries, 497.
—— described, 537.
Cenobitical monasteries, 140.
Cethern of the brilliant deeds, 42, 65.
Chain of silence or of attention, 504.
Chalice, the Ardagh, 246.
Chalk used on shields, 60.
Champion, the king's, 27, 46.
Charcoal, 369, 370, 438, 441, 444.
Chariots and charioteers, 4, 42, 43, 45.
—— described, 483 to 486.
Chariot-racing, 510.
Charlemagne, 194, 227, 242.
Charms and spells, 102, 103, 104.
Chase and capture of wild animals, 510 and following.
Chastity and modesty prized, 284.
Cheese, 360, 361.
Chess, 29.
—— described, 314.
—— taught, 184.
Chiefs and nobles, 18, 19, 77, 91.
Children of Lir, story of, 237.
Children, position of, 285, 286, 287, 520.
Chimneys, 298.
China, great wall of, 424.
Chisels, 448.
Chivalry, 65.
Christchurch, Dublin, 549.
Christianity, chap. vi.
Chronicon Scotorum, 230.
Churches and monastic buildings, 155 to 163.

Churns, 318.
Cimbaeth, k. of Ireland, 330.
Circular gold plates, 413.
Cities and towns, 6, 290.
Clann children, a group of relations supposed to be descended from a common ancestor, 81.
Clannaboy, or Clandeboye, 20.
Clapping of hands in divination, 99.
Clare County (37, 38), 16, 406.
Classes of Irish Music, 259.
—— of kings, 17.
—— of people, five main, 77.
—— of Tales, 233, 234.
Classification of Irish Literature, 214.
—— of upper garments, 384.
Claudian, the Roman poet, 33, 34.
Claymore, a great sword, 55.
Cleena, the fairy queen, 110, 111.
Cloak of darkness, 103.
Cloaks, 385 to 388; 391.
Clochan, a beehive-shaped hut, 153, 290.
Clod-mallet, 427.
Clogher in Tyrone, 120.
Clonard in Meath (29), 138, 175, 182, 482.
Clonmacnoise (34), 161, 176, 209, 229, 230, 486, 495.
Clonroad near Ennis, 339.
Clontarf (36), Battle of, 67, 104, 113, 207, 226.
Cloon-O, 99.
Clowns, 29, 501.
Coal, 302, 441.
Coal-mines, 441.
Cobthach the Slender, k. of Ireland, 280, 334.
Cockles used in dyeing, 468.
Cognisance on shields, 60.
Cogue, a drinking-cup, 317.
Coinage, coins, 11, 476.
Cóir Anmann, 232.
Coleraine (7), 42.
Colgan, the Rev. John, 220.
Colic, 272.
Collas, the Three, 330.
Collar of Moran, 128.
Colleges: see Schools.
Colloquy of the Ancient Men, 237.
Colman, bishop of Lindisfarne, 146, 178.
—— St., of Cloyne, 271.
—— St., of Templeshanbo, 526.
Colonisations by Irish, 32.
Colours of garments, 7, 383, 385.
Coltsfoot, 370.
Columbanus, St., 151, 176.
Columb's house at Kells, 140.

Columkille or Columba, St., 65, 122, 140, 143, 144, 145, 146, 163, 183, 189, 219, 220, 222, 518, 526.
Combs, 379.
Comgall, St., of Bangor, 175.
Comgan or Mac da Cherda, 522.
Commentaries on Law, 74.
Commerce, 11, 494, 495.
Committee of Nine for Br. Laws, 73.
Common descent from an ancestor, 80, 81.
Commons land, 83, 429, 431.
Communication by water, 491 to 493.
Compasses (for circles), 446.
Compensation, Law of, 86, 87, 88.
Comrar, a stone coffin or cist, 543, 544.
Conall Cernach, 39, 114, 377.
—— son of Blathmac, 457.
Conan Mael, 43.
Conari or Conaire the Great, k. of Ireland, 28, 31, 99, 131, 211, 516, 517.
—— the Second, k. of Ireland, 37.
Concobar mac Nessa, 27, 39, 100, 115, 235, 276, 329.
Condiment, 357.
Confession of St. Patrick, 34, 154, 218.
Congal Claen, prince of Ulster, 357.
Conleth, St., bishop of Kildare, 453.
Conn the Hundred Fighter, or of the Hundred Battles, k. of Ireland, 113, 210.
Connaught, 13, 16, 122, 165, 235.
—— extent of, anciently, 13, 16.
Connla the Comely, story of, 210, 211.
Conquests of Irish, 32.
Consumption (illness), 272.
Conventions and fairs, 326, 496, 497.
Convents and nuns in Ireland, 153.
Convulsions (illness), 272.
Cooks and Cooking, 351, 501.
Cooley, the Carlingford peninsula, 235.
Copenhagen, 147.
Copper, 434, 435, 437.
Copperas as medicine, 277.
Corc, k. of Munster, 337.
Corcomroe Abbey in Clare, 160.
Cork (56), 356.
Cormac mac Ait, king, 24, 26, 43, 44, 92, 115, 132, 310, 324, 325, 327, 342, 344, 361, 456.
Cormac Mac Cullenan, 201, 230.
Cormac's chapel at Cashel, Pref. xxiv; 158.
Cormac's Glossary, 201, 230.
Corn (grain), its preparations, 361, 362, 426, 427.

Cornish language, 197, 198, 200.
Corn-mills, 456.
Corn-ricks, 427.
Cornwall, 435.
Coroticus, Patrick's epistle to, 154.
Corpse, rights of a, 531, 532.
—— branch-covering for, 534.
Corrody, paid maintenance i monastery, 520.
Corrievreckan, 493 and note.
Costume illustrated, 378, 386, 387, 389, 390, 391, 393.
Cottage industries, 10, 463, 466.
Couches, 301 to 305.
Coursing with hounds, 510.
Court officers of kings, 25.
Courts of Justice, 5, 90.
Cow-herds, 430.
Cowl, 389.
Cows, 428.
—— as a standard of value, 477.
Coyne and livery, 85.
Craftsmen, social position and protection of, 452 to 455.
Craglea or Crageevill, near Killaloe (38), 110, 111, 338.
Crane or heron, 357.
—— for lifting, 447.
Crannoge, an insulated dwelling, 313.
Creeveroe, at Emain, 330.
Cremation, 534, 535, 536.
Cremation-ashes thrown into water, 506.
Crescents, gorgets, and necklets, 40 to 410.
Cridenbél, the satirist, 280.
Criffan the Great, k. of Irel. (A.D. 366 to 379), 33, 34.
Criffan, son of Cahirmore, 510.
Crimson, in dyeing, 467.
Crofton Croker's Fairy Legends, 342.
Croghan, palace of (21, 22), 112, 235, 300, 455, 497, 498.
—— described, 331.
Cromlechs, 543 to 546.
Cromm Cruach, the idol, 118, 119, 205.
Croom or Crom in Limerick (44), 69.
Crops, 426.
Crosiers, 453.
Cross of Cong, 246, 247, 249, 250.
Cross placed over graves, 549.
Crossan, a gleeman, 516, 517.
Crosses, 249, 416, 485, 486.
Crown or diadem, 25, 415, 416, 417.
Cualann, district of (36), 481.
Cuan O'Lochain, 321.
Cuculainn, 39, 48, 49, 59, 114, 115, 126, 196, 235, 277, 303, 418, 484.
Cuilmen, a great book, 209.

INDEX. 557

Cullen in Tipperary, 450.
Cummascach mac Ailello, his bell, 168.
Cummian or Cummain Fota, St., 176, 222.
Cupping and cupping-horn, 276.
Curath-mir, 'the champion's bit,' 114, 345.
Curds, 360, 361.
Curoi mac Daire, 42.
Curragh of Kildare, 333.
—— fair and races of, 499, 509, 510.
Curraghs or wicker boats, 471, 491, 492.
Cuthbert, St., 145.
Cutts Waterfall on the Bann, 40.
Cycles, astronomical and chronological, 193, 194.
—— of Historical Tales, 234.
Cyclopean building, 308.

Da Derga and his hostel, 99, 131, 211, 212, 237.
Dagda, the, a Dedannan god, 108, 115, 280.
Dagger, 56, 67.
Dagobert, k. of France, 177.
Dáire or Dáre, king of Ulster in St. Patrick's time, 526.
Dalaradia (8, 12, 18), 64.
Dalcassians, the O'Briens, inhabiting Clare, 16, 22, 111.
Dallan Forgaill, the poet, 210.
Dalriada, also called Dalicudini (7, 8), 37, 38.
Dalteen, an attendant on a horse soldier, 67.
Dam in a stream, 513.
Dana or Danann, the goddess, 109.
Danaus, k. of the Argives, 426.
Dancing, 501.
Danes, 59, 71, 116, 162, 195, 206, 227, 234, 458: see Scandinavians and Norsemen.
"Danish" forts and raths, 312.
Dathi, king of Ireland, 36.
—— his pillar-stone, 546.
David and Goliath, 50.
Davies, Sir John, 72, 86.
Death and burial, chap. xxvii.
Death-bell, 532.
De Berminghams, the, 337.
De Courcy, John, 27, 42, 312.
Dedannans; in Irish Tuatha de Danann, 31, 53, 105, 109, 110, 112, 115, 117, 130, 235, 331.
Deer, 428, 506, 507, 511.
Dega, St., the artificer, 453.
Degads or Clanna Degad, 42.
Degrees in Irish colleges, 180.

Deirdre, Naisi's wife, 376.
Dela, five sons of, 13.
de Lacy, Hugh, the elder, 291, 311.
Delphi, oracle of, 101.
Demons, 114, 117, 121.
Dermot and Gráinne's beds: see Cromlechs.
Dermot Mac Murrogh, k. of Leinster, 58, 211.
—— O'Dyna, 43, 327.
—— (son of Fergus), k. of Ireland, 321.
Derryloran in Tyrone, 275.
Descent of land, 85.
Designs in embroidery, 470.
Desiol, turning sunwise, 65, 127, 128.
Desmond or South Munster (48, 55, 56, 51), 16, 18, 69.
Destitution provided for, 520.
Destruction of books, 206.
Devenish Island (16), round tower of, 162, 451.
Diadem, 410, 415, 416.
Dialects of Celtic, 197.
Diancecht, the leech-god, 264, 265.
Diarrhœa, 272.
Dicuil, St., and his holy well at Lure, 151.
—— the Irish Geographer, 149, 195.
Dillesk, dulse, or duilesc, 367.
Dingle in Kerry (48), 468.
Dinner, 343.
Dinnree or Dinnrigh (46), 332, 333.
Dinnsenchus, 119, 211, 212, 232.
Dioscorides, the physician, 348.
Diseases, 270.
Distaff, 463.
Distress, and procedure by, 87, 503.
Divination and diviners, 98, 101.
Division of Ireland, 13 to 17.
Do-at, two knobs or discs, 410, 411, 412.
Dodder, the river, 481.
Dog, 504.
—— divination from howling of, 99.
Domestic vessels, 314.
Domnall (son of Aed mac Ainmirech), 384, 518.
Donegal (5, 6), 144, 230.
Donn (son of Milesius), fairy king of Knockfierna, 110.
Donnybrook, 481.
Donogh, son of King Blathmac, 457.
Doon, Rock of, 22.
Doonglara, royal residence, 340.
Doorkeeper, 296.
Dooros-Heath, 448, 449.
Down, Downpatrick (18), 39, 41.
Dowry (in marriage), 283.
Dowth on the Boyne, 537.
Dragons in lakes, 524.

Draughts (the game), 516.
Drawingroom, 300.
Drayton's Polyolbion quoted, 253.
Dress, 7, 382, and following pages.
Dressmaking, 469, 470.
Drink, various kinds of, described, 348.
Drinking-horn, 315.
Drinking-vessels, 295, 314, 318.
Drink of forgetfulness, 97.
Dripping, 356.
Drisheen, a sort of pudding, 356.
Drogheda, 249, 290.
Drowes, river (9), 13.
Drowning as a punishment, 90.
Druidesses, 100, 101.
Druids and druidism, 95 to 102; 122, 129, 137, 139, 169, 179, 180, 318.
—— Irish and Gaulish compared, 101.
"Druids' altars," 545.
Drumcliff, near Sligo (15), 163.
Drumketta, Ir. Druim-Cete, 189, 518.
Drunkenness reprehensible, 348.
Dublin (36), 245, 290, 435, 481, 482, 483.
Duilech, St., of St. Doulogh's, 156.
Duma, a mound, a burial-mound, 540 to 543.
Duma na Bo at Tara, 325.
Duma-nan-Giall or Mound of the Hostages at Tara, 324.
Dun, a fortified residence, 306, 307.
Dun Aengus on Aran Island (32), 308, 309, 329.
Dunbolg (40), 335, 353.
Dunbrody Abbey in Wexford, 160.
Dun-Cethern, 42.
Duncriffan at Howth, 329.
Dun-da-benn, now Mountsandall, 39.
Dundalgan near Dundalk (23, 24), 39, 40.
Dundrum Castle (18), 42, 312.
Dungal, the Irish monk, 194, 222.
Dun-keltair near Downpatrick, 39, 41.
Dunlang O'Hartigan, 104.
Dunlavin in Wicklow, 336.
Dun-nan-ged, Feast of, 113, 357.
Dunnasciath, royal residence, 329.
Dun-Rury, now Dundrum, in Down (18), 42, 312.
Dunseverick in Antrim, 329, 481.
Duns Scotus, 176.
Dunstan, St., 143, 145, 195.
Dun-Torgeis, near Castlepollard, 329.
Durrow in King's County (34), high cross of, 416.

Dwelling-houses : see House.
Dyeing, 466.
—— the eyebrows, 377.
—— the eyelids, 148.
—— the finger-nails, 376.
—— peasants' knowledge of, 469.
Dysert-Aengus in Limerick, 221.

EADFRID, bishop of Lindisfarne, 177.
Eagles, 4, 99.
Early rising, 432.
Earrings, 417, 418.
Ecclesiastical and religious writings, 217.
—— schools, 174 to 184.
Eclipses, 194, 195, 226.
Ecliptic, the, 195.
Education, chap. vii.
—— among the lay community, 179.
—— in fosterage, 184, 287.
Educational poems, 184.
—— test for admission to the Fena, 43.
Edward I., 358.
—— III., 354.
Eels, 512.
Eevinn or Eevill, the banshee, 104, 110, 111.
Effigies on monuments, 549, 550.
Eggs as food, 357.
Eginhard the Annalist, 227.
Egyptian monks in Ireland, 177.
Elder or boortree, 377.
Election of kings, 18, 19.
Elegy, 533.
Elements, worship of, 95, 121.
Elk, the Irish, 506, 507.
Emain, Emain Macha, or Emania (17), 27, 39, 109, 132, 229, 273, 298, 310, 455, 481, 497, 498.
—— described, 329.
Embroidery, 470, 501.
Emeralds, 401.
Emetics, 276.
Enamel and enamel work, 245, 246, 316.
Encampments, 63.
Endymion by Keats, 522.
England and English, 59, 85, 144, 295, 298, 305, 307, 347: see Britain.
Engravers, 445.
Ennis Abbey (38), 160.
Envoy or herald, 63.
Eoghan Mór, k. of Munster, 113.
Equestrians, 501 : see Horse-riding.
Equinoctial and equinoxes, 193.
Erc, bishop of Slane, and his hermitage, 137, 328, 357.
—— Concobar's grandson, 518.
Eremitical monasteries, 152, 153, 154

INDEX. 559

Fremon, k. of Ireland, 227.
Eric, a compensation fine, 88 : see Compensation.
Eric of Auxerre, 147.
Erysipelas, 272.
Esaia or Isaiah the prophet, 241.
Esau, 355.
Esker Riada, 482 and note.
Ethicus of Istria, 171, 173.
Evangelist, figure of, 387.
Eviction from house and land unknown, 85.
Evidence in court of law, 91.
Evil eye, 130, 131.
Exchange, mediums of, 475.
Extempore composition, 186.
Eyebrows and eyelids, dyeing of, 148, 377.

FACE, shape of, 376.
Facsimiles of Irish MSS., 212, 213.
Fairies, 105 and following pp.; 210, 280.
Fairs, 6, 7, 90, 496 to 504.
Fairyland, 102, 110, 125, 310.
Fairy Palace of the Quicken Trees, Story of, 237.
Fairy palaces, 105, 106.
Faithche, a lawn, an exercise green, 310, 311.
Falcons, 4.
Family, the, 80, 283.
Family names, 288.
Faraday, Miss Winifred, 236.
Farm animals, 428 to 430.
—— implements, 427.
—— life, 432.
Faroe Islands, 150.
Fasting, legal procedure by, 88.
Fe, an aspen-rod for measuring bodies and graves, 534.
Feast of Bricriu, 114, 211.
Feathers for beds, 303.
—— for ornamental roofs, 293.
—— for chariot awnings, 485.
Fechin, St., 153.
Fe-Fiada, 103, 104, 112.
Feilire of Oengus, or Aengus, 212, 220.
Féine, Féne, a céile or free rentpayer, a farmer, 71, 79, 84, 198.
Féis or Fés, a meeting, festivity, or convention, 91, 497.
Féis of Tara, 326, 497, 498.
Felim O'Conor, k. of Connaught, his tomb, 68, 550.
Female physicians, 268.
Fena of Erin (Irish Fianna), 38, 43, 44, 45, 235, 236, 377, 510.
—— how they cooked, 351.

Fences, 83, 421, 422.
Fénechas, the ancient Irish law, 71.
Ferdiad, the champion, 42, 303.
Ferdomnach, the scribe, 218, 219.
Fergil the Geometer, 176.
Fergus mac Léide, k. of Ulster, 116.
—— Mór, or Fergus mac Erc, 37, 38.
—— mac Roy, 39.
Ferleginn, chief professor, principal of a school or college, 178, 228.
Ferryboats, 4, 143.
Fer-side [Fershee], a male fairy, 110.
Festilogies, 220.
Fiacha, King, 425.
Fiacha Muillethan, k. of Munster, 342, 522.
Fibula : see Bunne-do-at.
Fiddle, 501.
Fidnemed, a sacred grove, 159.
Fili or file, a poet, a philosopher, 187.
Fillet for the forehead, 415.
Finachta the Festive, k. of Ireland, 182, 183.
Finan or Finnen of Lindisfarne, 146, 178.
Findabair, the princess, 365.
Findruine, white bronze, 391, 437, 438.
Fine, a group of persons related to each other, 81.
Fingal Ronain, story of, 237.
Finger-nails, 376.
Finnbarr, St., of Cork, 153.
Finnchua, or Findchua, Saint, of Brigown, 284.
Finnen or Finnian of Clonard, 138, 139, 175.
—— of Moville, 127.
Finn mac Cumail, 43, 44, 127, 236, 327.
—— mac Gorman, 211.
Finntan, nephew of Parthalon, 127.
Firbolgs, 13, 31, 52, 112.
Fire festival, 123.
—— perpetual, at Kildare and elsewhere, 143, 144.
—— worship, 123.
Firewood or firebote, 369.
Fish as food, 357.
Fishing, 512.
—— nets and spears for, 512.
—— weirs for, 513.
Fitzgerald, Gilbert, 159.
Fitz Geralds, the, 69.
Five items of common knowledge, 196.
—— roads leading from Tara, 328, 480, 481, 482.
—— ways of holding land, 82.
Fixity of tenure, 85.
Flag in battle, 64.

INDEX.

Flail, 427.
Flaith, a noble, 18, 77, 78, 79.
Flann of Monasterboice, 228.
Flavianus the Roman, 504.
Flax and its preparation, 465.
Flesc, a sort of bracelet, 78.
Fleshfork, 353, 354.
Fleshmeat and its accompaniments, 354.
Flint and steel, 370.
Flint workshop, 450.
Floors, how covered, 305.
Flour and meal, 362.
Flux for metals, 438.
Fog, the magic, 103.
Foillan, St , 252.
Food, 343 to 368.
—— in monasteries, 141, 343.
—— provision for, during battle, 66.
Fools, 29, 516.
Foot-races, 510.
—— wear, 396.
Fords, 4, 5.
Foreign expeditions, 8, 32.
—— merchants in Ireland, 501.
—— missions, 139, 144 and following pages; 147 and following pages.
—— students in monastic schools, 176.
Forge, 440 to 444.
Forks and knives at meals, 346, 347.
Formenius or Parmenius, 36.
Forrad or Forradh at Tara, 323, 324.
Fortchern, St. Patrick's smith, 453.
Forts of various kinds, 306 and following pages.
Fosterage, 286, 288, 509.
Foster-child's duty to foster-parents, 287, 520.
Founders and brasiers, 437.
Four Masters, the, 230.
Fowling, 511, 512.
Foxes, 4.
—— skins, 382.
France, 11, 149, 487.
Franciscan monastery of Adam and Eve, Dublin, 213.
Franks, 135, 290, 495.
Fraughans or whortleberries, 368.
Freemen, 77, 78, 79, 91.
Free circuits of kings, 23.
Frieze, 388.
Frock or jacket, 388, 389.
Frogs in Ireland, 524.
Froissart's account of knighthood, 48.
Fruit and fruit-trees, 337.
Fudir, an unfree tenant, 85, 91, 307.
Fuel, 369.
Fulling and fullers, 462, 464.
Funeral feast, 532, 534.

Funeral games, 497, 532.
—— obsequies, 532.
Furnace, 443, 444.
Furniture, 298 to 305.
Furs, 382.
Fursa, St., of Peronne, 252.

GAELIC LANGUAGE, 181, 197, 198.
Gaels, 35, 105.
Galloglass, a heavy-armed foot-soldier, 27, 68.
Galway (32), 482.
Game for hunting, 511.
Gamanraide of Connaught, 42.
Gap of danger, 46.
Garland of Howth, 242.
Garlic, 366.
Garnets, 401.
Garters, 394.
Gaul, 34, 36, 95, 295.
Gaulish druids, 95, 101, 102.
—— gods, 104.
—— language, 198.
—— workshops, ancient, 450.
Gauls, 105, 119, 125, 177, 306, 345 404, 484, 485.
Gavelkind, 83, 86.
Gavra, Battle of, 45.
Geese, 357.
Geis, a prohibition, a thing forbidden, 131.
Genealogies, 212, 232.
Geniti-glinni, sprites of the valley 114.
Geometry studied by Irish, 194, 195.
Geraldines, the, 69.
Germans, 177.
Germany, 149.
Gertrude, daughter of Pepin, 252.
Giants' graves : see Cromlech.
Giant's Sconce near Coleraine, 42.
Gibeah, slingers of, 49.
Gilla, modern giolla, a boy, a gilli or attendant, 67.
Giraldus Cambrensis, 57, 58, 80, 125 242, 252.
Girdles, 370, 391, 394.
Glaisín, woad for dyeing, 92.
Glandore in Cork (59), 111.
Glannagalt in Kerry, 97.
Glasnevin near Dublin, 175, 181.
Glass, 294, 295.
Glastonbury, 145, 195.
Gleemen, 516, 517.
Glossaries, 201.
Glosses, 198, 211.
—— described, 199.
Gloves, 394, 395.
Goad, 427, 490.

oaling or hurling, 513.
oats, 355.
obban Saer, the architect, 436.
—— St., 175.
oblins, 104 and following pp. ; 113.
od, names for, 104.
ods, pagan, 95, 101, 104.
oibniu, the Dedannan smith-god, 325, 435, 440.
ioidels or Gaels, 35.
ioidelic or Gaelic language, 197.
iold, 9, 244, 399, 476, 477, 501.
—— in Ireland and England compared, 400, 420.
—— mines, 245.
—— and silver as mediums of exchange, 476, 477, 478.
—— balls for hair, 418, 419.
—— objects in Nat. Museum, List of, 420
-olden Vale, the, 337.
ioldsmiths, 437, 449.
ioliath, 463.
ioll mac Morna, 43.
iood People, *i.e.* fairies, 107.
'ordon, Bernard, the physician, 270.
orgets, 404 to 410.
oshawks, 4.
ospels, 217, 240, 242, 243.
Gossipred, 287.
Gongane Barra in Cork (55), 153, 154.
Gouge (a carpenter's), 448, 449.
Gout in the hands, 272.
Government by kings, chap. ii.
Gráinne, d. of Cormac mac Art, 327.
Grain-rubber, 461.
Grammars, Ancient Irish, 201.
Grammatica Celtica of Zeuss, 200, 201.
Granard (22), 119.
Graves and graveyards, 534 to end.
Gravy, 356.
Grazing, 431, 432.
Grazing animals, classification of, 431.
Greaves (for legs), 59.
Greek and Roman writers on Ireland, 494.
Greek language in monastic schools, 175, 180, 181.
Greeks, 23, 54, 64, 97, 238, 260, 264, 265, 276, 283, 308, 345, 347, 377, 425, 450, 500, 502.
Green as a national colour, 384.
Greenan, a summer-house, 293, 300.
Greenan Lachtna, palace, 338.
Greenan-Ely, 331 : see Ailech.
Grey Abbey in Down, 160.
Greyhounds, 505.
Grian of the Bright Cheeks, 111.

Griffith, Sir Richard, 434.
Grinding corn, chap. xxi.
Grindstone, 449.
Groom, the chief's or king's, 29.
Ground colour in dyeing, 466.
Groups of society, 80.
Gryffith ap Conan, k. of Wales, 252.
Guaire the Hospitable, 304.
Guest-house of monastery, 142.
Guests, 373.
—— order of, at table, 343, 344.

HAGGARD, 6, 311, 427.
Hair and hair dressing, 377 to 380; 418.
Hallowe'en or All Hallows night, 112.
Halter (for animals), 427.
Hammer, 441, 447.
Handel's Harmonious Blacksmith, 260.
Handicrafts taught, 184: see Crafts.
Hands, clapping of, in divination, 99.
—— well-shaped, 376.
Handstone as a weapon, 49.
Hanging as a punishment, 90.
Hare, the, 4, 508.
Harlots, 517.
Harmony in Irish music, 260.
Harp, 251, 254, 255, 256, 257, 501
Harpers, Irish, 251 to 257.
—— travelling through Scotland, 263.
Hash or pottage, 355.
Hat or cap, 395.
Hatchet or axe, 445, 446.
Haughton, the Rev. Samuel, 226.
Hawks, 4.
Hazel and hazel-nuts, 100, 102, 367.
Head laid on bosom as a salutation, 518.
Head-gear, 395.
Headstones, 547, 548, 549.
Healy, the Most Rev. Dr., 137.
Heaven, the pagan, 124, 509.
Hebrews, 527.
Hebrides, the, 69, 512.
Hell-gate of Ireland, 112.
Helmet, 59.
Hennessy, W. M., 342.
Henry II., 357.
—— VIII., 139.
Heptarchy, the, 30.
Herald, 63.
Herb-doctors, 280.
Herb-garden, 6, 365.
Herbs in medicine, 265, 277, 280.
—— popular knowledge of, 280.
Herding and herdsmen, 432.
Heremon, first Milesian king, 120.
Hermits, Irish, 136, 152, 153.

2 o

562 INDEX.

Herons, 357.
Hiberi, Hiberni, *i.e.* the Irish, 348.
Hides and skins, 382, 383.
— used for beds, 303.
— as tablecloths, 347.
— exported, 495.
— used for curraghs, 491, 492.
High crosses, 249, 416, 485, 486.
Hired soldiers, 47.
Historian : see Shanachie.
Histories of Ireland, 231.
History of music, 251.
Hobbies and hobellers, 487.
Holed-stones, 423, 424.
Holyhead, 35.
Holy Island, in Lough Derg, 8.
— wells : see Wells.
Homer, 54, 64.
Homestead, 298, 299.
Homicide, 89, 90.
Honey, 350, 351, 362.
— treated of, 363.
Honours and rewards for learning, 190.
Hood (for head), 387, 389, 395.
Hoops and hooped vessels, 314.
Hornblowing as a trade-signal, 464, 465.
Horncastle's Irish Music, 262.
Horns, 257, 501.
— for drinking, 315.
Horse and foot, 67.
Horse-riding, 4, 487 to 490; 501, 510.
Horse-rod for guiding, 489, 490.
Horses, 29, 487.
— and stables, keeper of, 29.
Horse-shoeing, 490.
Horsewhip, 490.
Hospitalia (Irish) on the Continent, 375.
Hospitality, 5, 372, 373.
Hospitals, 279.
Hostages, 22, 325.
Hostels, public, 4, 187.
— described, 372.
Hot-air bath, 277.
Hounds, 504, 505, 506.
House, the, chap. xvi.
— builders of, 5.
— of manuscripts, 205.
— steward, 28.
Household of kings, 25.
Howth (36), 329.
Human sacrifice, 102, 119.
Hunting, 3, 377, 504, 505, 506, 507, 508, 510, and following pages.
Hurling or goaling, 513.
Hurts or whortleberries, 368.
Husband and wife, 283 to 286.
Hy Many, 18.
Hymns, 222.

I-Brazil, the enchanted island, 124.
Iceland, 149.
Ictian Sea, the English Channel, 33.
Idol, idols, 95, 118.
Ierne and Iernis, Ireland, 494.
Illumination of MSS., 238 to 244; 454.
Immortality of the soul, 102, 125.
Inauguration of kings, 19, 324.
Incantations, 97, 129, 265.
Inchagoill, in Lough Corrib, 547.
India and Indians, 88, 527.
Industrial education, 184, 287.
Industries : see Trades and Industries.
Ingcel the marauder, 99.
Inishcaltra (38), 8.
Inishmurray off Sligo coast (15), 144, 153, 279.
Ink and ink-horn, 203.
Innisfallen island and college, 229.
Insanity, 96, 97.
Inscriptions, 546, 547, 548, 549.
— tombs with, 547.
Interest on loans, 519.
Interior arrangements of house, 301 to 305.
Intermarriages between Irish and British, 35.
Intoxication, 348.
Inver Colpa, 13.
Iona (island), 143, 144, 145, 146, 185, 219.
Irish language and literature, chap. viii.
— modern students of, 202.
Irish music, chap. xiii.
— collections of, 262.
— musicians as teachers, 252.
Iron, 434.
Isaiah the prophet, 241.
Isle of Man, 36, 108: see Manx.
Isthmian games of Greece, 499, 502, 503.
Italy and Italians, 149, 163, 244, 295.

Jacob, the patriarch, 355.
James I., 86.
Jameson, a Scotch writer, 252.
Javelin, 67.
Jerpoint in Kilkenny, 160.
Jesters, jugglers, and gleemen, 29, 516.
Jet, 402.
Jewels, jewellery, 10, 29, 401, 402, 501.
Jews, 65, 130.
John, King, and his castle, Limerick, 297.
— Scotus Erigena, 176.

INDEX.

Joints (meat), distributed according to rank, 345.
Jones, Dr., bishop of St. David's, 35.
Judges : see Brehon and Brehon Laws.
Judgments in form of maxims and illustrations, 91, 92.
Jugglers, 29, 501, 516, 517.
Justice, administration of, 86 to 92.

KALE, 366.
Kavanagh, Art Mac Murrogh, 487.
Kavanagh horn, the, 315.
Keating, Geoffrey, 199, 231, 303.
Keats, the poet, 521, 522.
Keening or crying for the dead, 533.
Keens or death-tunes, 260.
Keeper of the king's jewels, 29.
Kellach, St., of Killala, 98.
Kells in Kilkenny, 482.
—— in Meath (29), 140.
Keltar of the Battles, 39, 54.
Kemble, J. M., an English antiquary, 417.
Kennfaela the Learned, 274, 275.
Kent, 86, 145.
Kermand Kelstach, the Ulster idol, 119.
Kern, a light-armed foot-soldier, 67.
Kerry diamonds, 401.
Keth mac Magach, 42.
Keys and locks, 297.
Key-shield of the Mass, 222.
Kildare (35), 143, 242, 245, 500.
Kilfinnane Moat, 307.
Killaloe (38), 111, 339.
Killarney (49), 227, 229, 435.
Killeen Cormac, 133, 134.
Kilmainham, 144.
Kilmallock Abbey, 159, 160
Kiln for corn-drying, 299.
—— for lime-burning, 450.
Kilt, 385, 389, 390.
Kilternan cromlech, 544, 545.
Kincora, palace of, at Killaloe (38), 331, 339.
Kinel, a race, a tribe, or aggregation of tribes, supposed to be descended from a common ancestor, 30.
Kinel Connell, the people of Tirconnell (now Donegal), 65.
Kineth O'Hartigan, 321.
Kings, chap. ii.; 77, 92, 131, 307, 372, 416, 453.
King John's Castle, Limerick, 297.
King with crown, 416.
King's Chair at Tara, 325.

Kiss as a salutation, 518.
Kistvaens, 543, 544.
Kitchen, 354.
—— garden, 6, 365.
—— or condiment, 357.
Kneading trough, 363.
Kneeling as a salutation, 519.
Knees, bare, 391, 392.
Knife for cutting rushes, 305.
—— for making pens, 203.
Knives and forks at meals, 346, 347.
Knights and knighthood, 48.
Knockainy, 110.
Knockaulin, 332, 333, 508.
Knockfierna near Croom in Limerick, 110.
Knockgraffon in Tipperary, 342, 522.
Knocklong, siege of, 342.
Knockmoy Abbey in Galway, 24, 160.
Knowth on the Boyne in Meath, 537.
Kongs Skuggsjo, an old Norse book, 323.
Kuno Meyer, Dr., Pref. ix; 237.

LABRAID, King, 418.
Ladle for metal casting, 438.
Laebhan, St. Patrick's smith, 453.
Laegaire the Victorious, 39, 114.
—— king of Ireland, 73, 98, 100, 119, 124, 131, 169, 327.
Laery Lorc, k. of Ireland, 280.
Lake-dwellings, 313.
Lakes, monsters in, 524.
Lamps and lanterns, 372.
Lance: see Spears.
Land and land laws, 81 to 86.
Land as support of church, 142.
—— laws relating to, 81 to 86.
—— tillage and grazing of, chap. xix.
—— measures of, 472, 473.
—— for tillage, 142, 425.
Lanigan, Dr., 145.
Lann or land, a plate of metal, a sword-blade, a griddle, 415.
Lapdog, 505.
Lard, 356, 365.
Lathe, 447, 448.
Latin language, 175, 180, 181, 215.
—— explaining Gaelic, 199, 200
Laura, an Eastern eremitical monastery, 153.
Lavra the Mariner, k. of Ireland, 334.
Lawn or green of a rath, 310, 311.
Laws: see Brehon Laws.
Laws, books of, 73.
—— relating to land, 81 to 86.
—— made to destroy Irish trade, 495.

Lay community: education amongst, 178 to 180.
Lay or secular schools, 8, 174, 178.
Lead, 435.
—— for roofs, 293.
Learning and education, 169.
Learning among the laity, 178 to 180.
—— esteemed and rewarded, 9, 184 to 191.
—— extent of, in monastic schools, 175, 176.
—— in pagan times, 168.
—— not confined to monasteries, 178, 179.
Leather, 59, 471.
—— covers for books, 453.
—— bags, 471.
—— bottles, 148.
—— used on shields, 59. 60, 62.
—— work as an art, 10, 239, 470.
Leaven or yeast, 362.
Lebar Brecc, 211.
—— Laigen, 208, 211.
—— na hUidhre: see Book of the Dun Cow.
Lecan in Sligo, 212.
Leeks and onions, 366.
Leggings, 391.
Legs bare, 391, 393.
Leighlin Bridge (40), 334.
Leinster province, 13, 16, 108, 124, 226, 284, 500.
—— ancient extent of, 13, 16.
Lending and borrowing, 519.
Leper-houses and leprosy, 271, 273, 274.
Lepreachán or leprechaun, a kind of fairy, 115, 116.
Leth Conn and Leth Mow, 482 note.
Letters, Irish (alphabet), 173.
Lewy, k. of Ireland, 37.
Lhuyd, the Welsh antiquarian, 35.
Liambain, 332: see Dunlavin.
Lia Fail, the inauguration stone at Tara, 20, 324.
Libraries, 205.
Lichen for dyeing, 467, 468.
Liemania, St. Patrick's sister, 548, 549.
Liffey, the river, 244, 481, 483, 509.
Light in houses, 370, 371, 372.
Lily of Medicine (a book), 270.
Lime, 312, 450.
—— used on shields, 60.
Limekilns, 450.
Limerick (44), 297.
Limitations of Kings, 25.
Limited Monarchy, 25.
Lindisfarne, 145, 146, 177, 178.
Linen, 382, 388, 465.
Lir, Story of, 237.

Lis-Doonglara, 340.
Lis, liss, lios, or less, an earthen fort, 107, 289, 300, 306, 309, 310: see Rath.
Lismullin near Tara, 456.
Lissoleem near Bruree, 340, 341.
Lists of Tales, 234.
Litany of Aengus the Culdee, 177.
Literature, ancient Irish, classified, 214.
Lives of Saints, 219, 220.
Lizards, 524.
Lochru, the druid, 100.
Locks and keys, 297.
Locomotion and commerce, chap. xxiv.
Loeg, Cuculainn's charioteer, 115, 196.
Loire river, 34.
Lón or Luin, Keltar's spear, 54.
Looking-glasses. 381.
Loom: see Weaving.
Lorne, son of Erc, 37.
Lost books of Erin, 208.
Loughbrickland in Down, 39.
Loughcrew hills, cemetery, 244.
Lough Derg on the Shannon (38), 108, 338.
—— Ennell in Westmeath (28), 329.
—— Foyle (7), 132.
—— Key in Roscommon, 229.
—— Melvin (15, 16), 13.
—— Neagh (11), 357.
—— Owel in Westmeath (28), 481.
—— Swilly, 132.
Louth, county (23), 16, 235.
Louvain, 220.
Lucet Mael, the druid, 100.
Lucky and unlucky days, 98.
Lug or Lugh of the Long Arms, the Dedannan hero-god, 126, 130, 479.
Lugnaed or Lugnaedon, and his headstone, 547, 548, 549.
Lugnasad, the 1st August, 500.
Lullabies, 260.
Lunacy, 96, 97.
Luncheon, 343.
Lunula or lunette, 405.
Lure in France, St. Dicuil's well at, 151.
Lycaon, the Trojan, 54.

MAC and O, 288.
Mac Adam, Robert, 383.
Mac Ailello and his bell, 168.
Mac Carthen, St., 28, 217.
Mac Carthy, Cormac, k. of Munster, 158.
—— Denis Florence, 12.
Mac Carthys, 69, 266.

INDEX. 565

Mac Coghlans of Delvin, 267.
Mac Con, k. of Ireland, 92.
Mac Criffan, Aed, 207, 211.
Mac Dara's Island and church (31, 32), 155.
Mac Dermott, Brian, 229.
Mace or club, 51.
Macecht, St. Patrick's smith, 453.
Mac Firbis, Duald, 201, 230, 232.
—— family of, 212, 213.
Mac Geoghegan, Connell, 230.
Mac Gorman, bishop and scribe, 207.
Mac Gréine, the Dedannan king, 123.
Macha of the golden hair, queen of Ireland, 109, 330.
Machaon, the Greek physician, 276.
Mac Kelleher, monk and scribe, 207, 209.
Mac Mahons, the, 267.
Mac Morrogh, Dermot, king of Leinster, 58, 211.
Macnamaras, the, 267.
Mac Rannall, Richard, 351.
Mad dogs, 505, 506.
Madness, 96, 97.
Mael; see Mail.
Maengal or Marcellus, 252.
Magh and its compounds: see Moy.
Magh Adhair in Clare, 22.
Magh Slecht or Plain of Prostrations (22), 118, 119, 164.
Magic Fog, 103.
—— and magicians, 96, 103: see Sorcery.
Maguire, Cathal, the annalist, 120, 229.
Maguires, the, 266.
Maidoc, St., of Ferns, 353.
Maigue, the River, 341.
Maildune: see Voyage of.
Mailmuri mac Ceileachair, 207, 209.
Mailoran's Mill, 426, 457.
Mainchine, an Irish monk in Carthage, 150.
Maive, queen of Connaught, Irish *Medb*, 100, 235, 310, 332, 365.
—— Queen (another), 310, 328.
Mallets, 447.
Malt for ale, 350.
Mannanan mac Lir, the Irish sea-god, 107, 108, 115.
Manchan, St., his shrine, 390.
Mantle or cloak, 384, 385 to 388, 391.
—— of invisibility, 103, 104.
—— of the peasantry, 388.
Manure, 425.
Manuscripts, House of, 205.
Manx halfpenny, 108.
—— language and names, 36, 197, 198.

Markets in fairs, 495, 497, 501.
Marriage, 283 to 286.
—— hollow at Tailltenn, 499.
Marshal, 344.
Martin, the writer on the Hebrides, 69.
—— St., of Tours, 218.
Martyrologies, 220.
Martyrology of Donegal, 220.
Masons and masonry, 437, 450 to 452.
Mast or wood-mast, 368, 429.
Materia Medica, 277.
Mayday, 120, 123, 479.
Maynooth College, 213.
Mead or Metheglin, 348, 350.
Meal and flour, 362.
Meals, in general, 343.
Measures, standards of, 311, 472.
Meath, province, 14, 15, 16.
Medical MSS., 268.
Medical attendance in battle, 65.
Medical herbs, 265, 277, 280.
Medicine and medical doctors, 109, 143; chap. xiv.
Meetings, 496 to 504.
Menelaus the Greek, 276.
Men of learning, 184.
Mensal land, 15, 19, 22, 82.
Mercenary soldiers, 46, 47.
Merionethshire, 35.
Messan, a lapdog, 505.
Metals treated of, 484, 485.
Metal-casting, 438, 439.
—— work and workers, 246 to 249, 439.
Metempsychosis, 102, 126.
Mether, a drinking-vessel, 317, 318.
Meyer, Dr. Kuno, Pref. ix; 237.
Midach, Diancecht's son, 265.
Milan Glosses, 200, 320.
Milesian colony, 31, 105, 109, 110, 112, 117, 235.
Military asylums, 47.
Military formation and marching, 66.
Military ranks, orders, and services, 38.
Militia, several kinds of, 38.
Milk and its products, 142, 359.
Milking, 432.
—— tunes for, 260.
Mill, 142, 325; chap. xxi.
Mines and minerals, 9, 433, 434, 435.
Minn, a diadem, 410, 415, 416.
Mirrors, 381.
Missionaries, Irish, 144 to 152.
Mistletoe, 99, 102.
Moat or mote, a raised fort, 306.
—— of Castletown, near Dundalk, 40.

Moat of Kilfinnane, 307.
Mobi or Movi, of Glasnevin, 175, 181.
Molaise, St., 175.
Monasteranenagh, 160, 499.
Monasterboice (23, 24), 228.
Monasteries, 8, 136, 137, 139 and following pages; 290, 432.
—— hospitality in, 5, 142.
—— paid maintenance in, 520.
Monastic life, 139 and following pages.
—— liss or rampart, 163.
—— schools, 8, 174 to 184.
Money, 476, 477, 478.
Mongan of Rathmore, 126, 127.
Montalembert, 146, 147.
Montgomeryshire, 35.
Monsters in lakes, 524.
Moon, 193, 195.
—— age of, 196.
Moore, Thomas, 34, 144.
—— his melodies, 262, 263.
Morann, the great judge, 128.
Mordants in dyeing, 466.
Morrigan, the war-fury, 112, 113.
Mór-tuath, great tuath, several tuaths united, 17, 18, 30.
Moses, 479.
Mould for making furnace, 444.
Moulds for casting, 439.
Mountebanks, 501.
Mountsandall, 39.
Mowing, 427.
Moylena, Battle of, 113.
Moy Mell, the pagan heaven, 124.
Moyola, river in Derry, 245.
Moyrath, Battle of, 113, 114, 212, 235, 274.
Moyry Pass near Dundalk, 481.
Moy Slecht: see Magh Slecht.
Muirchu's Life of St. Patrick, 169, 526.
Mullaghshee at Ballyshannon (9), 109, 110.
Mullenoran, 457.
Munster, 13, 16, 37, 109, 110, 466.
—— ancient extent and sub-divisions of, 13, 14, 15, 16.
Murkertagh O'Brien, k. of Ireland, 331, 338.
Music, chapter xiii., 195, 348, 500, 501.
—— Irish teachers of, 252.
Musical branch, 258, 504.
—— instruments, 254 to 259, 501.
Mussel-producing pearls, 402.
Mustache, 380.
Mutton, 354.
Muzzles for dogs, 505.
Mythology, Irish pagan, 104 to 118.

NAAS (35), 332.
—— described, 334.
Nails of fingers, 376.
Napkins at table, 347.
National colour, absence of, 384.
National Museum, Dublin, list of, gold objects in, 420.
Nature and natural beauty, love of, among Irish, 521 to 524.
Navan fort or ring, 330: see Emain.
Nechtan, k. of Leinster, 337.
Necklaces, 402.
Necklets, 402 to 410.
Needle and thread, 469.
Needlework, 469, 470: see Sewing.
Neit, the Irish war-god, 113.
Nemed, a sanctuary, 158.
Nemedian colony, 31.
Nemnach, well at Tara, 325.
Nemon, Neit's wife, 113.
Nenagh (38, 39), 499.
Nennius, his History and the Irish version of it, 212.
Nether garments, 391.
Nets for birds and fish, 511, 512.
Nettles as food, 366.
New Grange on the Boyne, 108, 244, 538.
Newry (18), river, 424.
Newtown Abbey in Meath, 160.
Niall Glunduff, k. of Ireland, 288.
Niall of the Nine Hostages, 34.
Nigra, Chevalier, a great Italian scholar in Celtic, 215.
Nine waves, 271.
Nith, stream near Tara, 325, 456.
Nivelle in Belgium, 252.
Noah's ark, 223.
Nobber in Meath, 254.
Nobles, 18, 77: see Chiefs.
Non-free classes, 79, 80.
Non-noble freemen, 78, 79.
Norse, Norsemen, the, 36: see Scandinavians and Danes.
Northumbria, 145, 146.
Nuada Necht, king, 31.
Nuns and convents in Ireland, 153, 154.
Nurse tunes, 260.
Nuts, 100, 102, 367.
Nutt, Alfred, 523.

O and MAC, 288.
Oak tree, 99, 100, 102.
—— bark for tanning, 471.
—— mast, 368, 429.
Oaths, 104, 121, 123, 124.
Oatmeal, 362.
Oats, 426.

INDEX.

O'Brien, Murkertagh, k. of Ireland, 331, 338.
O'Briens, the, 16, 69, 111, 267, 339: see Dalcassians.
Obsequies, funeral, 532.
O'Cahan, the inaugurator, 22.
—— Rory Dall, 253.
O'Callanans, 266.
O'Carolan, Turlogh, the musician, 254, 262.
O'Cassidys, 266.
Occupation-tunes, 260, 261.
O'Clery, Conary and Cucogry, 230.
—— Michael, 201, 220.
—— his Calendar, 220.
—— his Glossary, 201.
O'Connallon, Thomas, the harper, 253.
O'Conor, Felim: see Felim.
—— Roderick, king of Ireland, 17, 31.
—— Turlogh, king of Ireland, 249.
O'Conors, the, 22.
O'Corra's sons, story of, 317.
O'Curry, Prof. Eugene, Pref. vi; 53, 75, 127, 161, 208, 305.
O'Davoren's Glossary, 201.
O'Donnells, the, 22, 65, 218.
O'Donovan, John, LL.D., 75, 161, 201, 220, 230, 321, 332.
O'Duffy, Muredach, archbishop of Tuam, 249.
Oenach: see Fairs.
Offa's Dyke, 424.
O'Flahertys, the, 266.
O'Freel, the inaugurator, 22.
Ogham, 98, 169 to 173, 203.
O'Gonnilloe near Killaloe, 245.
O'Hagan, the inaugurator, 22.
O'Hartigan, Dunlang, 104.
—— Kineth, the poet, 321, 344.
O'Hechan, Mailisa Mac Braddan, the artist of the Cross of Cong, 249.
O'Hickeys, the, 267.
O'Kennedys, the, 267.
O'Lavan, the artist, 315.
Old age, provision for, 520.
O'Lees, the, 266.
Olioll: see Ailill.
Ollave, Ir. ollamh, a person holding the highest degree of any profession or art, a doctor, 29, 180 and following, 185, 436, 498.
Ollamh Fodla, king, 497.
O'Lochan, Cuan, 321.
O'Loghlin, Donall, king of Ireland, 166.
Olympic Games of Greece, 499, 502, 503.
O'Mulconry, Ferfesa, 230.

One foot, one hand, one eye (sorcery), 102, 103.
O'Neill, Shane, 27, 47, 371, 395.
O'Neills, the, 22, 69, 288.
Onions and leeks, 366.
Open-air treatment in hospitals, 273, 274.
Ophthalmia, 272.
Opus Hibernicum, 147, 244, 249, 316, 399.
Ordeals, 128, 129, 169.
Orders, the Three, of Irish saints, 135 and following pages: see Three orders.
Ore, 433, 434, 435.
Orkney Islands, 512.
Ornamentation of MSS., 239 to 244.
Ornaments, personal, 399 to 419.
Orpheus, 260.
O'Shiels, the, 267.
Oscar, son of Ossian, 43.
Ossar, the lapdog, 99.
Ossian, Irish Oisín, son of Finn, 43, 126.
Ossianic Tales, 199, 523.
Ossory (39, 45, 46), 18, 482, 500.
Oswald, king of Northumbria, 145, 146, 177.
O'Tinnri, Maclodar, the physician, 266.
Otter and otter skins, 382, 383, 508, 511.
Over-kings of Ireland, 31.
Owen: see Eoghan.
Outdoor relief, 521.
Oxen, 427, 428, 486.
Oxford, 176.

PAGAN artistic metal-work, 246, 399.
—— ornamentation, 244.
Paganism, chap. v.
Painters, 445.
Painting the cheeks, 377.
Palaces, 24, 320 to 342.
Palladins, 133, 135.
Pallas, the goddess, 107.
Pallas Grean, 111.
Palsy, 272.
Pancakes, 361.
Pantry, 300.
Paps, the, mountains near Killarney, 109.
Parchment, 202, 205.
Parmenius or Formenius the hermit, 36.
Parnell, Thomas, 342.
Parsnips, 366.
Parthalon, 127.
Parthalonian colony, 31, 271.

INDEX.

Pasturage, 421.
Patrick, St., 28, 34, 73, 98, 100, 118, 119, 120, 122, 128, 133, 135, 136, 154, 155, 164, 165, 169, 171, 174, 205, 217, 220, 318, 328, 453, 454, 470, 526.
—— Druidical prophecy of his coming, 98.
Patrickstown fairy-moat, 107.
Pearls, 10, 401, 402.
Peat or turf, 369.
Pen and penknife, 203.
Penwork as an art, 239.
Penal Laws, 72, 495.
Pentarchy, the Irish, 17.
Pepin, Mayor of the Palace, 194.
Person and toilet, 376 to 382.
Personal ornaments, 399 to 419.
Pet animals, 525.
Petrie, Dr. George, Pref. xii; 161, 162, 321, 324.
—— his Irish Music, 262.
Phantom Island, 125.
Phantoms, 104 and following pages; 117.
Phœnicians, 121, 494.
Phœnix Park, near Dublin, 513.
Physicians, 264 to 268, chap. xiv. in general.
—— Goddess of, 109.
—— in the army, 66.
Picts, 33, 37, 226, 227.
—— and Scots, 31.
Pigs, 25, 429, 430, 511.
Pigsty, 299.
Pillar-stones, 120, 423.
Pincers or tongs of smith, 441.
Pinginn, a penny, a coin and weight, 474 to 478.
Pinkerton, the Scotch historian, 219.
Pins, 391, 392.
Pipes, musical, 256, 257, 501.
Pitfalls for animals, 511.
Place, time, person, and cause of writing a book, Preface, x.
Plagues, 270.
Plane, a carpenter's, 447.
Pleaders and advocates, 91.
Pledging articles, 519.
Plough and ploughing, 427.
Plough-whistles, 261.
Pocket, 394.
Poems, educational, 184.
Poetry, ancient Irish, 214 to 216.
Poets, 109, 186 and following, 304: see Ollave.
—— circuits or visitations of, 187.
—— saved at Drumketta, 189.
—— writing-staves of, 202, 203, 204.
Poison, 280.
Poitou in France, 348.
Polyolbion, Drayton's, 253.

Pooka, Ir. púca, the fairy, 116.
Poor laws in ancient Ireland, 520, 521.
—— scholars, 181.
Popular cures and herb-knowledge, 280.
Porcelain ornaments, 294.
Pork, 354.
Porridge, 362, 363.
Posts supporting roof, 293.
Pottage or hash, 355.
Potters and potter's wheel, 320.
Pounds for cattle, 87, 525.
Prayer, 95, 144, 152.
Precious stones, 401.
Press for shaping timber, 447.
Privileges of kings, 23.
Prizes for performances at fairs, 501.
Probe, a doctor's, 277.
Procedure by distress, 87.
—— by fasting, 88.
Professions, 9.
—— hereditary, 184, chap. viii. in general.
Property, test of rank, 77.
Prosody, Irish, 214 to 216.
Prosper of Aquitaine, 133.
Protection of crafts, 452 to 455.
Provinces, the ancient, 13, 14, 15.
Psalms, 218.
Psalter of Cashel, 230.
Ptolemy, the geographer, 494.
Puddings, 356.
Punishment, modes of, 89.
Purple in dyeing, 467, 468.
Purse, 394.
Pursuit of Dermot and Grainne, 327.
Pythoness, 101.

QUAIGH, a drinking-cup, 317.
Queens, 17, 92.
Quern, 142, 459.
Quicken, quickbeam, or rowantree, 100, 102, 355.
Quin in Clare, 160, 420.

RACES, 500, 509.
Racks for hanging small articles on, 302.
Radnorshire, 35.
Rahan (34), church doorway, 454.
Rake (the instrument), 428.
Rampart boundaries, 424.
Rath, a circular earthwork for a dwelling, 112, 306, 309, 310: see Lis.
—— in Westmeath, 329.
Rathbeagh on the Nore, 329.

INDEX.

Rath Caelchon at Tara, 326.
Rathcoran near Baltinglass, 335.
Rathcroghan in Roscommon: see Croghan.
Rath Gráinne at Tara, 327.
Rath-Keltair at Downpatrick, 39, 41.
Rath-Laegaire at Tara, 327.
Rathmaive near Tara, 310, 328.
Rathmiles near Tara, 328.
Rathnagree near Baltinglass, 336.
Rath-na-seanaid at Tara, 323.
Rath-righ or Rath-na-Righ at Tara, 310, 323.
Ravens, 98, 99.
Razors, 380, 381.
Reaping and reaping-hooks, 426.
Re-birth, 126, 127.
Rechtaire, a house-steward, 28.
Recitation of stories and poetry, 179, 238, 500.
Red Branch Knights, 38, 39, 42, 45, 47, 48, 54, 235, 265, 329, 330, 345, 346, 510.
Reeds for roofs, 293.
Reeves, Rt. Rev. William, 220.
Reins: see Bridles.
Relics, use of, in battle, 65.
Relieving officer, 521.
Relig-na-Rig at Croghan, 332.
Rennet, 361.
Rent, 82, 84, 85.
Reptiles and serpents, 117, 524, 525.
Restrictions of kings, 25.
Retaliation and law of, 86.
Renda, same as Carbery Riada, 37, 227.
Revenue of kings, 22, 25.
Rhapsodists of the Greeks, 500.
Rheumatism cured, 277.
Rhyme and rhyming, 215, 216.
Rhyming rats to death, 188.
Ring-money, 478.
Rings and bracelets, 400, 401, 501.
Roads, 4, 328, 480 to 483.
Roberts, an English writer, 298, 347, 358.
Rock of Cashel, the, 337, 338.
Roe of a salmon, 362.
Roman and Greek writers on Ireland, 32, 494.
Romanesque style of architecture, 158, 159.
Roman wall, 424.
Rome and the Romans, 23, 33, 54, 64, 97, 135, 145, 146, 177, 347, 348, 377, 504.
Roofs of houses, 293.
Roscommon abbey, 229.
Ro-sualt, a fabulous monstrous fish, 525.
Round towers, 160, 451.

Rowan tree, 355.
Royal residences, 24, 320 to 342.
Roydamna, a crown prince, 19, 500.
Ruadan of Lorrha, St., 321.
Runners or couriers, 29.
Rushes for beds, 303.
——— for floors, 305.
——— for roofs, 293.
Rushlights, 372.
Ruskin quoted, 383.
Rye, 426.

Sacred armistice of the Greeks, 503.
Sacred Island, i.e. Ireland, 494.
Saddles, 487, 488.
Saffron-dye, 388, 468.
Sai-re-Cerd, 'a sage in handicraft,' 455.
Saint: see under the respective names.
——— David's Monastery in Wales, 144.
——— Doulogh's Church near Dublin, 156.
——— Gall in Switzerland, 194, 200, 252.
——— John's Day (24th June), 123.
——— Nicholas' College, Galway, 232.
Saints' love of animals, 526.
Saints, three orders of: see Three Orders.
Salmon, 357, 362, 512.
——— in wells, 164.
Salt, 351, 358.
Saltair-na-Rann, 192, 196, 221.
Saltair, or Psalter of Cashel, 209.
——— of Tara, 498.
Salutation, modes of, 518.
Salzburg, 194.
Samain (1st of November), 112, 118, 479, 497, 498.
Samera, the chief, 114.
Sanctuary, 158.
Sapphires, 401.
Sarcophagi, 537 to 546.
Satchels, for books, 206.
Satin, 382, 385.
Satire and satirists, 188.
Sausages, 356.
Saw (a carpenter's), 445.
Saxons, 33, 290.
Scabbard, 55, 56.
Scallcrow, or royston crow, 113.
Scandinavians, 287: see Danes and Norsemen.
Scathach, the female champion, 277.
Scattery Island (43), 128.
School life and school methods, 181.

INDEX.

Schools, lay, 8, 174, 178.
—— monastic or ecclesiastical, 8, 137, 174 to 184.
—— pagan, 174, 179, 180.
Science, knowledge of, 191.
Scissors, 462.
Scotch and Irish music, 263.
Scotch Gaelic, 197, 198.
Scotch harpers learning from Ireland, 252.
Scotchmen, 27, 47, 55, 120, 252, 355.
Scotch pipes, 256.
Scotland, 20, 32, 33, 36, 37, 38, 60, 95, 112, 122, 144, 163, 165, 198, 227, 253, 261, 263, 292, 302, 307, 310, 345, 383, 461, 492, 499: see Hebrides.
Scots (*i.e.* the Irish), 32, 33, 37, 133, 135, 146, 178, 227, 290.
Scott's novels referred to, 302, 345.
Screpall, a coin, a weight, 474, 476.
Scribes, Irish, 202, 204, 239 to 244.
Scripture, 143, 150, 218.
Sculpture, 249.
Scythe, 427.
Sea, the, 528.
Seals as food, 355.
—— skins of, 382.
Seasons, the four, 478, 479.
Sechnall, St., 222.
Secular clergy, 136, 137.
Séd, a jewel, 10, 29, 401, 402.
—— a cow as an article of value, 402, 478.
Séds or jewels, keeper of, 29.
Sedulius, 176.
Seirkieran in King's County, 144.
Senait Mac Manus in Lough Erne, 229.
Senan, St., of Scattery, 128.
Senchan Torpest, the poet, 188.
Senchus Mór, 73, 74.
Seneschal, 28.
Sentinels and watchmen, 63.
Separation of man and wife, 285.
Sept, a group of people connected by blood, 80.
Sepulchral chambers, 537 to 546.
—— monuments, 540.
Sepulchres: see Cemeteries.
—— Greek, 538.
Serpents and reptiles, 117, 524, 525.
Seven Churches, 158.
—— degrees of wisdom, 180.
—— Romans buried in Aran, 177.
Sewing, 383, 469, 471: see Needlework.
Shakespeare's plays, 130, 188.
Shanachie, a historian, a storyteller, 6, 64, 186, 232, 238, 344.
Shanid Castle in Limerick (43), 69.
Sharpening tools, 449.

Shaving, 380, 381.
Shears and shearing, 462.
Sheath for a sword, 55, 56.
Shee, a fairy, a fairy-palace, 103, 105, 106, 109, 124.
Sheep, 430.
Sheephouse, 299.
Shees open at Samain, 112.
Sheets for beds, 303.
Sheevra, a kind of fairy, 115.
Shellfish used in dyeing, 468.
Shells as a land-improver, 425.
—— for lime, 450.
Shepherd, 430.
Shetland Islands, 150.
Shiel, Dr, of Ballyshannon, 267.
Shield, 59, 344, 345, 446.
Shield-bearer or squire, 344.
Shingles for roofs, 293.
Ships and boats, 491 to 493.
Shirt, 394.
Shoeing horses, 460.
Shoemaker, the fairies', 116.
Shoes and sandals, 347, 396 to 399.
Shoes, magical, 116.
—— of metal, 397, 398.
—— taken off at meals, 347.
Shovel, 427, 428.
Showmen, 501.
Shrine of St. Maidoc, 378.
—— of St. Manchan, 390.
—— of St. Patrick's bell, 165, 166, 167.
Shrines for relics and books, 147, 217, 438.
Shroud and winding-sheet, 533.
Sickles, 426.
Sick maintenance, 274.
Sid-Aeda at Ballyshannon, 109.
Sid Buidb or Sidh Bhuidhbh, Bodb Derg's palace, 108.
Síde or Sid, a fairy, a fairy dwelling, an elf-mound: see Shee.
Sieves, 363.
Silence at meetings, how obtained, 504.
Silk, 382, 385.
Silver, 244, 245.
—— dishes at dinner, 365.
—— and gold as mediums of exchange, 476, 477, 478.
Skellig Island off Kerry, 153.
Skreen Hill in Meath, 45.
Slainge, first king of Ireland, 31.
Slán, wells so called, 122.
Slane on the Boyne (29), 137, 357, 481.
Slaves and slavery, 80.
Sledges and hammers, 441, 447.
Sleeping accommodation, 300.
Sleeping-draught, 277.

INDEX.   571

Sleight-of-hand tricks, 517.
Slieve Anierin, a mountain in Leitrim, 435.
―― Fuait or Fuaid near Newtown-Hamilton in Armagh (17), 481.
―― Golry in Longford, 368.
―― Mish in Kerry (49), 117.
Slievenamon in Tipperary, 111.
Sligo (15), 160.
Sling and sling-stones, 49.
Sloe-bush or blackthorn and its fruit, 368.
Smallpox, 271.
Smelting, 245, 434, 435.
Smiths and smithwork, 101, 109, 437, 440 to 444.
―― goddess of, 109.
Smith's song, 260.
Snakes, 524.
Sneezing, divination from, 98.
Soap, 381.
Soldiers tied in pairs, 67.
Solinus, 55, 491.
Solstices, 193.
Sons of Usna, 39.
Sorcerers and sorcery, 102.
Soul, immortality of, 102, 125.
Sound as a distance measure, 473.
Spades, 427, 428.
―― for turf, 369.
Spancel, 432.
Spears and spearheads, 51, 438, 511.
Speckled Book, 211.
Spells and charms, 102, 103, 104.
Spenser, Edmund, 188, 517.
Spindles, 463.
Spinning, 463.
Spits for roasting, 351.
Sprouts (vegetables), 355.
Spunk, tinder, 370.
Spurs, none used, 490.
Staigue Fort in Kerry, 308.
Standards or banners, 64.
Standing up as mark of respect, 518.
Stars, observation of, 98, 196.
Steel, 449: steelyard, 475.
Stilicho, the Roman general, 34.
Stirabout or porridge, 362, 363.
Stirrups, none used, 490.
Stitching wounds, 276.
Stock, lending of, to tenants, 22, 84.
Stokes, Miss Margaret, Frontispiece, Preface, xii.
―― her pilgrimages in search of traces of Irish saints, 150.
―― Whitley, D.C.L., LL.D., 201, 219, 221, 222, 229, 232, 237, 334.
Stone, building in, 436, 450 to 452.
―― circles, 543.
―― of the Divisions, 14.

Stone vessels, 314.
―― for weapons and tools, 434.
Stone-carving, 249.
Stones, adoration of, 118, 119, 120, 424.
Stories: see Tales.
Story-telling, 238.
Stowe missal, 242.
Strainer, 349.
Stratagem in war, 66.
Strategy, tactics, and modes of fighting, 62.
Straw for beds, 303.
―― for floors, 305.
―― for thatching, 293.
Strawberries, 368.
Strongbow, *i. e.* Richard, earl of Clare, his tomb, 549.
Stroove and Stroove Bran in Donegal, 97.
Structure of society, 77.
Stuarts, the, 38.
Styles for writing on waxed tablets, 205.
―― of Irish music, the three, 260.
Subordination of military ranks, 63.
Subsidies, 83.
Subterranean chambers in forts, 307, 308.
Sullivan, Dr. W. K., Pref. vii.
Sun, the, 122.
―― worship, 122, 123.
Sundays and holidays, 141, 343.
Sundial, 193.
Surnames, 21.
Swearing by arms, 121.
―― by elements, 123, 124.
―― by the gods, 104.
Sweating-houses (medicine), 277, 278, 279.
Swimming, 5, 184.
Swine: see Pigs.
Swineherds, 430.
Switzerland, 149, 163, 314.
Swords (arms), 55, 56.
Symmachus, the Roman, 504.
Synchronisms of Flann, 228.

TABLECLOTH, 347.
Tables (in houses), 346.
Tablet-staves for writing on, 202 to 205.
Tacitus, 494.
Tailltenn (29), 15, 329, 344, 497, 498, 499.
Táin-bo-Quelna, 210, 211, 212, 265, 346.
―― described, 235.
Tairill, St. Patrick's brasier, 453.

Tales, historical and romantic, chap. xi.
—— educational function of, 179, 181.
—— general character of, 237.
Taliesin, the ancient Welsh bard, 127.
Tallaght (35, 36), near Dublin, 271.
Tanist, the elected successor to a living king or chief, 19.
Tanistry, 86.
Tanning, 471.
Tara (29), 15, 17, 20, 90, 92, 96, 100, 131, 169, 211, 246, 289, 292, 298, 310, 312, 318, 329, 344, 456, 497.
—— described, 321 to 328.
—— brooch, 246, 247, 248, 249, 414.
—— Feis of, 497, 498.
—— Luachra, 341.
Tartan, 383.
Tasach, St. Patrick's brasier, 453.
Teaching in handwork, 184.
—— and teachers, 100, 101, chap. vii.
Tech Cormac at Tara, 324.
—— Midchuarta at Tara: see Banqueting-Hall.
Teltown: see Tailltenn.
Temair: see Tara.
Tempull Caimhain in Aran, 157.
Temples, 95.
Tenants, 82, 83, 84, 85.
Tenure of land, 81 to 86.
Terminus, the Roman god, 120.
Termon, a sanctuary, 158.
Territorial boundaries, 422, 423, 424.
—— subdivision of Ireland, 13.
Testament, the, 143, 150, 218: see Scripture and Bible.
Testaments: see Wills.
Thatch of roofs, 293.
Theodosius, the Roman general, 33, 34.
Thomond or North Munster (43, 44, 45), 16, 18.
Thread: see Sewing and Spinning.
Three Orders of Saints, 135; First Order, 135 to 138; Second, 135, 138 and following pages; Third, 136, 152, 153.
—— waves of Erin, 62.
Threlkeld, the writer on Irish botany, 280.
Threshing, 427.
Throne, a king's, 24.
Tide, time of flow of, 196.
—— at Clontarf on day of battle, 226.
Tigernach O'Breen, the annalist, 229.
Tigernmas, king of Ireland, 118, 244.
Timber as working material, 433.
Time and its measures, 478, 479, 480.

Timpan, a musical instrument, 255, 256, 501.
Tin, 435, 437.
Tinder, 360.
Tirconnell, now the Co. Donegal (6, 9, 10), 18, 22.
Tirechán's notes on St. Patrick, 218.
Tirnanoge, the land of youth, 12, 124, 126.
Tlachtga (29), 15, 329, 497, 499.
Toads in Ireland, 524.
Tober Finn at Tara, 327.
Tobernagalt in Glennagalt, 97.
Todd, the Rev. Dr., 220, 222, 226.
Toilet and person, 377 to 382.
Toilet articles (small), 381, 382.
Tolka, the river, near Dublin, 182.
Tombstones: see Sepulchral monuments.
Tomregan in Cavan, 274.
Tongs or pincers, 441.
Tonn Cleena, Cleena's wave, at Glandore, 111, 529.
—— Rudraidhe, 529.
—— Tuaithe, 529.
Tonsure, 148.
Tools, various, 445 and following.
Topazes, 401.
Tornant moat near Dunlavin, 336.
Torques, 403, 404.
Towns and cities, 6, 290.
Trades and tradesmen, 10, 79, 452 to 455.
Trades connected with clothing, chap. xxii.
Transformation and transmigration after death, 102, 126.
Translations into Irish, 214.
Traps for animals, 511, 512.
Treatment of diseases, 273 to 280.
Trees, 433.
—— reverenced by the druids, 99.
Trefining or trepanning (surgery), 274, 275.
Tribe, the, 81, 82.
Tribe-land, 82.
Tribute to kings and chiefs, 22, 84: see Boru.
Trim Castle (29), 291.
Trinity College, Dublin, 213.
—— well at Carbury in Kildare (29, 35), 337.
Tripartite Life of St. Patrick, 219.
Triscatal, Concobar's champion, 27.
Trough, 315, 441.
Trousers, 391, 488.
Trout in wells, 164.
Troy, war of, 212.
Truce at fairs, 502, 503.
Trumpets and horns, 68, 257, 258, 259, 344.

INDEX.   573

Tuam (27), 249.
Tuan mac Cairill, the sage, 127.
Tuath, a territory, 15, 17, 30, 77, 273.
—— size of, 16.
Tuatha de Dananu : see Dedannans.
Tuathal, the Legitimate, king of Ireland, 14, 329.
Tubbrid church in Tipperary, 231.
Tubs, 315, 316.
Tucking cloth, 462, 464.
Tullahogue in Tyrone, 22.
Tulsk in Roscommon, 332.
Tumblers (showmen), 501, 517.
Tumulus, or burial-mound, on the Boyne, 541.
Tuning-key of a harp, 256.
Turbary, 432.
Turf or peat, 369, 432.
—— spades, 369.
Turgesius, the viking, 329.
Turners, 447.
Turning right-hand-wise and left-hand-wise : see Desiol.
Twelve Apostles of Erin, 139.
Tying soldiers in pairs, 67.
Tyrian purple, 468.
Tyrone (10, 11), 18, 245.

UCHADAN, the artificer, 245.
Ulster, 13, 16, 37, 38, 60, 64, 132, 189, 235, 358, 450, 465.
—— ancient extent of, 14, 16.
Ultan, bishop of Ardbraccan, 218.
—— and the orphans, 530.
—— brother of Fursa, 252.
Ultonian Knights : see Red Branch.
Ulysses, 103, 381.
Underclothing, 393.
Underground chambers in forts, 307.
Universe, description of, in Irish, 192.
Unlucky days, 98.
Urns for ashes of the dead, 535, 541, 543, 545, 546.
Ushnagh (28), 14, 15, 120, 329, 344, 497, 498, 499.
Usna, Sons of, 39, 236, 376.

VALUE, standards of, 475.
Van Helmont of Brussels, 266.
Vapour bath, 277.
Various social customs, chap. xxvi.
Veal, 354.
Vegetables for table, 355, 365, 366, 367.
Veils, 395, 396.
Vellum, 202, 205.

Venison, 354.
Venus, the goddess, 103.
Vessels, 314 to 320.
Virgil or Virgilius of Aghaboe, bishop of Salzburg, 194.
Visitation of chiefs and officials, 23, 373.
—— of poets, 187.
Vitrified forts, 310.
Voices of birds, divination from, 98.
Voyage of St. Brendan, 492.
—— of Maildune, 210, 212, 237, 304, 348.
Vulcan, 440.

WAGGONS, 4.
Waistcoat, absence of, 385.
Wakes or dead watches, 532, 533.
Wales, 144, 283, 302, 303, 307, 468, 487.
—— Irish conquests and colonisations in, 32, 33, 34, 35.
War-cries, 69.
Ward, Hill of, in Meath, 15.
War and warfare, 7, 8, and chap. iii.
War-goddesses or war-furies, 112.
War-marches (music), 261.
War-service, 45.
Ware, Sir James, Pref. vii.
Washing hands and face, 381.
—— the body after death, 533.
Watchdogs, 505.
Watchmen and sentinels, 63.
Water, communication by, 491 to 493.
—— digging for, 425.
—— mills, chap. xxi.
—— worshipped, 122.
Water-bottles, 471.
Watercress, 366.
Wave of Erin, of Man, of the North, and of Britain, 529.
Waves, nine, 271, 528.
—— The Three, of Erin, 62, 529.
Wax candles, 371.
Waxed tablets for writing on, 205.
Weapons, swearing by, 121.
—— use of, taught, 184.
—— worshipped, 121.
Weaving, 463, 464.
Weeping aloud for the dead, 533.
Weight and standards of, 474, 475.
Weirs, 513.
Wells, 122, 151, 163.
Welsh, the, 47, 252, 287, 346, 468, 492.
—— language and literature, 35, 197, 200.
—— music, 252.

Westwood, Prof J. O., 240.
Wexford (46), 245.
Wheat, 426.
Whetstone, 449.
Whey, 360, 361.
Whip, 490.
Whiskey, 350.
Whortleberries or hurts, 368.
Wickerwork houses, 291, 292, 293.
—— shields, 59.
Wicklow (40, 41), 9, 133, 435.
Wife, 91, 283 to 286.
Wild boars, 511.
William of Malmesbury, 145, 195.
Will of Cahirmore, 510.
Wills or testaments, 531.
Wind: colours and qualities of winds, 527, 528.
Windgap in Kilkenny, 482.
Windows, 294, 295.
Wine, 348, 495.
Wisdom, seven degrees of, 180.
Witches and witchcraft, 100.
Witnesses, 91, 286.
Wizards, 101.
Woad plant for dyeing, 467.
Wolf, 506.
Wolf-dog, 504, 505, 506, 511.
Women, 212.
—— position of, 283, 284: see Wife.
Wood as working material, 433.
—— building in, 290 to 293; 436, 444.
Wood-carvers, 445.
Woods and forests, 1, 433.

Wool and woollens, 382, 462 to 470.
Wordsworth, the poet, 522.
Work in monasteries, 139 and following pages.
Workers in wood, metal, and stone, chap. xx.
Workshops, ancient, 449, 450.
Worship of the elements, 121.
—— of idols, 118.
—— of weapons, 121.
Wounds closed up by stitching, 276.
Wren, the, 98.
Writing and writing-materials, 202.
Writing known to pagan Irish, 169 to 173.
Wurzburg Glosses, 200.

YEAR and its subdivisions, 478, 479.
Yeast or leaven, 362.
Yellow Book of Lecan, 208, 212.
Yellow colour, 383, 488.
—— hair, 376.
—— plague, 153, 178, 271, 530.
Yew rod for divination, 98.
Yew tree and wood, 100, 102, 363, 444, 445.
York, 176.

ZEUSS, 200, 215.
Zinc, 435, 437.
Zurich, lake, 36.

WORKS
BY
P. W. JOYCE, M.A., LL.D., T.C.D.;
M.R.I.A.

ONE OF THE COMMISSIONERS FOR THE PUBLICATION OF THE ANCIENT LAWS OF IRELAND;
HON. PRESIDENT OF THE ROYAL SOCIETY OF ANTIQUARIES, IRELAND;
LATE PRINCIPAL, MARLBOROUGH STREET TRAINING COLLEGE, DUBLIN.

Two Splendid Volumes, richly gilt, both cover and top. With 361 Illustrations. Price £1 1s. net.

A SOCIAL HISTORY OF ANCIENT IRELAND.

A Complete Survey of the Social Life and Institutions of Ancient Ireland. All the important Statements are proved home by references to authorities and by quotations from ancient documents.

Of the 31 Chapter headings, 27 are the same as those given below for the Smaller Social History.

One Vol., Cloth gilt. 598 pages, 213 Illustrations. Price 3s. 6d. net.

A SMALLER SOCIAL HISTORY OF ANCIENT IRELAND,

Treating of the Government, Military System, and Law; Religion, Learning, and Art; Trades, Industries, and Commerce; Manners, Customs, and Domestic Life of the Ancient Irish People.

Traverses the same ground as the larger work above; but besides condensation, most of the quotations and nearly all the references to authorities are omitted in this book.

PART I.—**Government, Military System, and Law.**—Chapter I. A Preliminary Bird's-eye View—II. Government by Kings—III. Warfare IV. The Brehon Laws.

PART II.—**Religion, Learning, and Art**—Chapter V. Paganism—VI. Christianity—VII. Learning and Education—VIII. Irish Language and Literature—IX. Ecclesiastical and Religious Writings—X. Annals, Histories, and Genealogies—XI. Historical and Romantic Tales—XII. Art—XIII. Music—XIV. Medicine and Medical Doctors.

PART III.—**Social and Domestic Life.**—Chapter XV. The Family—XVI. The House—XVII. Food, Fuel, and Light—XVIII. Dress and Personal Adornment—XIX. Agriculture and Pasturage—XX. Workers in Wood, Metal, and Stone—XXI. Corn Mills—XXII. Trades and Industries connected with Clothing—XXIII. Measures, Weights, and Mediums of Exchange—XXIV. Locomotion and Commerce—XXV. Public Assemblies, Sports, and Pastimes—XXVI. Various Social Customs and Observances—XXVII. Death and Burial. Index.

Third Edition. Thick Crown 8vo. 565 pages. Price 10s. 6d.

A SHORT HISTORY OF IRELAND
FROM THE EARLIEST TIMES TO 1608.

Cloth gilt. 528 pages. Price 3s. 6d.
Published in December, 1897: now in its 70th Thousand.

A CHILD'S HISTORY OF IRELAND,
WITH
Specially drawn Map and 160 Illustrations,

Including a Facsimile in full colours of a beautiful Illuminated Page of the Book of Mac Durnan, A.D. 850.

Besides having a very large circulation here at home, this book has been adopted by the Australian Catholic Hierarchy for all their Schools in Australia and New Zealand; and also by the Catholic School Board of New York for their Schools.

Cloth. 312 pages. 24th Thousand. Price 2s.

A CONCISE HISTORY OF IRELAND
FROM
THE EARLIEST TIMES TO 1837.

With Introductory Chapters on the Literature, Laws, Buildings, Music, Art, &c., of the Ancient Irish People.

Cloth. 160 pages. Price 9d.

OUTLINES OF THE HISTORY OF IRELAND
FROM
THE EARLIEST TIMES TO 1905.
50th Thousand.

"This little book is intended mainly for use in schools; and it is accordingly written in very simple language. But I have some hope that those of the general public who wish to know something of the subject, but who are not prepared to go into details, may also find it useful. . . . I have put it in the form of a consecutive narrative, avoiding statistics and scrappy disconnected statements."—*Preface.*

Seventh Edition. Crown 8vo. Cloth gilt. Vol. I., Price 5s.; Vol. II., 5s.
(Sold together or separately.)

THE ORIGIN AND HISTORY OF IRISH NAMES OF PLACES.

Fcap. 8vo. Cloth. Price 1s.

IRISH LOCAL NAMES EXPLAINED.

In this little book the original Gaelic forms, and the meanings, of the names of five or six thousand different places are explained. The pronunciation of all the principal Irish words is given as they occur.

New Edition. Cloth. Price 3s. 6d.

OLD CELTIC ROMANCES.

Twelve of the most beautiful of the Ancient Irish Romantic Tales translated from the Gaelic.

Fcap. 8vo. Cloth. Price 1s.

A GRAMMAR OF THE IRISH LANGUAGE.

Cloth. 220 pages. With many Illustrations. Price 1s. 6d.

A READING BOOK IN IRISH HISTORY.

This book contains forty-nine Short Readings, including "Customs and Modes of Life": an Account of Religion and Learning; Sketches of the Lives of Saints Brigit and Columkille; several of the Old Irish Romantic Tales, including the "Sons of Usna," the "Children of Lir," and the "Voyage of Maildune"; the history of "Cahal-More of the Wine-red Hand," and of Sir John de Courcy; an account of Ancient Irish Physicians, and of Ancient Irish Music, &c., &c.

Fourth Edition. 4to. Price—Cloth, 3s.; Wrapper, 1s. 6d.

ANCIENT IRISH MUSIC,

Containing One Hundred Airs never before published, and a number of Popular Songs.

Paper cover. 4to. Price 1s.

IRISH MUSIC AND SONG.

A Collection of Songs in the Irish language, set to the old Irish airs.

(Edited by Dr. JOYCE for the " Society for the Preservation of the Irish Language.")

Paper cover. Crown 8vo. Price 6d. net.

IRISH PEASANT SONGS IN THE ENGLISH LANGUAGE.

With the old Irish airs: the words set to the Music.

Twentieth Edition. 86th Thousand. Fcap. 8vo. Cloth. Price 3s. 6d.

A HAND-BOOK OF SCHOOL MANAGEMENT
AND METHODS OF TEACHING.

DA 930.5 .J87 1906
SMC
Joyce, P. W. (Patrick
 Weston), 1827-1914.
A smaller social history
 of ancient Ireland,
AJZ-8067 (mcab)

CPSIA information can be obtained
at www.ICGtesting.com
Printed in the USA
LVOW10s0231010817
543261LV00026B/1277/P